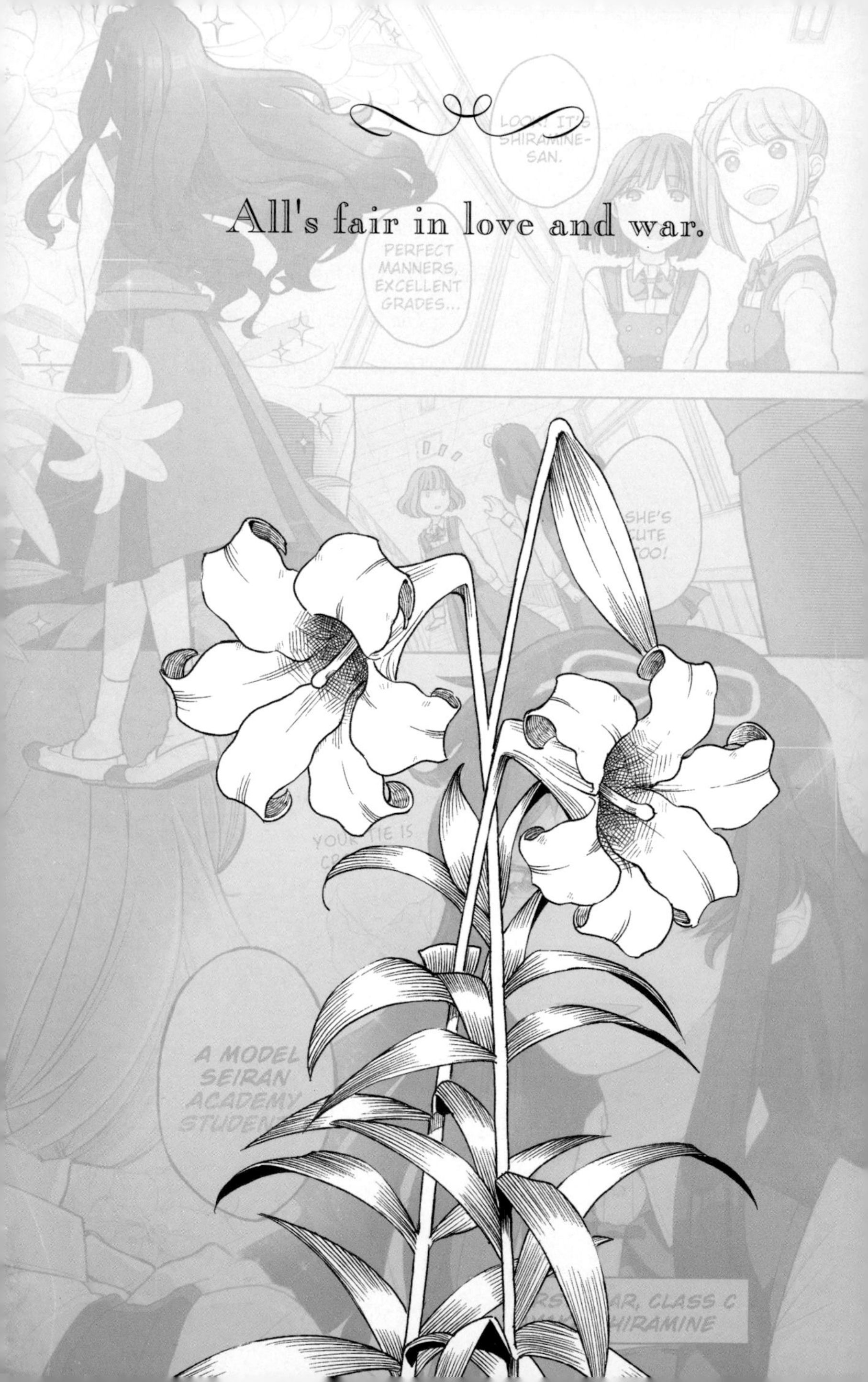
All's fair in love and war.
LOOK! IT'S SHIRAMINE-SAN.
PERFECT MANNERS, EXCELLENT GRADES...
SHE'S CUTE TOO!

Kiss and White Lily for My Dearest Girl 1 Contents

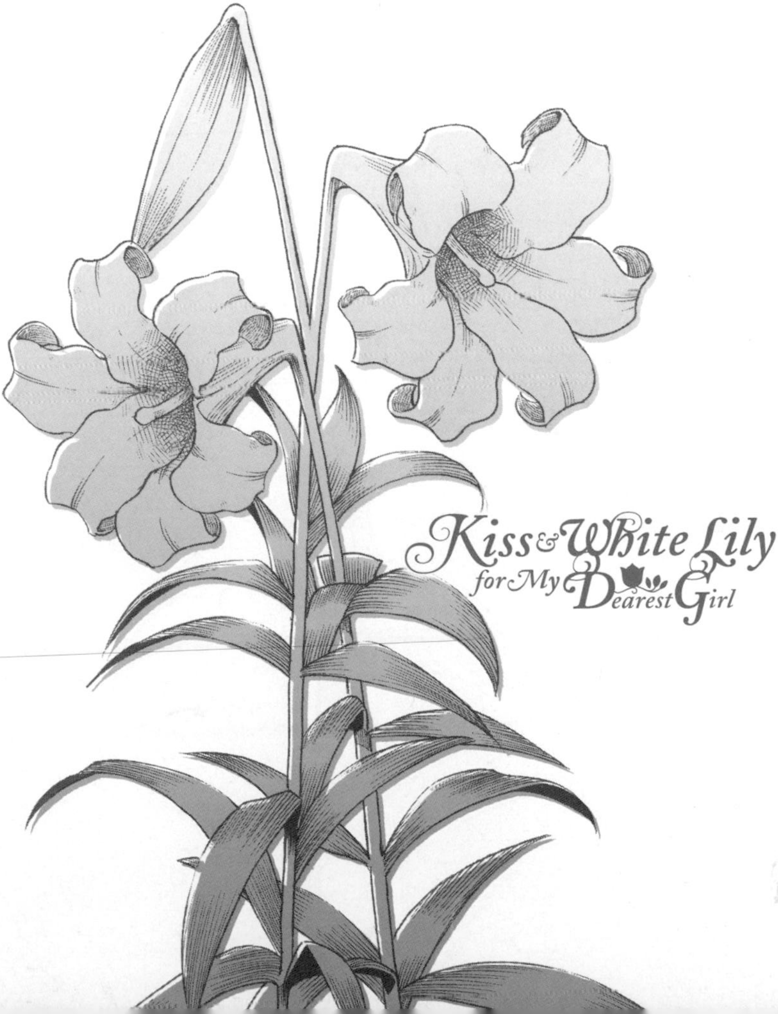

Kiss & White Lily
for My Dearest Girl

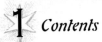

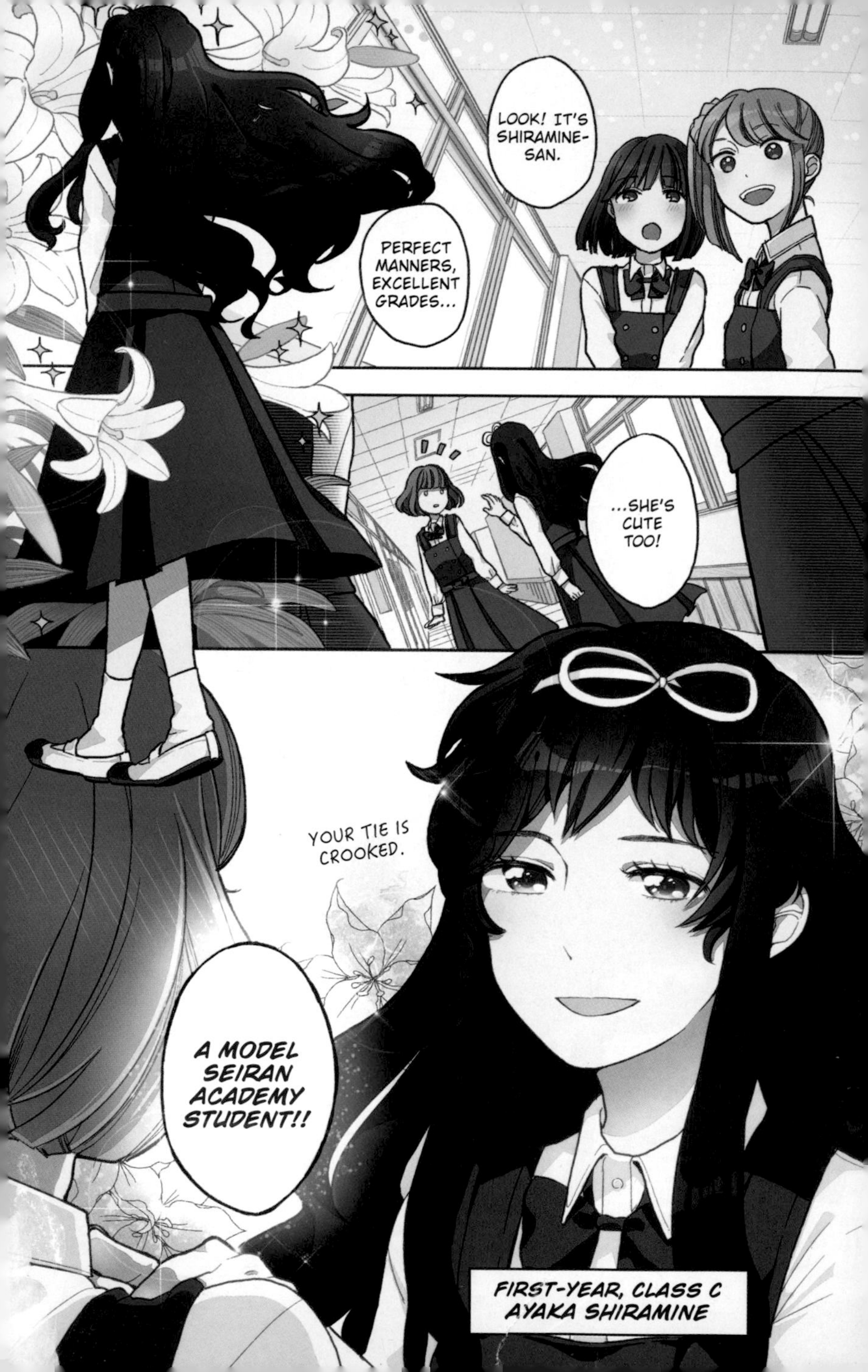
LOOK! IT'S SHIRAMINE-SAN.
PERFECT MANNERS, EXCELLENT GRADES...
...SHE'S CUTE TOO!
YOUR TIE IS CROOKED.
A MODEL SEIRAN ACADEMY STUDENT!!
FIRST-YEAR, CLASS C AYAKA SHIRAMINE

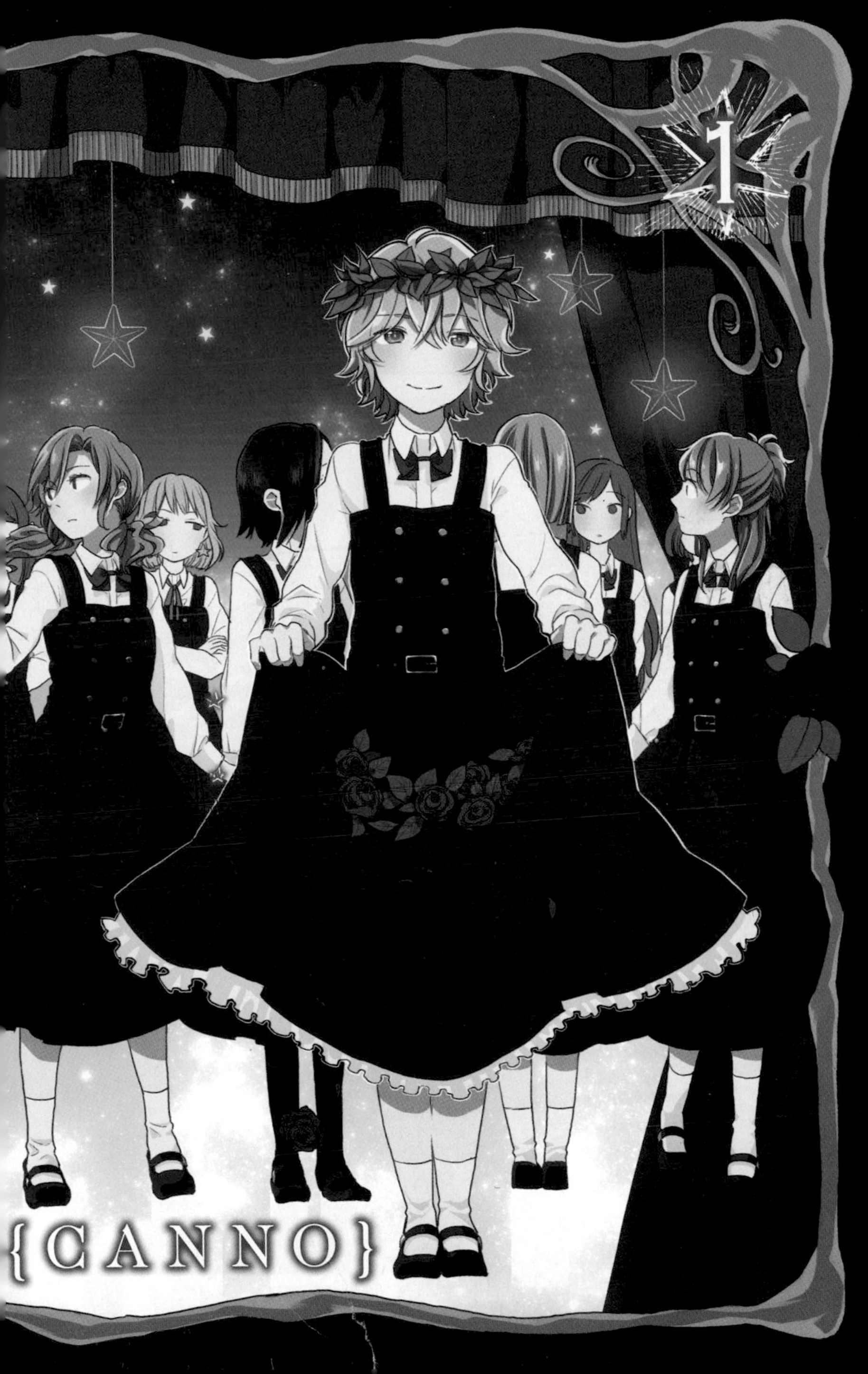
1
{CANNO}

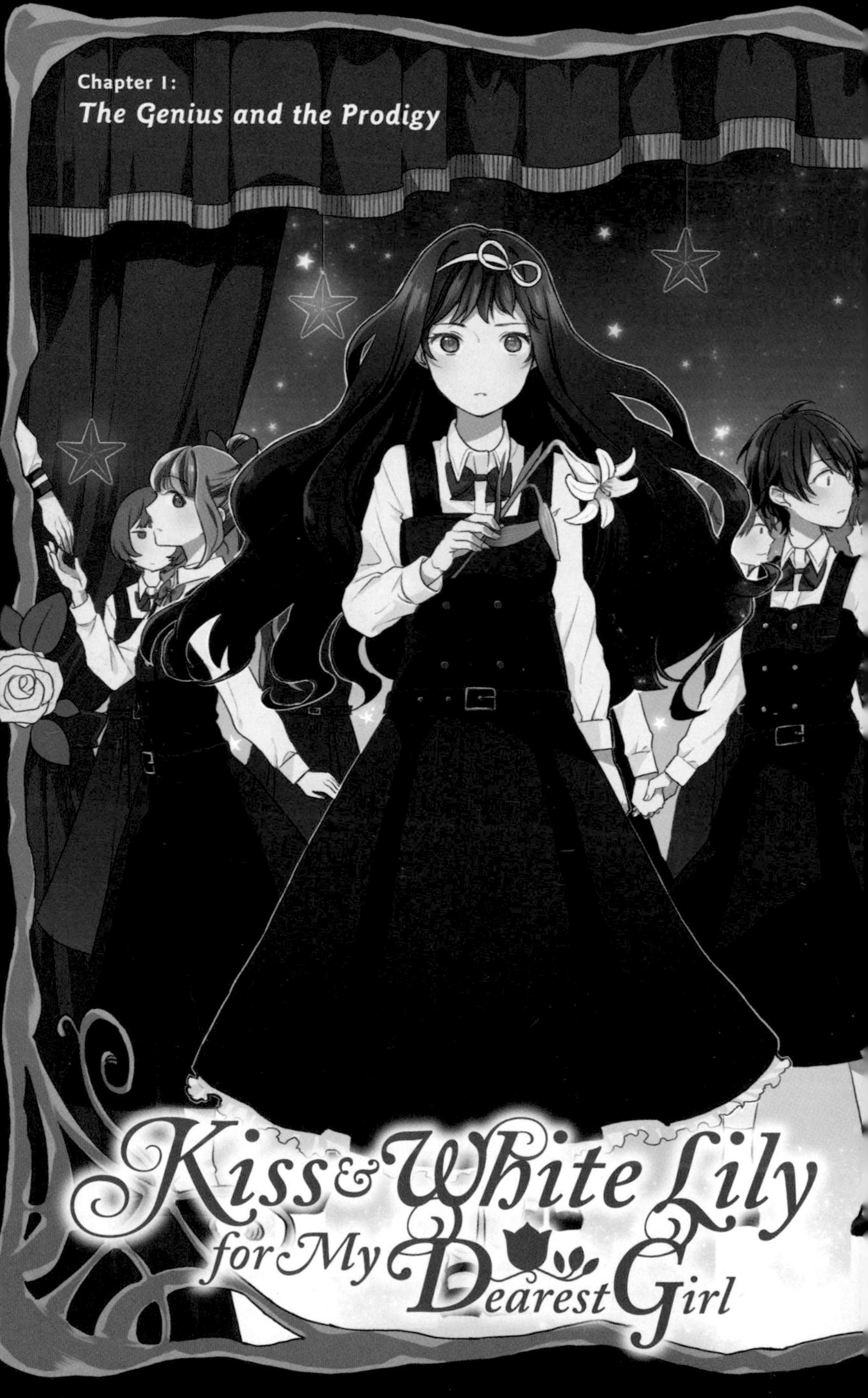
Chapter 1:
The Genius and the Prodigy
Kiss & White Lily for My Dearest Girl

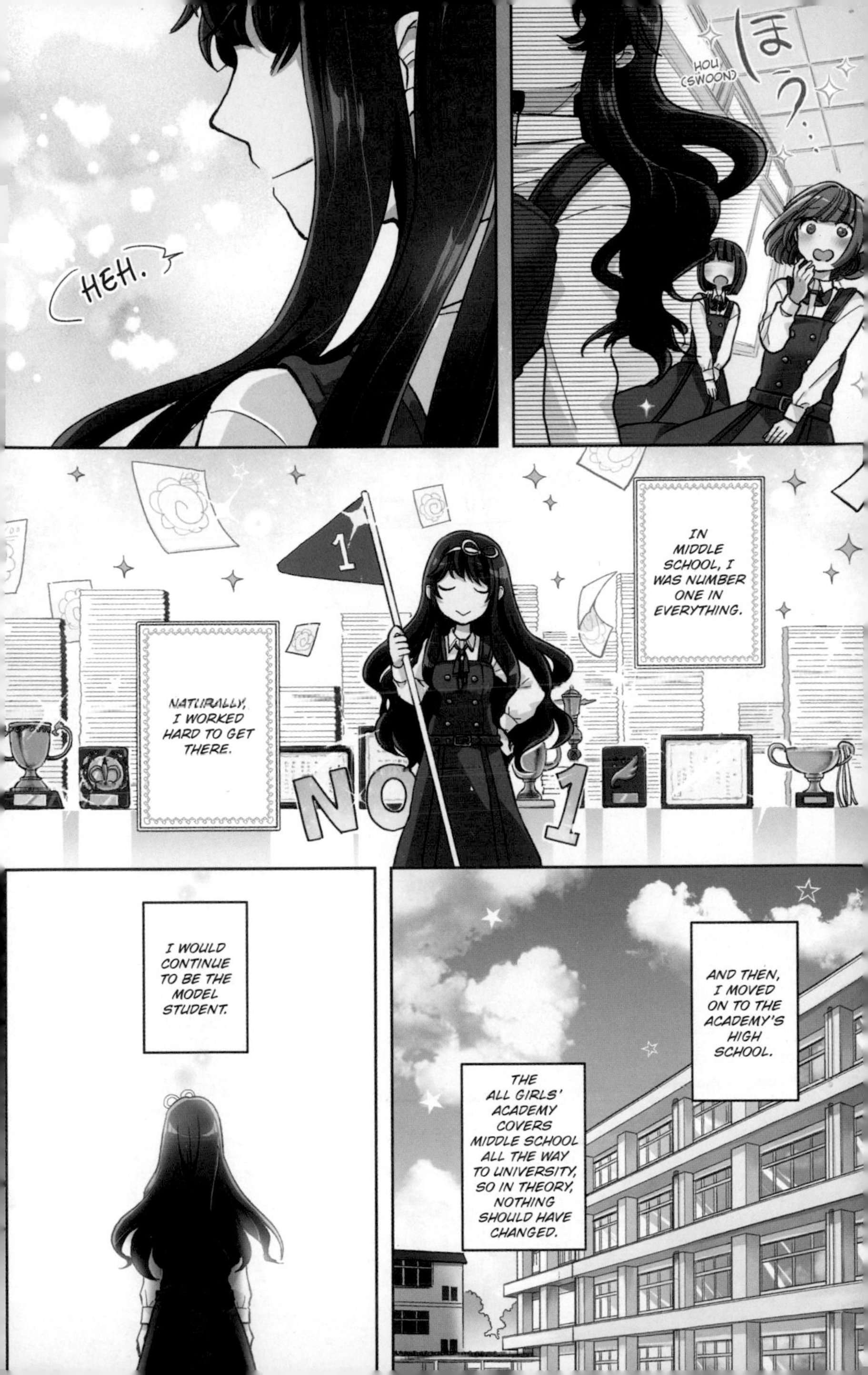
ほう…
HOU (SWOON)
HEH.
IN MIDDLE SCHOOL, I WAS NUMBER ONE IN EVERYTHING.
NATURALLY, I WORKED HARD TO GET THERE.
NO 1
AND THEN, I MOVED ON TO THE ACADEMY'S HIGH SCHOOL.
THE ALL GIRLS' ACADEMY COVERS MIDDLE SCHOOL ALL THE WAY TO UNIVERSITY, SO IN THEORY, NOTHING SHOULD HAVE CHANGED.
I WOULD CONTINUE TO BE THE MODEL STUDENT.

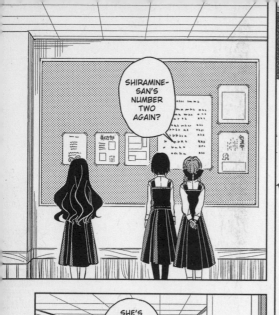

SHIRAMINE-SAN'S NUMBER TWO AGAIN?

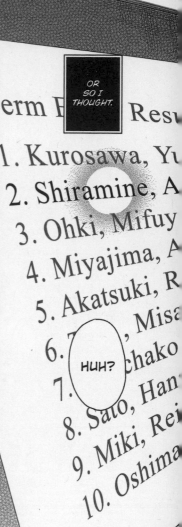

erm E Resu

1. Kurosawa, Yu

2. Shiramine, A

3. Ohki, Mifuy

4. Miyajima, A

5. Akatsuki, R

6. T , Misa

HUH?

7. chako

8. Sato, Han

9. Miki, Rei

10. Oshima

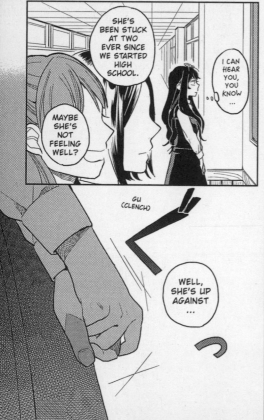

SHE'S BEEN STUCK AT TWO EVER SINCE WE STARTED HIGH SCHOOL.

I CAN HEAR YOU, YOU KNOW ...

MAYBE SHE'S NOT FEELING WELL?

GU (CLENCH)

WELL, SHE'S UP AGAINST ...

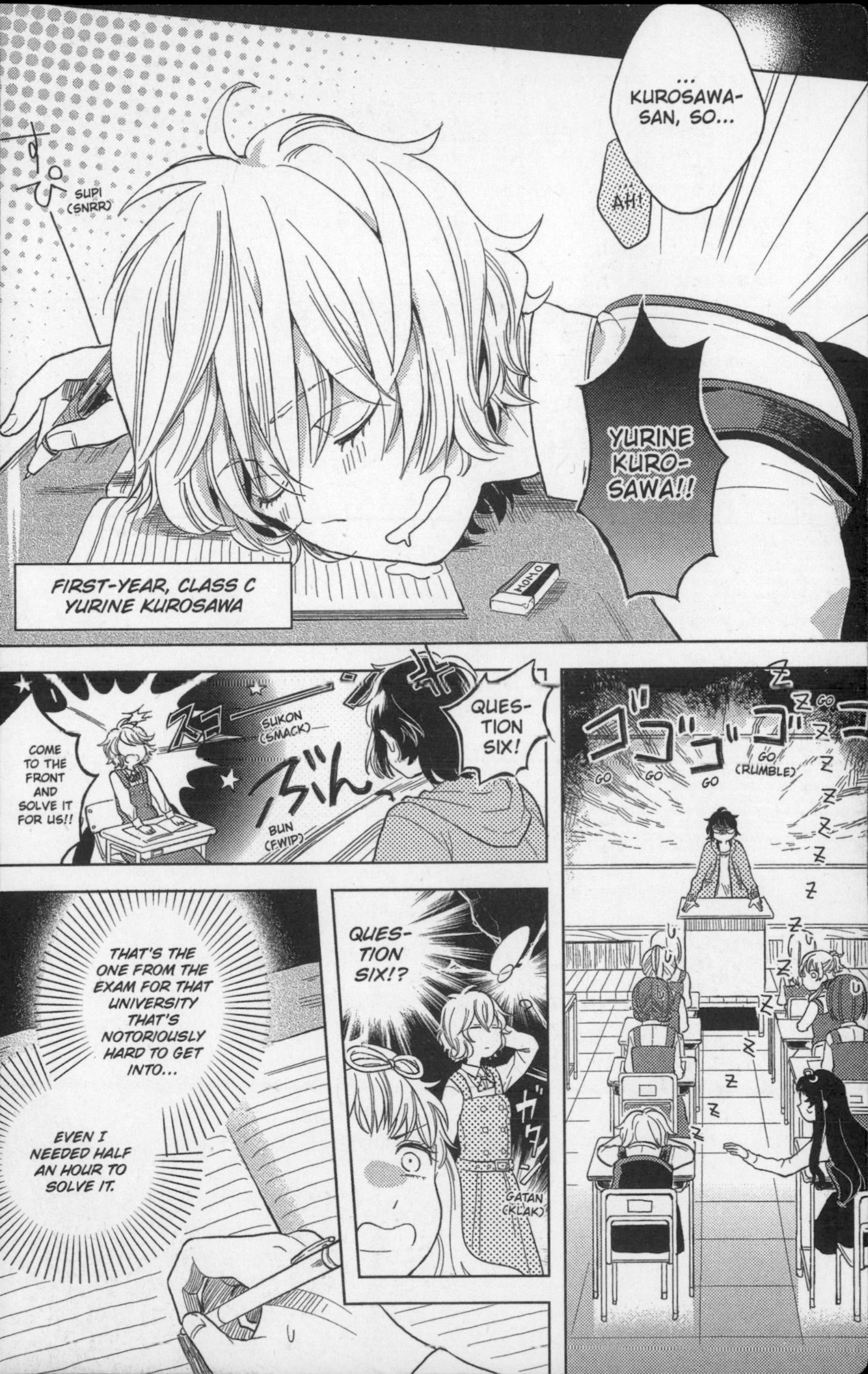
... KUROSAWA-SAN, SO...
AH!
YURINE KURO-SAWA!!
SUPI (SNRR)
FIRST-YEAR, CLASS C YURINE KUROSAWA
GO GO GO GO (RUMBLE)
QUES-TION SIX!
SUKON (SMACK)
BUN (FWIP)
COME TO THE FRONT AND SOLVE IT FOR US!!
QUES-TION SIX!?
GATAN (KLAK)
THAT'S THE ONE FROM THE EXAM FOR THAT UNIVERSITY THAT'S NOTORIOUSLY HARD TO GET INTO...
EVEN I NEEDED HALF AN HOUR TO SOLVE IT.

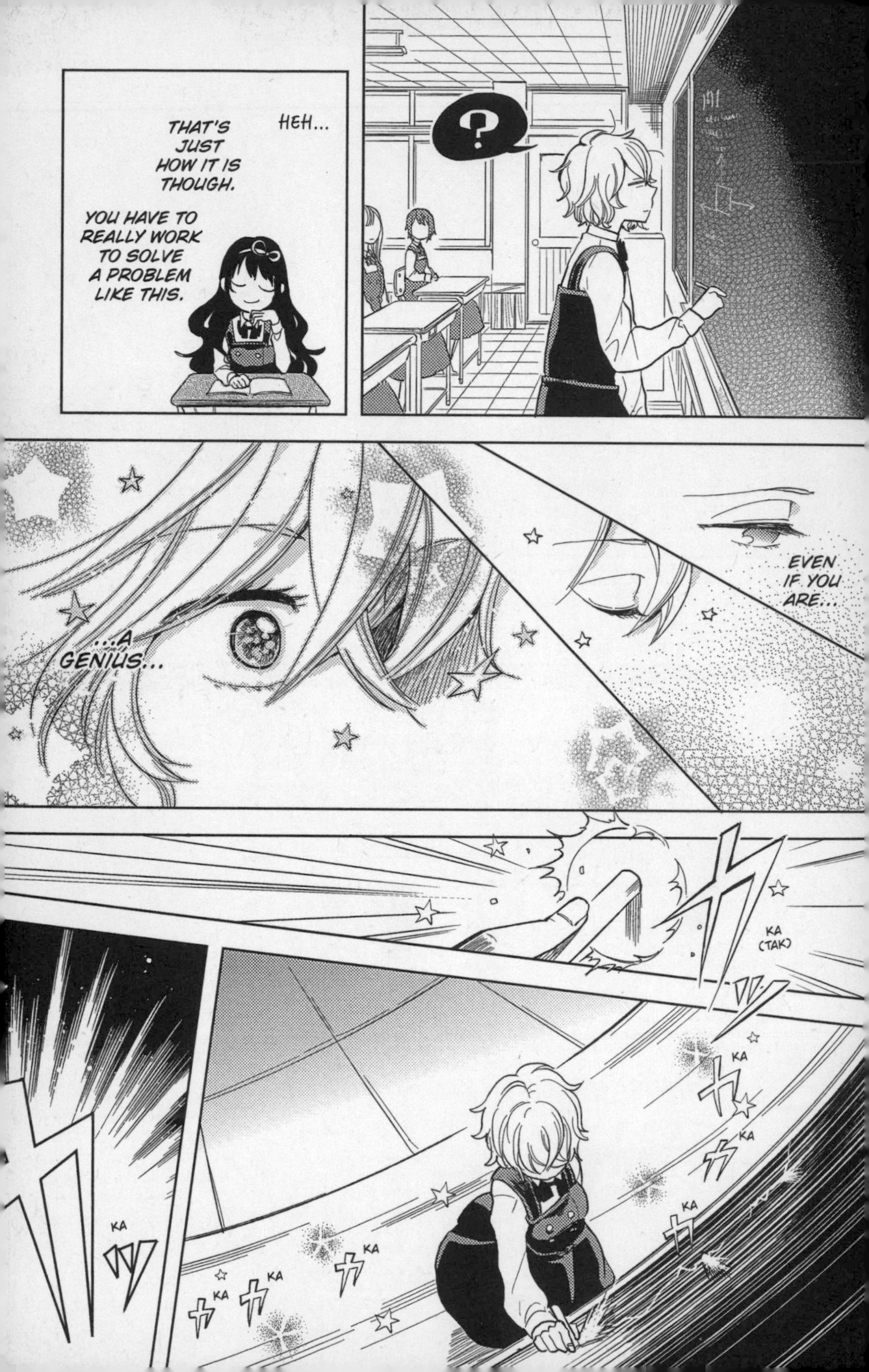
?
HEH...
THAT'S JUST HOW IT IS THOUGH.
YOU HAVE TO REALLY WORK TO SOLVE A PROBLEM LIKE THIS.
EVEN IF YOU ARE...
...A GENIUS...
KA (TAK)
KA
KA
KA
KA
KA
KA
KA

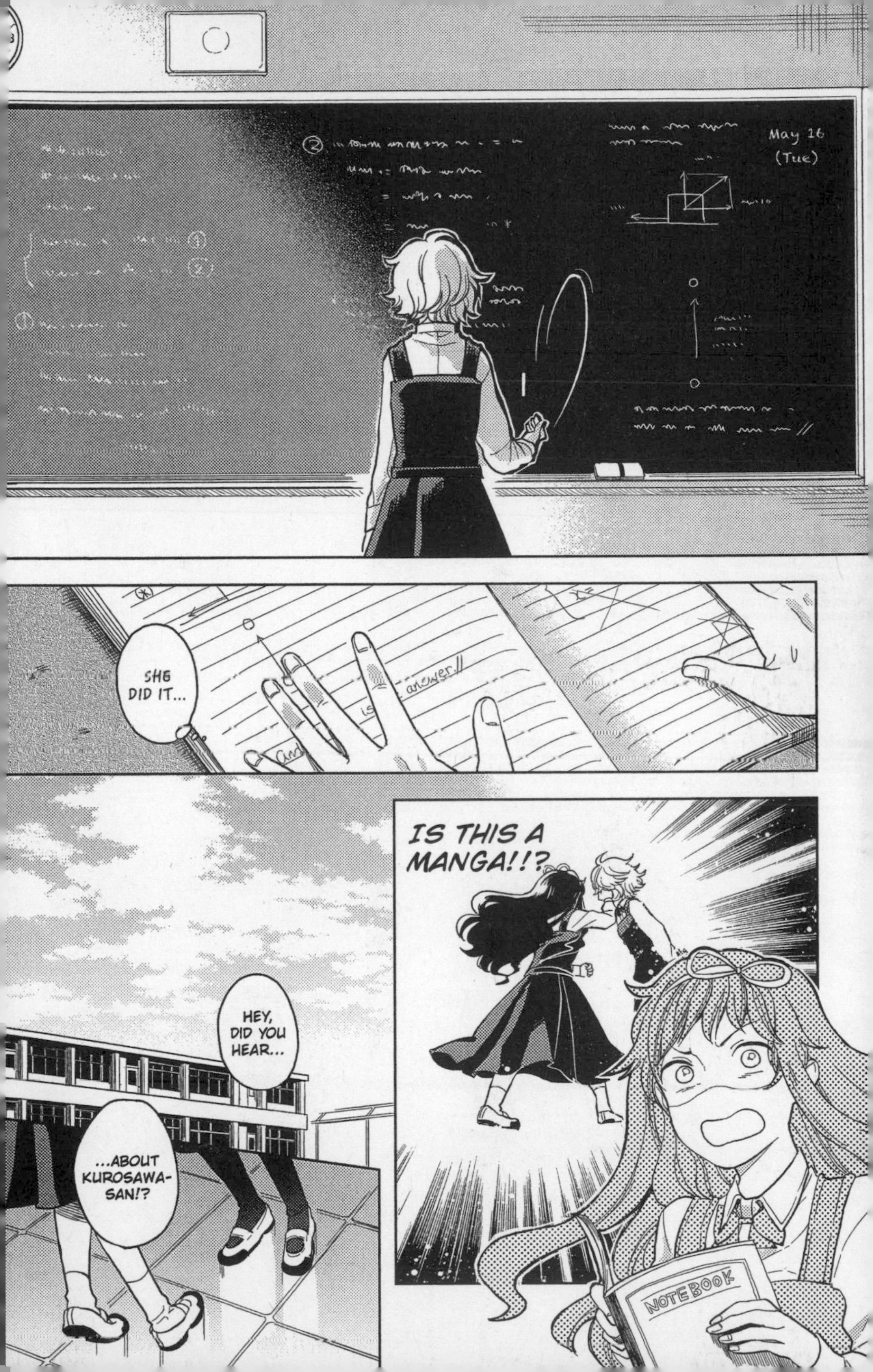
May 16 (Tue)
SHE DID IT...
IS THIS A MANGA!!?
NOTEBOOK
HEY, DID YOU HEAR...
...ABOUT KUROSAWA-SAN!?

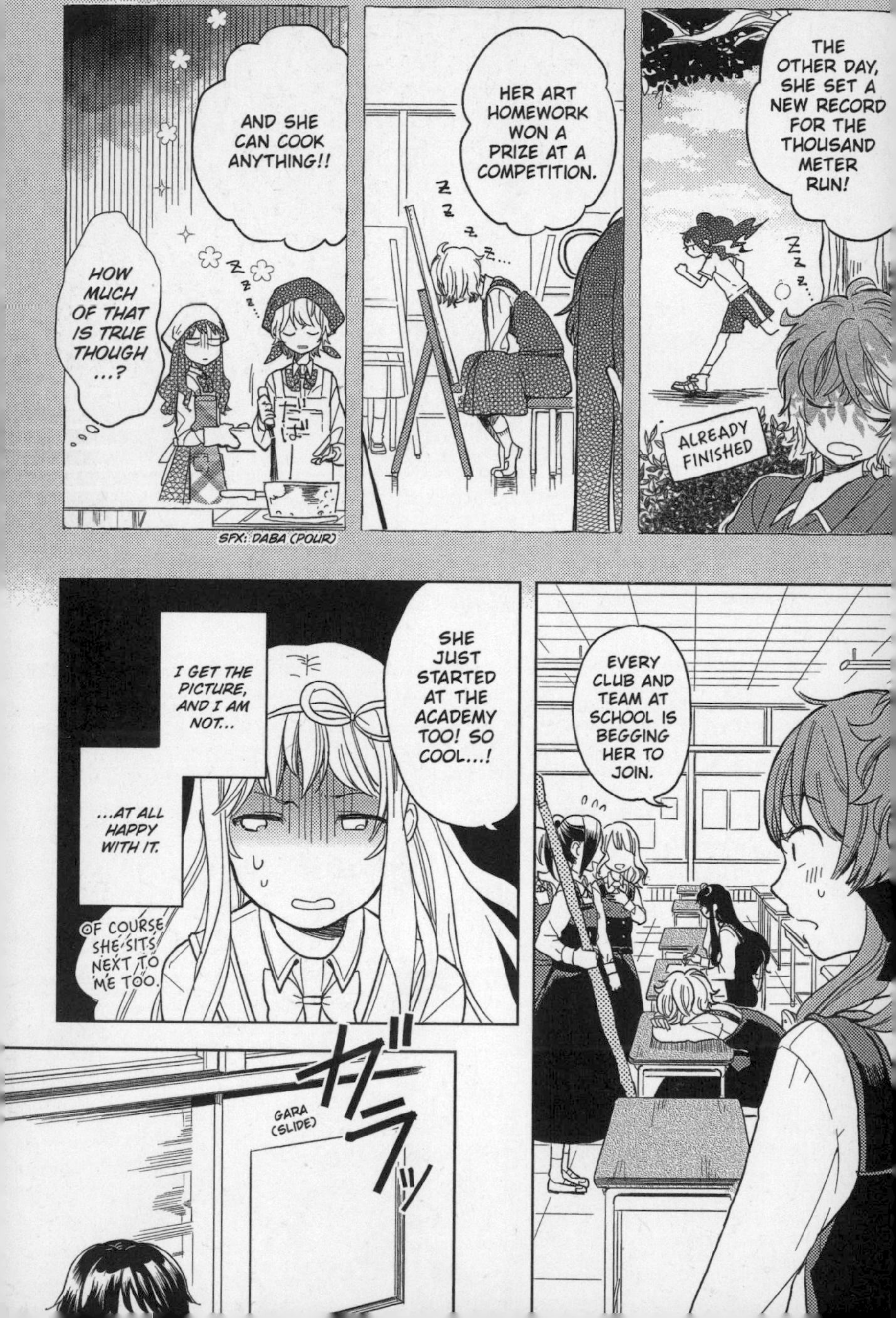
THE OTHER DAY, SHE SET A NEW RECORD FOR THE THOUSAND METER RUN!
ALREADY FINISHED
HER ART HOMEWORK WON A PRIZE AT A COMPETITION.
AND SHE CAN COOK ANYTHING!!
HOW MUCH OF THAT IS TRUE THOUGH...?
SFX: DABA (POUR)
EVERY CLUB AND TEAM AT SCHOOL IS BEGGING HER TO JOIN.
SHE JUST STARTED AT THE ACADEMY TOO! SO COOL...!
I GET THE PICTURE, AND I AM NOT...
...AT ALL HAPPY WITH IT.
OF COURSE SHE SITS NEXT TO ME TOO.
GARA (SLIDE)

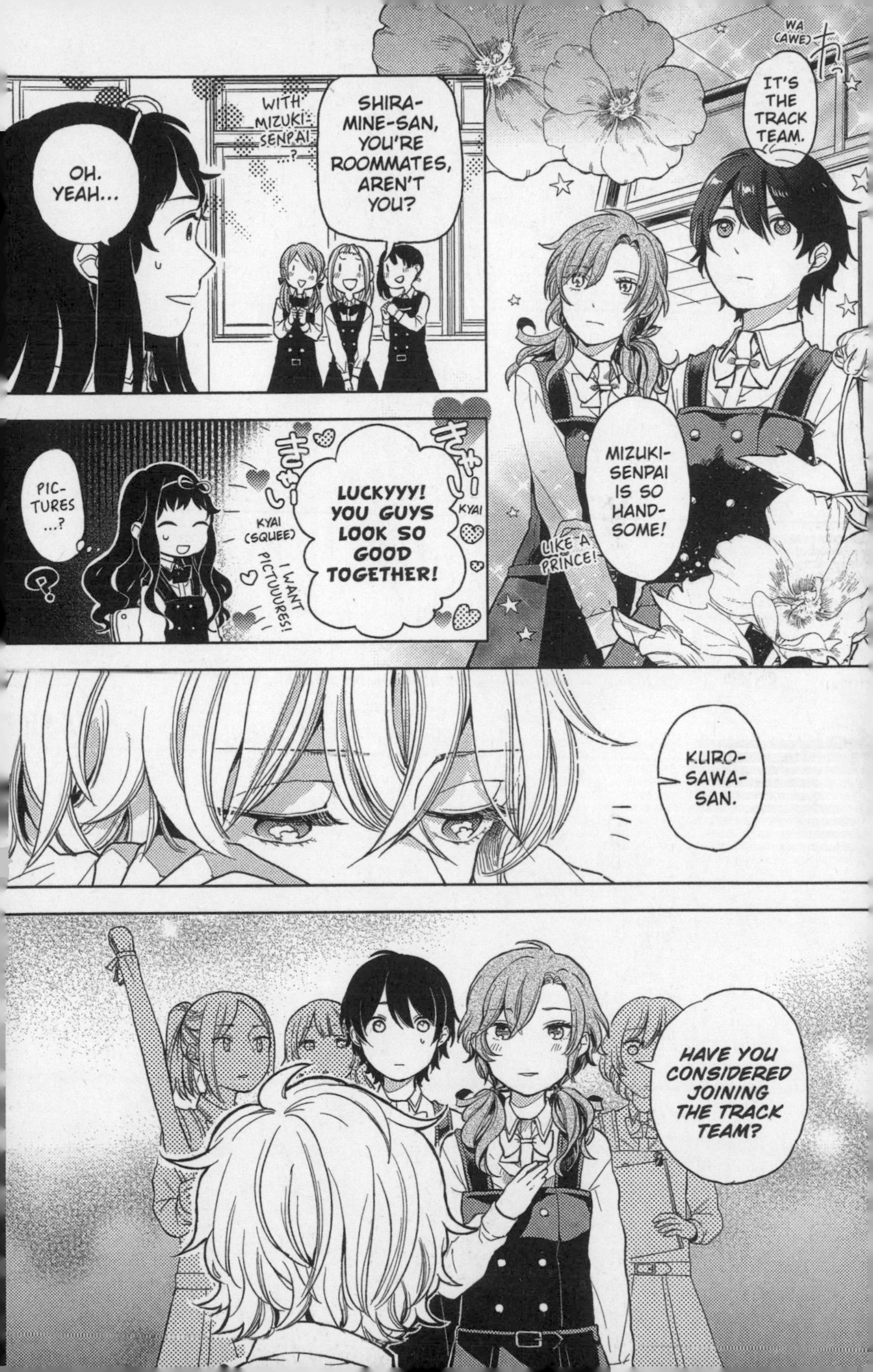
WA (AWE)
IT'S THE TRACK TEAM.
MIZUKI-SENPAI IS SO HANDSOME!
LIKE A PRINCE!
SHIRA-MINE-SAN, YOU'RE ROOMMATES, AREN'T YOU?
WITH MIZUKI-SENPAI?
OH. YEAH...
LUCKYYY! YOU GUYS LOOK SO GOOD TOGETHER!
KYAI
KYAI (SQUEE)
I WANT PICTUUURES!
PIC-TURES...?
KURO-SAWA-SAN.
HAVE YOU CONSIDERED JOINING THE TRACK TEAM?

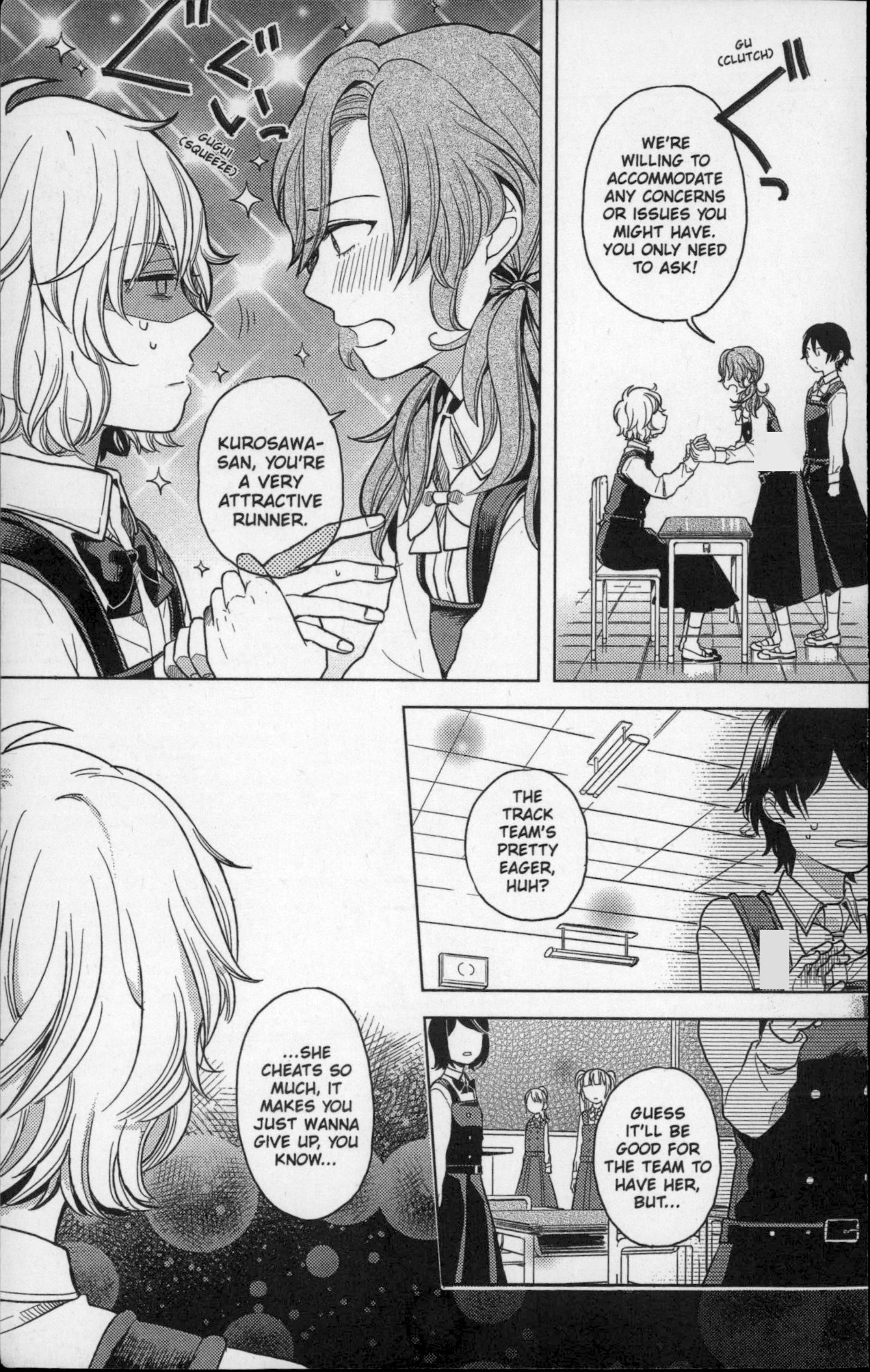
GU (CLUTCH)
WE'RE WILLING TO ACCOMMODATE ANY CONCERNS OR ISSUES YOU MIGHT HAVE. YOU ONLY NEED TO ASK!
GUGUI (SQUEEZE)
KUROSAWA-SAN, YOU'RE A VERY ATTRACTIVE RUNNER.
THE TRACK TEAM'S PRETTY EAGER, HUH?
GUESS IT'LL BE GOOD FOR THE TEAM TO HAVE HER, BUT...
...SHE CHEATS SO MUCH, IT MAKES YOU JUST WANNA GIVE UP, YOU KNOW...

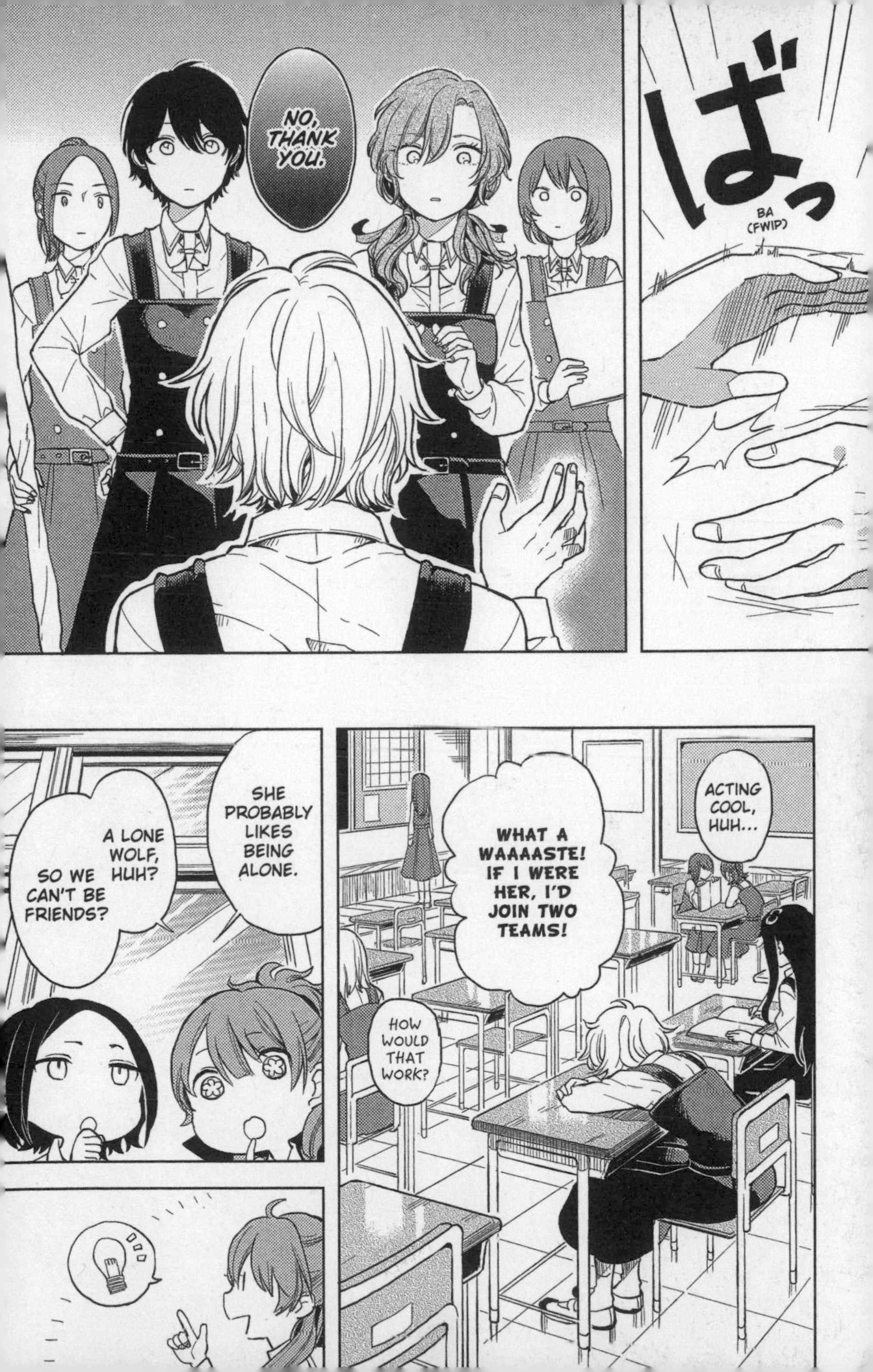
ばっ
BA (FWIP)
NO, THANK YOU.
ACTING COOL, HUH...
WHAT A WAAAASTE! IF I WERE HER, I'D JOIN TWO TEAMS!
HOW WOULD THAT WORK?
SHE PROBABLY LIKES BEING ALONE.
A LONE WOLF, HUH?
SO WE CAN'T BE FRIENDS?

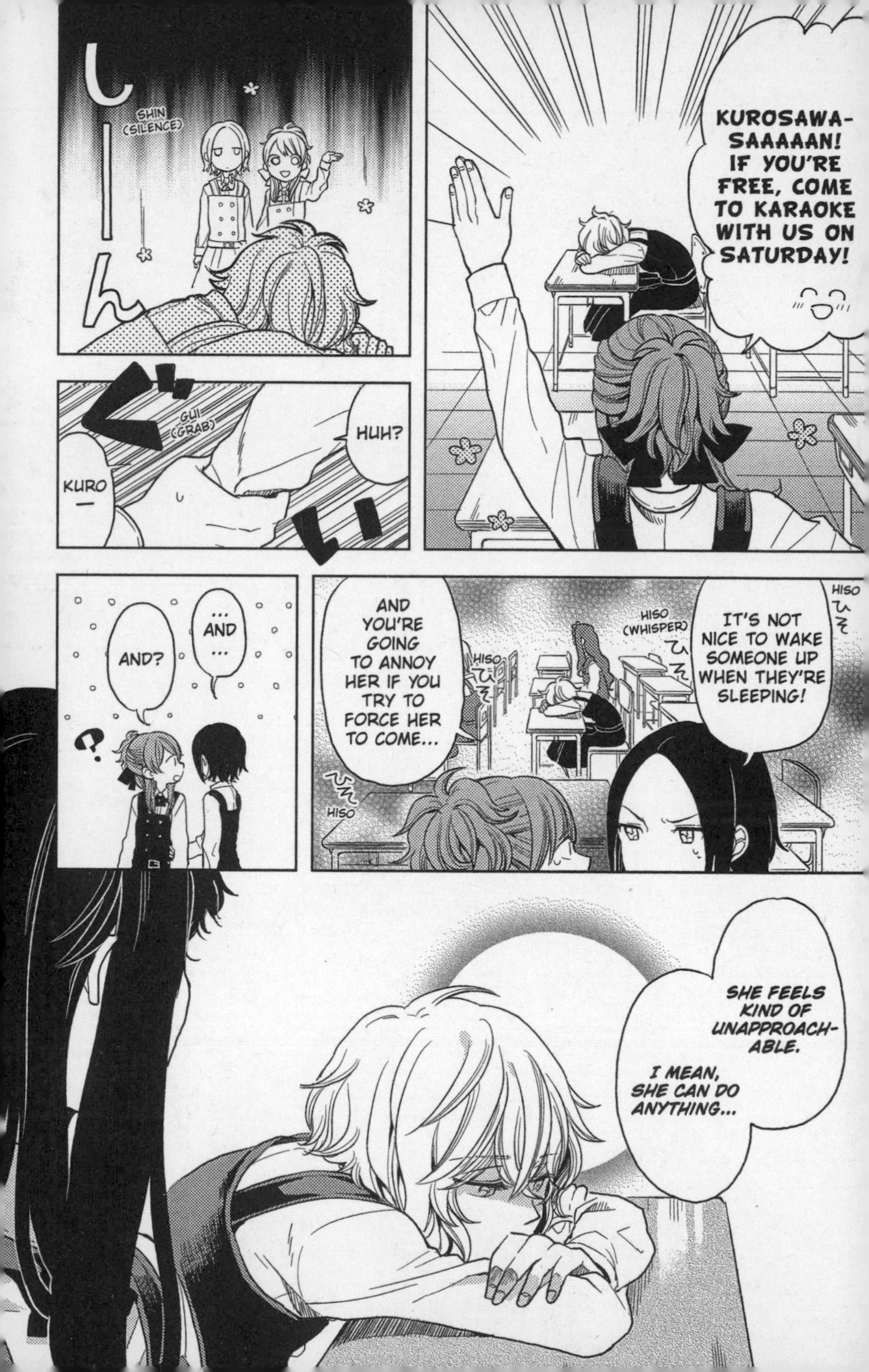
KUROSAWA-SAAAAAN! IF YOU'RE FREE, COME TO KARAOKE WITH US ON SATURDAY!
SHIN (SILENCE)
GUI (GRAB)
HUH?
KURO—
HISO
HISO (WHISPER)
IT'S NOT NICE TO WAKE SOMEONE UP WHEN THEY'RE SLEEPING!
HISO
AND YOU'RE GOING TO ANNOY HER IF YOU TRY TO FORCE HER TO COME...
HISO
... AND ...
AND?
SHE FEELS KIND OF UNAPPROACHABLE.
I MEAN, SHE CAN DO ANYTHING...

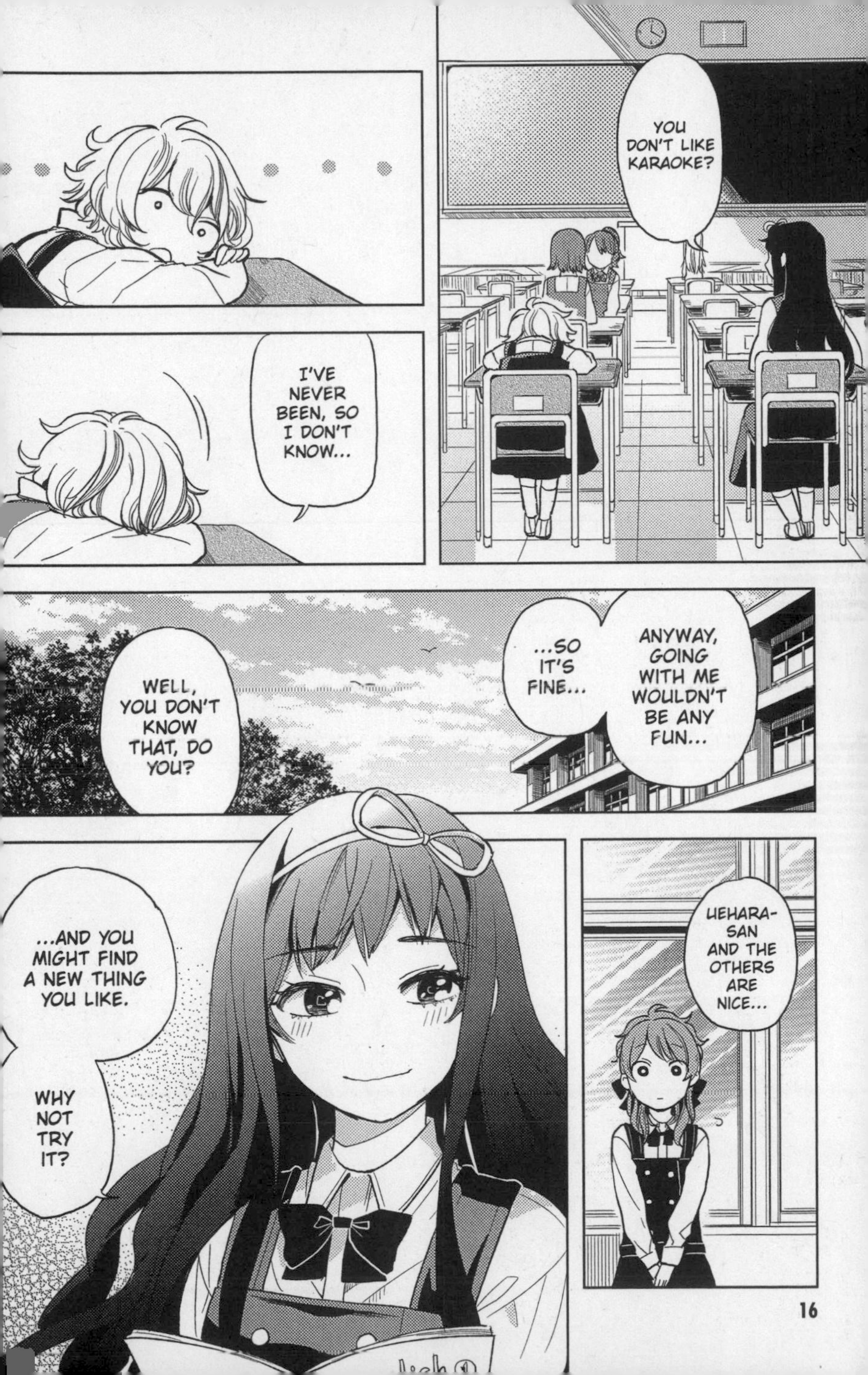
YOU DON'T LIKE KARAOKE?
I'VE NEVER BEEN, SO I DON'T KNOW...
ANYWAY, GOING WITH ME WOULDN'T BE ANY FUN...
...SO IT'S FINE...
WELL, YOU DON'T KNOW THAT, DO YOU?
UEHARA-SAN AND THE OTHERS ARE NICE...
...AND YOU MIGHT FIND A NEW THING YOU LIKE.
WHY NOT TRY IT?

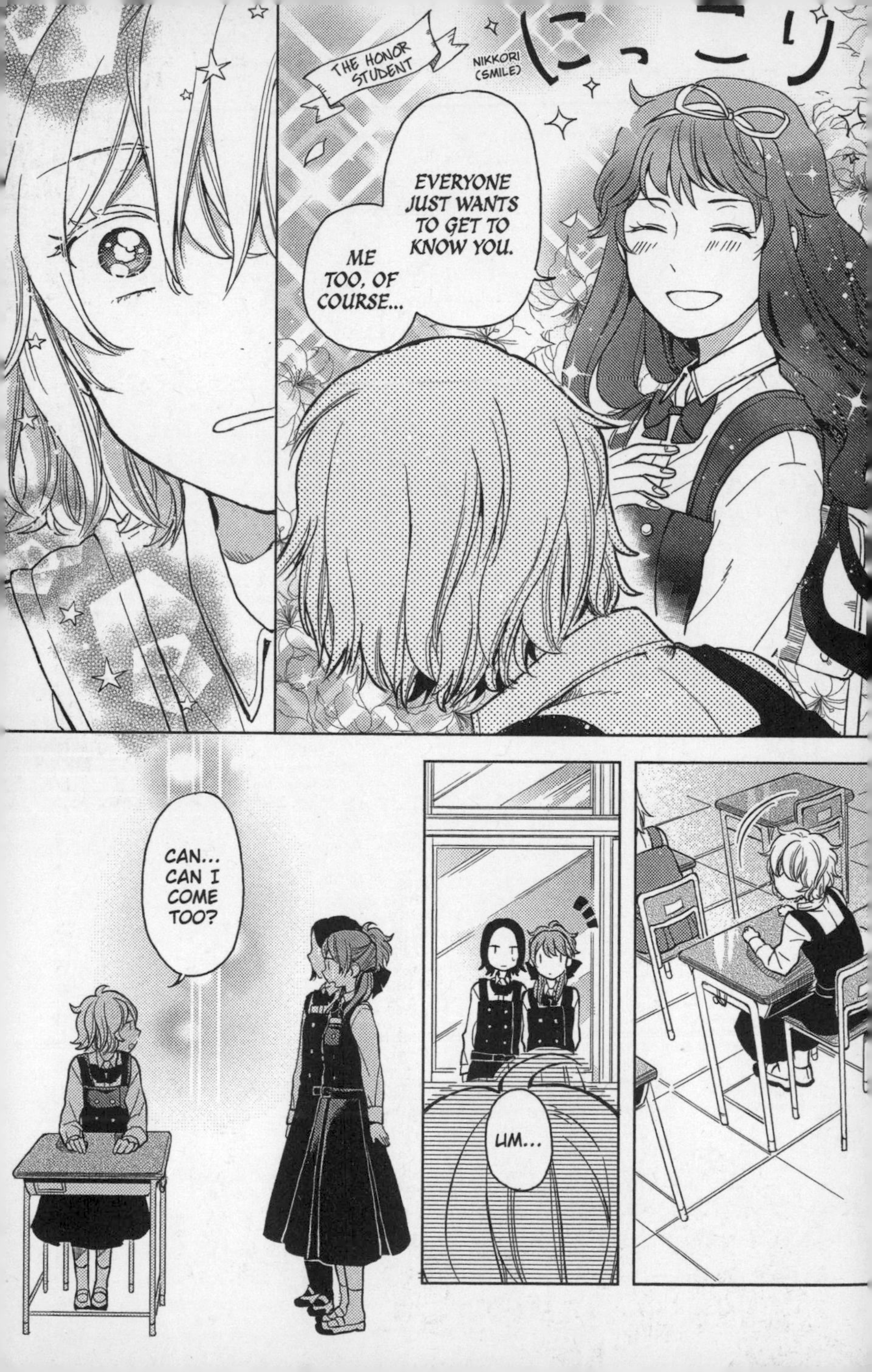
にっこり
NIKKORI (SMILE)
THE HONOR STUDENT
EVERYONE JUST WANTS TO GET TO KNOW YOU.
ME TOO, OF COURSE...
UM...
CAN... CAN I COME TOO?

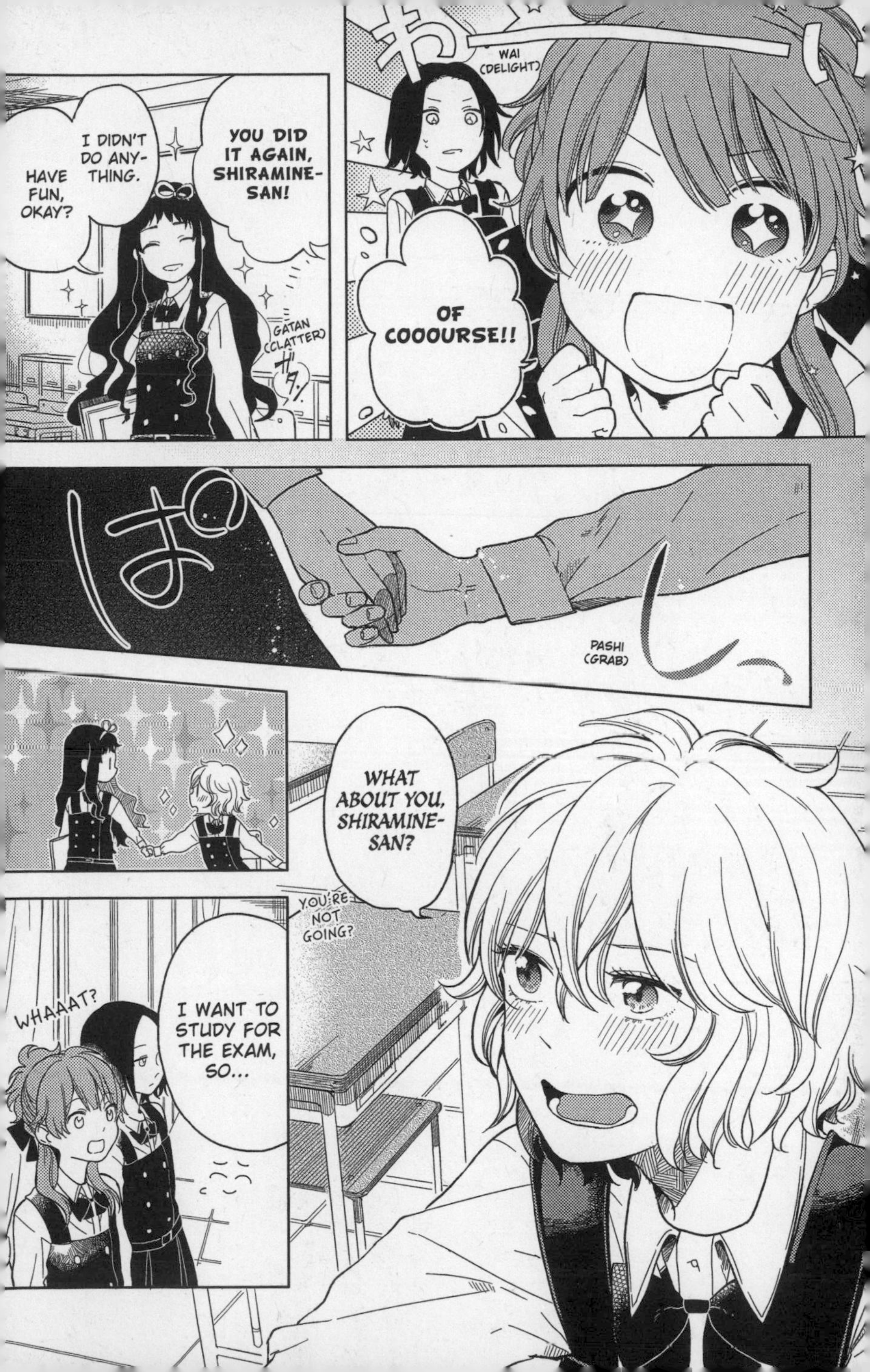
WAI (DELIGHT)
OF COOOURSE!!
YOU DID IT AGAIN, SHIRAMINE-SAN!
I DIDN'T DO ANYTHING. HAVE FUN, OKAY?
GATAN (CLATTER)
PASHI (GRAB)
WHAT ABOUT YOU, SHIRAMINE-SAN?
YOU'RE NOT GOING?
I WANT TO STUDY FOR THE EXAM, SO...
WHAAAT?

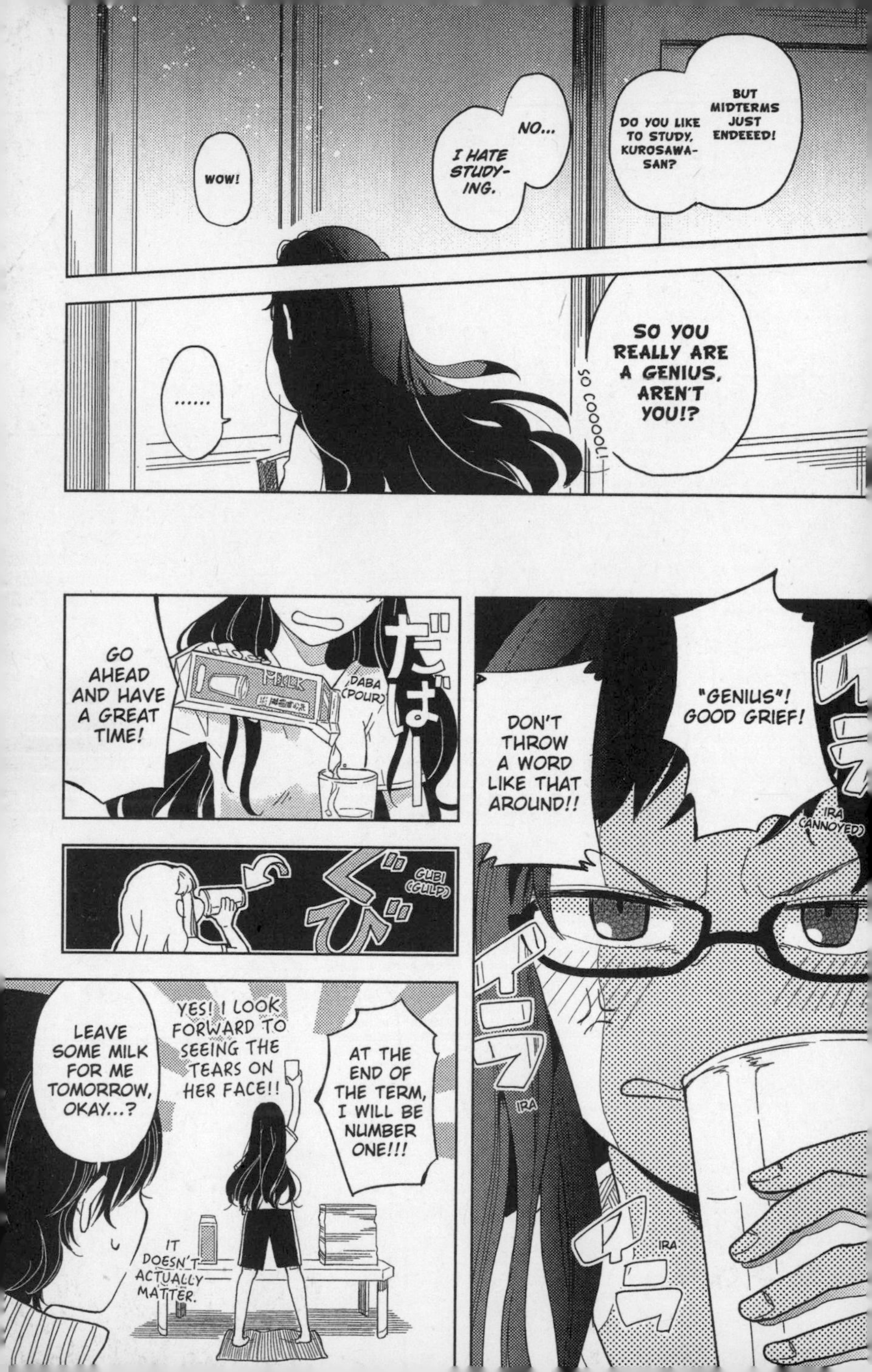
BUT MIDTERMS JUST ENDEEED!
DO YOU LIKE TO STUDY, KUROSAWA-SAN?
NO...
I HATE STUDYING.
WOW!
SO YOU REALLY ARE A GENIUS, AREN'T YOU!?
SO COOOOL!
......
IRA (ANNOYED)
"GENIUS"! GOOD GRIEF!
DON'T THROW A WORD LIKE THAT AROUND!!
IRA
IRA
だば
DABA (POUR)
GO AHEAD AND HAVE A GREAT TIME!
ぐび
GUBI (GULP)
AT THE END OF THE TERM, I WILL BE NUMBER ONE!!!
YES! I LOOK FORWARD TO SEEING THE TEARS ON HER FACE!!
LEAVE SOME MILK FOR ME TOMORROW, OKAY...?
IT DOESN'T ACTUALLY MATTER.

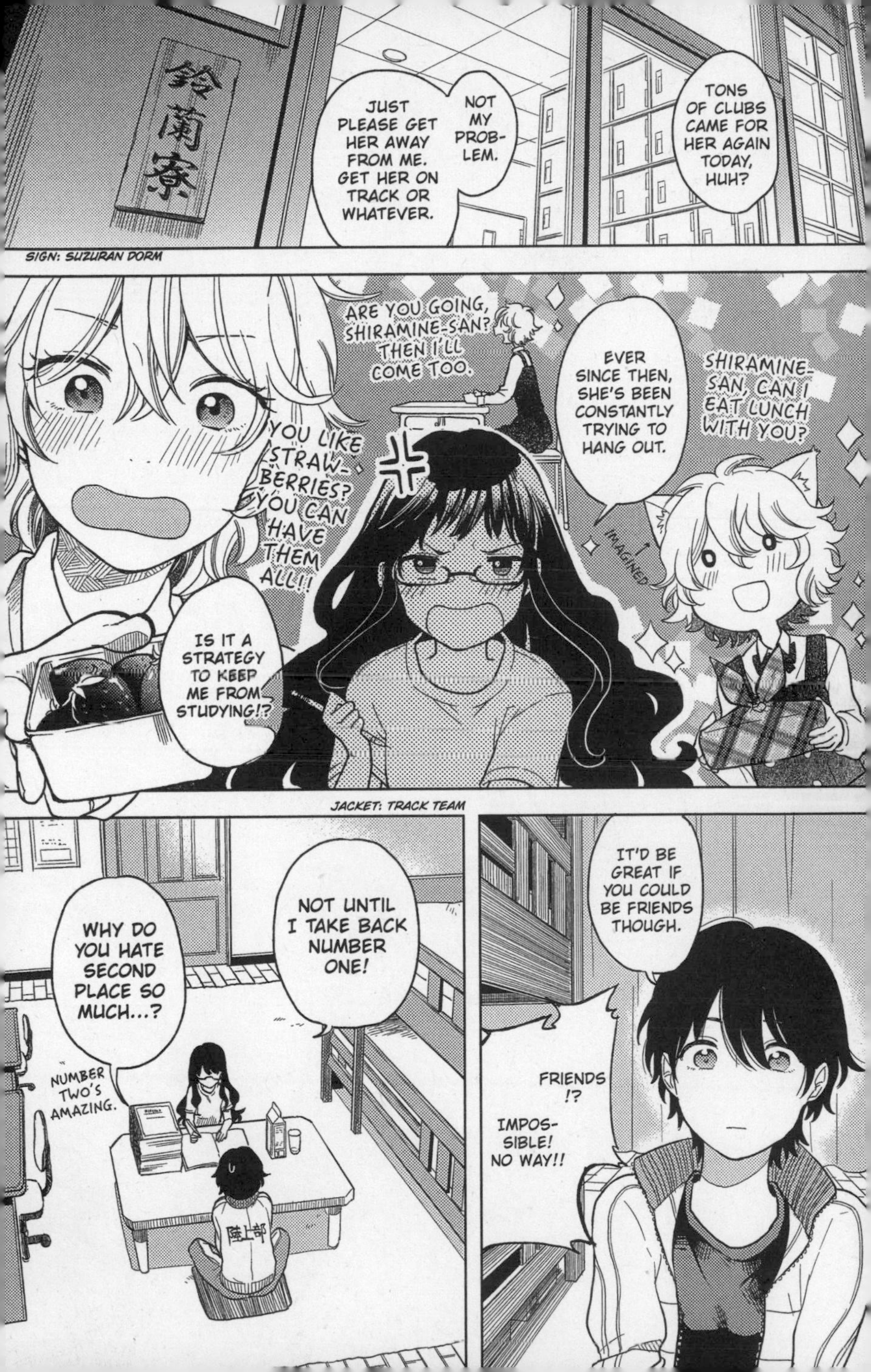
TONS OF CLUBS CAME FOR HER AGAIN TODAY, HUH?
NOT MY PROBLEM.
JUST PLEASE GET HER AWAY FROM ME. GET HER ON TRACK OR WHATEVER.
鈴蘭寮
SIGN: SUZURAN DORM
SHIRAMINE-SAN, CAN I EAT LUNCH WITH YOU?
EVER SINCE THEN, SHE'S BEEN CONSTANTLY TRYING TO HANG OUT.
IMAGINED
ARE YOU GOING, SHIRAMINE-SAN? THEN I'LL COME TOO.
YOU LIKE STRAWBERRIES? YOU CAN HAVE THEM ALL!!
IS IT A STRATEGY TO KEEP ME FROM STUDYING!?
JACKET: TRACK TEAM
IT'D BE GREAT IF YOU COULD BE FRIENDS THOUGH.
FRIENDS!?
IMPOSSIBLE! NO WAY!!
NOT UNTIL I TAKE BACK NUMBER ONE!
WHY DO YOU HATE SECOND PLACE SO MUCH...?
NUMBER TWO'S AMAZING.
陸上部

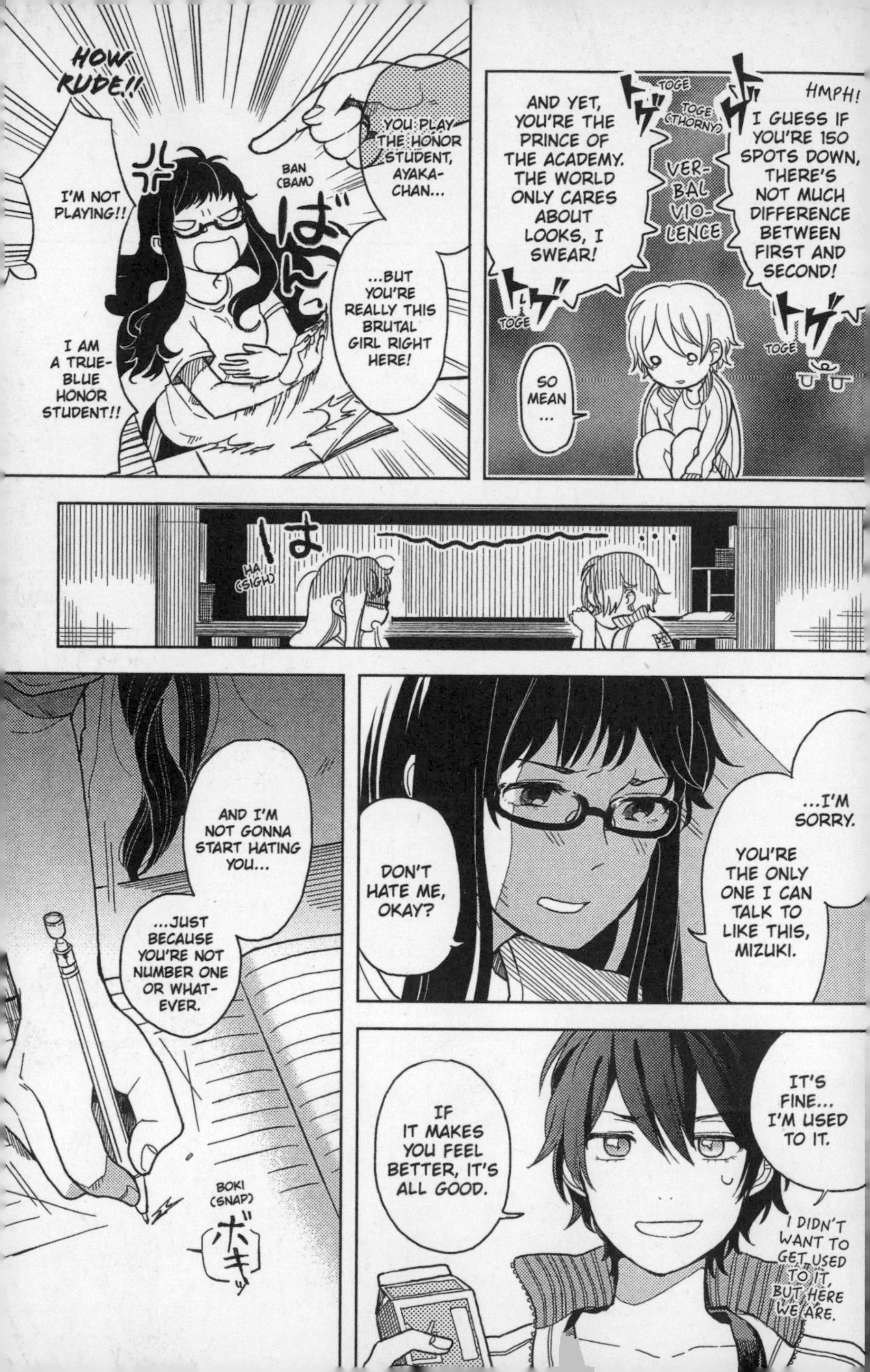
HMPH!
I GUESS IF YOU'RE 150 SPOTS DOWN, THERE'S NOT MUCH DIFFERENCE BETWEEN FIRST AND SECOND!
TOGE
TOGE (THORNY)
VERBAL VIOLENCE
AND YET, YOU'RE THE PRINCE OF THE ACADEMY. THE WORLD ONLY CARES ABOUT LOOKS, I SWEAR!
TOGE
TOGE
SO MEAN...
YOU PLAY THE HONOR STUDENT, AYAKA-CHAN...
...BUT YOU'RE REALLY THIS BRUTAL GIRL RIGHT HERE!
BAN (BAM)
HOW RUDE!!
I'M NOT PLAYING!!
I AM A TRUE-BLUE HONOR STUDENT!!
HA (SIGH)
...I'M SORRY.
YOU'RE THE ONLY ONE I CAN TALK TO LIKE THIS, MIZUKI.
DON'T HATE ME, OKAY?
IT'S FINE... I'M USED TO IT.
I DIDN'T WANT TO GET USED TO IT, BUT HERE WE ARE.
IF IT MAKES YOU FEEL BETTER, IT'S ALL GOOD.
AND I'M NOT GONNA START HATING YOU...
...JUST BECAUSE YOU'RE NOT NUMBER ONE OR WHATEVER.
BOKI (SNAP)

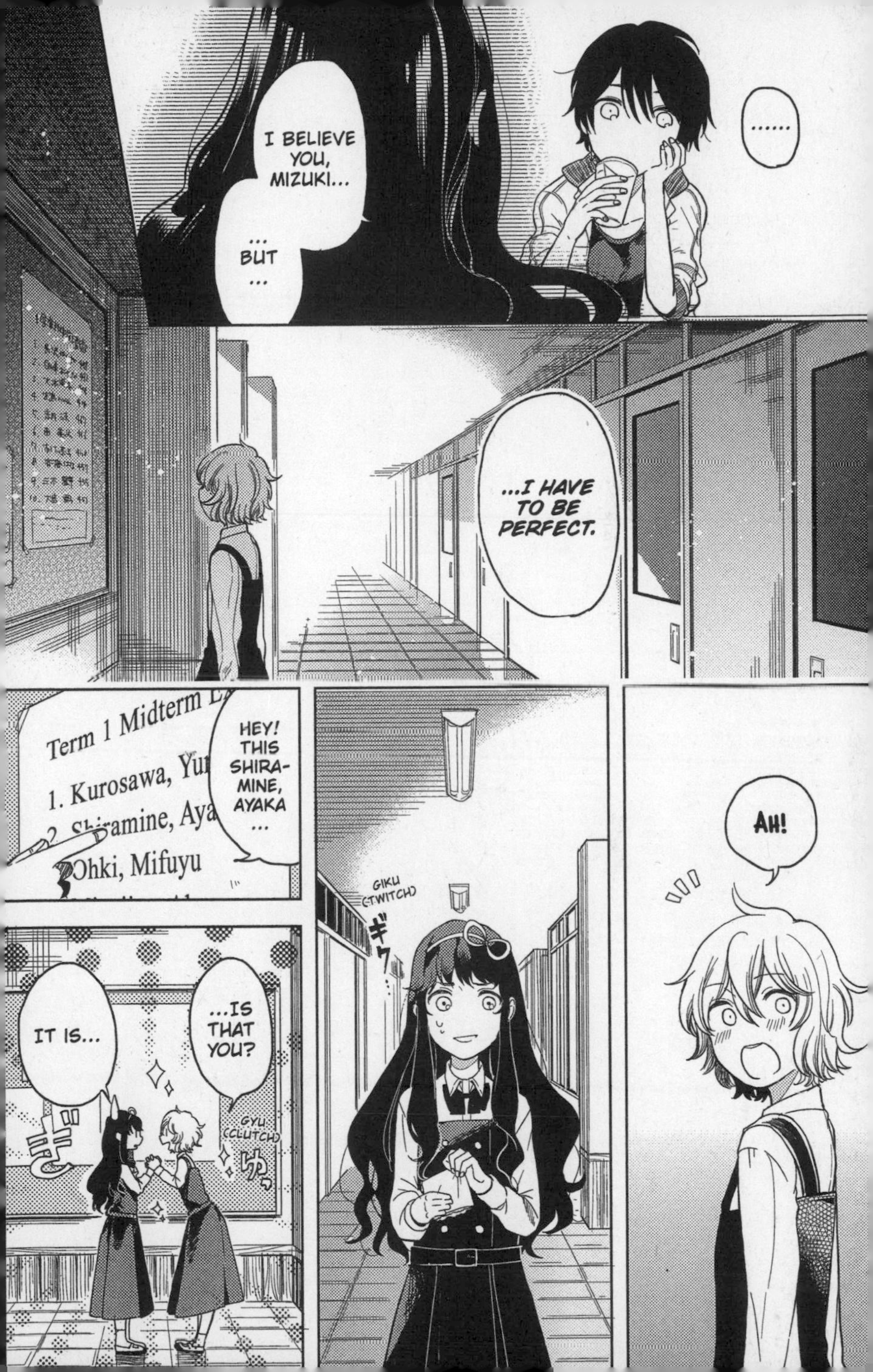
......
I BELIEVE YOU, MIZUKI...
... BUT ...
...I HAVE TO BE PERFECT.
AH!
GIKU (TWITCH)
ギク
Term 1 Midterm
1. Kurosawa, Yu
2. Shiramine, Aya
Ohki, Mifuyu
HEY! THIS SHIRAMINE, AYAKA ...
...IS THAT YOU?
IT IS...
GYU (CLUTCH)
ぎゅ

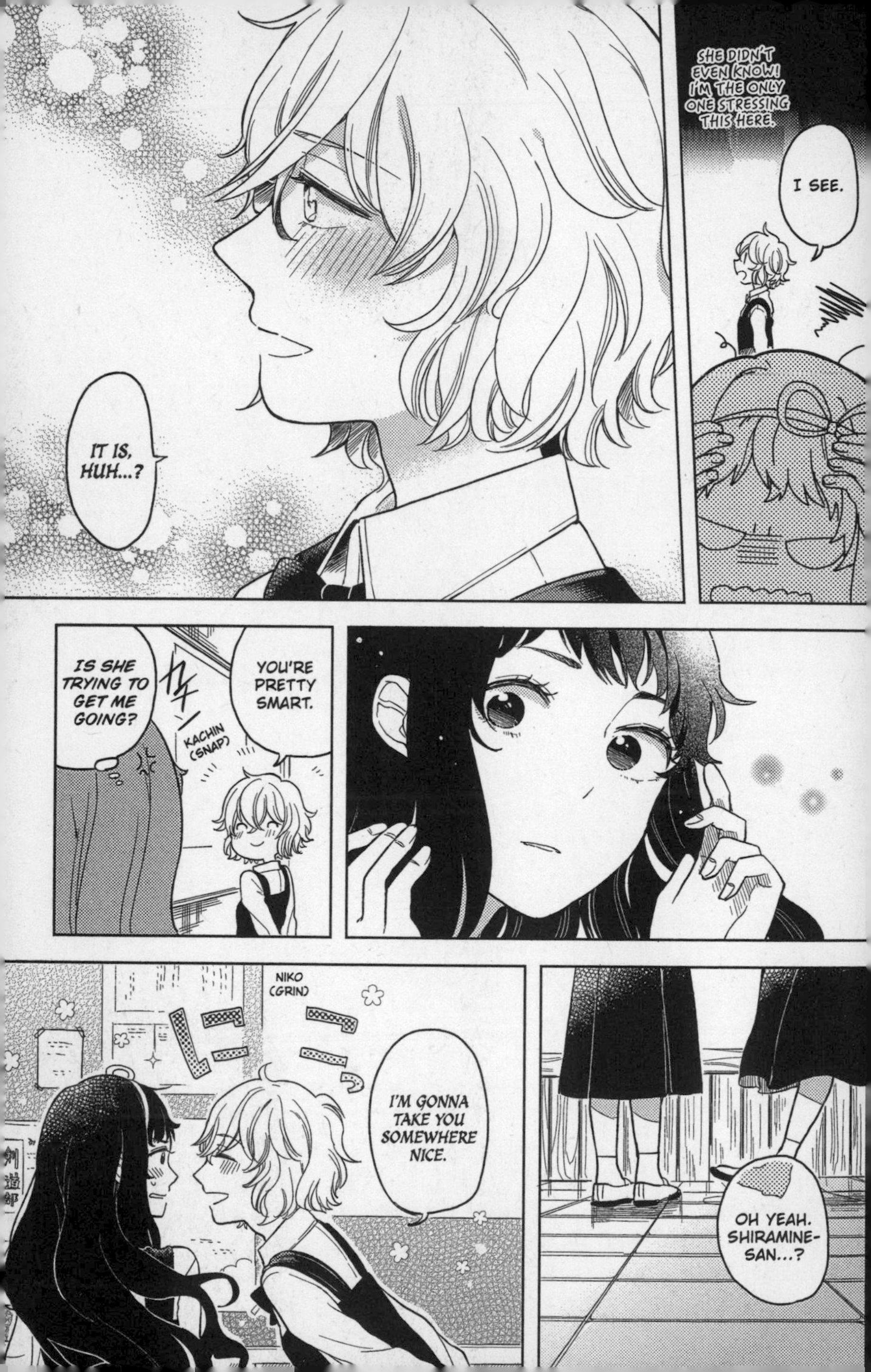
SHE DIDN'T EVEN KNOW! I'M THE ONLY ONE STRESSING THIS HERE.
I SEE.
IT IS, HUH...?
YOU'RE PRETTY SMART.
KACHIN (SNAP)
IS SHE TRYING TO GET ME GOING?
OH YEAH. SHIRAMINE-SAN...?
NIKO (GRIN)
I'M GONNA TAKE YOU SOMEWHERE NICE.
剣道部

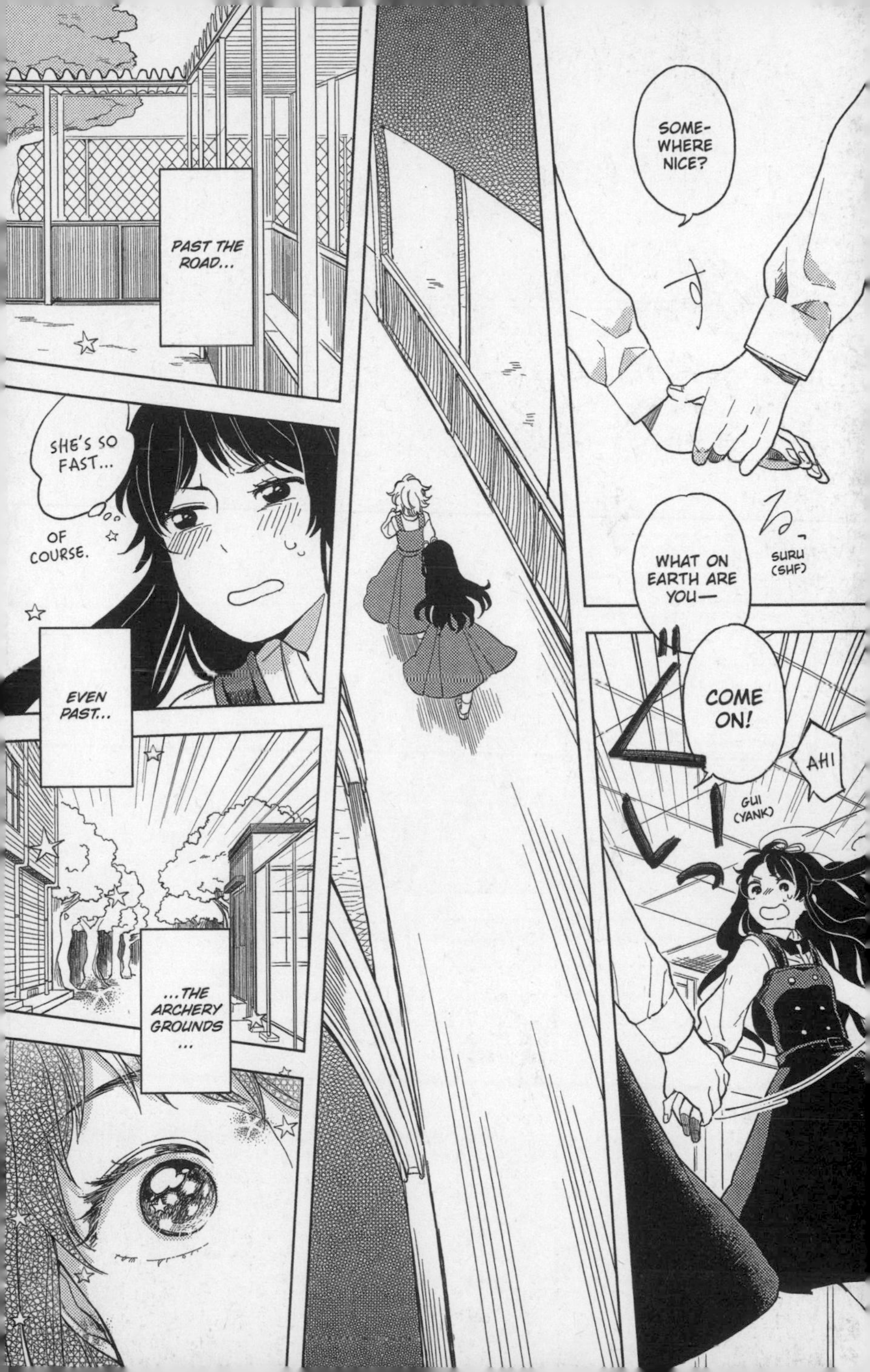
SOME-WHERE NICE?
SURU (SHF)
WHAT ON EARTH ARE YOU—
COME ON!
AHI
GUI (YANK)
PAST THE ROAD...
SHE'S SO FAST...
OF COURSE.
EVEN PAST...
...THE ARCHERY GROUNDS...

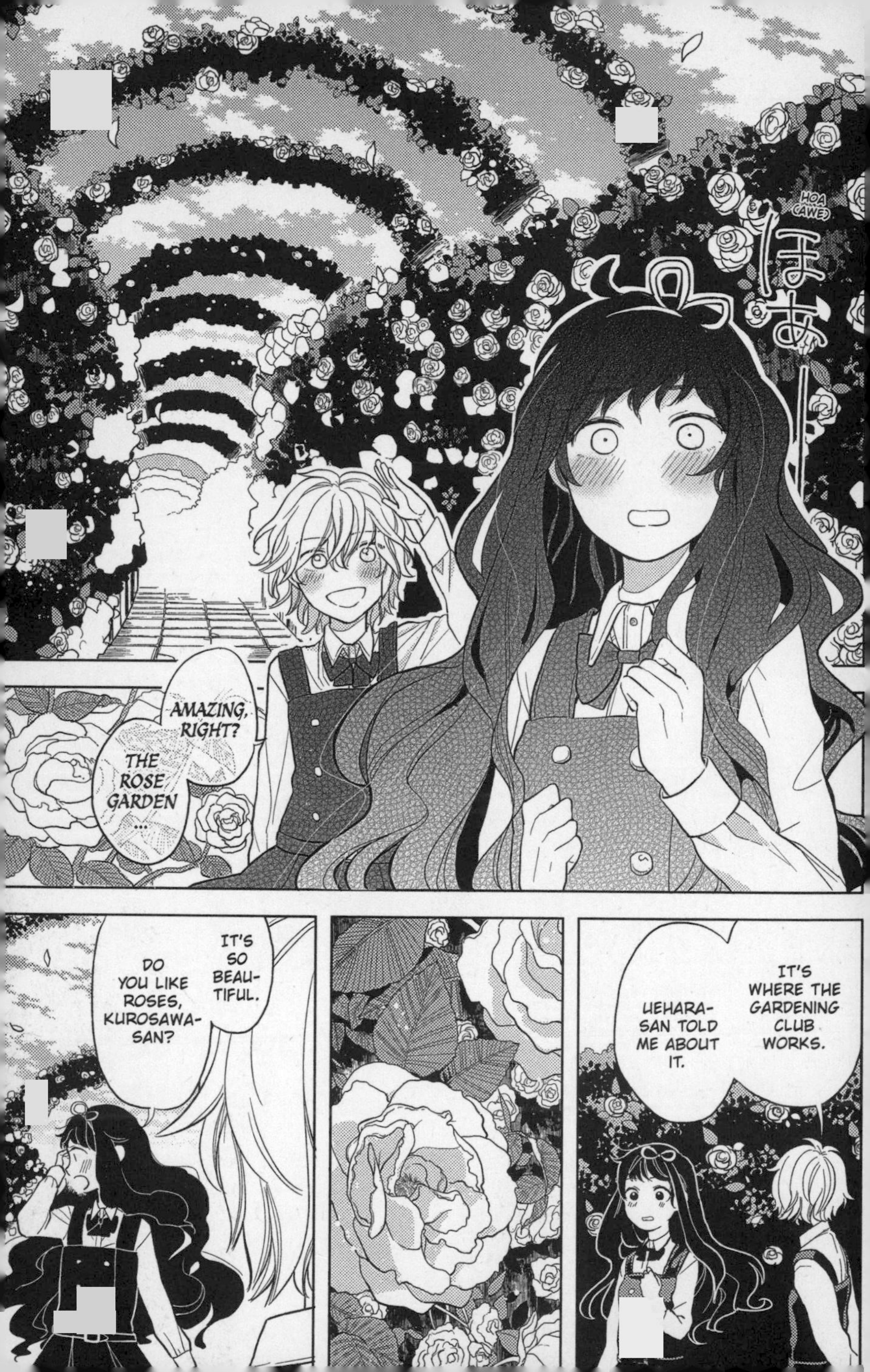
HOA (AWE)
ほあ
AMAZING, RIGHT?
THE ROSE GARDEN...
IT'S WHERE THE GARDENING CLUB WORKS.
UEHARA-SAN TOLD ME ABOUT IT.
IT'S SO BEAU-TIFUL.
DO YOU LIKE ROSES, KUROSAWA-SAN?

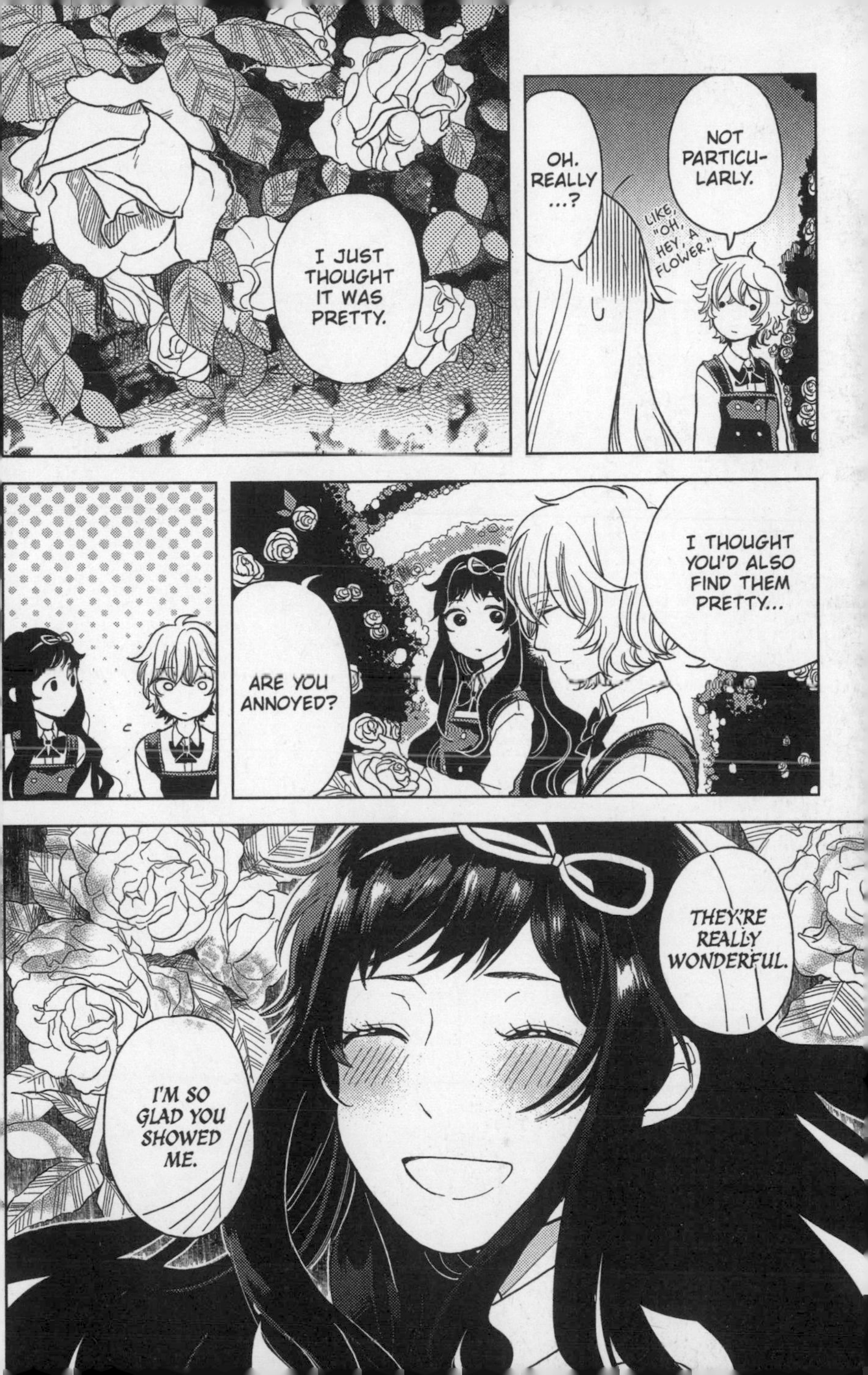
NOT PARTICU-LARLY.
LIKE, "OH, HEY, A FLOWER."
OH. REALLY ...?
I JUST THOUGHT IT WAS PRETTY.
I THOUGHT YOU'D ALSO FIND THEM PRETTY...
ARE YOU ANNOYED?
THEY'RE REALLY WONDERFUL.
I'M SO GLAD YOU SHOWED ME.

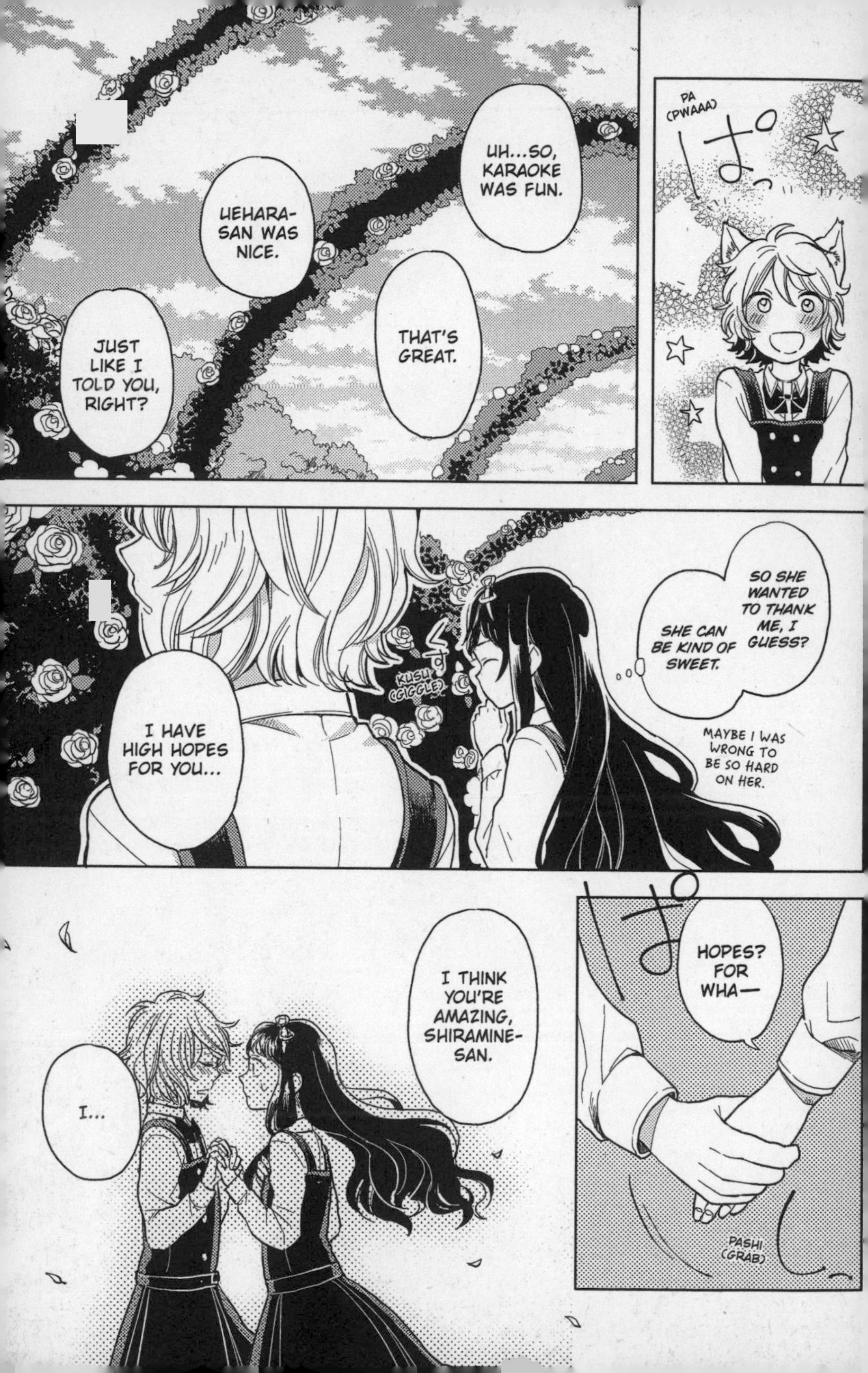
PA
(PWAAA)
ぱっ
UH...SO, KARAOKE WAS FUN.
UEHARA-SAN WAS NICE.
THAT'S GREAT.
JUST LIKE I TOLD YOU, RIGHT?
SO SHE WANTED TO THANK ME, I GUESS?
SHE CAN BE KIND OF SWEET.
MAYBE I WAS WRONG TO BE SO HARD ON HER.
くす
KUSU (GIGGLE)
I HAVE HIGH HOPES FOR YOU...
ぱ
HOPES? FOR WHA—
PASHI (GRAB)
I THINK YOU'RE AMAZING, SHIRAMINE-SAN.
I...

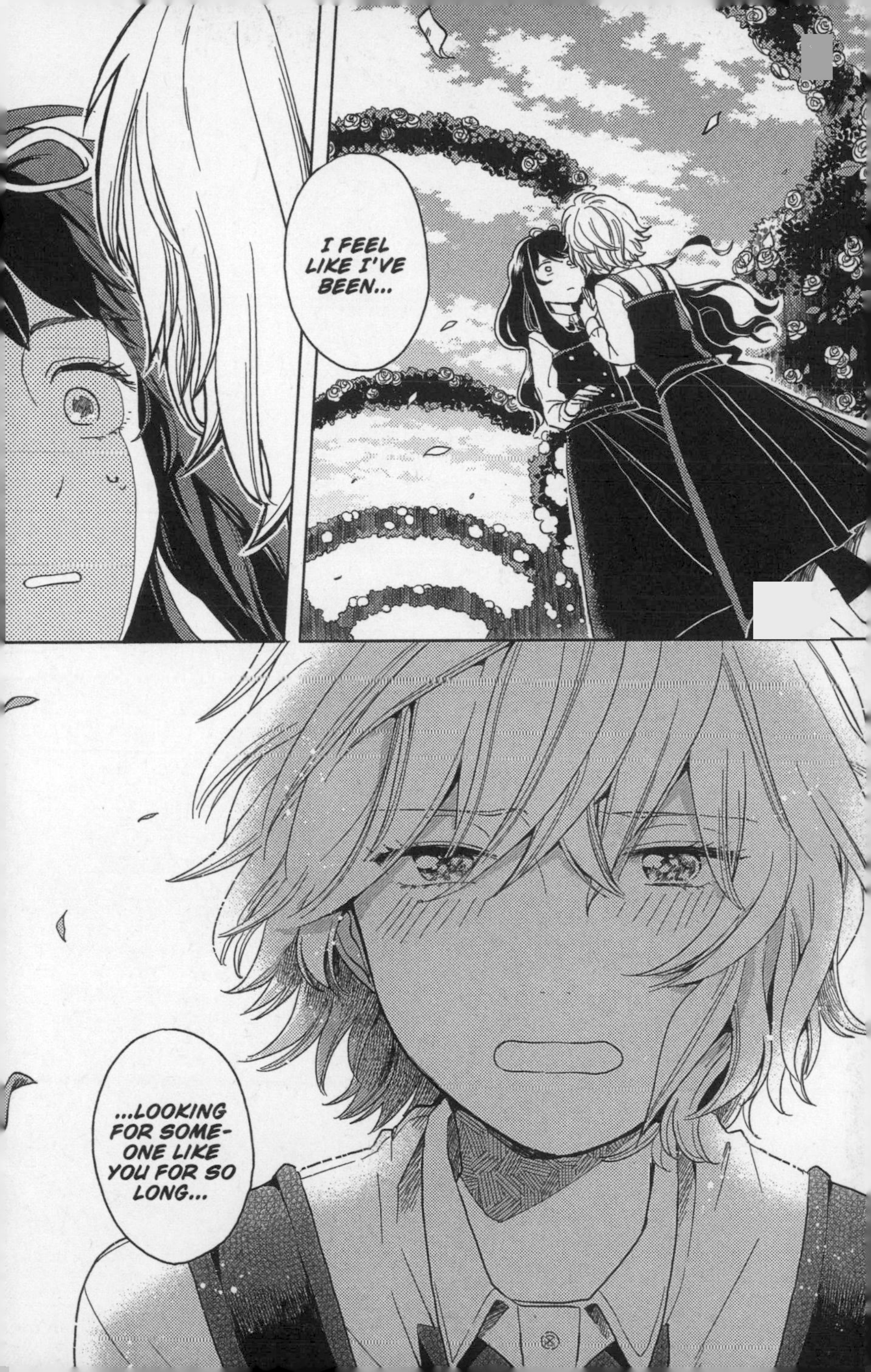
I FEEL LIKE I'VE BEEN...
...LOOKING FOR SOME-ONE LIKE YOU FOR SO LONG...

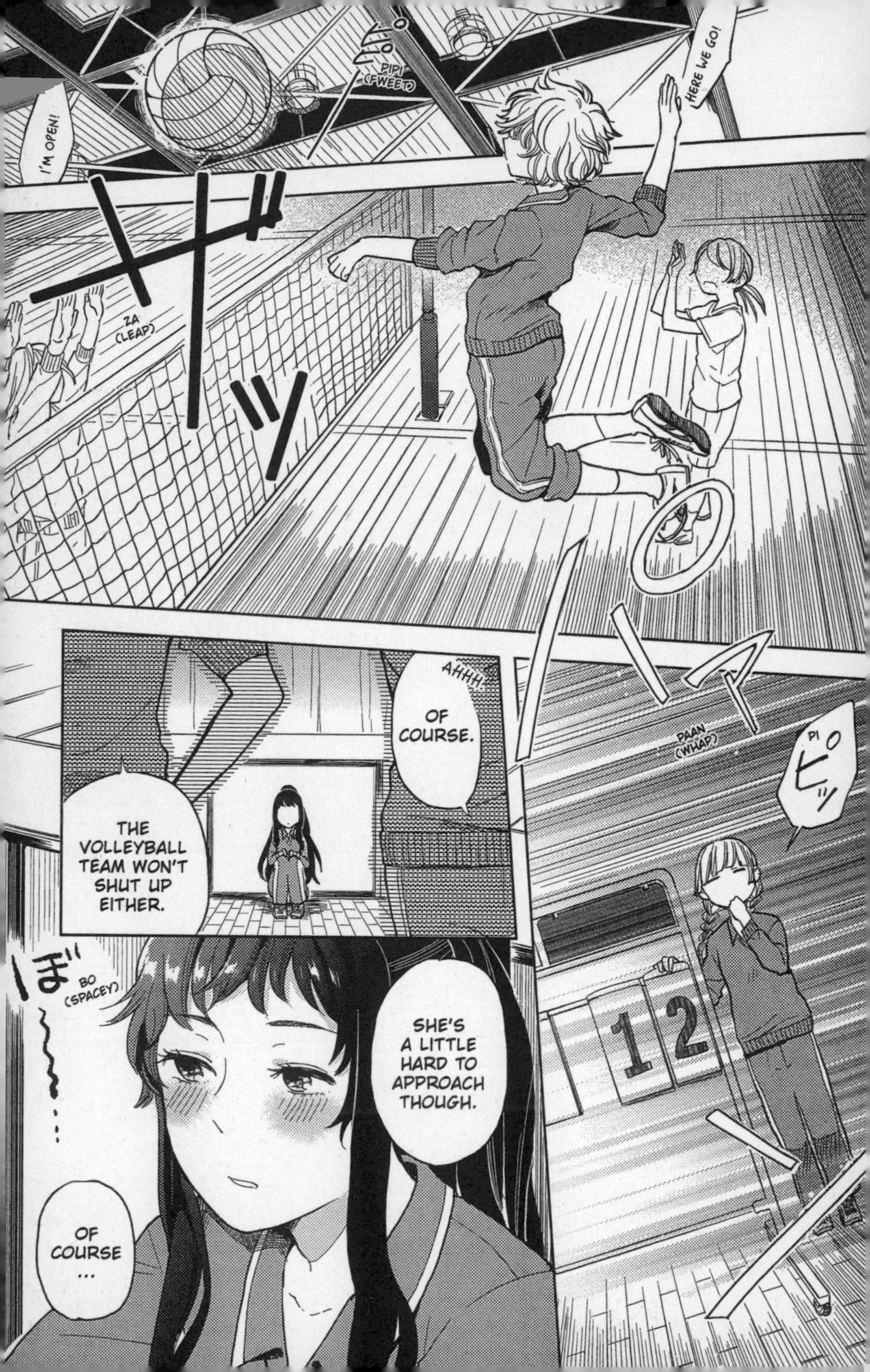
HERE WE GO!
PIPI (FWEET)
I'M OPEN!
ZA (LEAP)
PAAN (WHAP)
PI
AHHH.
OF COURSE.
THE VOLLEYBALL TEAM WON'T SHUT UP EITHER.
SHE'S A LITTLE HARD TO APPROACH THOUGH.
BO (SPACEY)
OF COURSE ...

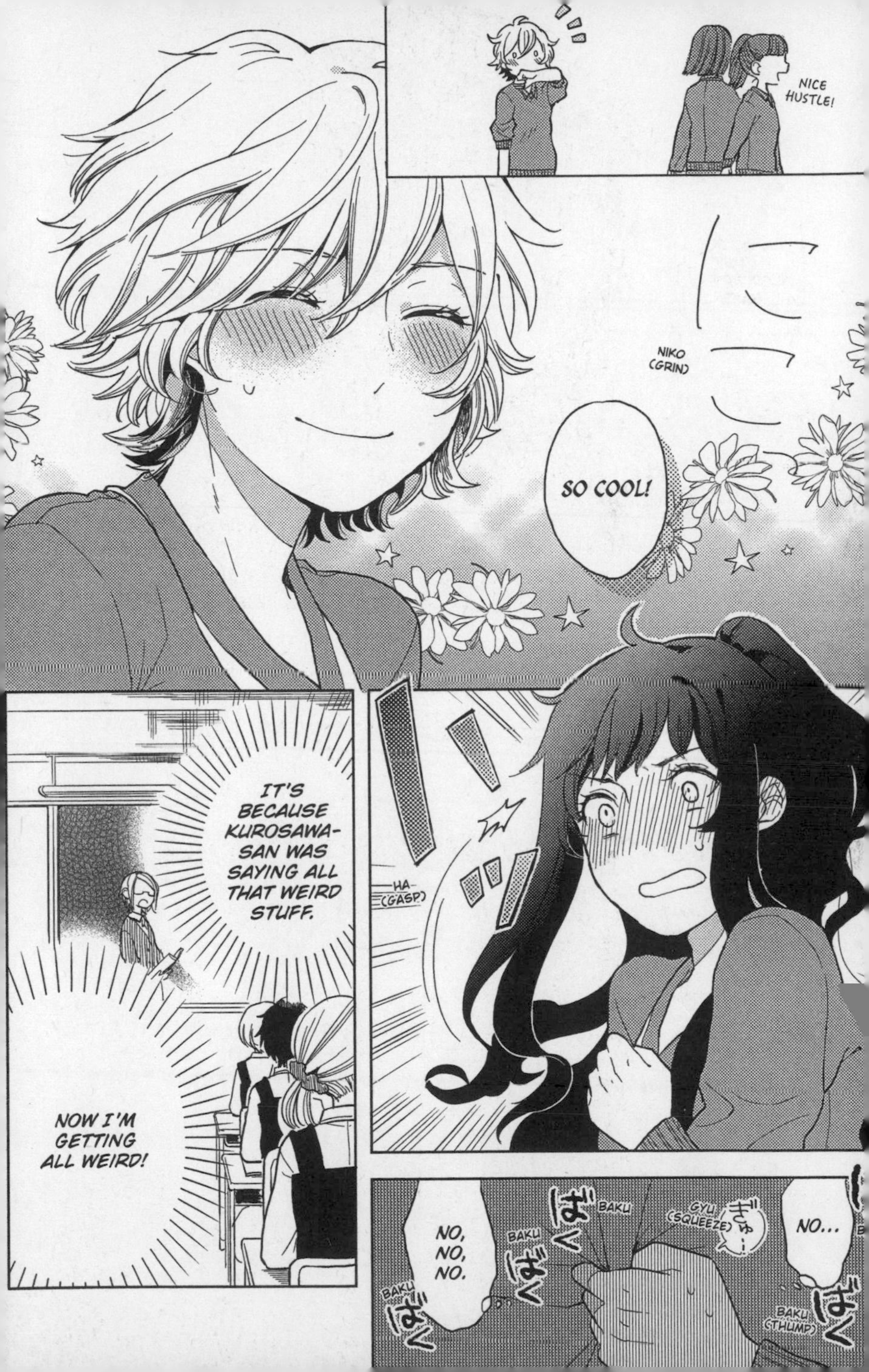
NICE HUSTLE!
NIKO (GRIN)
SO COOL!
HA- (GASP)
NO...
BAKU (THUMP)
GYU (SQUEEZE)
BAKU
BAKU
NO, NO, NO.
BAKU
IT'S BECAUSE KUROSAWA-SAN WAS SAYING ALL THAT WEIRD STUFF.
NOW I'M GETTING ALL WEIRD!

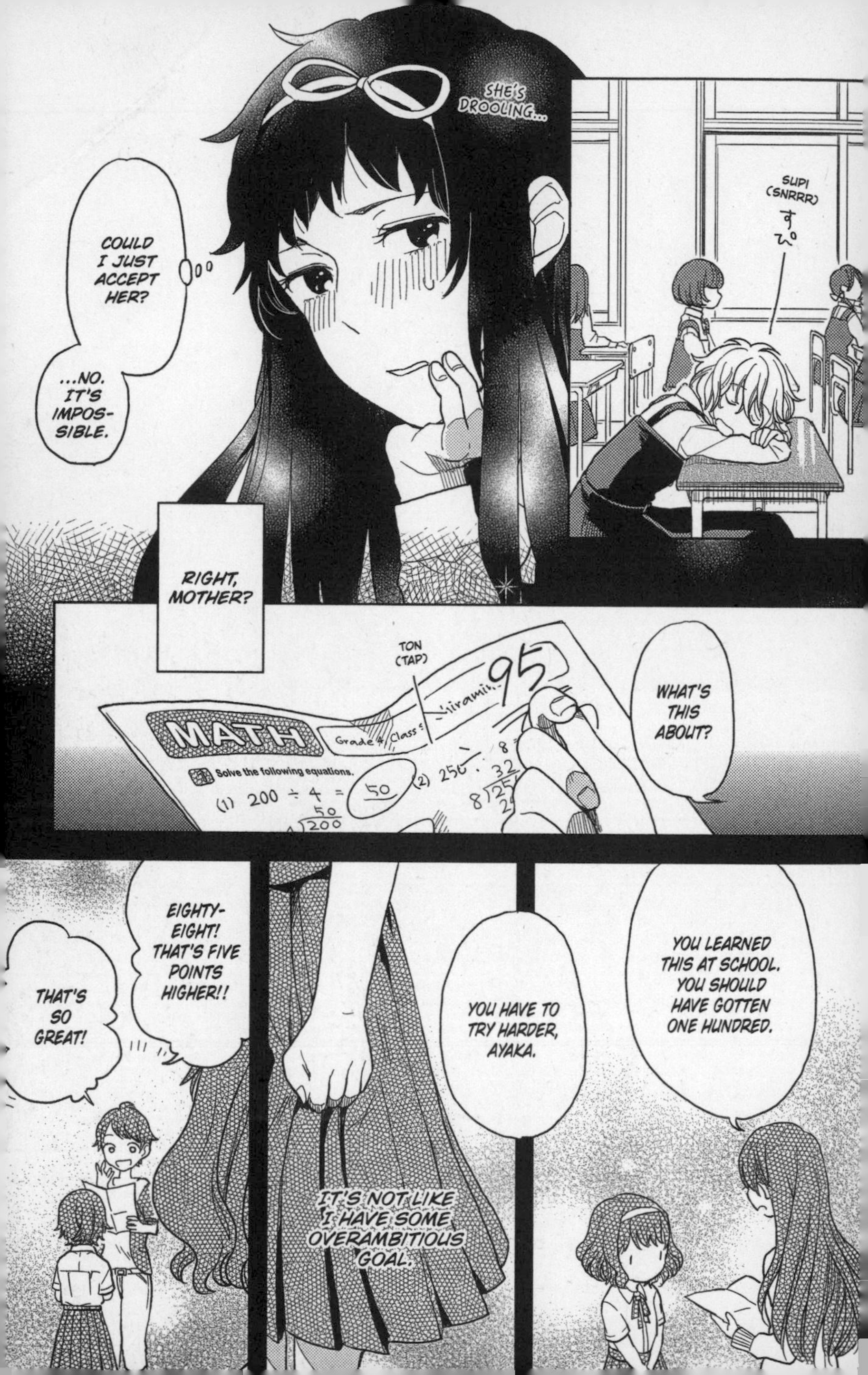
SUPI (SNRRR)
すぴ
SHE'S DROOLING...
COULD I JUST ACCEPT HER?
...NO. IT'S IMPOSSIBLE.
RIGHT, MOTHER?
TON (TAP)
95
MATH
Grade 4 Class 5
Solve the following equations.
(1) 200 ÷ 4 = 50
WHAT'S THIS ABOUT?
YOU LEARNED THIS AT SCHOOL. YOU SHOULD HAVE GOTTEN ONE HUNDRED.
YOU HAVE TO TRY HARDER, AYAKA.
IT'S NOT LIKE I HAVE SOME OVERAMBITIOUS GOAL.
EIGHTY-EIGHT! THAT'S FIVE POINTS HIGHER!!
THAT'S SO GREAT!

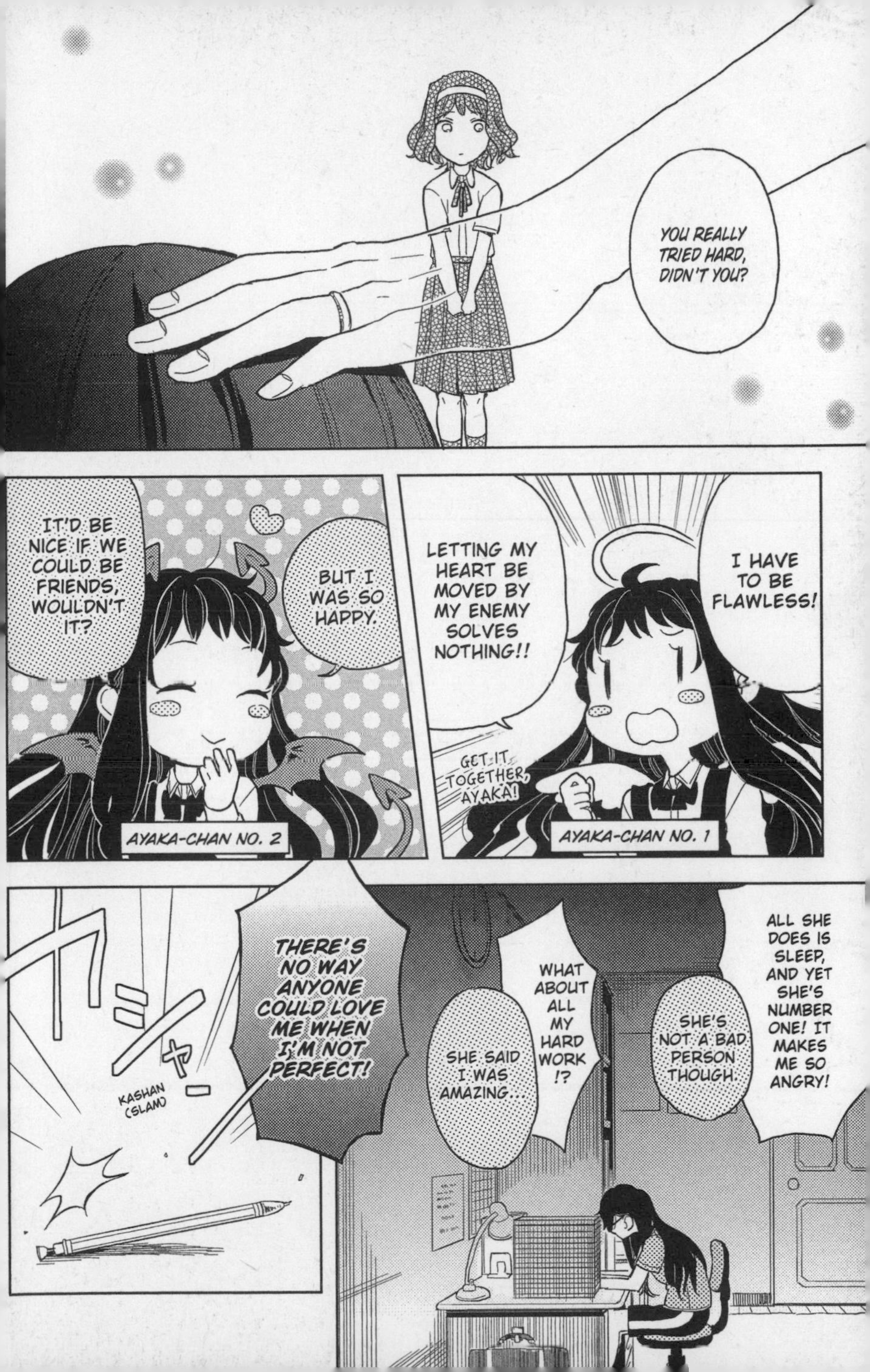
YOU REALLY TRIED HARD, DIDN'T YOU?
I HAVE TO BE FLAWLESS!
LETTING MY HEART BE MOVED BY MY ENEMY SOLVES NOTHING!!
GET IT TOGETHER, AYAKA!
AYAKA-CHAN NO. 1
BUT I WAS SO HAPPY.
IT'D BE NICE IF WE COULD BE FRIENDS, WOULDN'T IT?
AYAKA-CHAN NO. 2
ALL SHE DOES IS SLEEP, AND YET SHE'S NUMBER ONE! IT MAKES ME SO ANGRY!
SHE'S NOT A BAD PERSON THOUGH.
WHAT ABOUT ALL MY HARD WORK!?
SHE SAID I WAS AMAZING...
THERE'S NO WAY ANYONE COULD LOVE ME WHEN I'M NOT PERFECT!
KASHAN (SLAM)

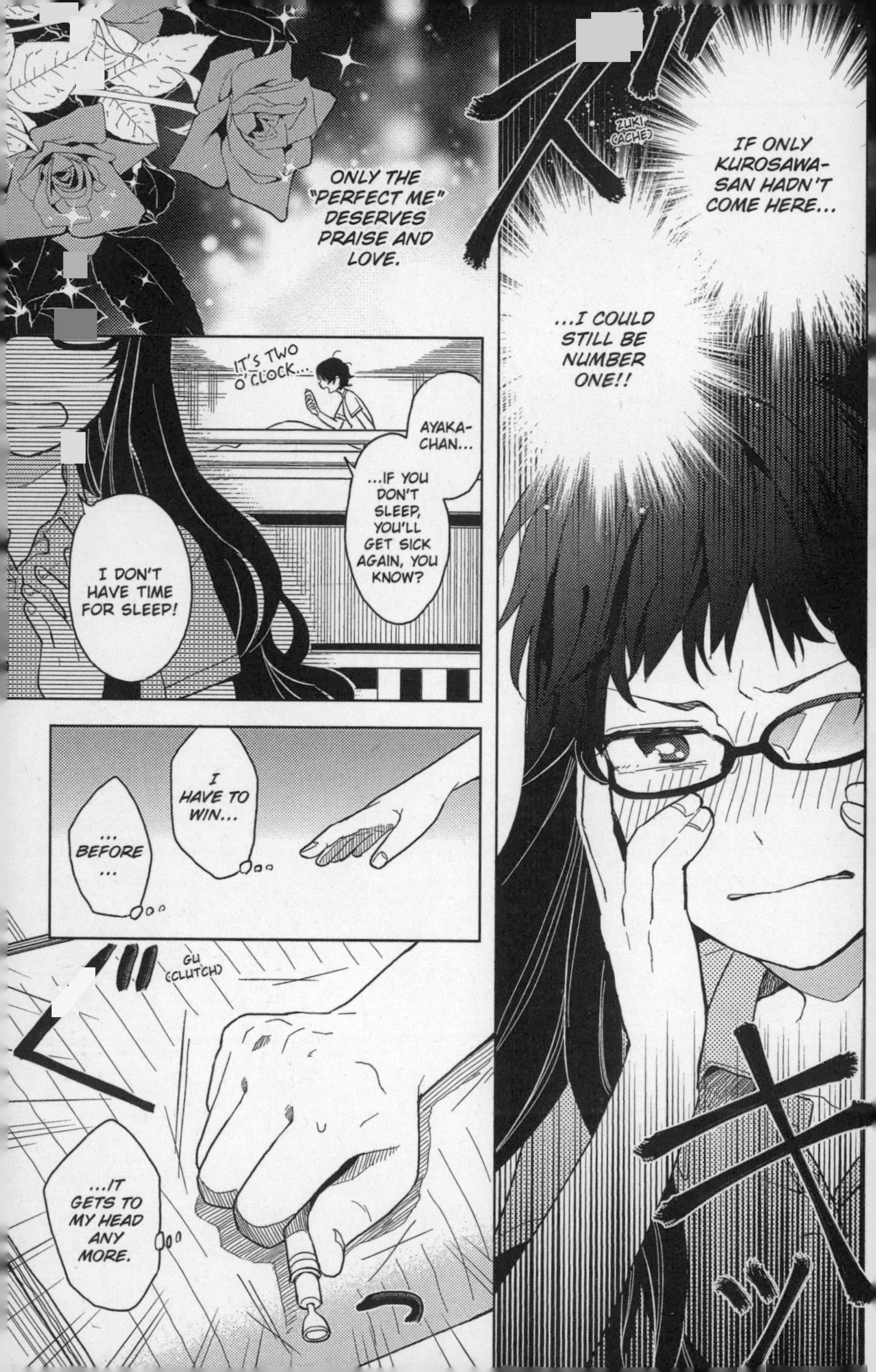
ZUKI (CACHE)
IF ONLY KUROSAWA-SAN HADN'T COME HERE...
...I COULD STILL BE NUMBER ONE!!
ONLY THE "PERFECT ME" DESERVES PRAISE AND LOVE.
IT'S TWO O'CLOCK...
AYAKA-CHAN...
...IF YOU DON'T SLEEP, YOU'LL GET SICK AGAIN, YOU KNOW?
I DON'T HAVE TIME FOR SLEEP!
I HAVE TO WIN...
...BEFORE...
GU (CLUTCH)
...IT GETS TO MY HEAD ANY MORE.

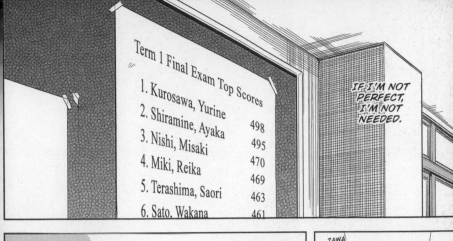

Term 1 Final Exam Top Scores

1. Kurosawa, Yurine
2. Shiramine, Ayaka   498
3. Nishi, Misaki   495
4. Miki, Reika   470
5. Terashima, Saori   469
6. Sato, Wakana   463
                       461

IF I'M NOT PERFECT, I'M NOT NEEDED.

Yurine 498

Ayaka 495

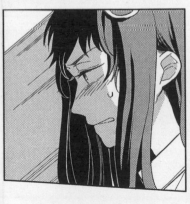

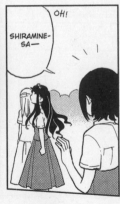

OH!

SHIRAMINE-SA—

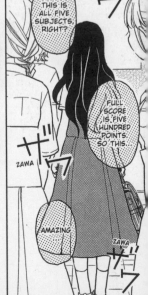

ZAWA (CHATTER)

OF COURSE IT'D BE KUROSAWA-SAN!

ZAWA

THIS IS ALL FIVE SUBJECTS, RIGHT?

FULL SCORE IS FIVE HUNDRED POINTS SO THIS...

ZAWA

AMAZING

ZAWA

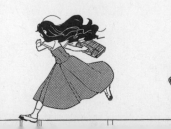

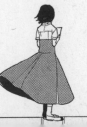

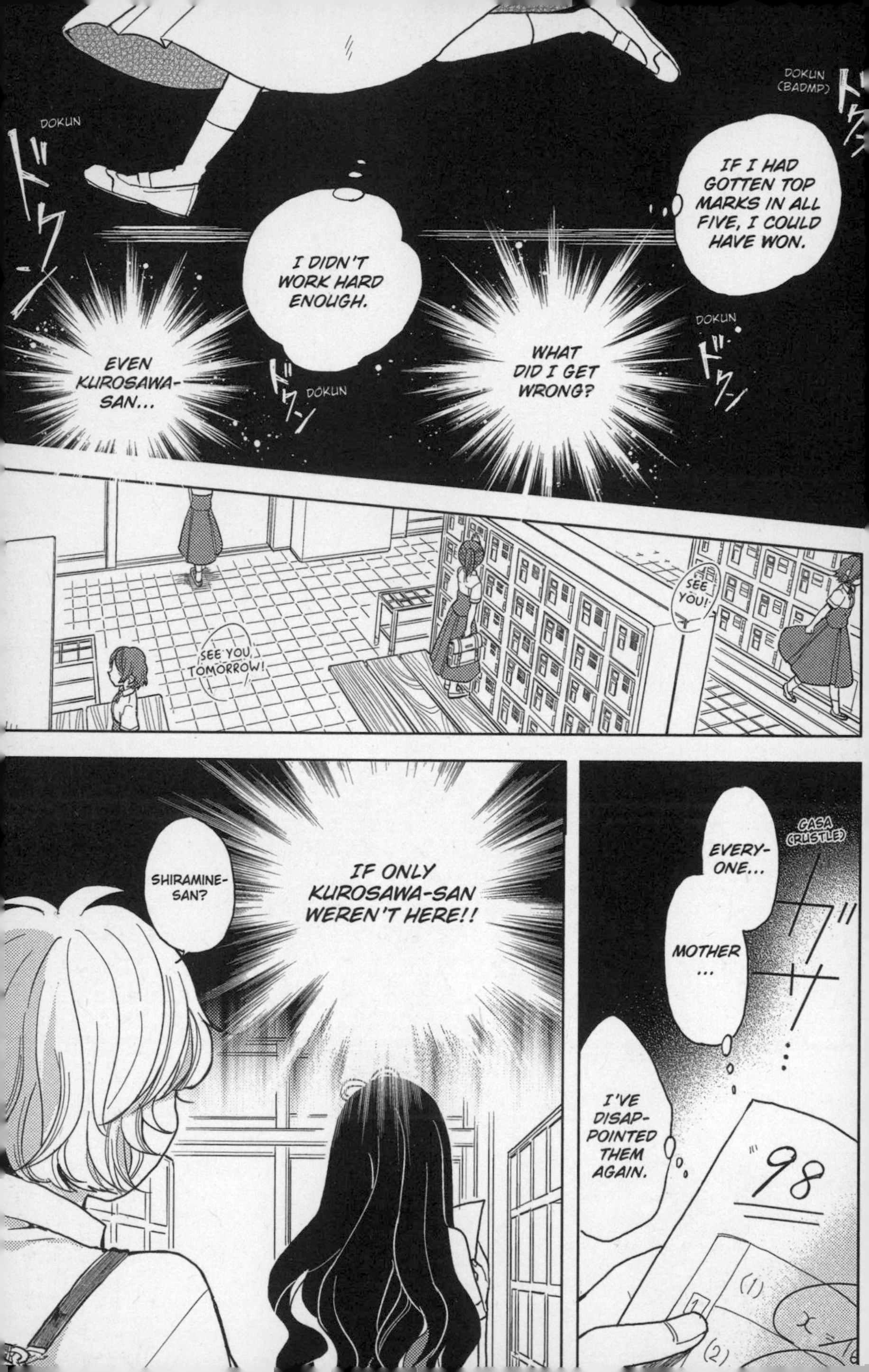
DOKUN (BADMP)
IF I HAD GOTTEN TOP MARKS IN ALL FIVE, I COULD HAVE WON.
I DIDN'T WORK HARD ENOUGH.
DOKUN
DOKUN
WHAT DID I GET WRONG?
DOKUN
EVEN KUROSAWA-SAN...
SEE YOU!
SEE YOU TOMORROW!
GASA (RUSTLE)
EVERY-ONE...
MOTHER...
I'VE DISAP-POINTED THEM AGAIN.
98
(1)
(2)
IF ONLY KUROSAWA-SAN WEREN'T HERE!!
SHIRAMINE-SAN?

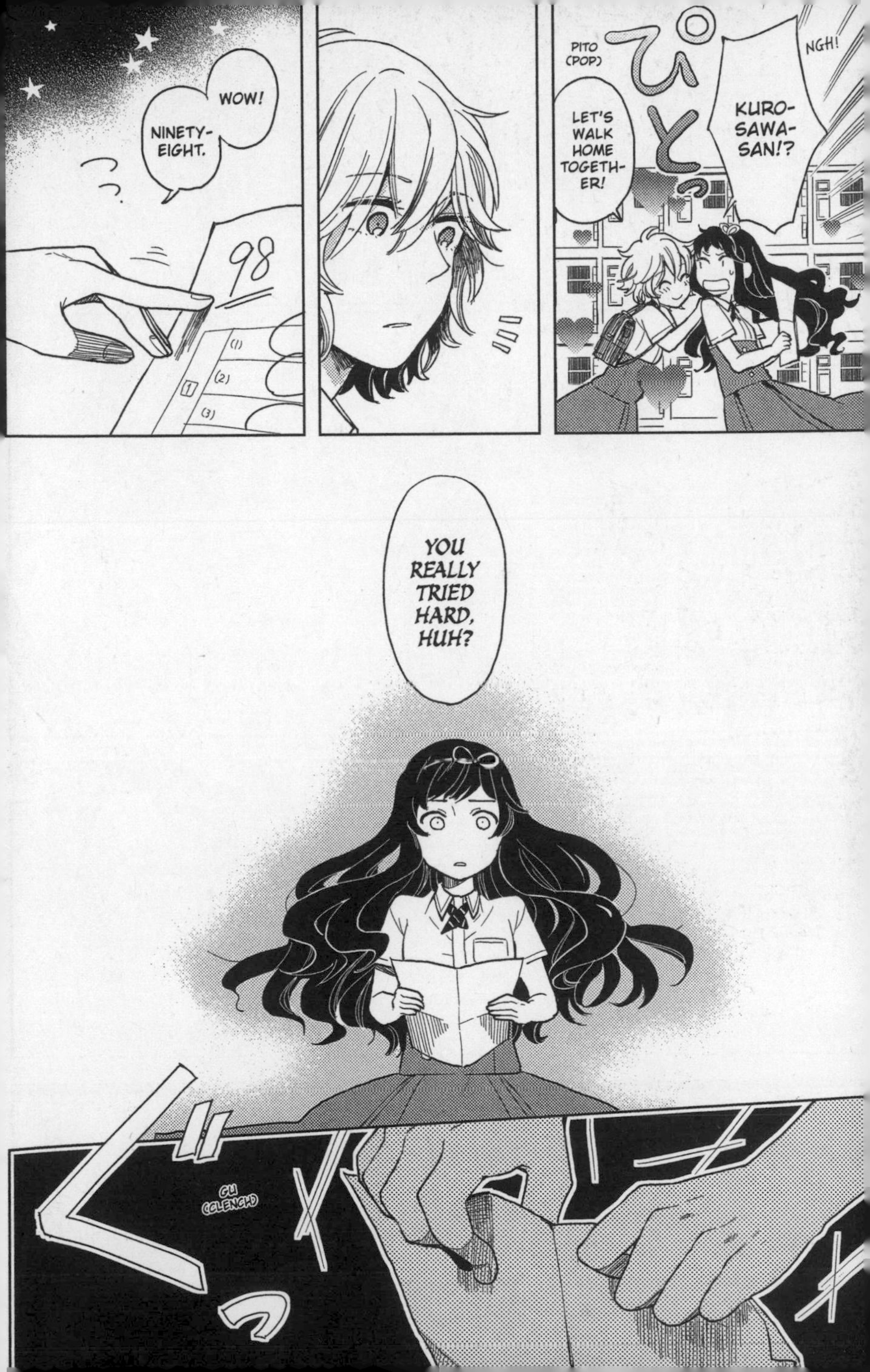
NGH!
KURO-SAWA-SAN!?
PITO (POP)
LET'S WALK HOME TOGETH-ER!
WOW!
NINETY-EIGHT.
98
YOU REALLY TRIED HARD, HUH?
GU (CLENCH)

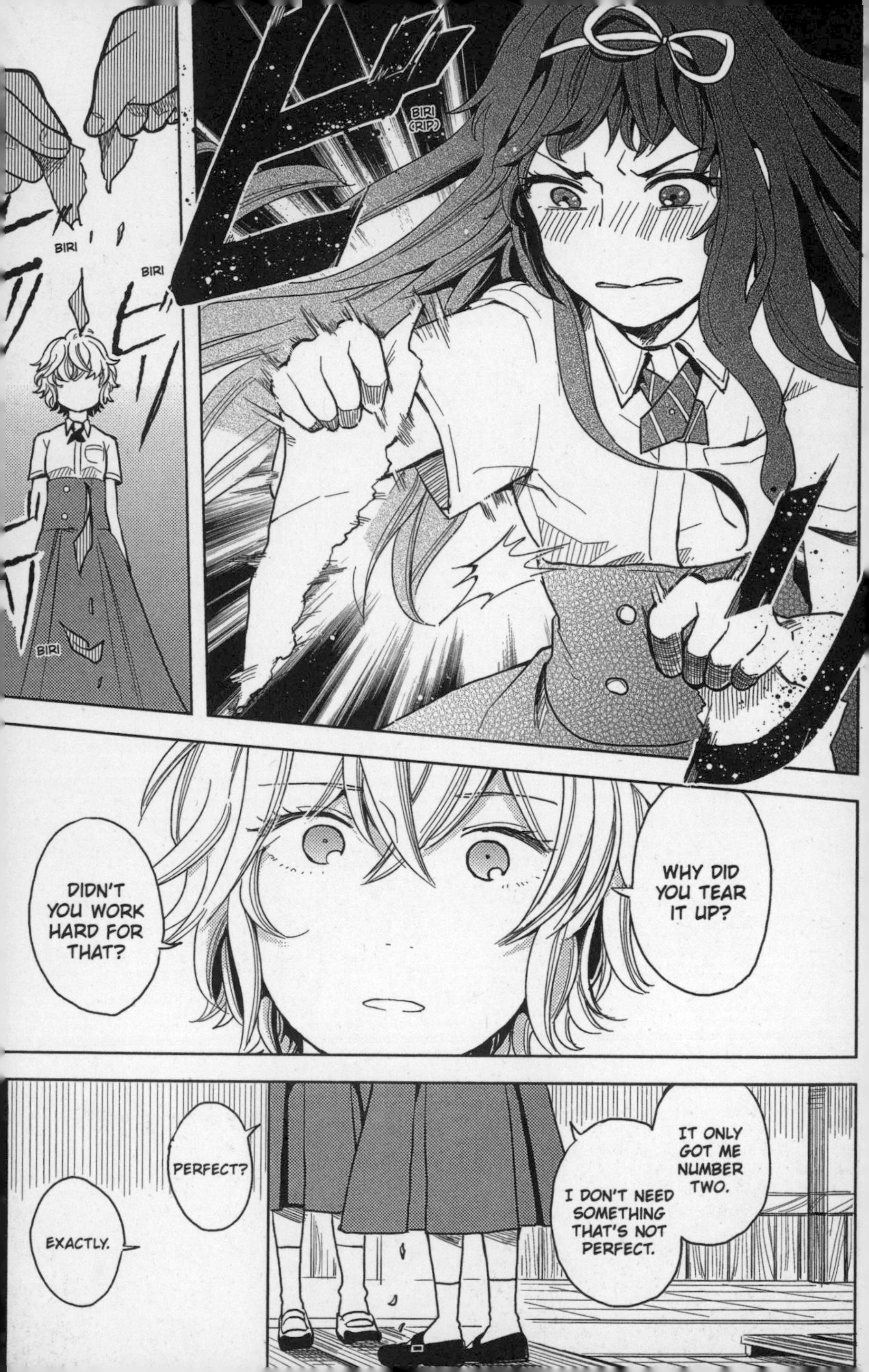
BIRI (RIP)
BIRI
BIRI
BIRI
WHY DID YOU TEAR IT UP?
DIDN'T YOU WORK HARD FOR THAT?
IT ONLY GOT ME NUMBER TWO.
I DON'T NEED SOMETHING THAT'S NOT PERFECT.
PERFECT?
EXACTLY.

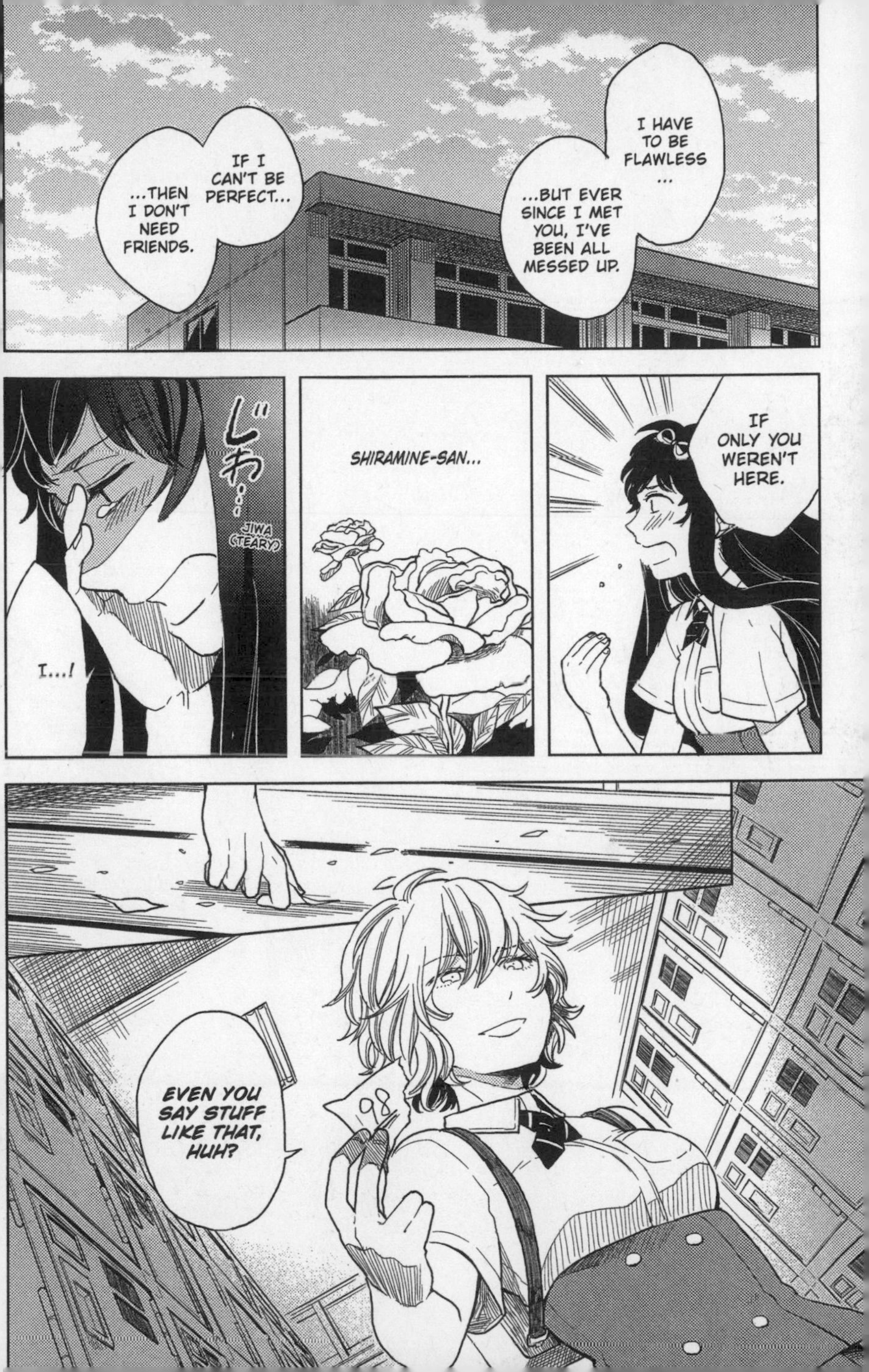
I HAVE TO BE FLAWLESS ...
...BUT EVER SINCE I MET YOU, I'VE BEEN ALL MESSED UP.
IF I CAN'T BE PERFECT...
...THEN I DON'T NEED FRIENDS.
IF ONLY YOU WEREN'T HERE.
SHIRAMINE-SAN...
じわ…
JIWA (TEARY)
I...!
98
EVEN YOU SAY STUFF LIKE THAT, HUH?

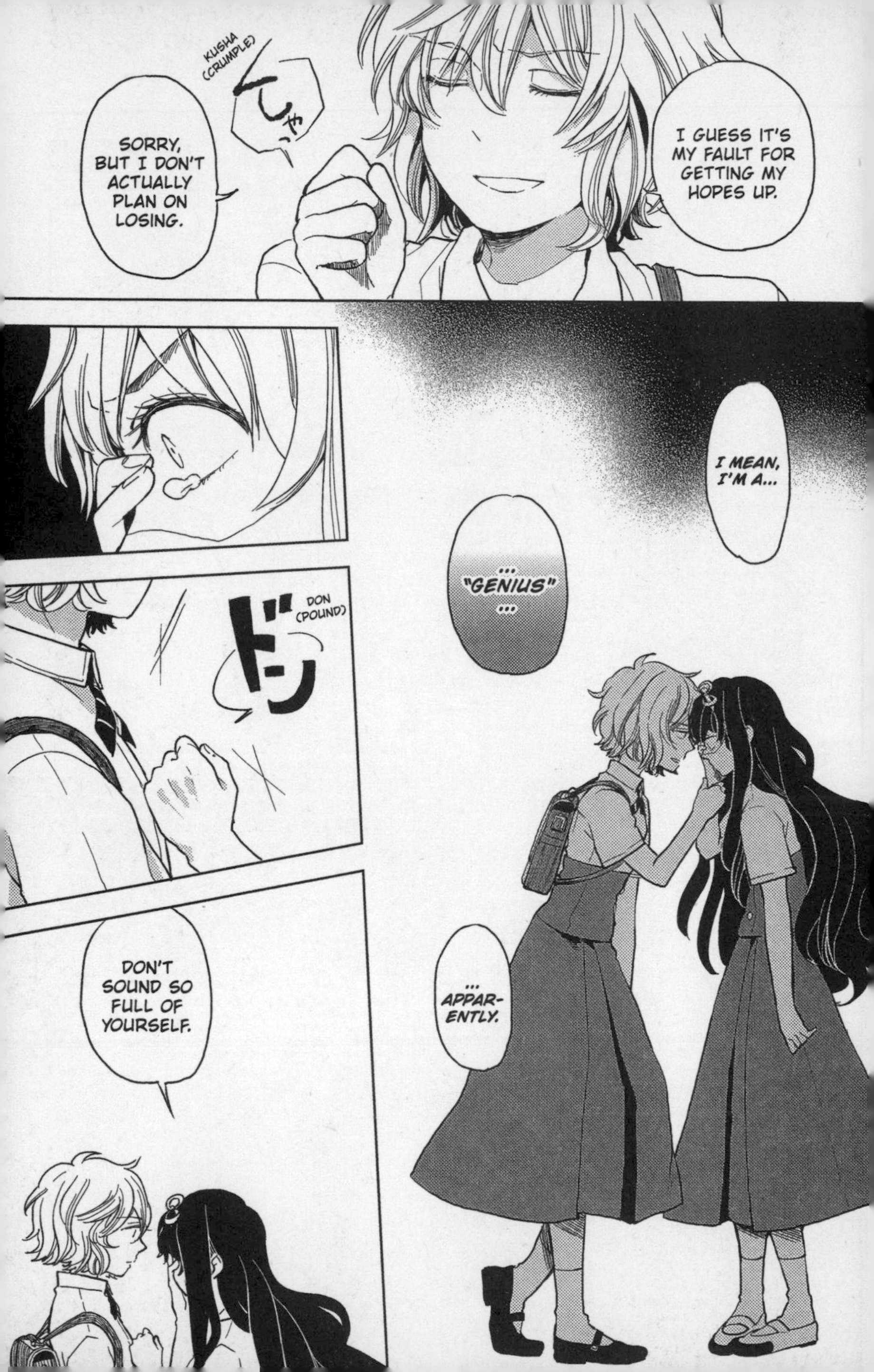
I GUESS IT'S MY FAULT FOR GETTING MY HOPES UP.
KUSHA (CRUMPLE)
SORRY, BUT I DON'T ACTUALLY PLAN ON LOSING.
I MEAN, I'M A...
... "GENIUS" ...
... APPARENTLY.
DON (POUND)
DON'T SOUND SO FULL OF YOURSELF.

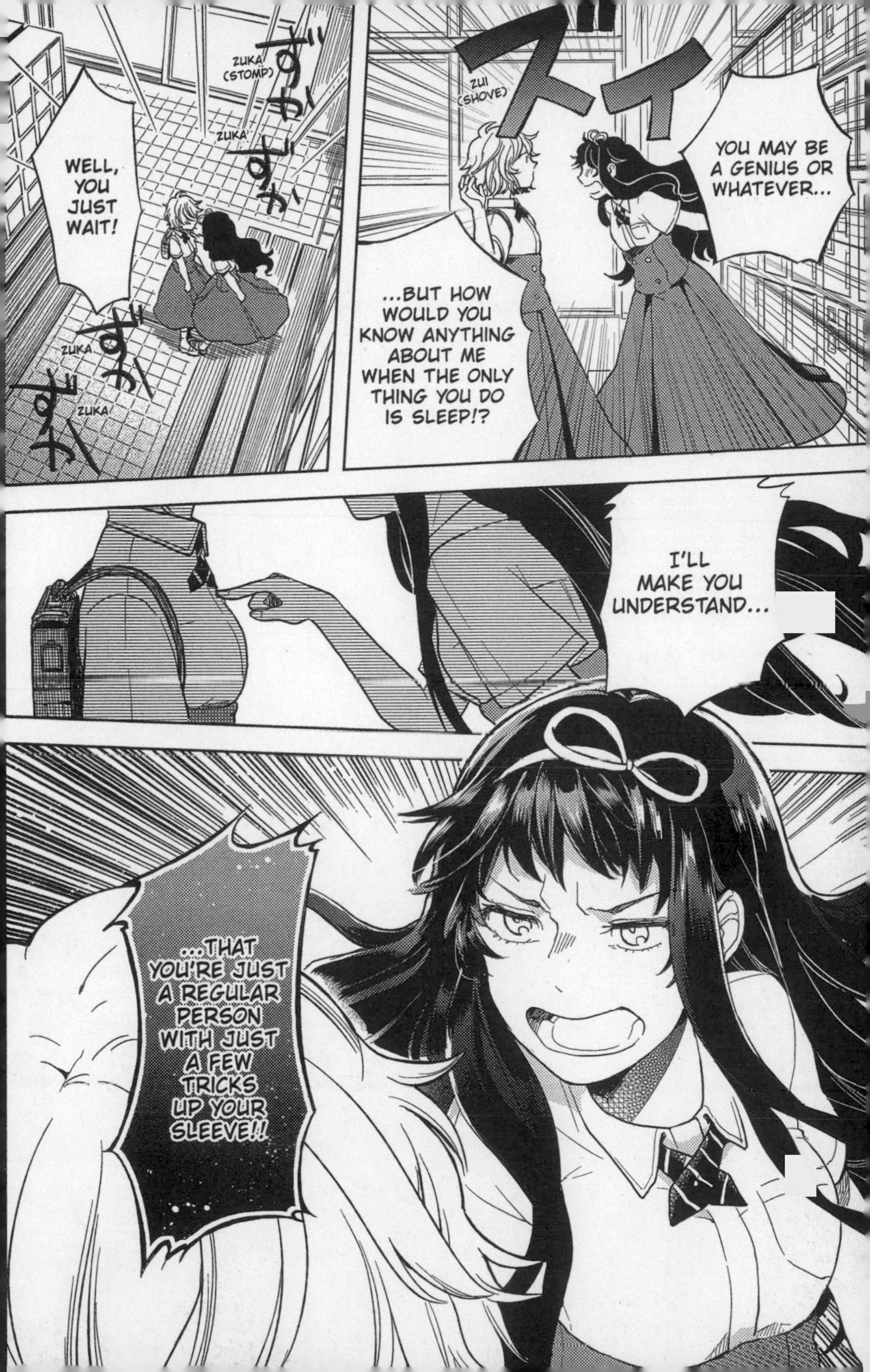

ZUI (SHOVE)
YOU MAY BE A GENIUS OR WHATEVER...
...BUT HOW WOULD YOU KNOW ANYTHING ABOUT ME WHEN THE ONLY THING YOU DO IS SLEEP!?
ZUKA (STOMP)
ZUKA
WELL, YOU JUST WAIT!
ZUKA
ZUKA
I'LL MAKE YOU UNDERSTAND...
...THAT YOU'RE JUST A REGULAR PERSON WITH JUST A FEW TRICKS UP YOUR SLEEVE!!

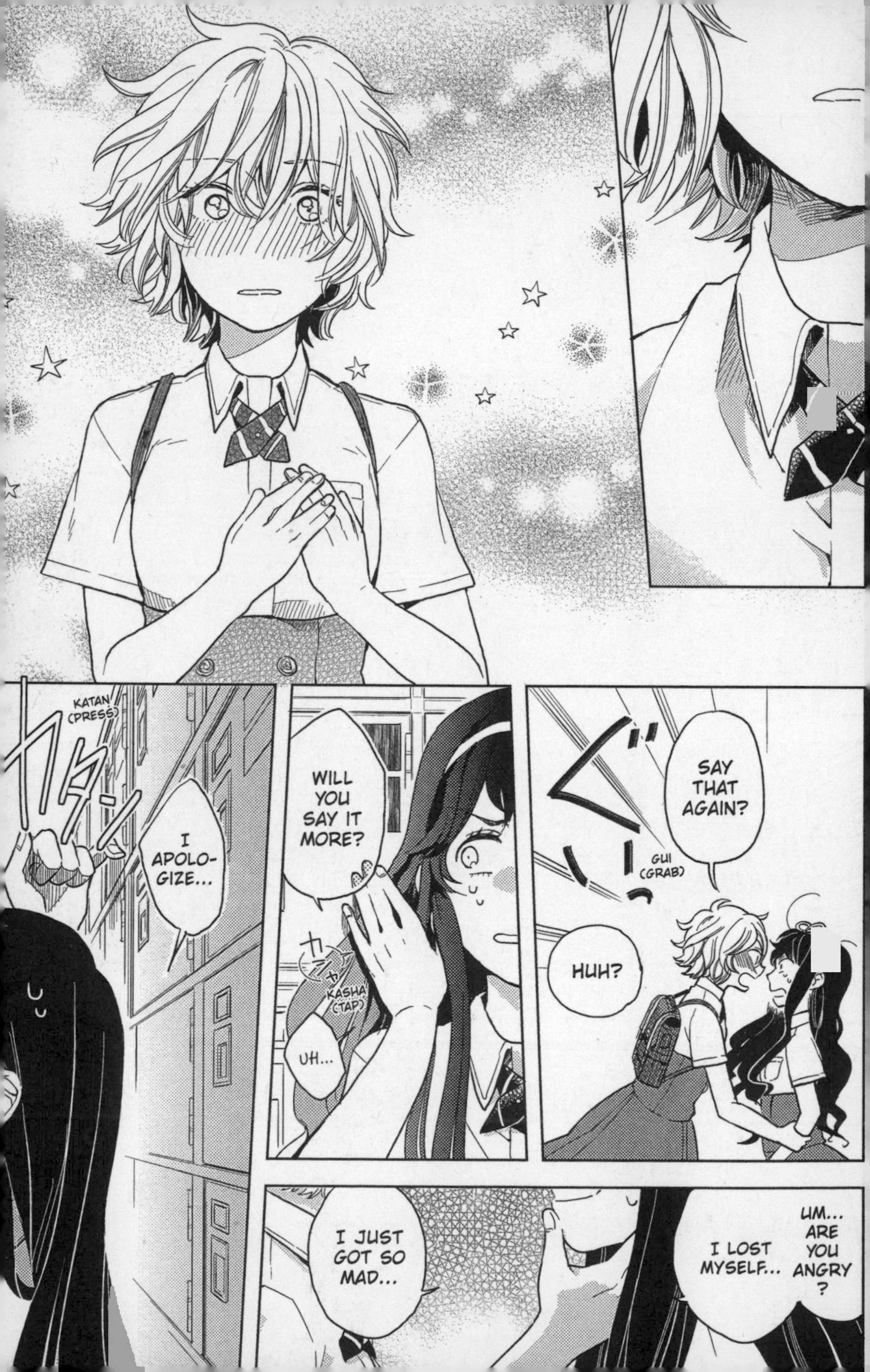
SAY THAT AGAIN?
GUI (GRAB)
HUH?
WILL YOU SAY IT MORE?
KASHA (TAP)
UH...
UM... ARE YOU ANGRY?
I LOST MYSELF...
I JUST GOT SO MAD...
KATAN (PRESS)
I APOLOGIZE...

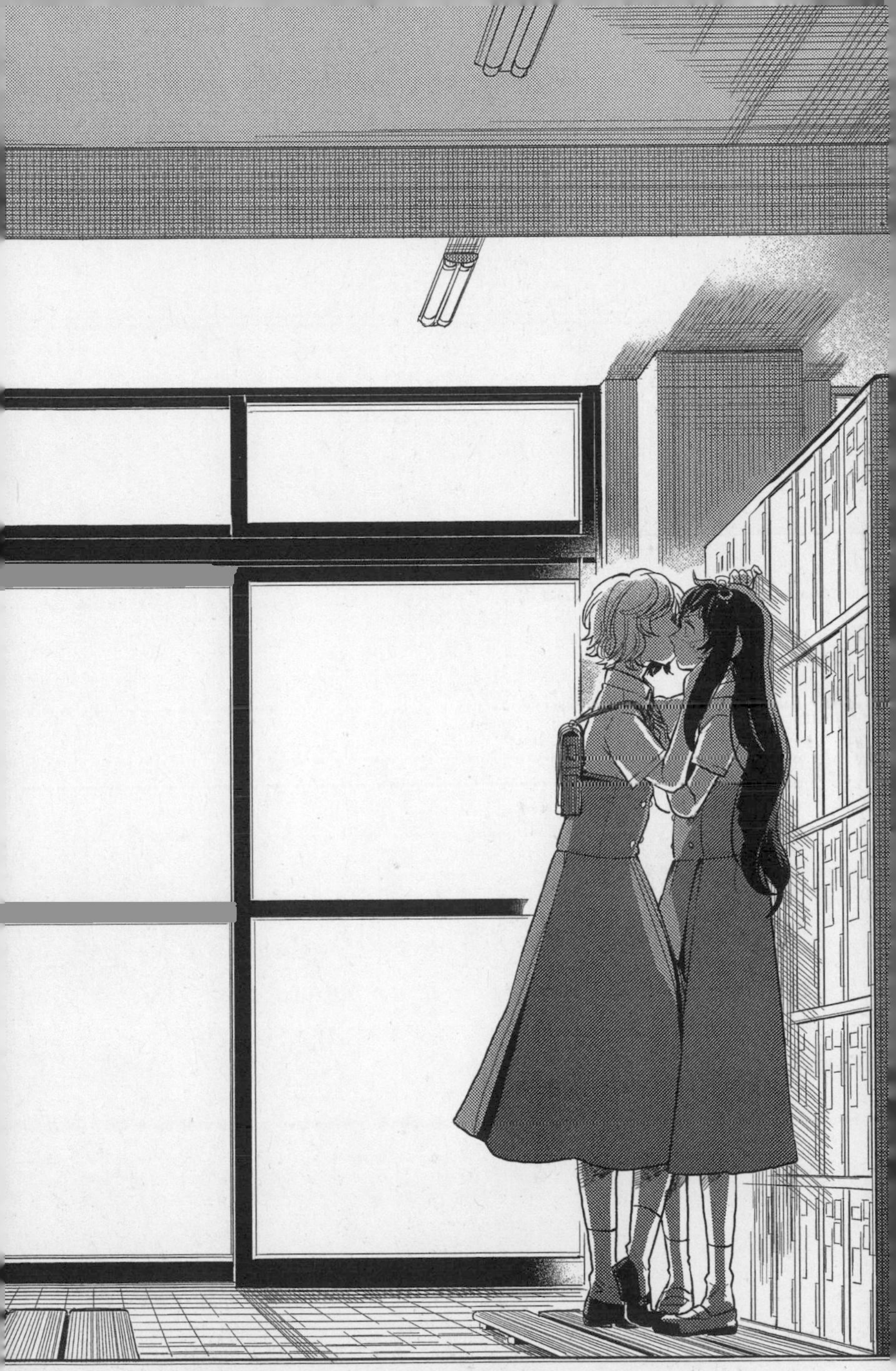

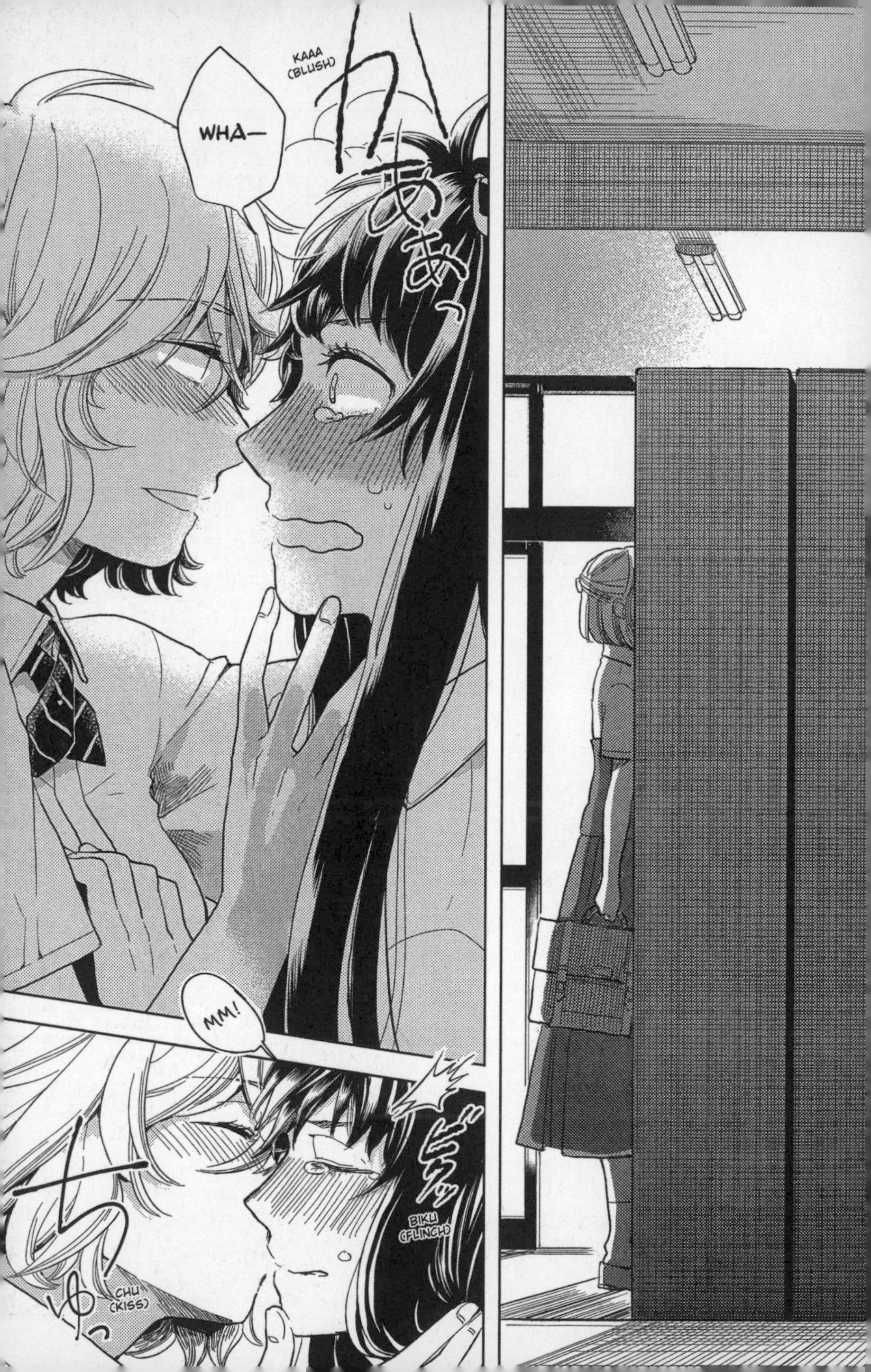
KAAA (BLUSH)
あぁっ
WHA—
MM!
BIKU (FLINCH)
CHU (KISS)

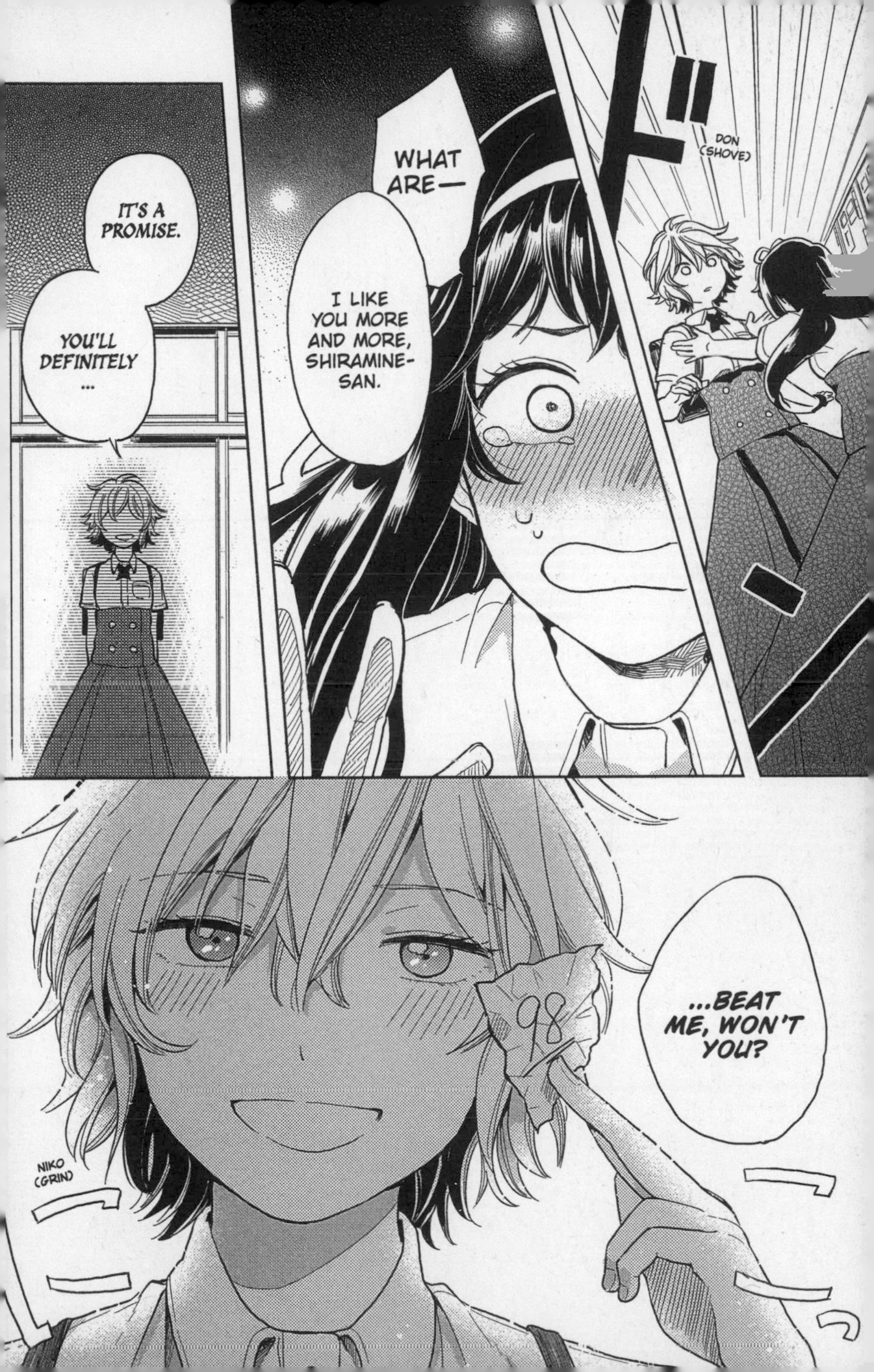
DON (SHOVE)
WHAT ARE—
I LIKE YOU MORE AND MORE, SHIRAMINE-SAN.
IT'S A PROMISE.
YOU'LL DEFINITELY ...
...BEAT ME, WON'T YOU?
98
NIKO (GRIN)

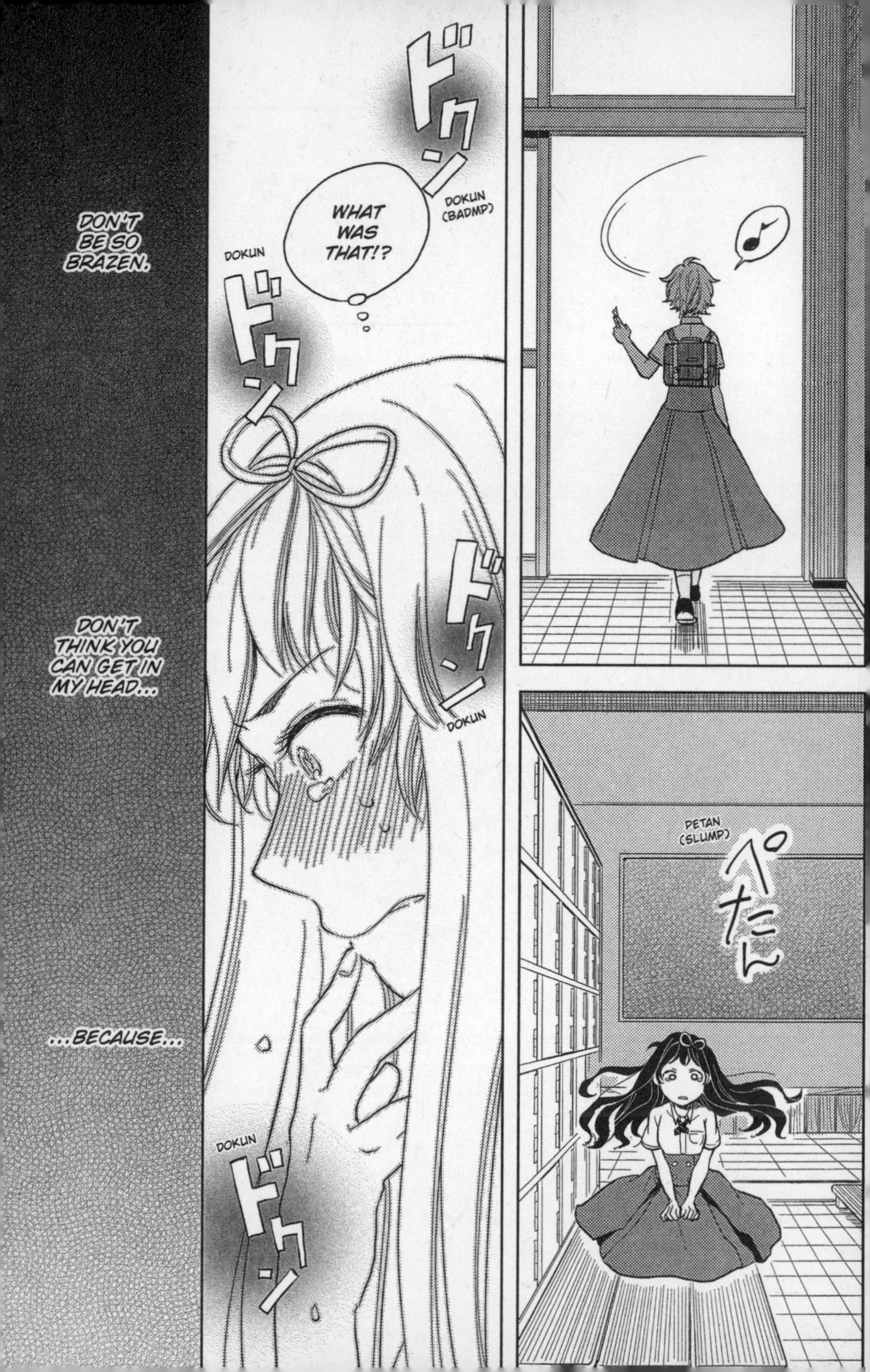
PETAN (SLUMP)
ペたん
ドクン
DOKUN (BADMP)
WHAT WAS THAT!?
DOKUN
ドクン
ドクン
DOKUN
DOKUN
ドクン
DON'T BE SO BRAZEN.
DON'T THINK YOU CAN GET IN MY HEAD...
...BECAUSE...

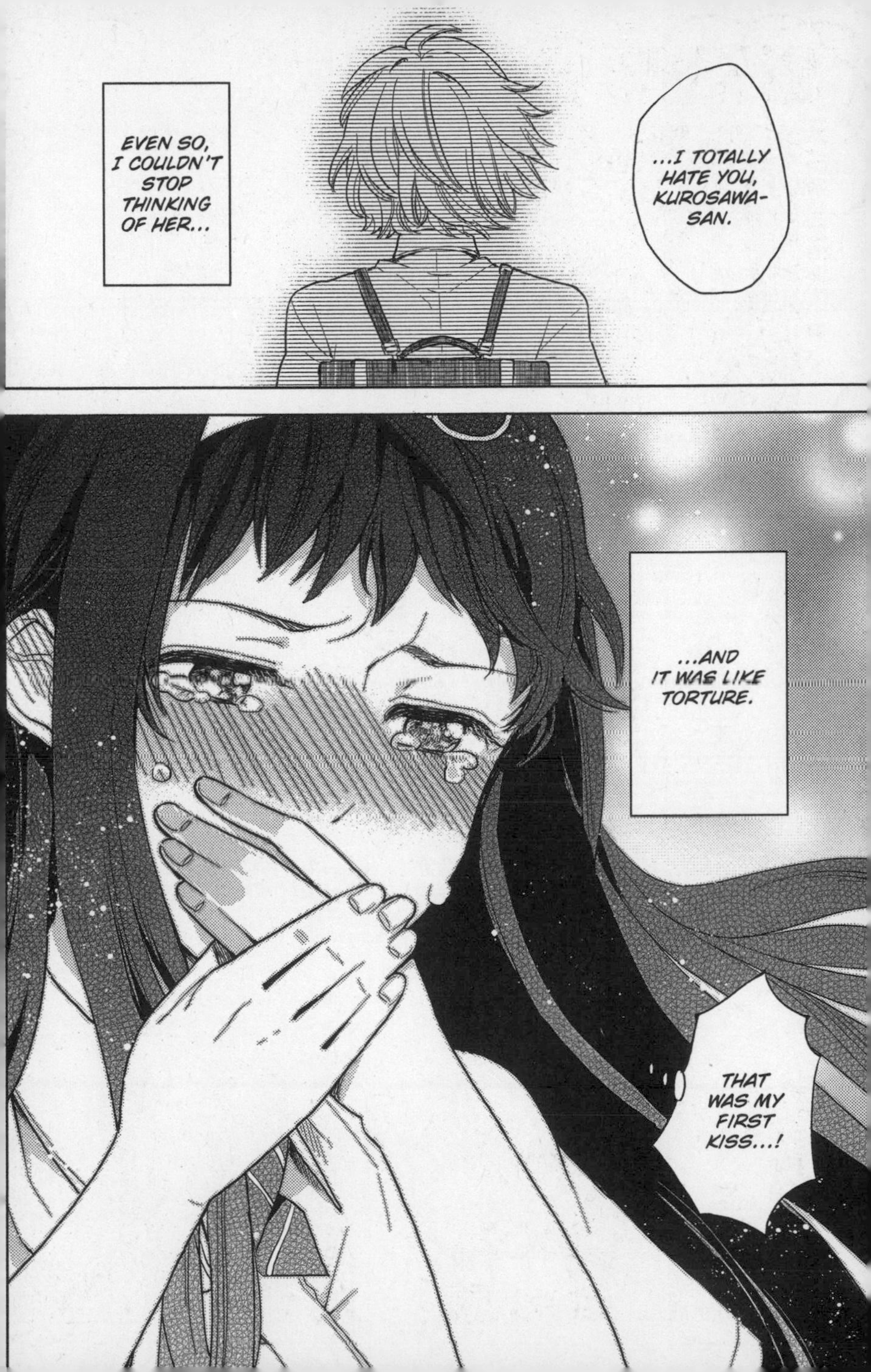
...I TOTALLY HATE YOU, KUROSAWA-SAN.
EVEN SO, I COULDN'T STOP THINKING OF HER...
...AND IT WAS LIKE TORTURE.
THAT WAS MY FIRST KISS...!

Right Person for the Job

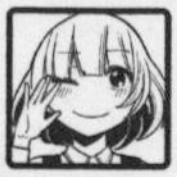

KANAKO

FIRST-YEAR, CLASS B
SHORT, DREAMY-EYED GIRL

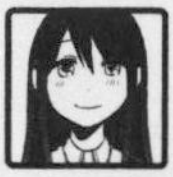

NAGI

MIDDLE SCHOOL THIRD-YEAR, CLASS 1
TALL, ORTHODOX BEAUTY

KISS THEATER: WHAT'S BEHIND THE STORY!?

PEOPLE OTHER THAN THE MAIN CHARACTERS HAVE STORIES TOO. HERE, WE PRESENT THE "LITTLE LOVE" STORIES HAPPENING BEHIND THE SCENES.

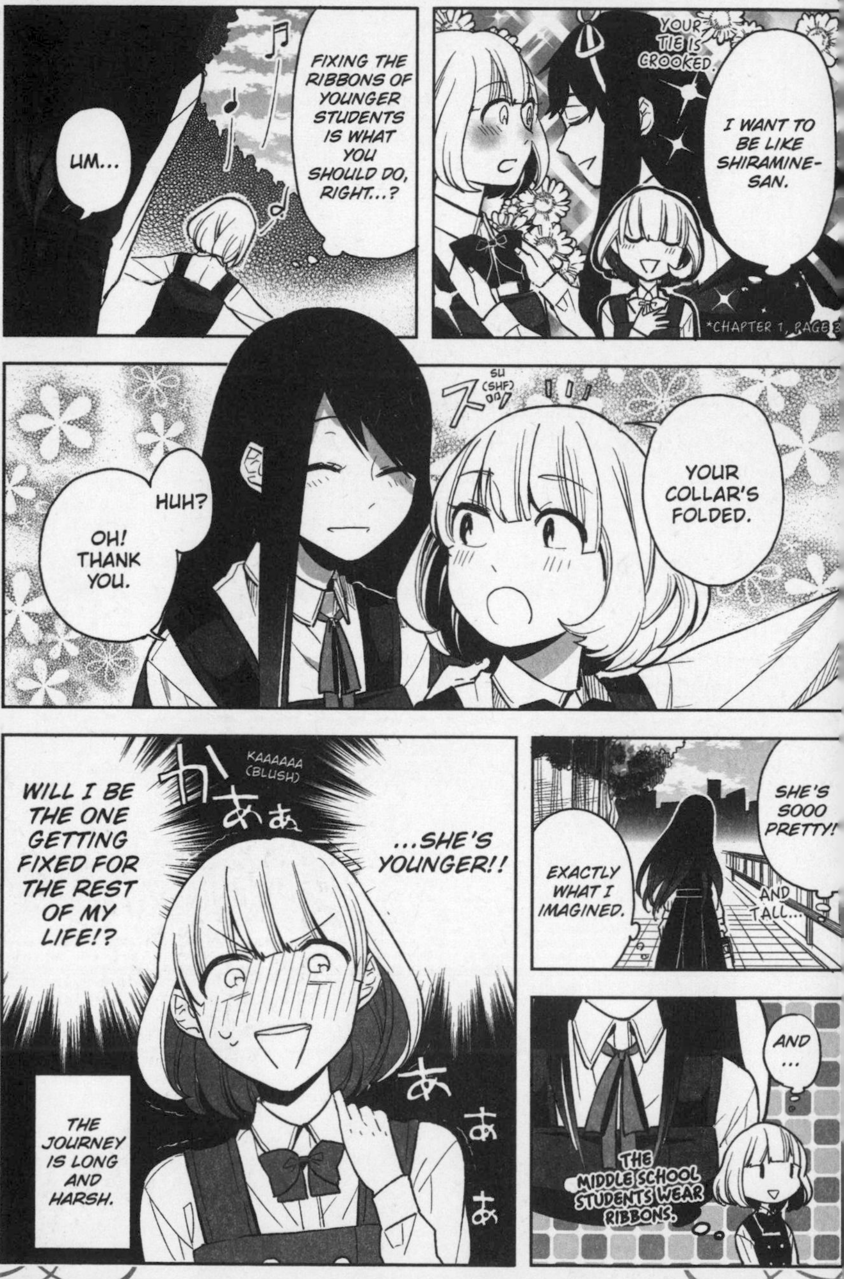
YOUR TIE IS CROOKED.
I WANT TO BE LIKE SHIRAMINE-SAN.
*CHAPTER 1, PAGE 3
FIXING THE RIBBONS OF YOUNGER STUDENTS IS WHAT YOU SHOULD DO, RIGHT...?
UM...
SU (SHF)
YOUR COLLAR'S FOLDED.
HUH?
OH! THANK YOU.
SHE'S SOOO PRETTY!
AND TALL...
EXACTLY WHAT I IMAGINED.
AND ...
THE MIDDLE SCHOOL STUDENTS WEAR RIBBONS.
KAAAAAA (BLUSH)
...SHE'S YOUNGER!!
WILL I BE THE ONE GETTING FIXED FOR THE REST OF MY LIFE!?
THE JOURNEY IS LONG AND HARSH.

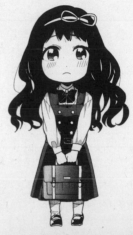

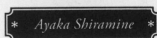
Ayaka Shiramine

A y a k a   S h i r a m i n e

A first-year honor student in the Seiran Academy High School. She works hard, gets excellent grades, and is quite sociable. She's lived her life proud of that image of herself, so she is baffled by her sudden rival, Yurine Kurosawa. Born a sore loser, she doesn't really mind hard work, but she's quite meddlesome. An only child.

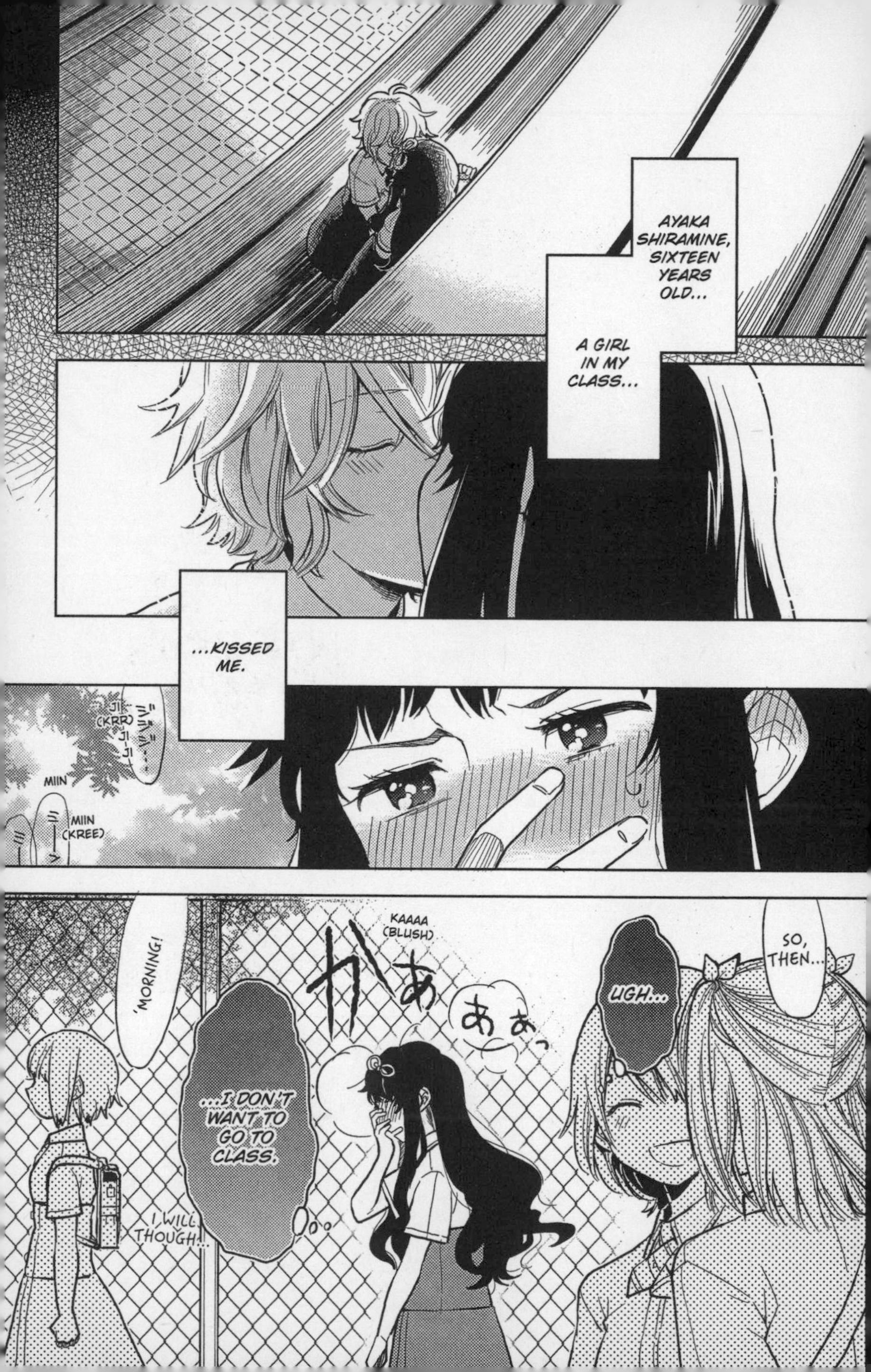
AYAKA SHIRAMINE, SIXTEEN YEARS OLD...
A GIRL IN MY CLASS...
...KISSED ME.
JI (KRR) JI-JI
MIIN MIIN (KREE)
SO, THEN...
UGH...
KAAAA (BLUSH)
'MORNING!
...I DON'T WANT TO GO TO CLASS.
I WILL THOUGH...

Chapter 2:
The Monster of Lonely Island

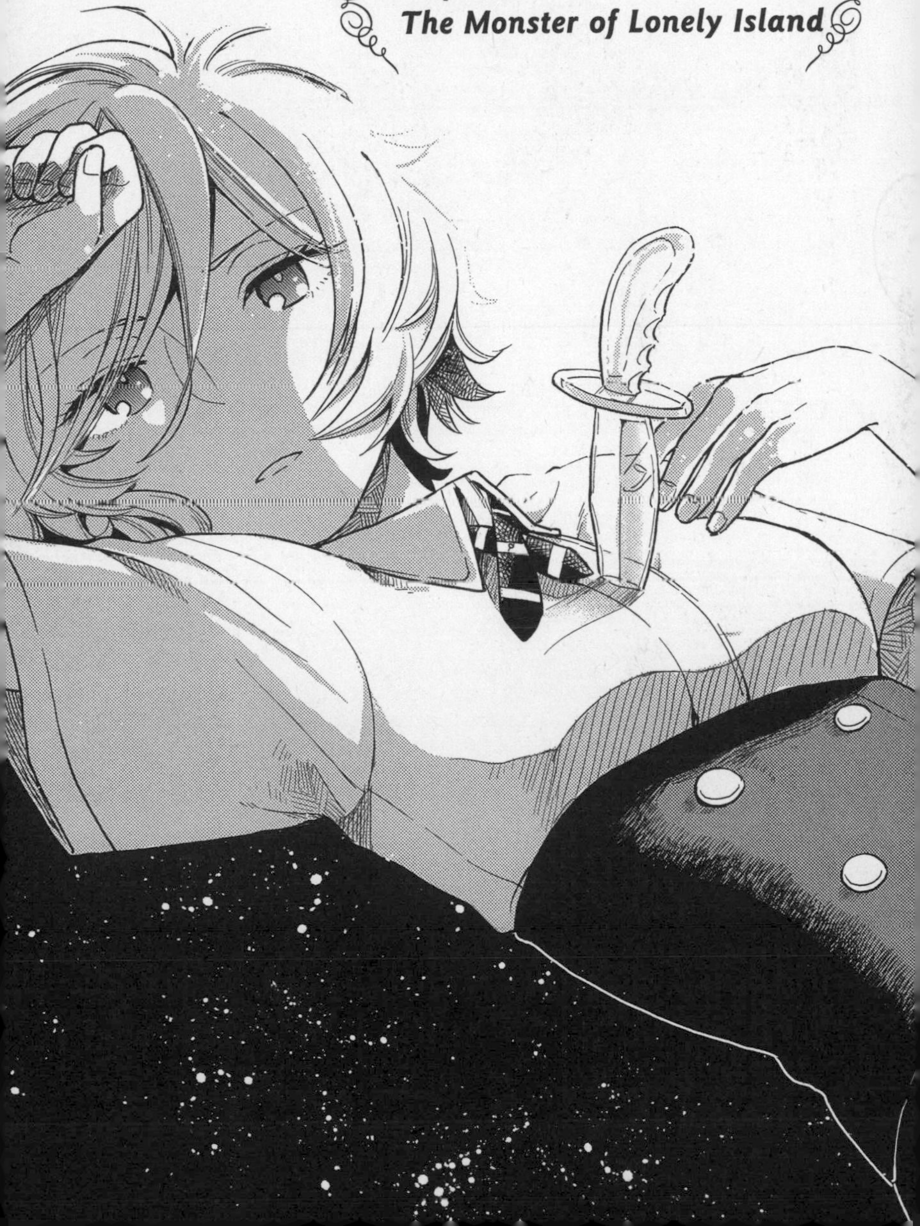

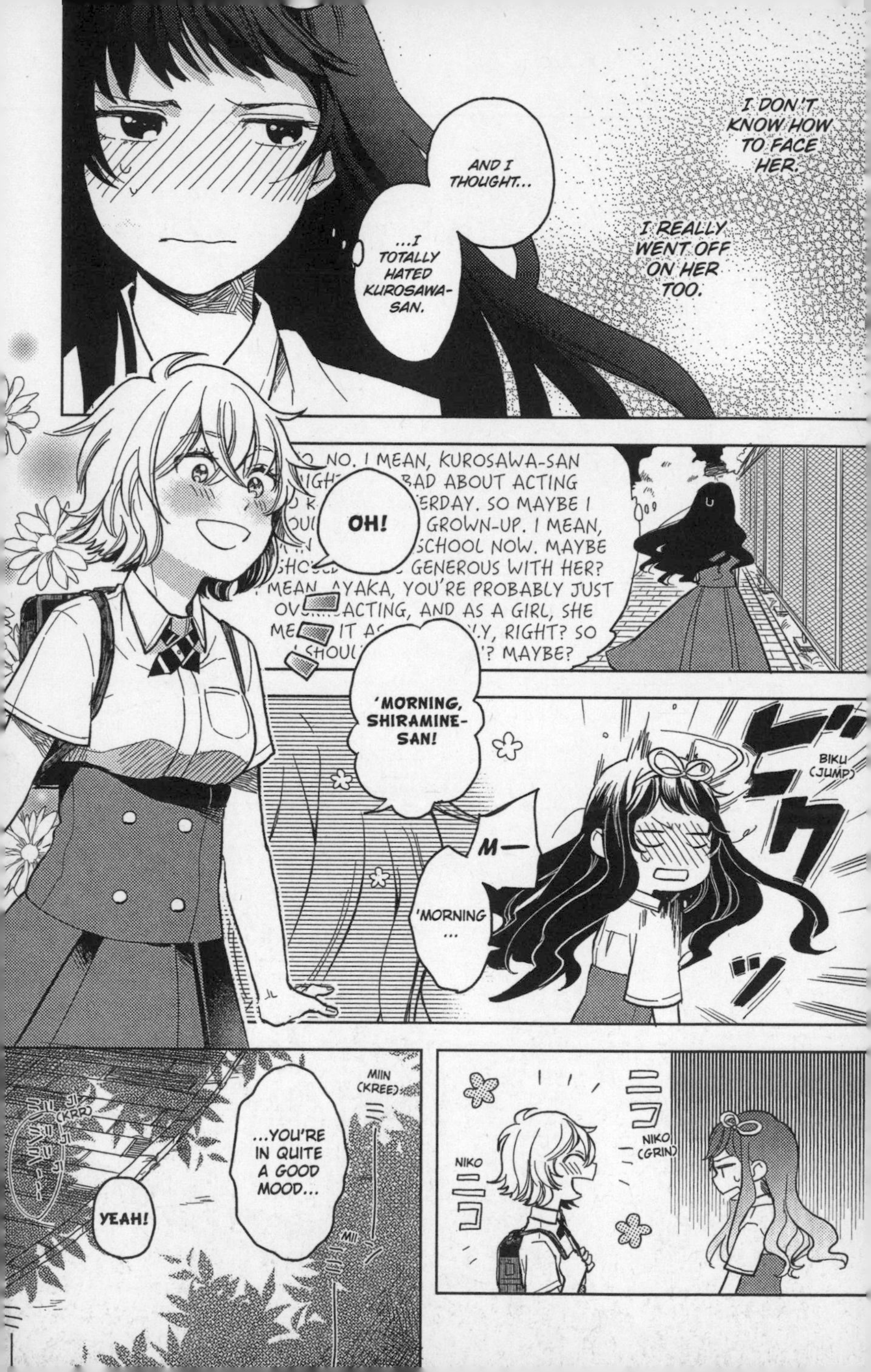

AND I THOUGHT...

...I TOTALLY HATED KUROSAWA-SAN.

I DON'T KNOW HOW TO FACE HER.

I REALLY WENT OFF ON HER TOO.

OH!

NO. I MEAN, KUROSAWA-SAN ...BAD ABOUT ACTING ...YESTERDAY. SO MAYBE I ...GROWN-UP. I MEAN, ...SCHOOL NOW. MAYBE ...GENEROUS WITH HER? ...MEAN, AYAKA, YOU'RE PROBABLY JUST OV...ACTING, AND AS A GIRL, SHE ME...IT A...Y, RIGHT? SO ...SHOUL...? MAYBE?

'MORNING, SHIRAMINE-SAN!

M—

'MORNING...

BIKU (JUMP)

...YOU'RE IN QUITE A GOOD MOOD...

MIIN (KREE)

YEAH!

NIKO

NIKO (GRIN)

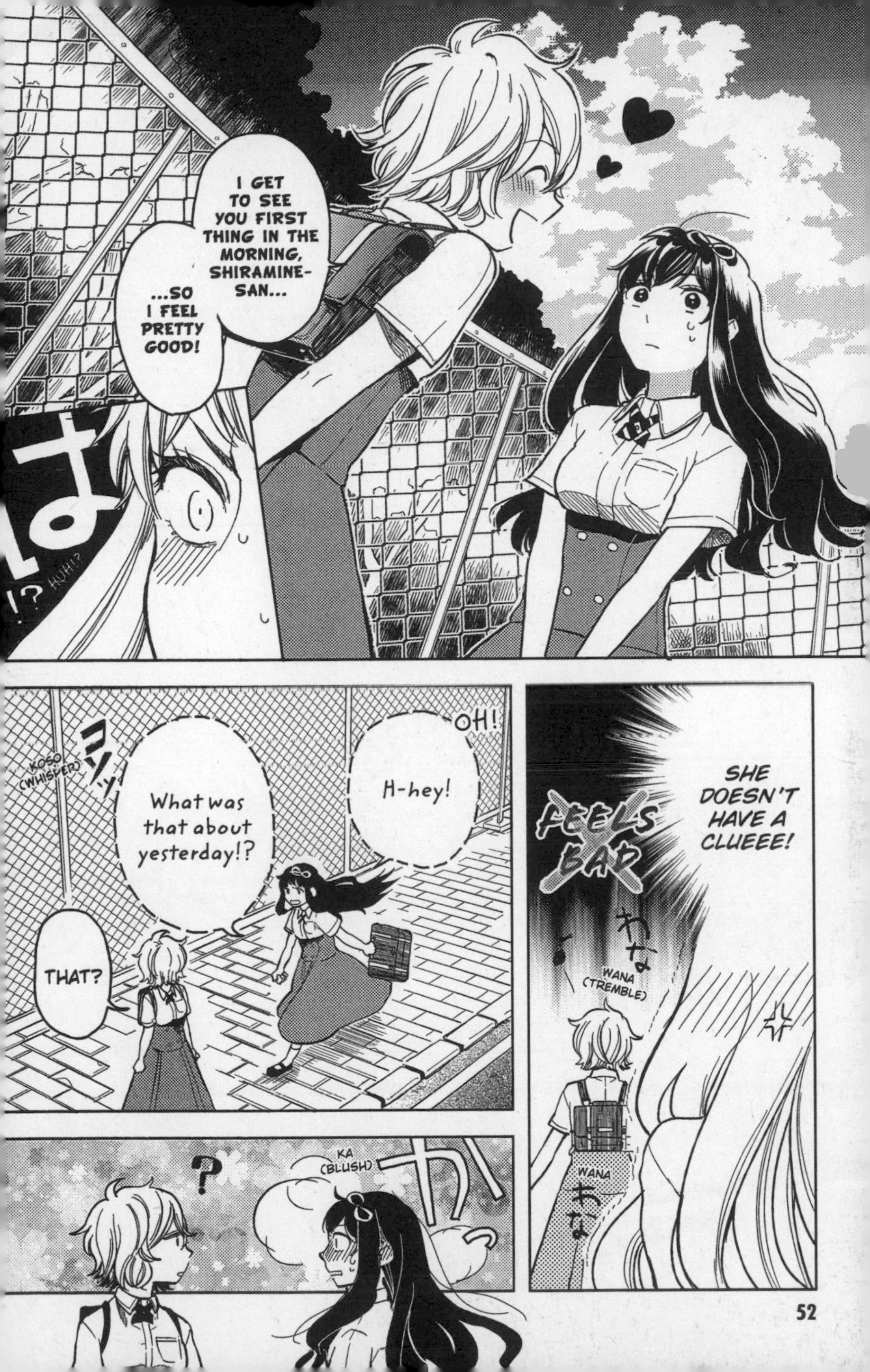

I GET TO SEE YOU FIRST THING IN THE MORNING, SHIRAMINE-SAN...
...SO I FEEL PRETTY GOOD!
は!?
HUH!?
FEELS BAD
SHE DOESN'T HAVE A CLUEEE!
わな
WANA (TREMBLE)
WANA
わな
OH!
H-hey!
What was that about yesterday!?
KOSO (WHISPER)
THAT?
?
KA (BLUSH)

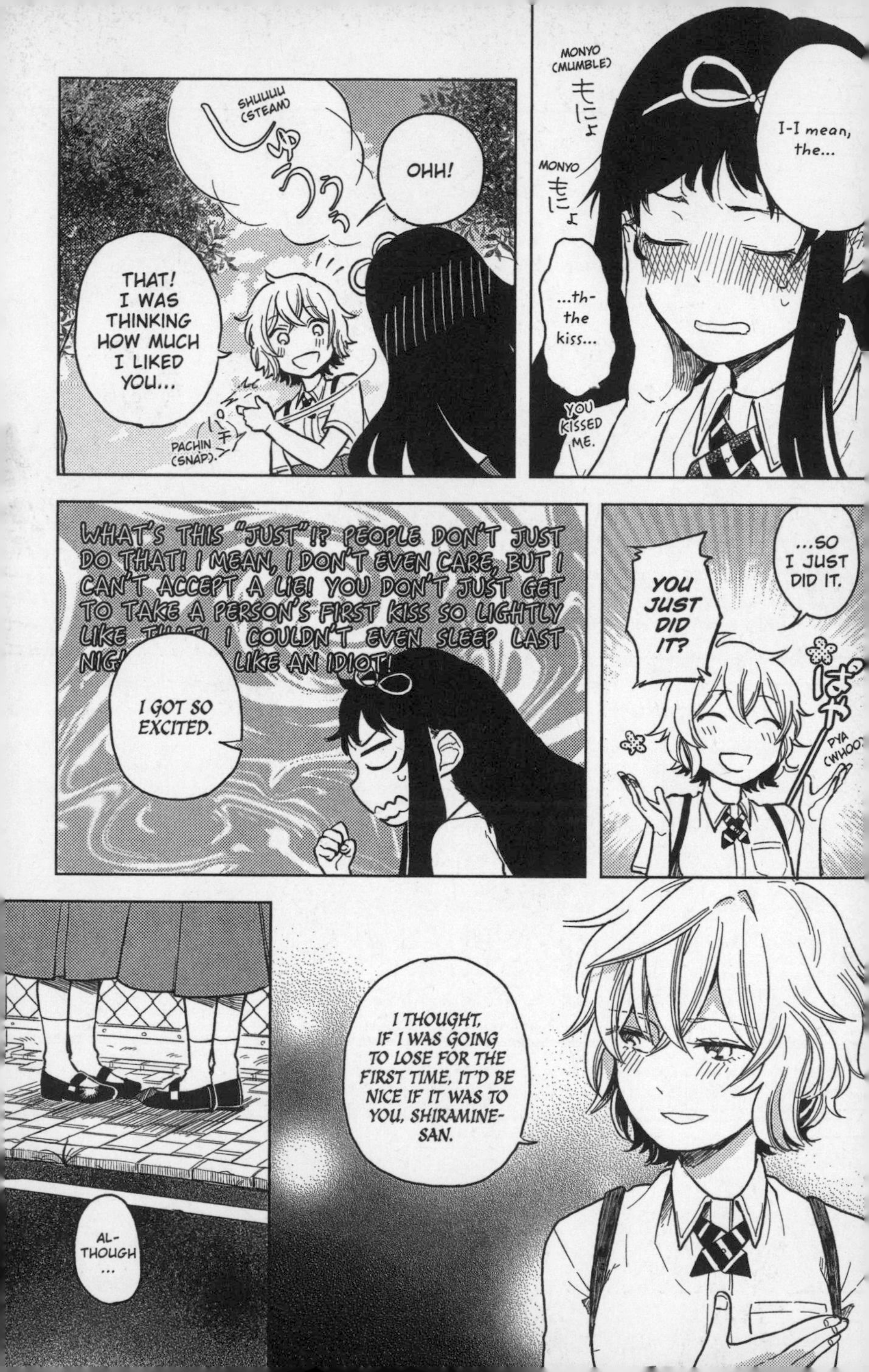
MONYO (MUMBLE)
もにょ
MONYO
もにょ
I-I mean, the...
...th- the kiss...
YOU KISSED ME.
SHUUUUU (STEAM)
OHH!
THAT! I WAS THINKING HOW MUCH I LIKED YOU...
PACHIN (SNAP)
パチ
...SO I JUST DID IT.
YOU JUST DID IT?
PYA
WHAT'S THIS "JUST"!? PEOPLE DON'T JUST DO THAT! I MEAN, I DON'T EVEN CARE, BUT I CAN'T ACCEPT A LIE! YOU DON'T JUST GET TO TAKE A PERSON'S FIRST KISS SO LIGHTLY LIKE
I COULDN'T EVEN SLEEP LAST
LIKE AN IDIOT!
I GOT SO EXCITED.
I THOUGHT, IF I WAS GOING TO LOSE FOR THE FIRST TIME, IT'D BE NICE IF IT WAS TO YOU, SHIRAMINE-SAN.
AL-THOUGH...

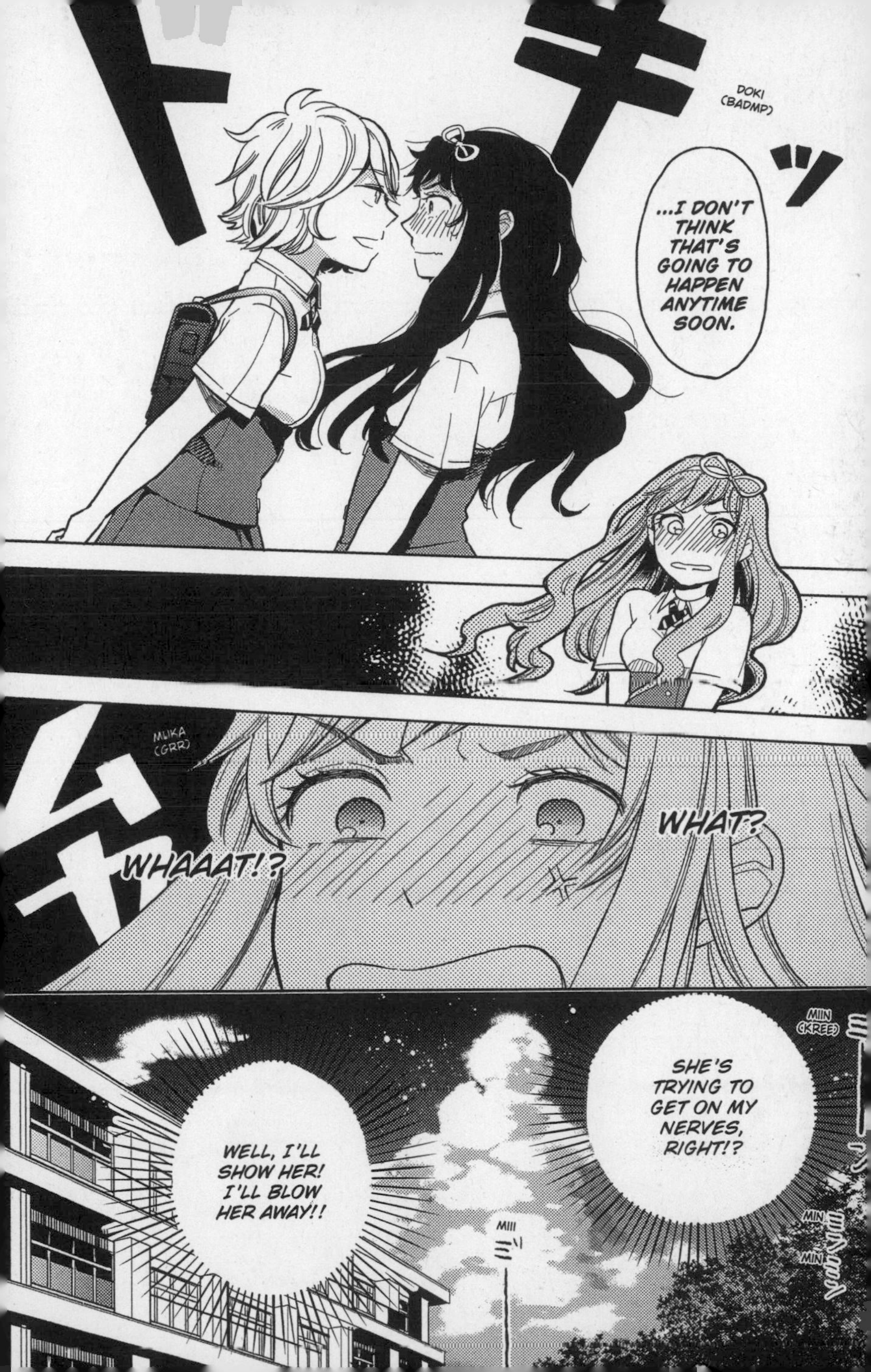
DOKI (BADMP)
...I DON'T THINK THAT'S GOING TO HAPPEN ANYTIME SOON.
WHAT?
MUKA (GRR)
WHAAAT!?
MIIN (KREE)
SHE'S TRYING TO GET ON MY NERVES, RIGHT!?
WELL, I'LL SHOW HER! I'LL BLOW HER AWAY!!
MIII
MIN
MIN

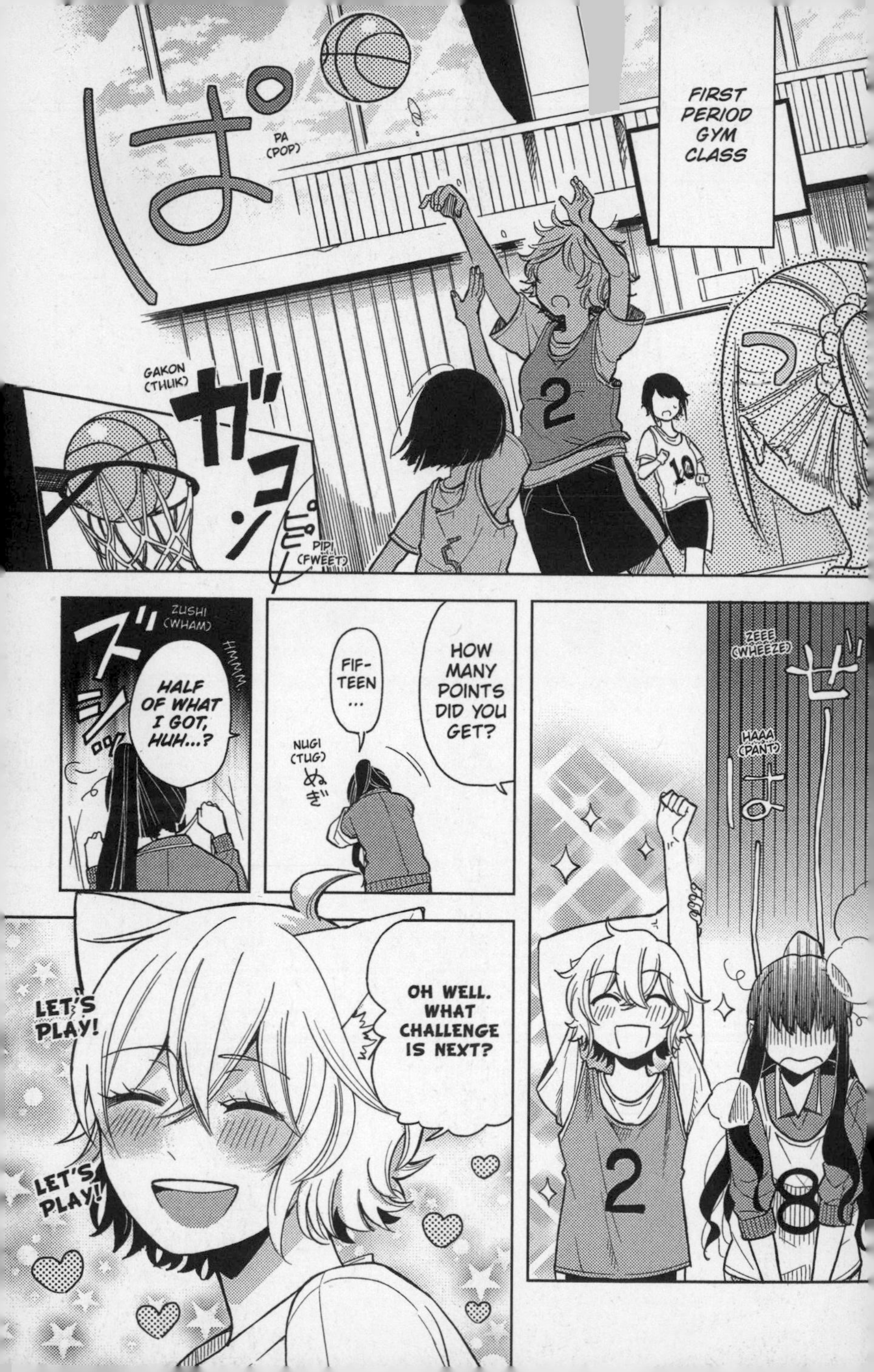
FIRST PERIOD GYM CLASS
ぱ
PA (POP)
ガコン
GAKON (THLIK)
ピピ
PIPI (FWEET)
ぜー
ZEEE (WHEEZE)
はー
HAAA (PANT)
HOW MANY POINTS DID YOU GET?
FIF-TEEN...
NUGI (TUG)
ぬぎ
ズシッ
ZUSHI (WHAM)
HALF OF WHAT I GOT, HUH...?
OH WELL. WHAT CHALLENGE IS NEXT?
LET'S PLAY!
LET'S PLAY!

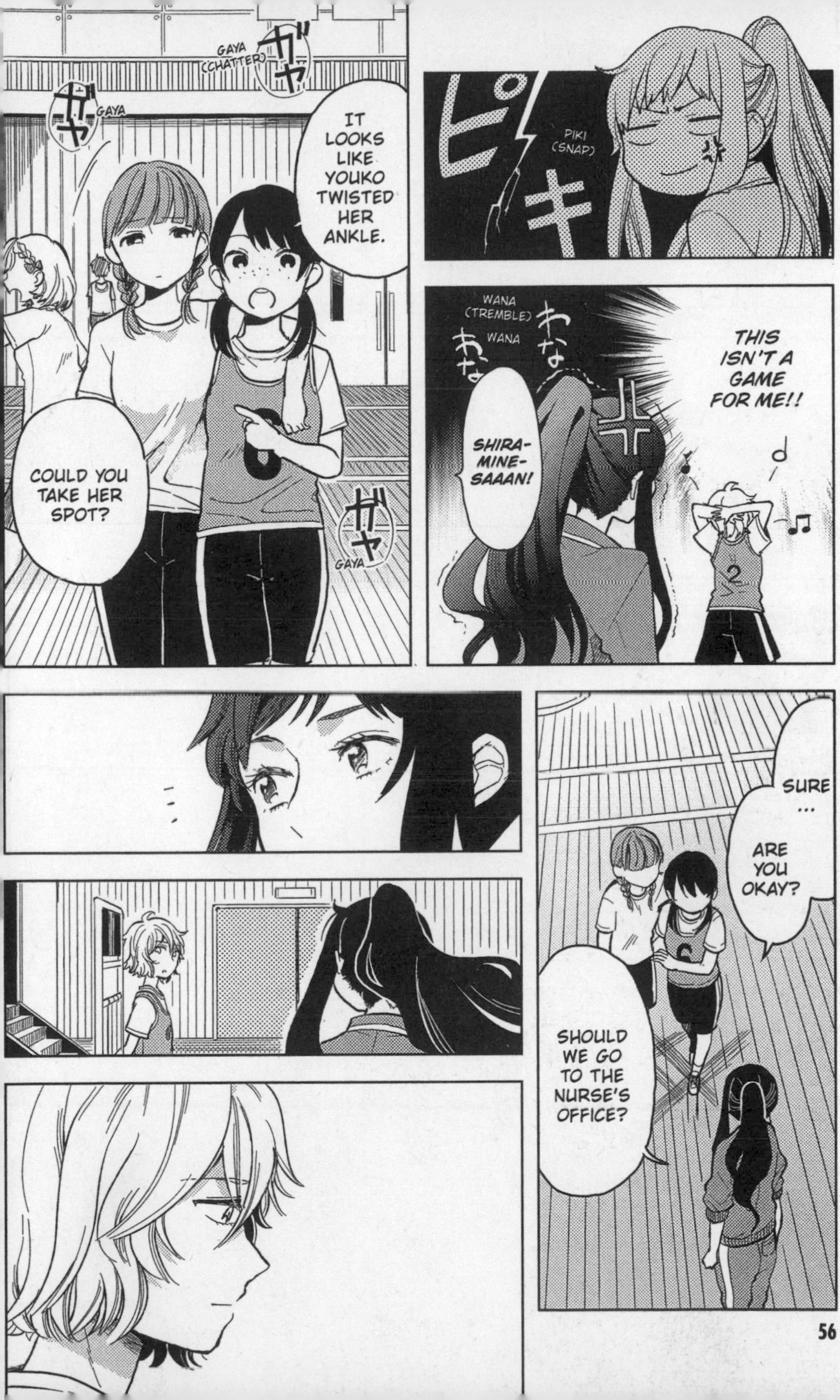
ピキ
PIKI (SNAP)
THIS ISN'T A GAME FOR ME!!
わな
WANA (TREMBLE)
わな
WANA
SHIRA-MINE-SAAAN!
ガヤ
GAYA (CHATTER)
ガヤ
GAYA
IT LOOKS LIKE YOUKO TWISTED HER ANKLE.
COULD YOU TAKE HER SPOT?
ガヤ
GAYA
SURE...
ARE YOU OKAY?
SHOULD WE GO TO THE NURSE'S OFFICE?
...

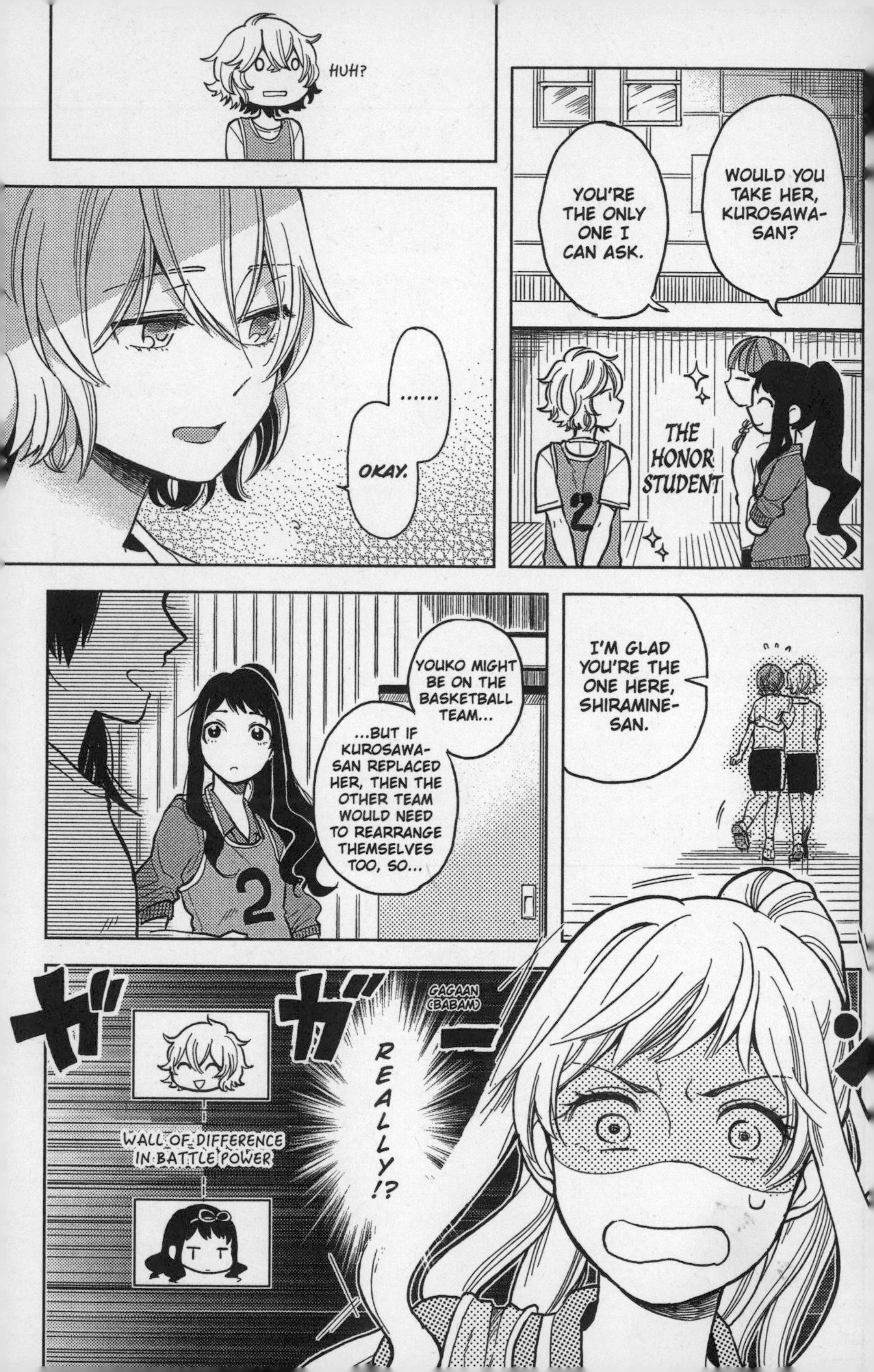
WOULD YOU TAKE HER, KUROSAWA-SAN?
YOU'RE THE ONLY ONE I CAN ASK.
HUH?
THE HONOR STUDENT
......
OKAY.
I'M GLAD YOU'RE THE ONE HERE, SHIRAMINE-SAN.
YOUKO MIGHT BE ON THE BASKETBALL TEAM...
...BUT IF KUROSAWA-SAN REPLACED HER, THEN THE OTHER TEAM WOULD NEED TO REARRANGE THEMSELVES TOO, SO...
GAGAAN (BABAM)
REALLY!?
WALL OF DIFFERENCE IN BATTLE POWER

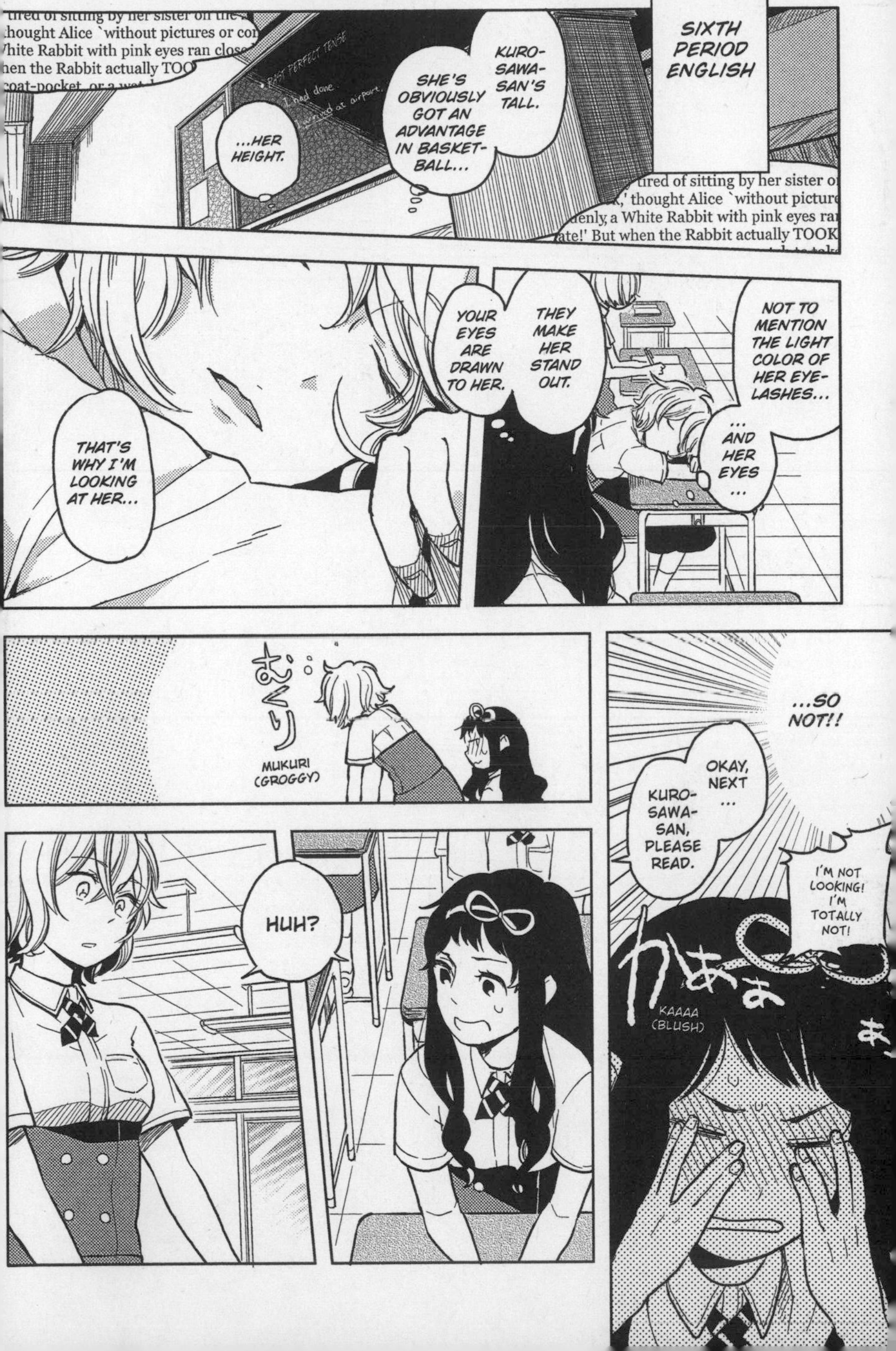
SIXTH PERIOD ENGLISH
KURO-SAWA-SAN'S TALL.
SHE'S OBVIOUSLY GOT AN ADVANTAGE IN BASKET-BALL...
...HER HEIGHT.
NOT TO MENTION THE LIGHT COLOR OF HER EYE-LASHES...
...AND HER EYES...
THEY MAKE HER STAND OUT.
YOUR EYES ARE DRAWN TO HER.
THAT'S WHY I'M LOOKING AT HER...
...SO NOT!!
OKAY, NEXT... KURO-SAWA-SAN, PLEASE READ.
I'M NOT LOOKING! I'M TOTALLY NOT!
かぁぁぁ
KAAAA (BLUSH)
むくり
MUKURI (GROGGY)
HUH?

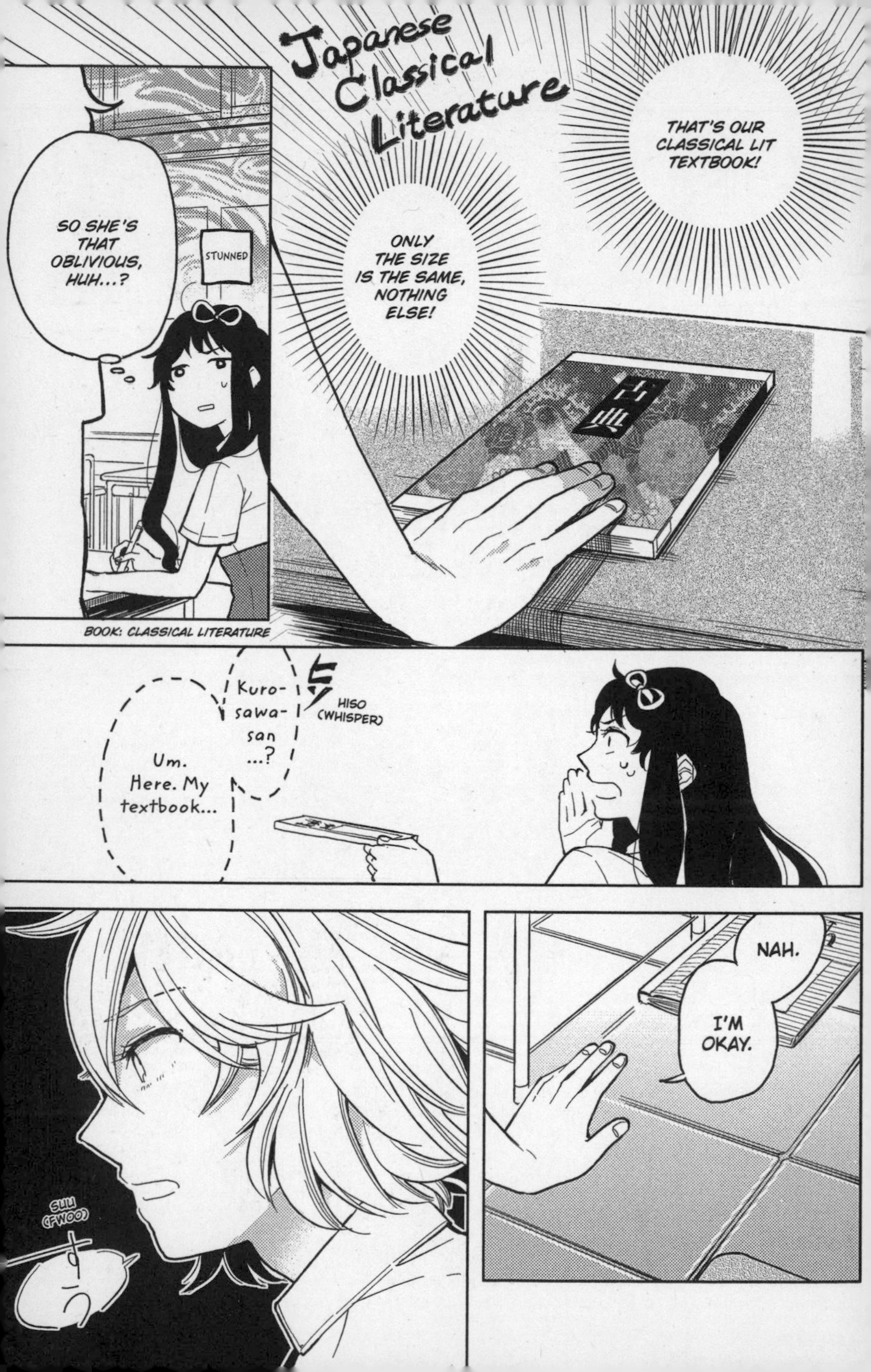
Japanese Classical Literature
THAT'S OUR CLASSICAL LIT TEXTBOOK!
ONLY THE SIZE IS THE SAME, NOTHING ELSE!
SO SHE'S THAT OBLIVIOUS, HUH...?
STUNNED
BOOK: CLASSICAL LITERATURE
HISO (WHISPER)
Kuro-sawa-san ...?
Um. Here. My textbook...
NAH.
I'M OKAY.
SUU (FWOO)

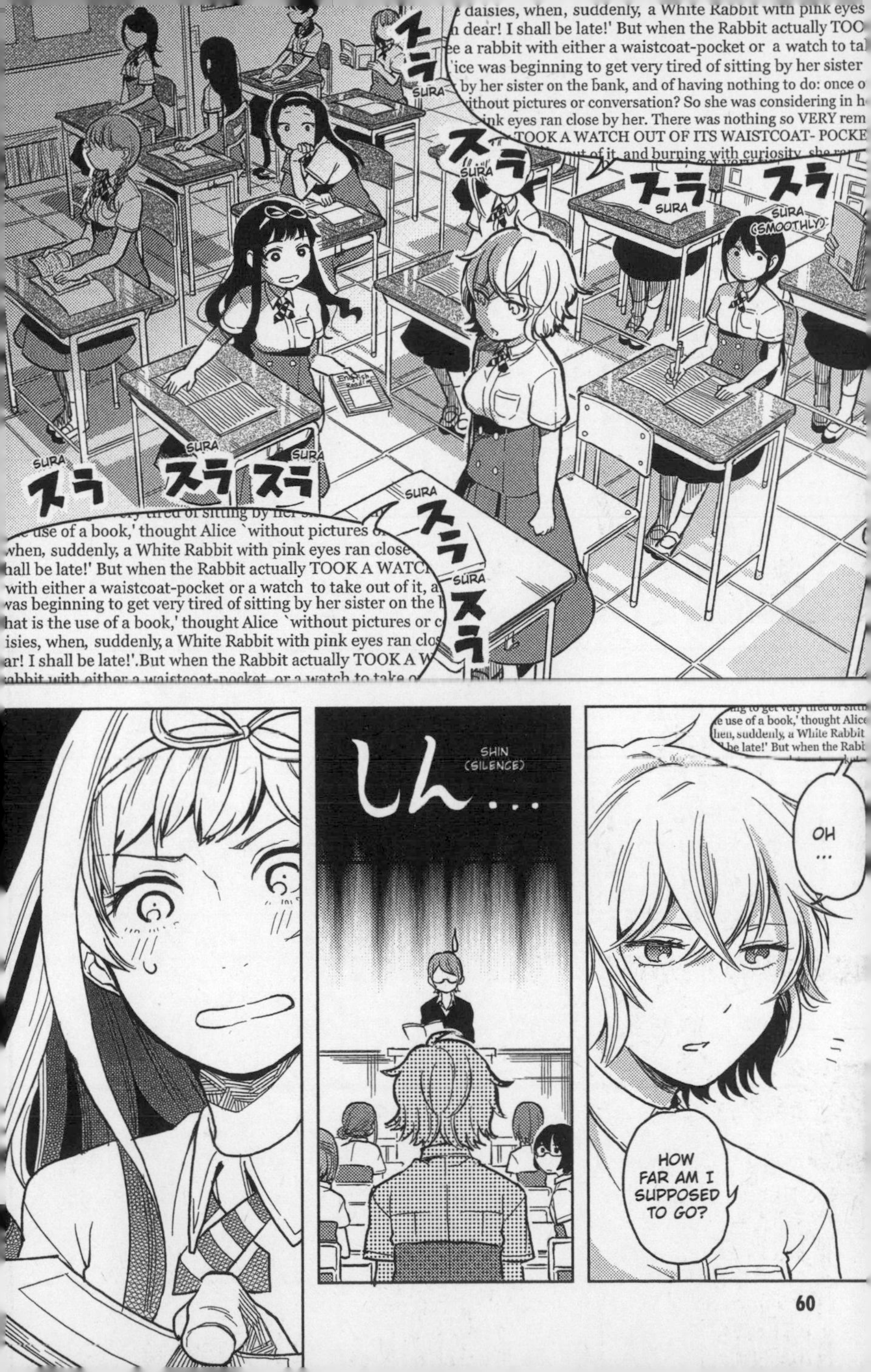
daisies, when, suddenly, a White Rabbit with pink eyes
dear! I shall be late!' But when the Rabbit actually TOO
e a rabbit with either a waistcoat-pocket or a watch to ta
'ice was beginning to get very tired of sitting by her sister
by her sister on the bank, and of having nothing to do: once o
ithout pictures or conversation? So she was considering in h
ink eyes ran close by her. There was nothing so VERY rem
TOOK A WATCH OUT OF ITS WAISTCOAT- POCKE
スラ
SURA
スラ
SURA
スラ
SURA
スラ
SURA (SMOOTHLY)
スラ
SURA
スラ
SURA
スラ
SURA
スラ
SURA
スラ
SURA
e use of a book,' thought Alice `without pictures o
when, suddenly, a White Rabbit with pink eyes ran close
hall be late!' But when the Rabbit actually TOOK A WATC
with either a waistcoat-pocket or a watch to take out of it, a
was beginning to get very tired of sitting by her sister on the b
hat is the use of a book,' thought Alice `without pictures or c
isies, when, suddenly, a White Rabbit with pink eyes ran clos
ar! I shall be late!'.But when the Rabbit actually TOOK A W
e use of a book,' thought Alice
hen, suddenly, a White Rabbit
be late!' But when the Rabb
OH ...
HOW FAR AM I SUPPOSED TO GO?
しん...
SHIN (SILENCE)

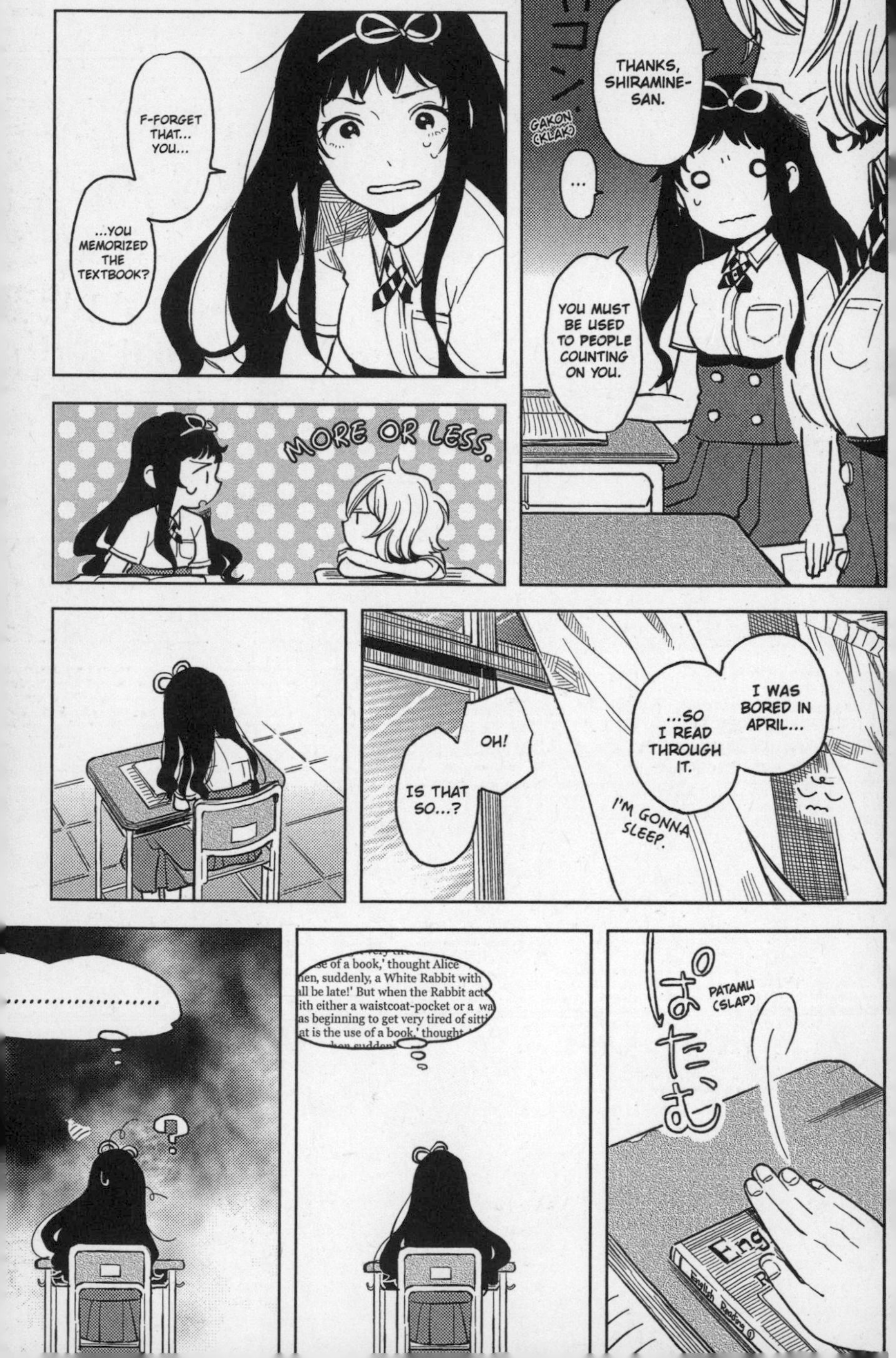

THANKS, SHIRAMINE-SAN.
ガコン
GAKON (KLAK)
...
YOU MUST BE USED TO PEOPLE COUNTING ON YOU.
F-FORGET THAT... YOU...
...YOU MEMORIZED THE TEXTBOOK?
MORE OR LESS.
I WAS BORED IN APRIL...
...SO I READ THROUGH IT.
I'M GONNA SLEEP.
OH!
IS THAT SO...?
ぱたむ
PATAMU (SLAP)
Eng
use of a book,' thought Alice
hen, suddenly, a White Rabbit with
all be late!' But when the Rabbit act
ith either a waistcoat-pocket or a wa
as beginning to get very tired of sitti
at is the use of a book,' thought
....

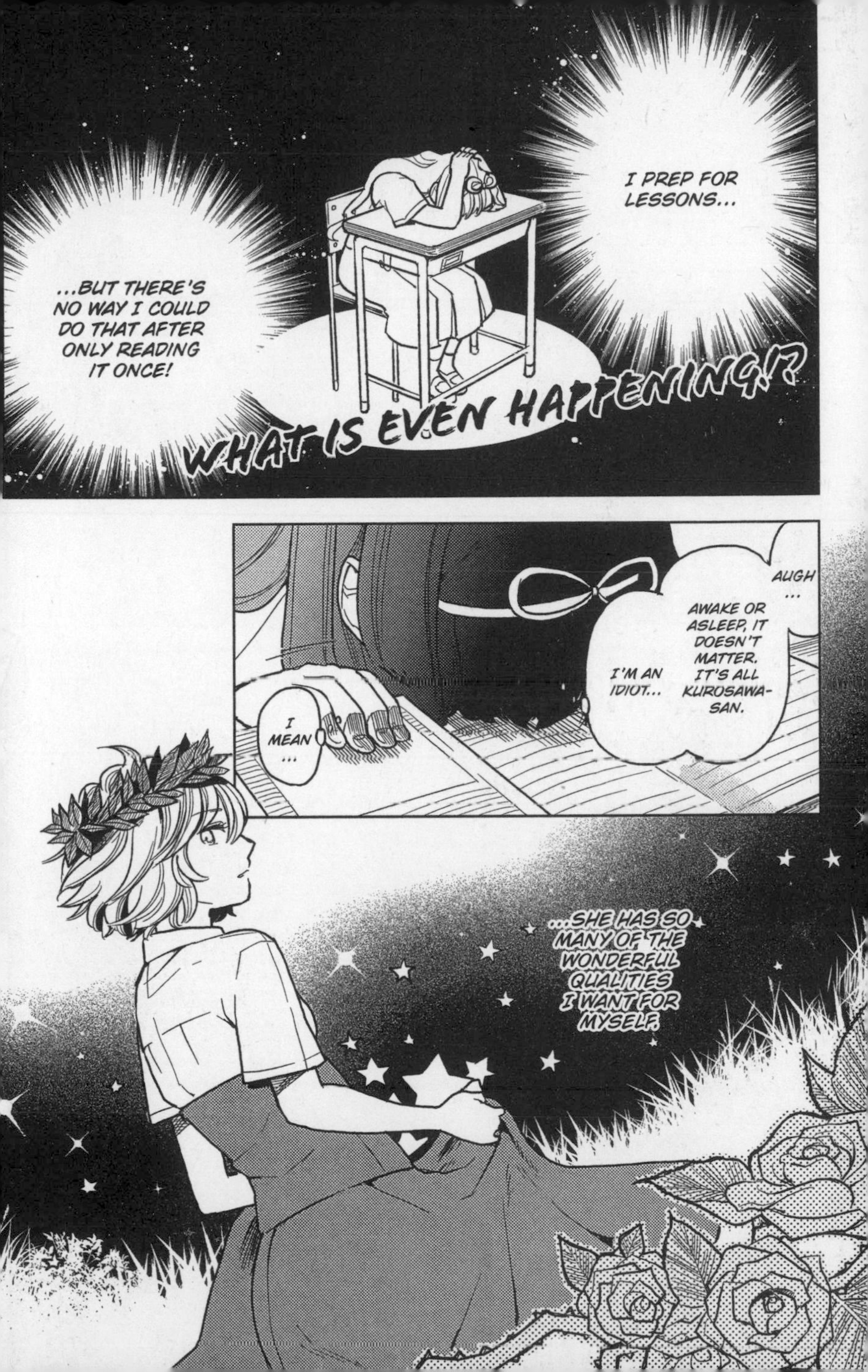
I PREP FOR LESSONS...
...BUT THERE'S NO WAY I COULD DO THAT AFTER ONLY READING IT ONCE!
WHAT IS EVEN HAPPENING!?
AUGH...
AWAKE OR ASLEEP, IT DOESN'T MATTER. IT'S ALL KUROSAWA-SAN.
I'M AN IDIOT...
I MEAN...
...SHE HAS SO MANY OF THE WONDERFUL QUALITIES I WANT FOR MYSELF.

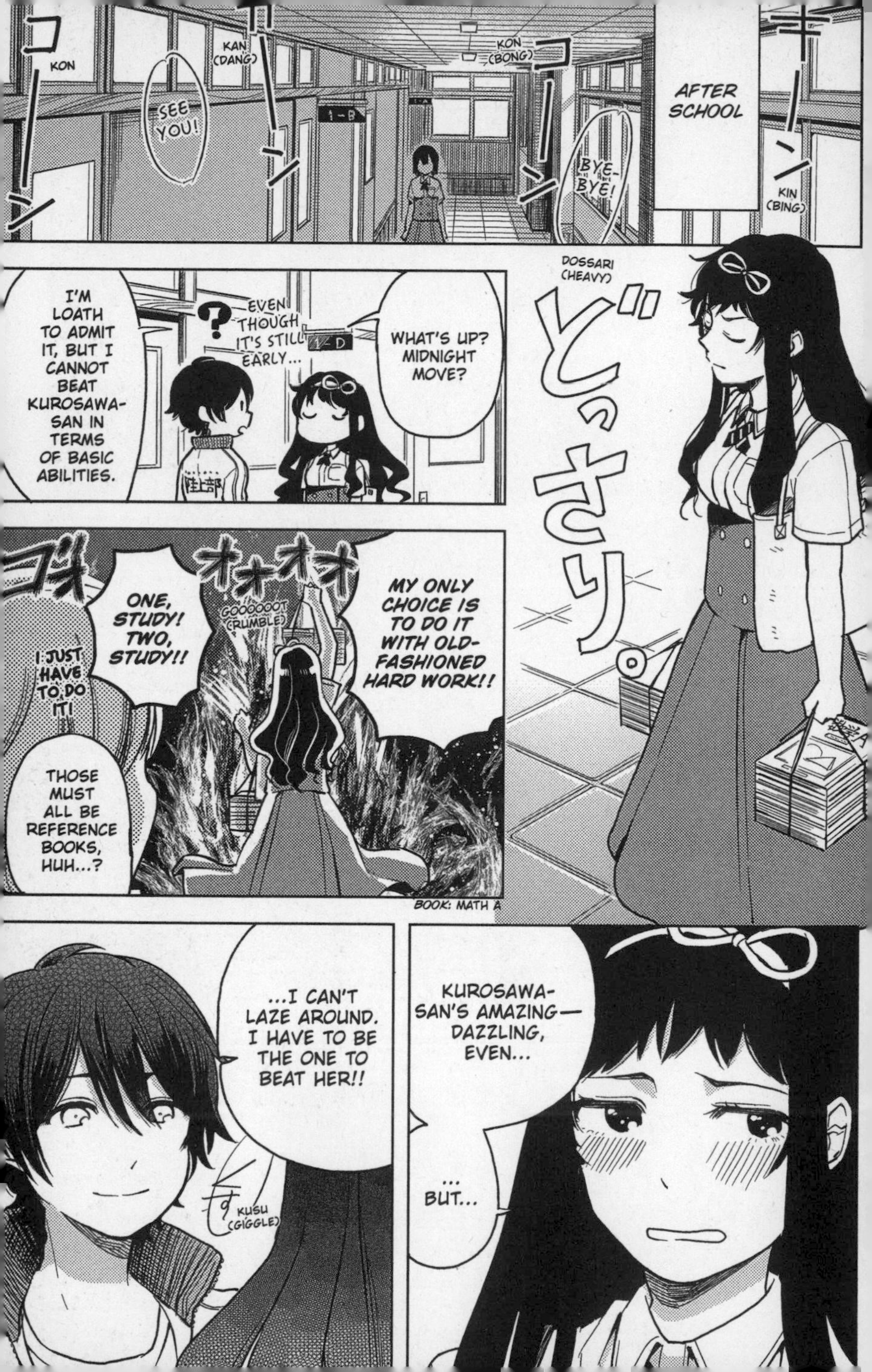
AFTER SCHOOL
KIN (BING)
BYE-BYE!
KON (BONG)
KAN (DANG)
SEE YOU!
KON
DOSSARI (HEAVY)
WHAT'S UP? MIDNIGHT MOVE?
EVEN THOUGH IT'S STILL EARLY...
?
I'M LOATH TO ADMIT IT, BUT I CANNOT BEAT KUROSAWA-SAN IN TERMS OF BASIC ABILITIES.
MY ONLY CHOICE IS TO DO IT WITH OLD-FASHIONED HARD WORK!!
GOOOOOOT (RUMBLE)
ONE, STUDY! TWO, STUDY!!
I JUST HAVE TO DO IT!
THOSE MUST ALL BE REFERENCE BOOKS, HUH...?
BOOK: MATH A
KUROSAWA-SAN'S AMAZING— DAZZLING, EVEN...
... BUT...
...I CAN'T LAZE AROUND. I HAVE TO BE THE ONE TO BEAT HER!!
KUSU (GIGGLE)

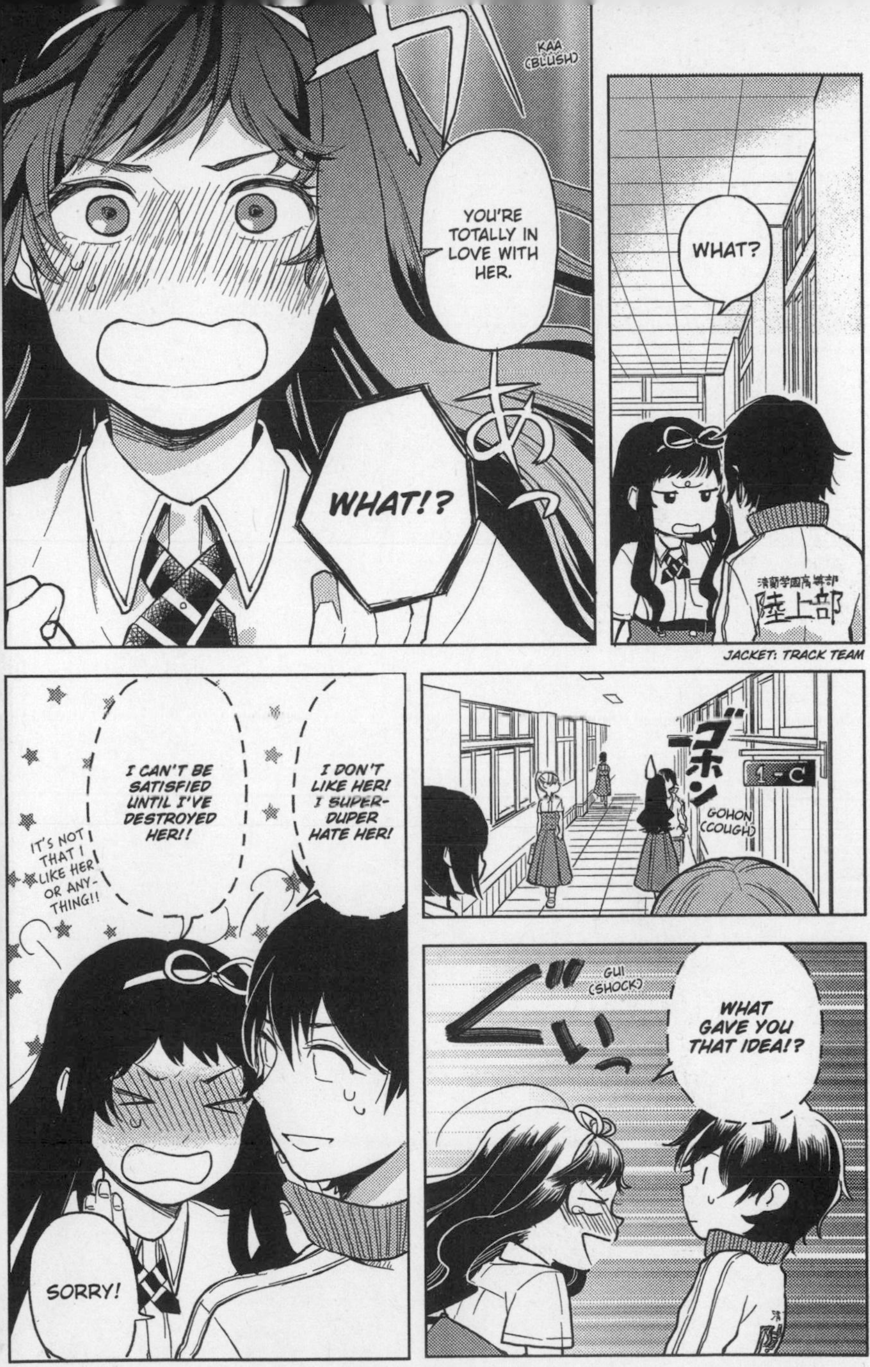
WHAT?
陸上部
JACKET: TRACK TEAM
KAA (BLUSH)
YOU'RE TOTALLY IN LOVE WITH HER.
WHAT!?
GOHON (COUGH)
WHAT GAVE YOU THAT IDEA!?
GUI (SHOCK)
I DON'T LIKE HER! I SUPER-DUPER HATE HER!
I CAN'T BE SATISFIED UNTIL I'VE DESTROYED HER!!
IT'S NOT THAT I LIKE HER OR ANY-THING!!
SORRY!

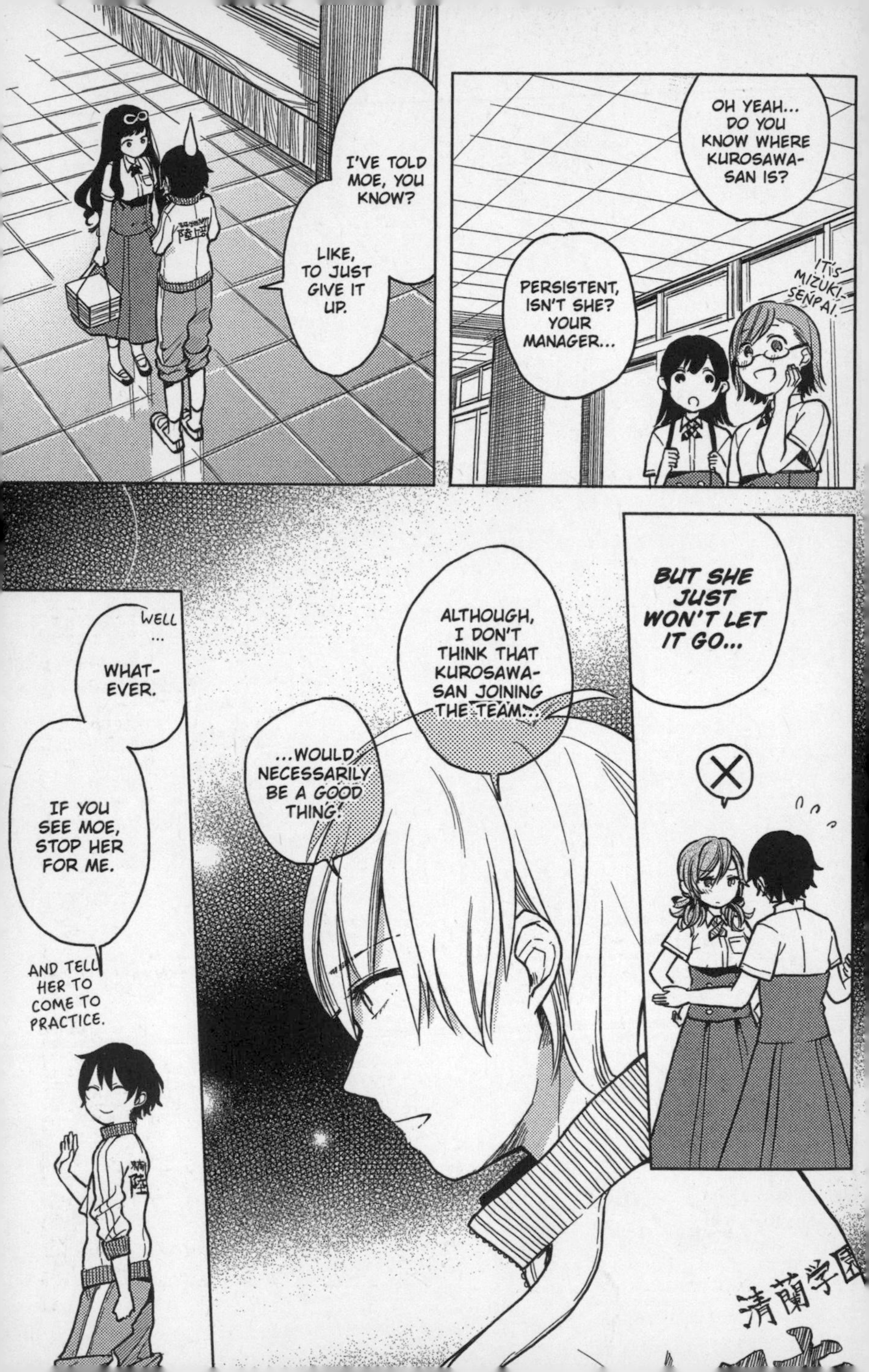
OH YEAH... DO YOU KNOW WHERE KUROSAWA-SAN IS?
IT'S MIZUKI-SENPAI.
PERSISTENT, ISN'T SHE? YOUR MANAGER...
I'VE TOLD MOE, YOU KNOW?
LIKE, TO JUST GIVE IT UP.
BUT SHE JUST WON'T LET IT GO...
ALTHOUGH, I DON'T THINK THAT KUROSAWA-SAN JOINING THE TEAM...
...WOULD NECESSARILY BE A GOOD THING.
清蘭学園
WELL... WHATEVER.
IF YOU SEE MOE, STOP HER FOR ME.
AND TELL HER TO COME TO PRACTICE.

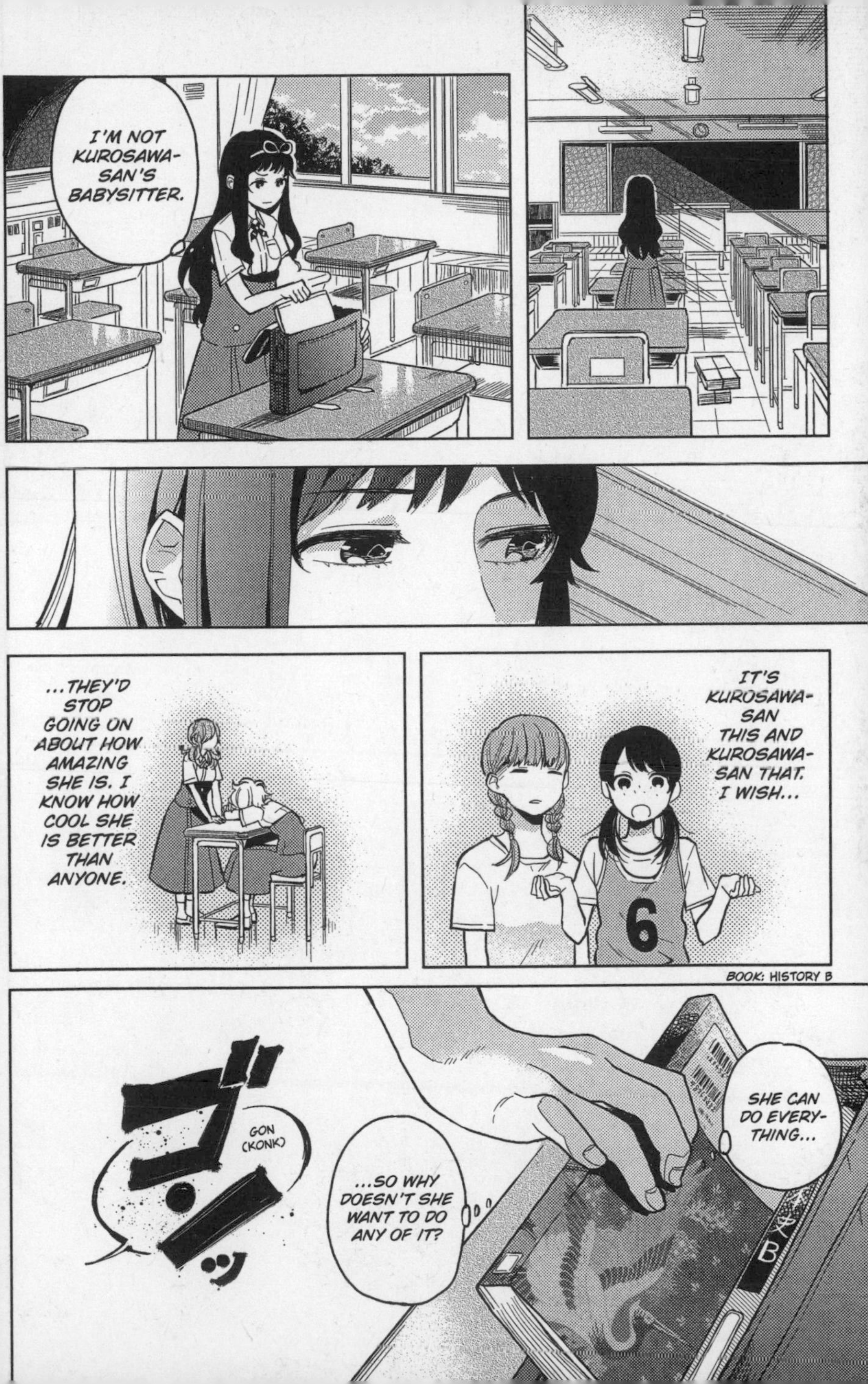
I'M NOT KUROSAWA-SAN'S BABYSITTER.
IT'S KUROSAWA-SAN THIS AND KUROSAWA-SAN THAT. I WISH...
...THEY'D STOP GOING ON ABOUT HOW AMAZING SHE IS. I KNOW HOW COOL SHE IS BETTER THAN ANYONE.
BOOK: HISTORY B
SHE CAN DO EVERY-THING...
...SO WHY DOESN'T SHE WANT TO DO ANY OF IT?
GON (KONK)

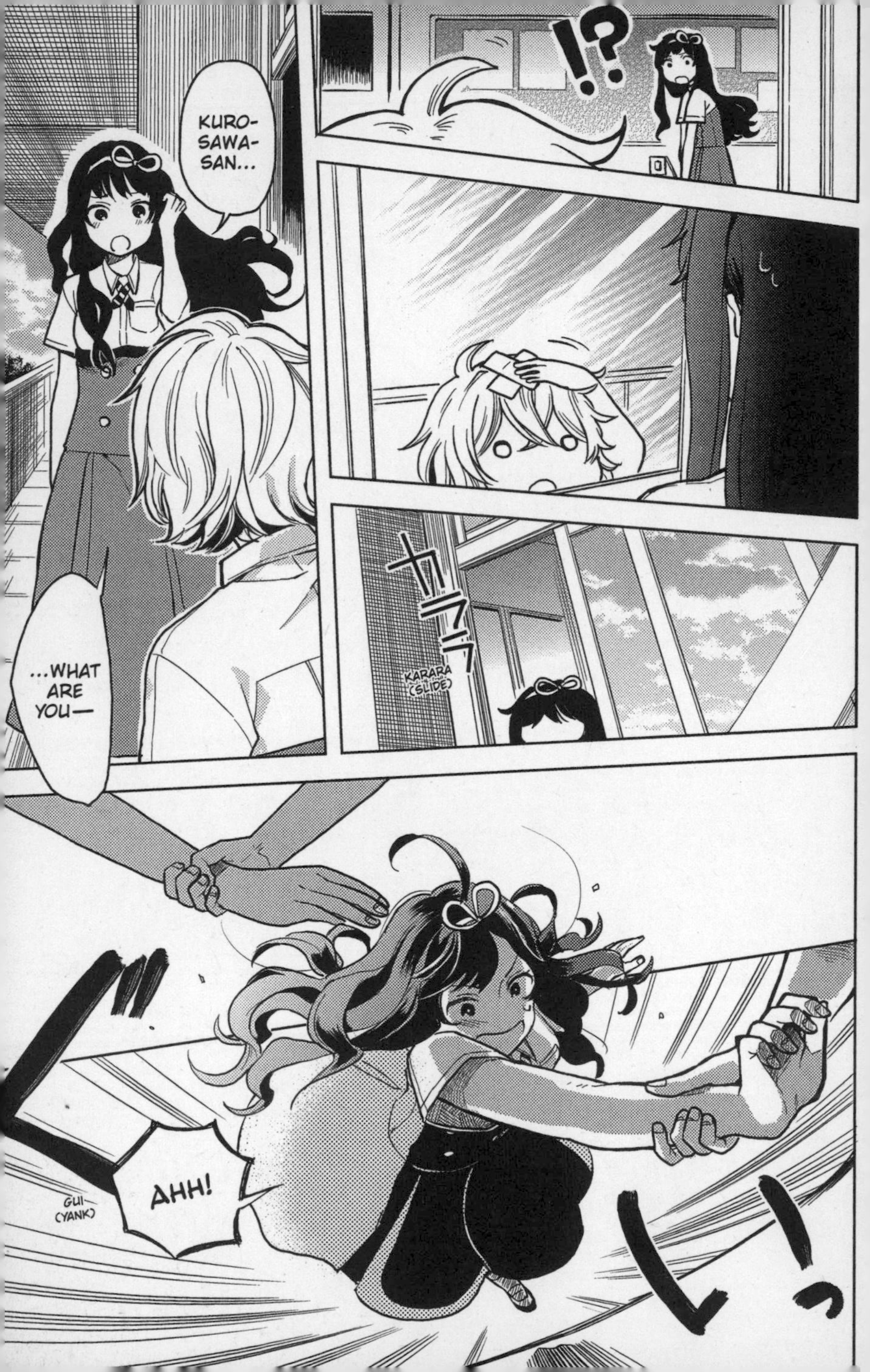
!?
KARARA (SLIDE)
KURO-SAWA-SAN...
...WHAT ARE YOU—
AHH!
GUI (YANK)

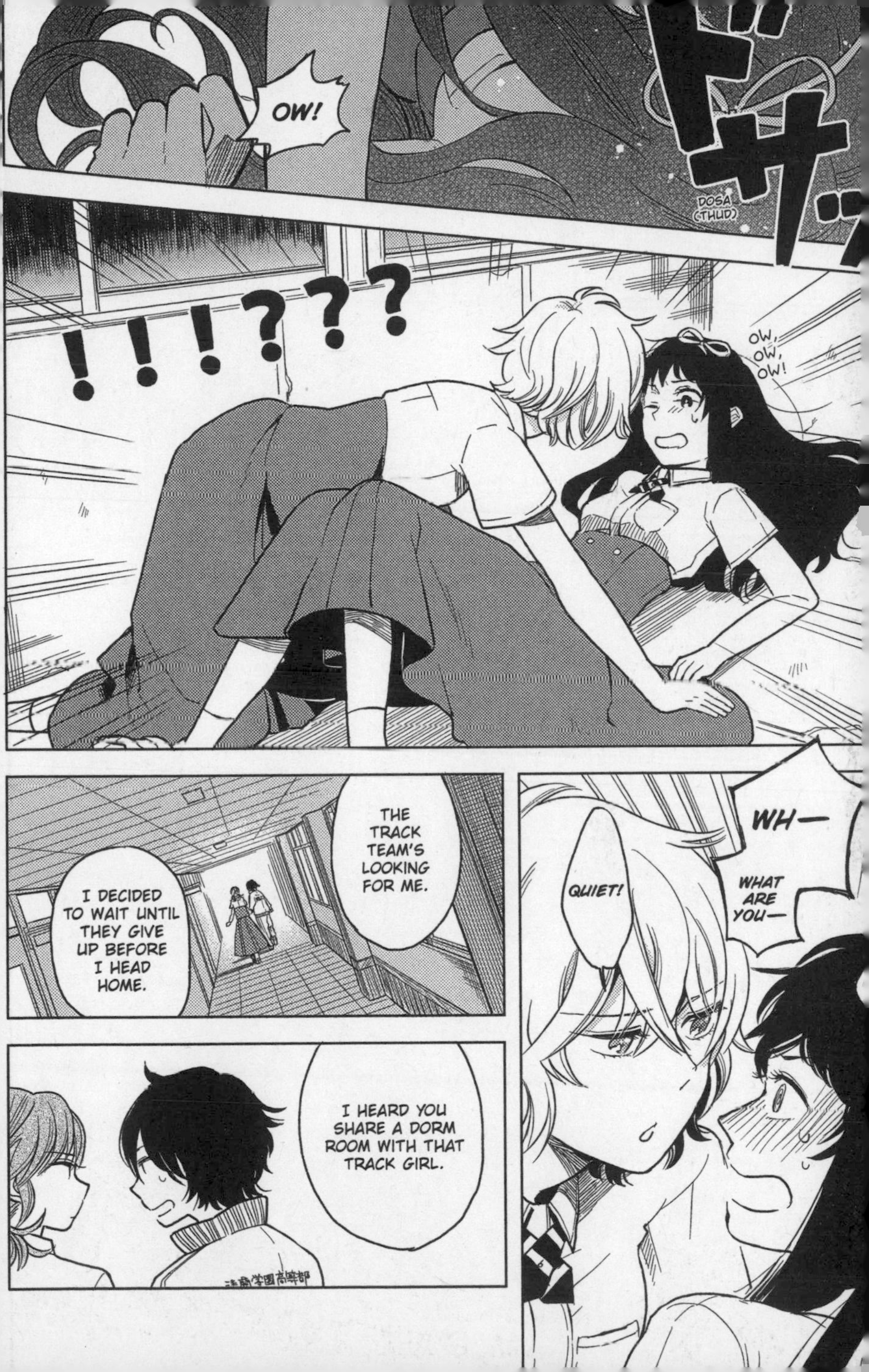
ドサッ
DOSA (THUD)
OW!
OW, OW, OW!
!!!???
WH—
WHAT ARE YOU—
QUIET!
THE TRACK TEAM'S LOOKING FOR ME.
I DECIDED TO WAIT UNTIL THEY GIVE UP BEFORE I HEAD HOME.
I HEARD YOU SHARE A DORM ROOM WITH THAT TRACK GIRL.

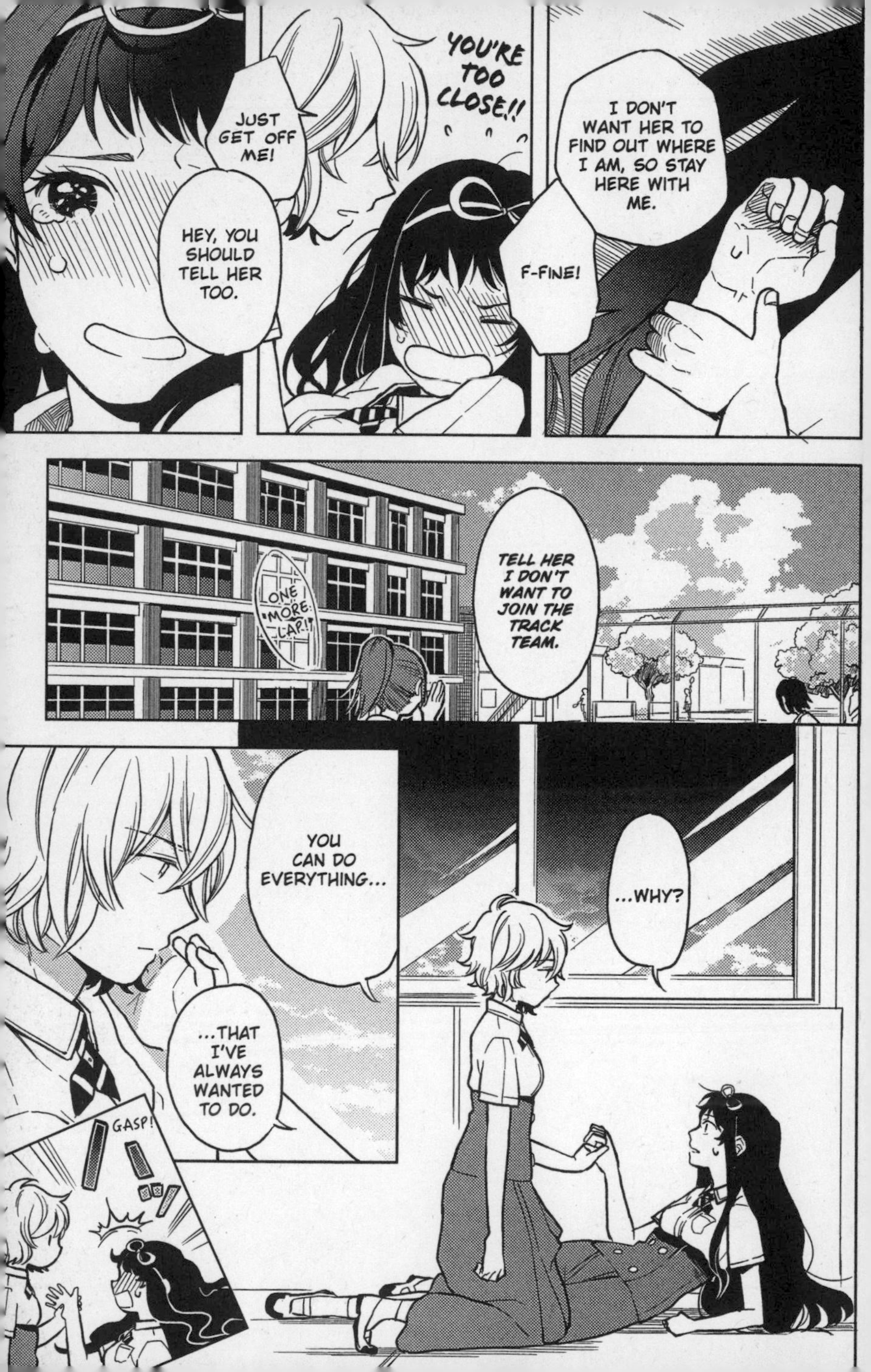
I DON'T WANT HER TO FIND OUT WHERE I AM, SO STAY HERE WITH ME.
F-FINE!
YOU'RE TOO CLOSE!!
JUST GET OFF ME!
HEY, YOU SHOULD TELL HER TOO.
TELL HER I DON'T WANT TO JOIN THE TRACK TEAM.
ONE MORE LAP!!
...WHY?
YOU CAN DO EVERYTHING...
...THAT I'VE ALWAYS WANTED TO DO.
GASP!

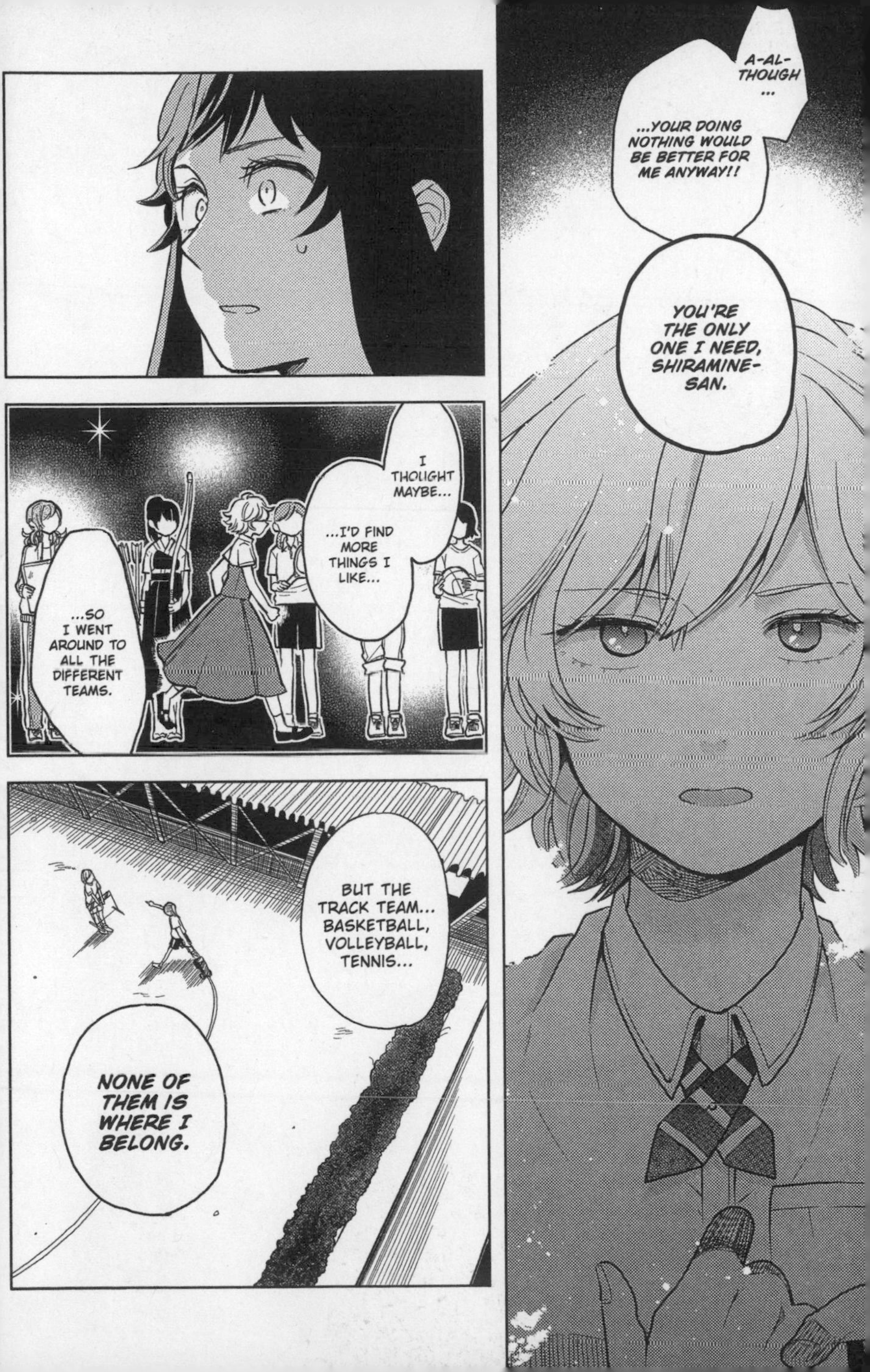
A-AL-THOUGH...
...YOUR DOING NOTHING WOULD BE BETTER FOR ME ANYWAY!!
YOU'RE THE ONLY ONE I NEED, SHIRAMINE-SAN.
I THOUGHT MAYBE...
...I'D FIND MORE THINGS I LIKE...
...SO I WENT AROUND TO ALL THE DIFFERENT TEAMS.
BUT THE TRACK TEAM... BASKETBALL, VOLLEYBALL, TENNIS...
NONE OF THEM IS WHERE I BELONG.

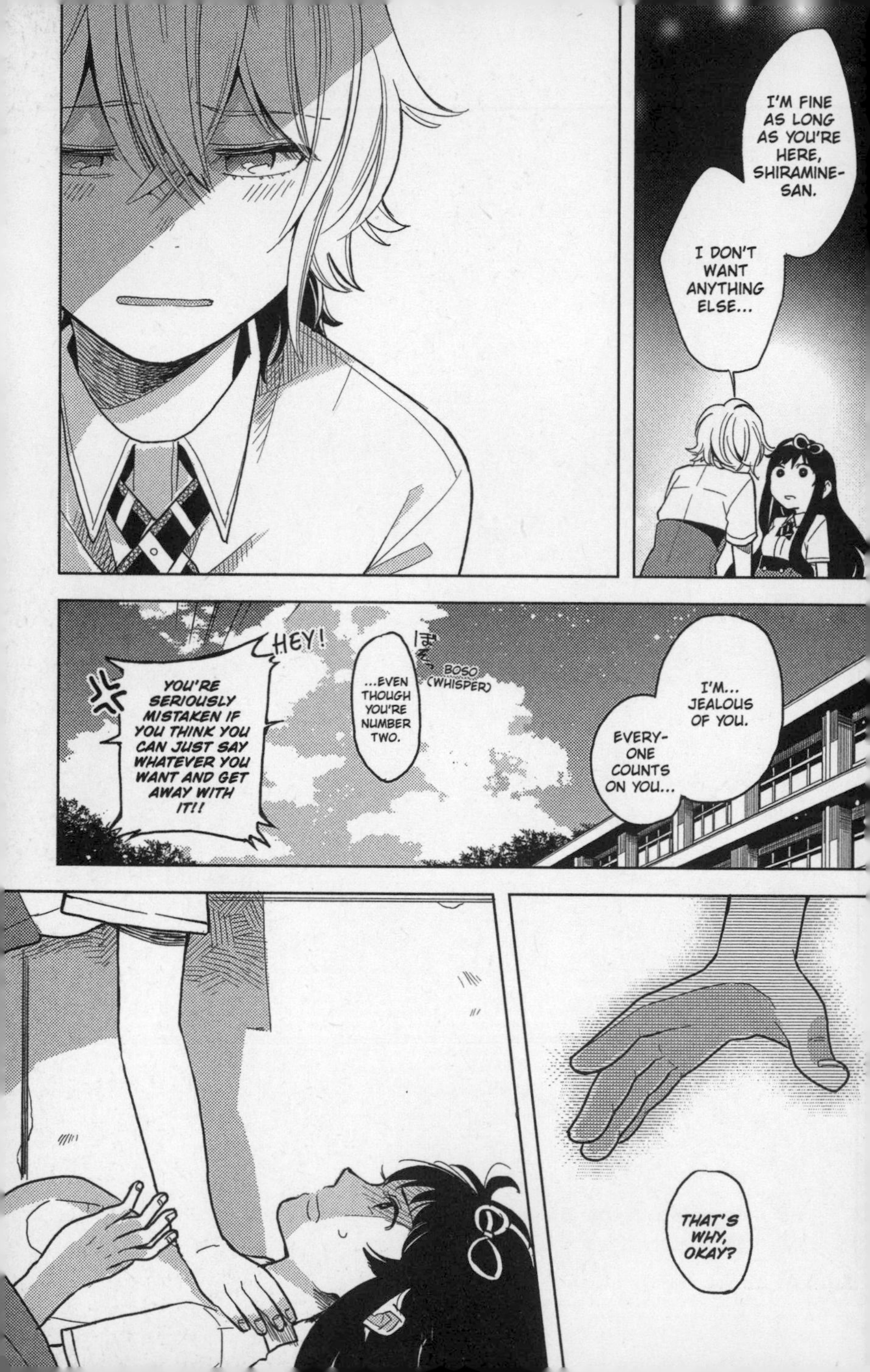
I'M FINE AS LONG AS YOU'RE HERE, SHIRAMINE-SAN.
I DON'T WANT ANYTHING ELSE...
I'M... JEALOUS OF YOU.
EVERY-ONE COUNTS ON YOU...
...EVEN THOUGH YOU'RE NUMBER TWO.
BOSO (WHISPER)
HEY!
YOU'RE SERIOUSLY MISTAKEN IF YOU THINK YOU CAN JUST SAY WHATEVER YOU WANT AND GET AWAY WITH IT!!
THAT'S WHY, OKAY?

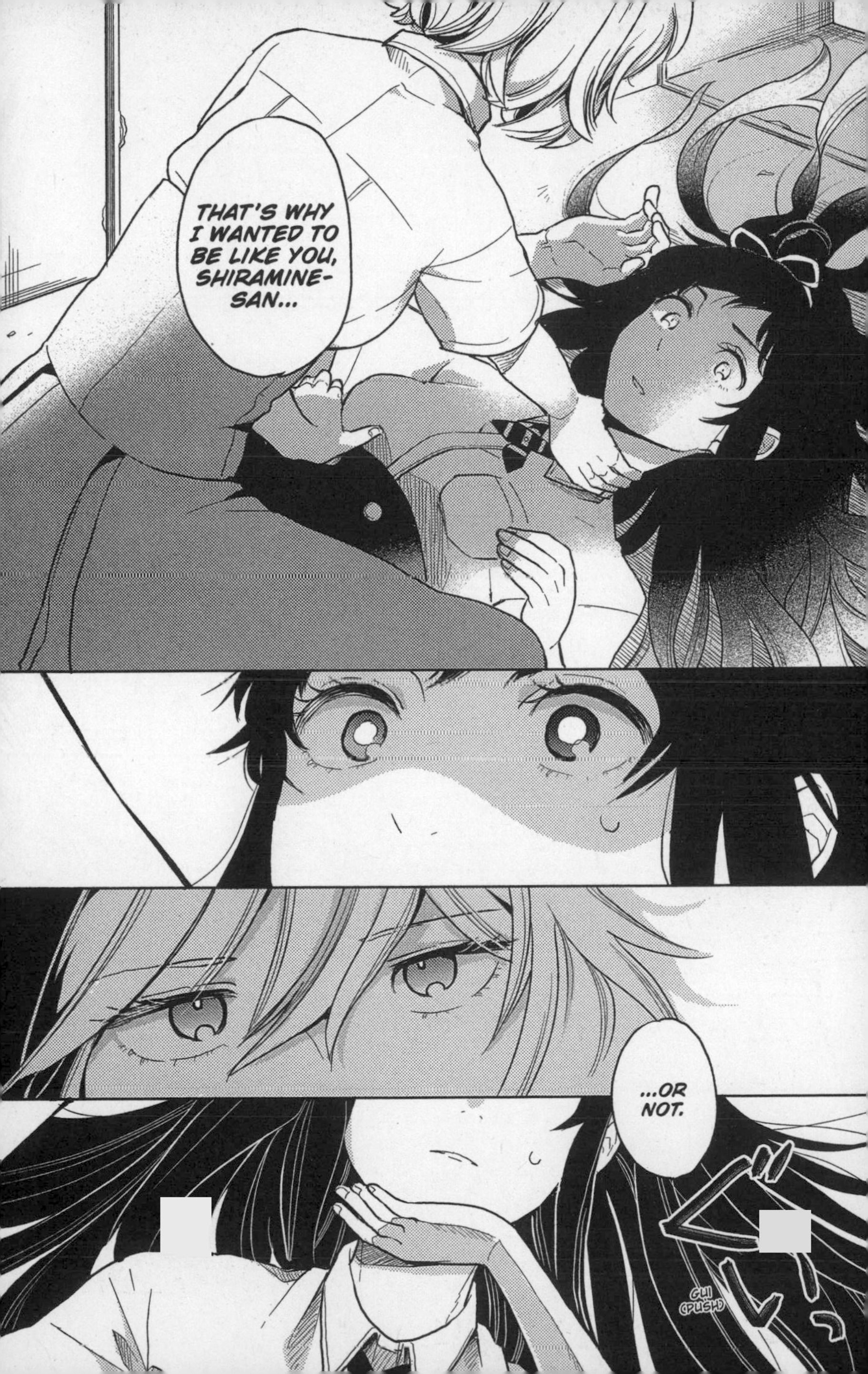
THAT'S WHY I WANTED TO BE LIKE YOU, SHIRAMINE-SAN...
...OR NOT.
GUI (PUSH)

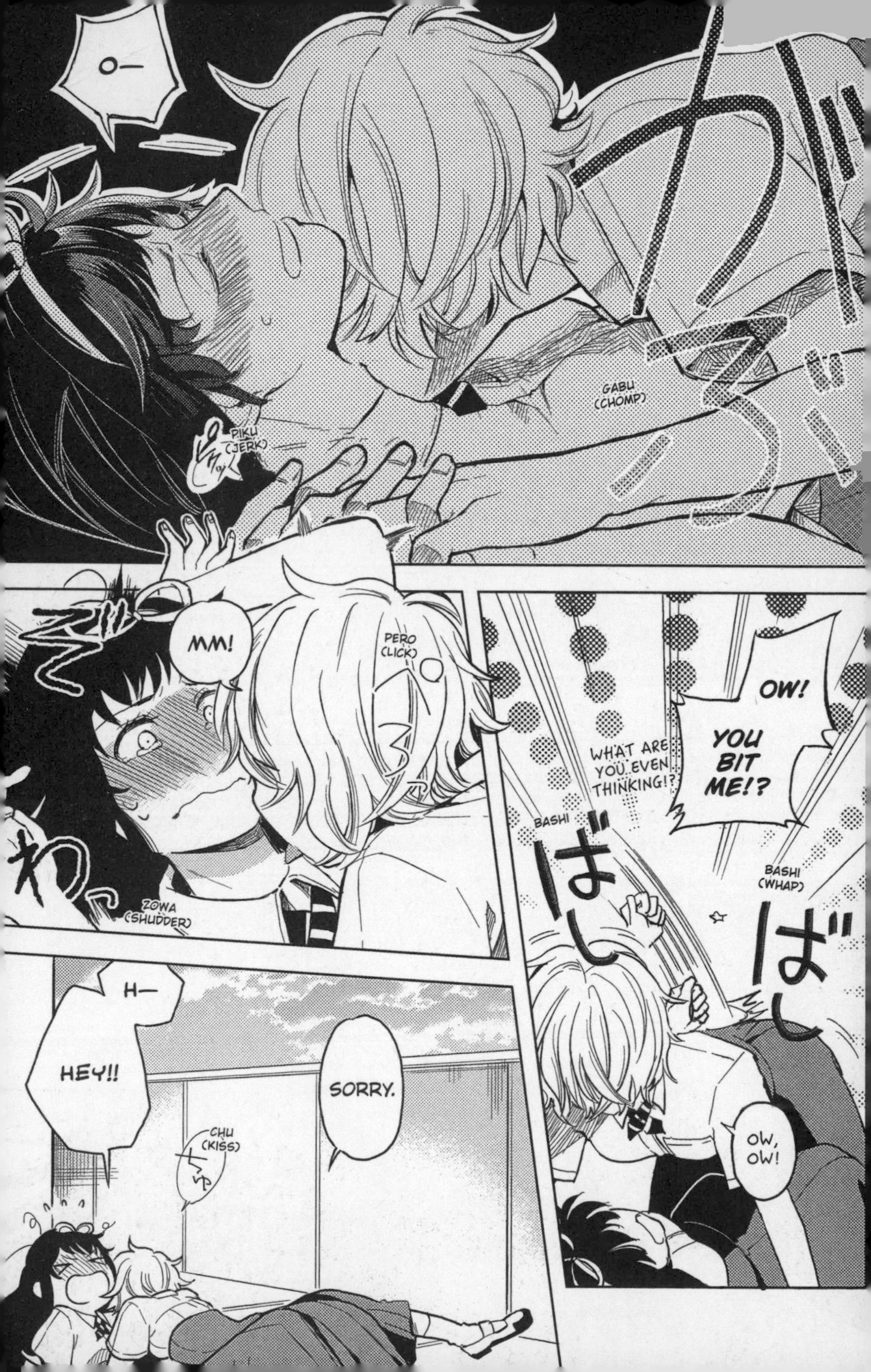
O—
GABU (CHOMP)
PIKU (JERK)
OW!
YOU BIT ME!?
WHAT ARE YOU EVEN THINKING!?
BASHI
ばし
BASHI (WHAP)
ばし
OW, OW!
PERO (LICK)
MM!
ZOWA (SHUDDER)
SORRY.
H—
HEY!!
CHU (KISS)

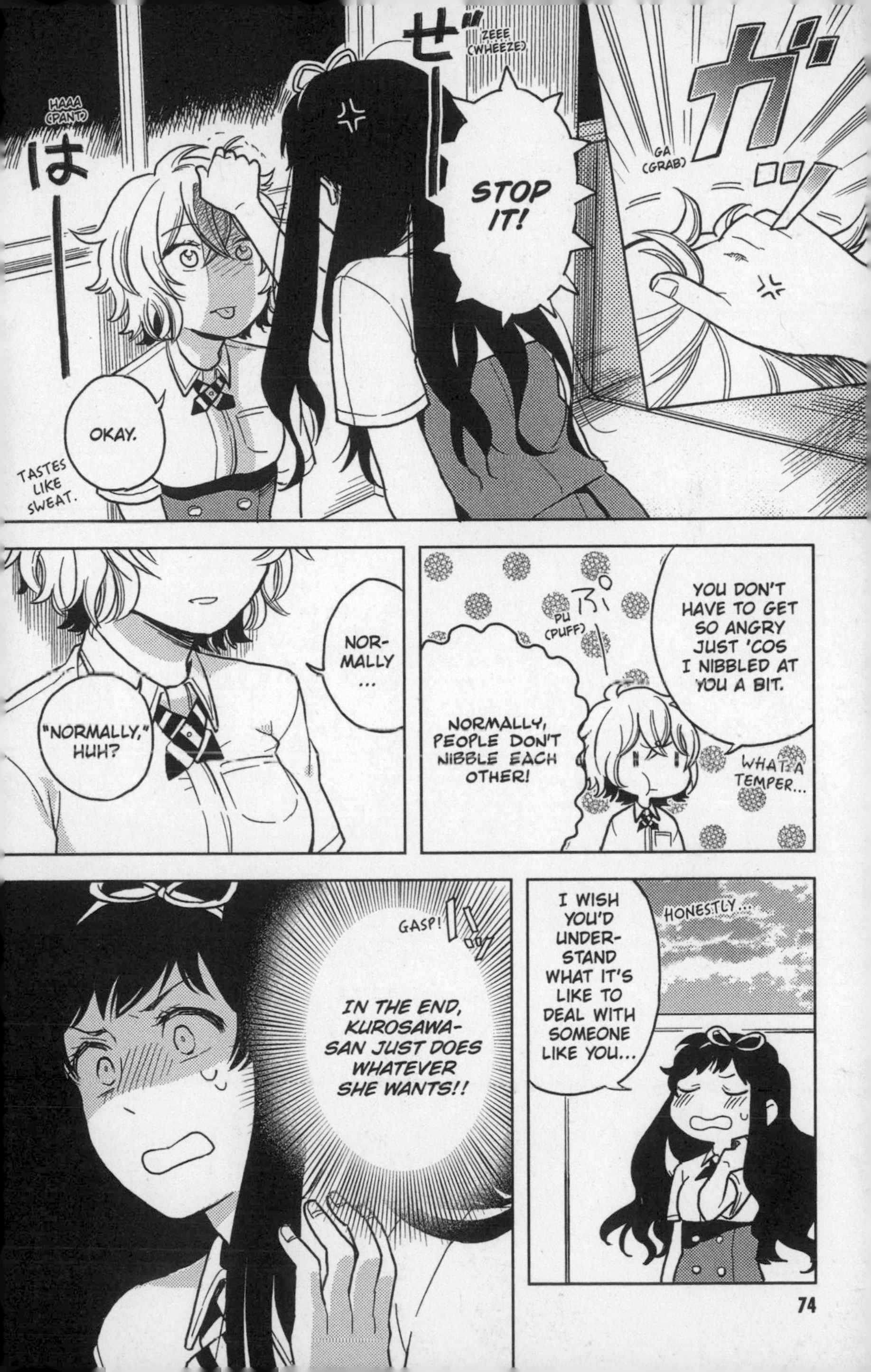
ガッ
GA (GRAB)
STOP IT!
ぜー
ZEEE (WHEEZE)
は
HAAA (PANT)
OKAY.
TASTES LIKE SWEAT.
YOU DON'T HAVE TO GET SO ANGRY JUST 'COS I NIBBLED AT YOU A BIT.
ぷ
PU (PUFF)
WHAT A TEMPER...
NORMALLY, PEOPLE DON'T NIBBLE EACH OTHER!
NOR-MALLY...
"NORMALLY," HUH?
HONESTLY...
I WISH YOU'D UNDER-STAND WHAT IT'S LIKE TO DEAL WITH SOMEONE LIKE YOU...
GASP!
IN THE END, KUROSAWA-SAN JUST DOES WHATEVER SHE WANTS!!

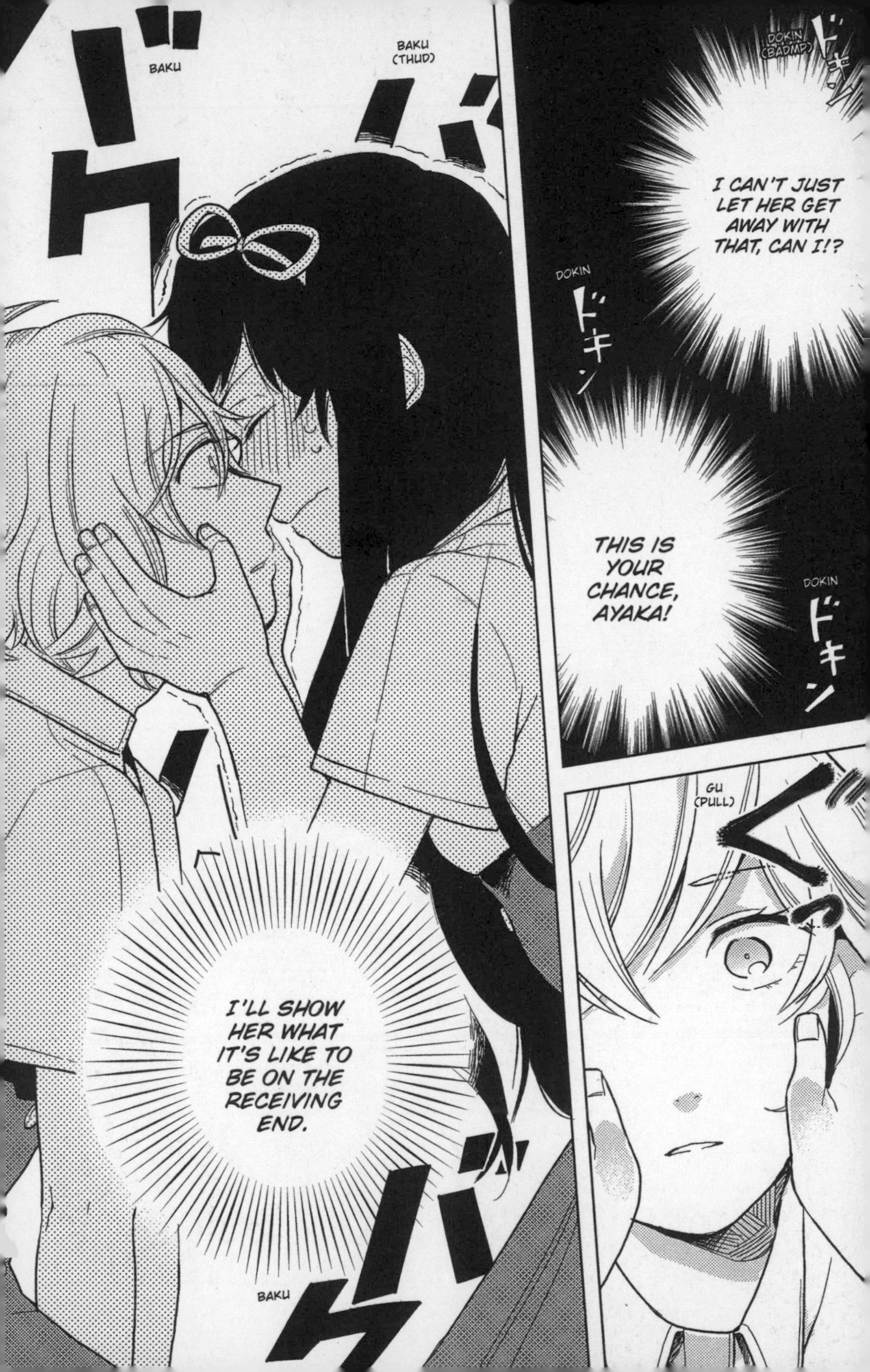
DOKIN (BADMP)
I CAN'T JUST LET HER GET AWAY WITH THAT, CAN I!?
DOKIN
ドキン
THIS IS YOUR CHANCE, AYAKA!
DOKIN
ドキン
GU (PULL)
BAKU
BAKU (THUD)
I'LL SHOW HER WHAT IT'S LIKE TO BE ON THE RECEIVING END.
BAKU

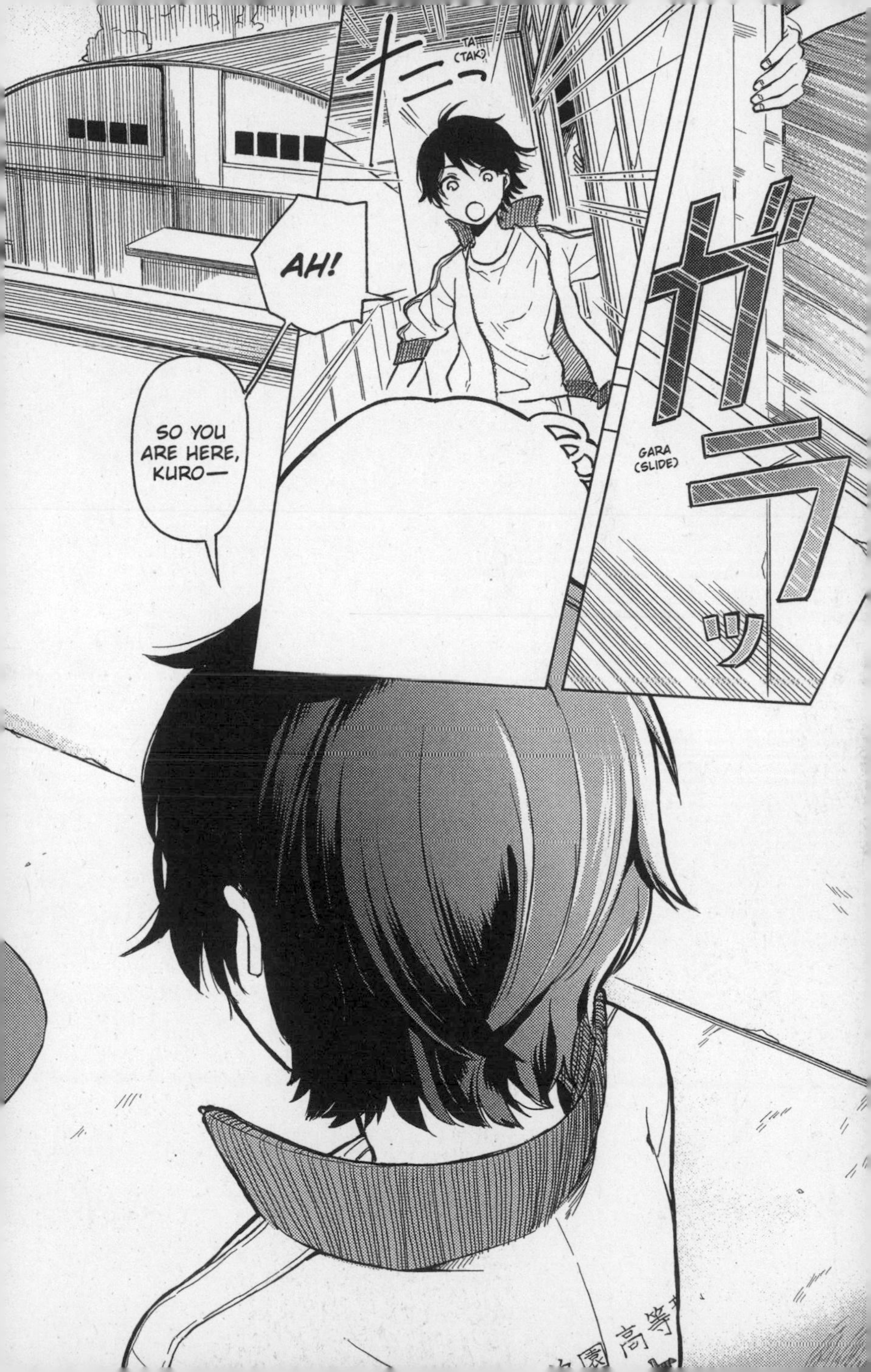
GARA (SLIDE)
TA (TAK)
AH!
SO YOU ARE HERE, KURO—

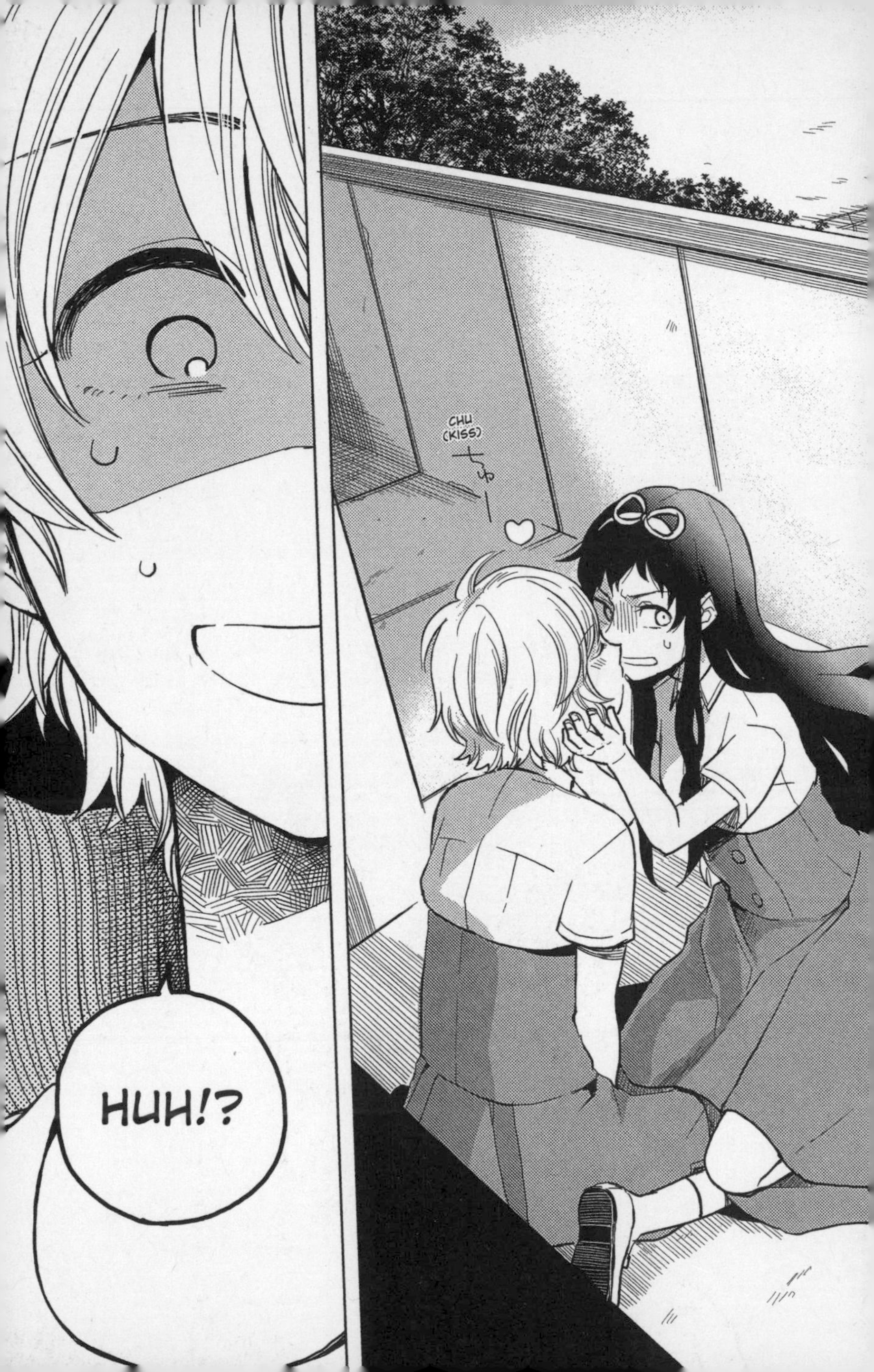
CHU
(KISS)
HUH!?

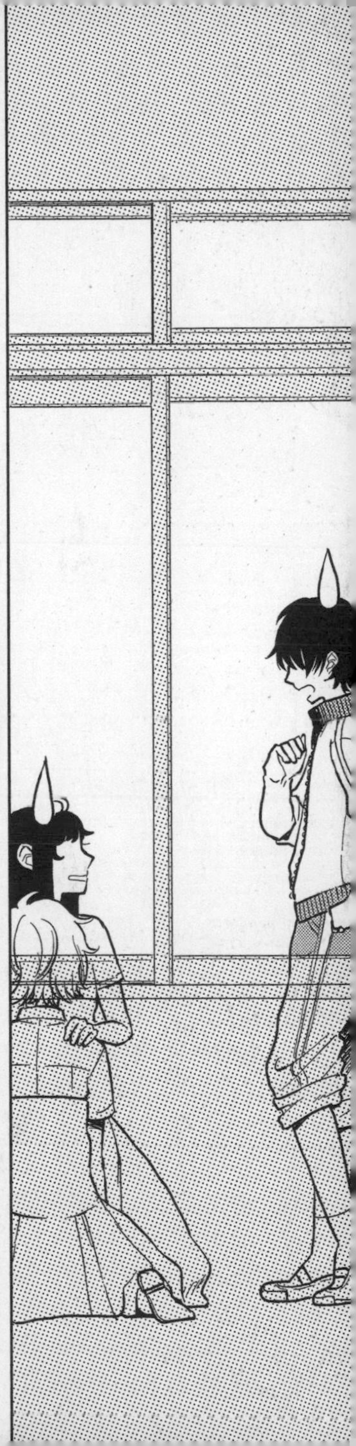

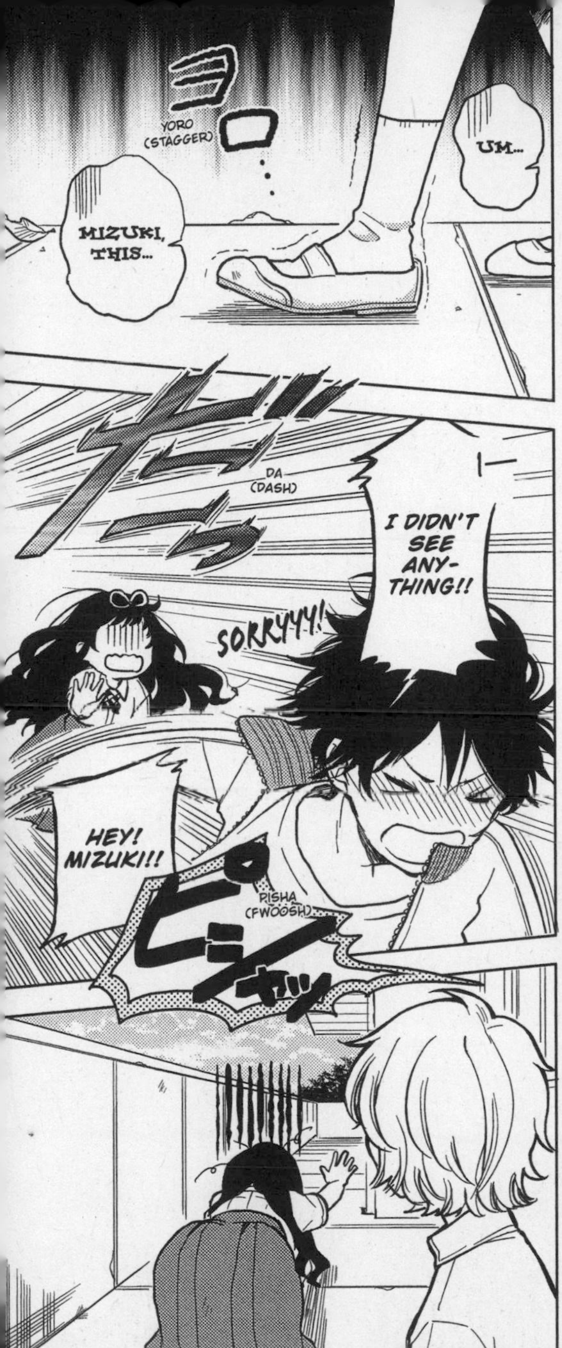
UM...
YORO (STAGGER)
MIZUKI, THIS...
I DIDN'T SEE ANY-THING!!
DA (DASH)
SORRYYY!
HEY! MIZUKI!!
PISHA (FWOOSH)

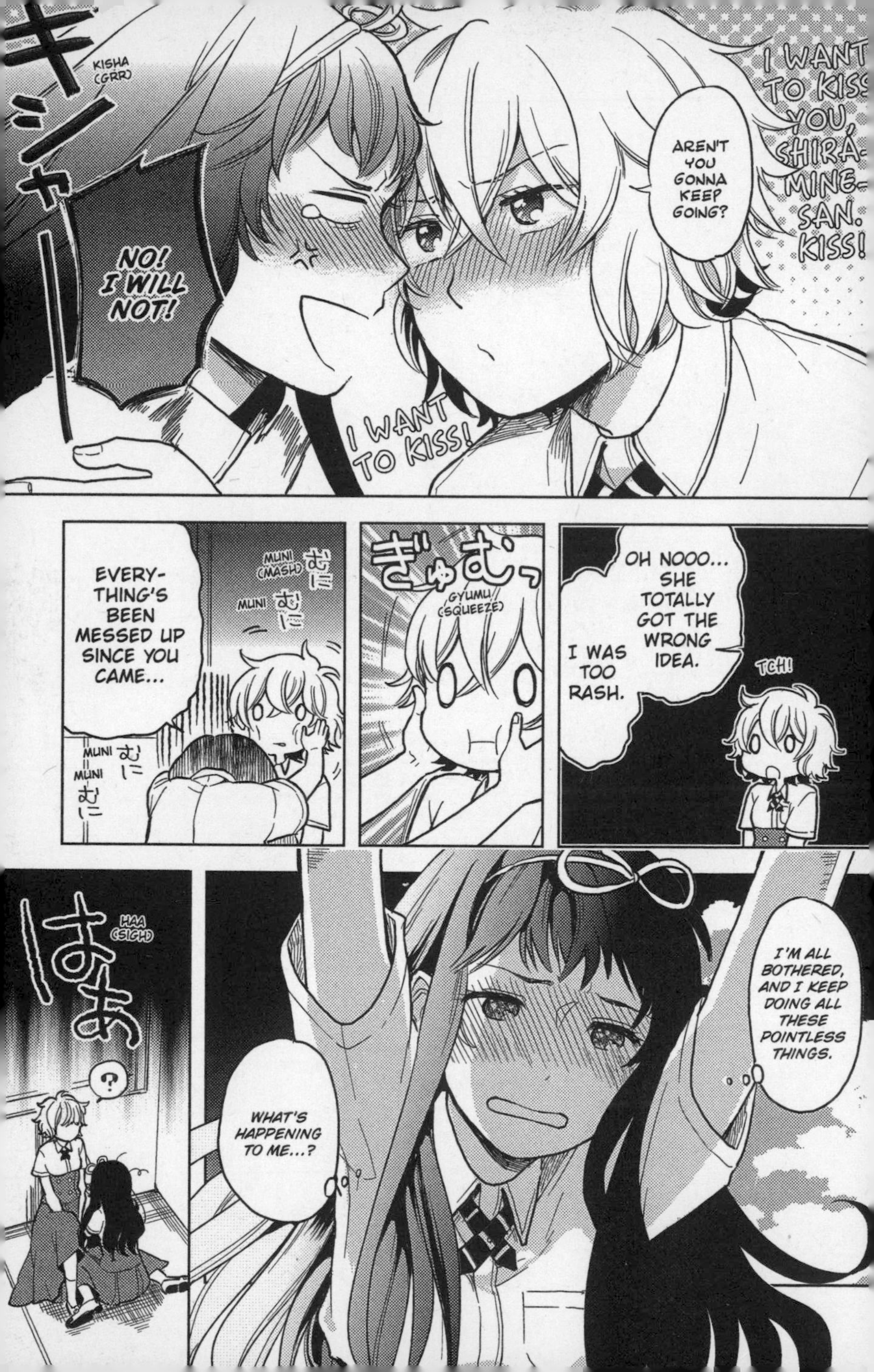
I WANT TO KISS YOU, SHIRA-MINE-SAN. KISS!
AREN'T YOU GONNA KEEP GOING?
I WANT TO KISS!
NO! I WILL NOT!
キシャー
KISHA (GRR)
OH NOOO... SHE TOTALLY GOT THE WRONG IDEA.
I WAS TOO RASH.
TCH!
ぎゅむっ
GYUMU (SQUEEZE)
EVERY-THING'S BEEN MESSED UP SINCE YOU CAME...
むに
MUNI (MASH)
むに
MUNI
むに
MUNI
むに
MUNI
I'M ALL BOTHERED, AND I KEEP DOING ALL THESE POINTLESS THINGS.
WHAT'S HAPPENING TO ME...?
はあ
HAA (SIGH)
?

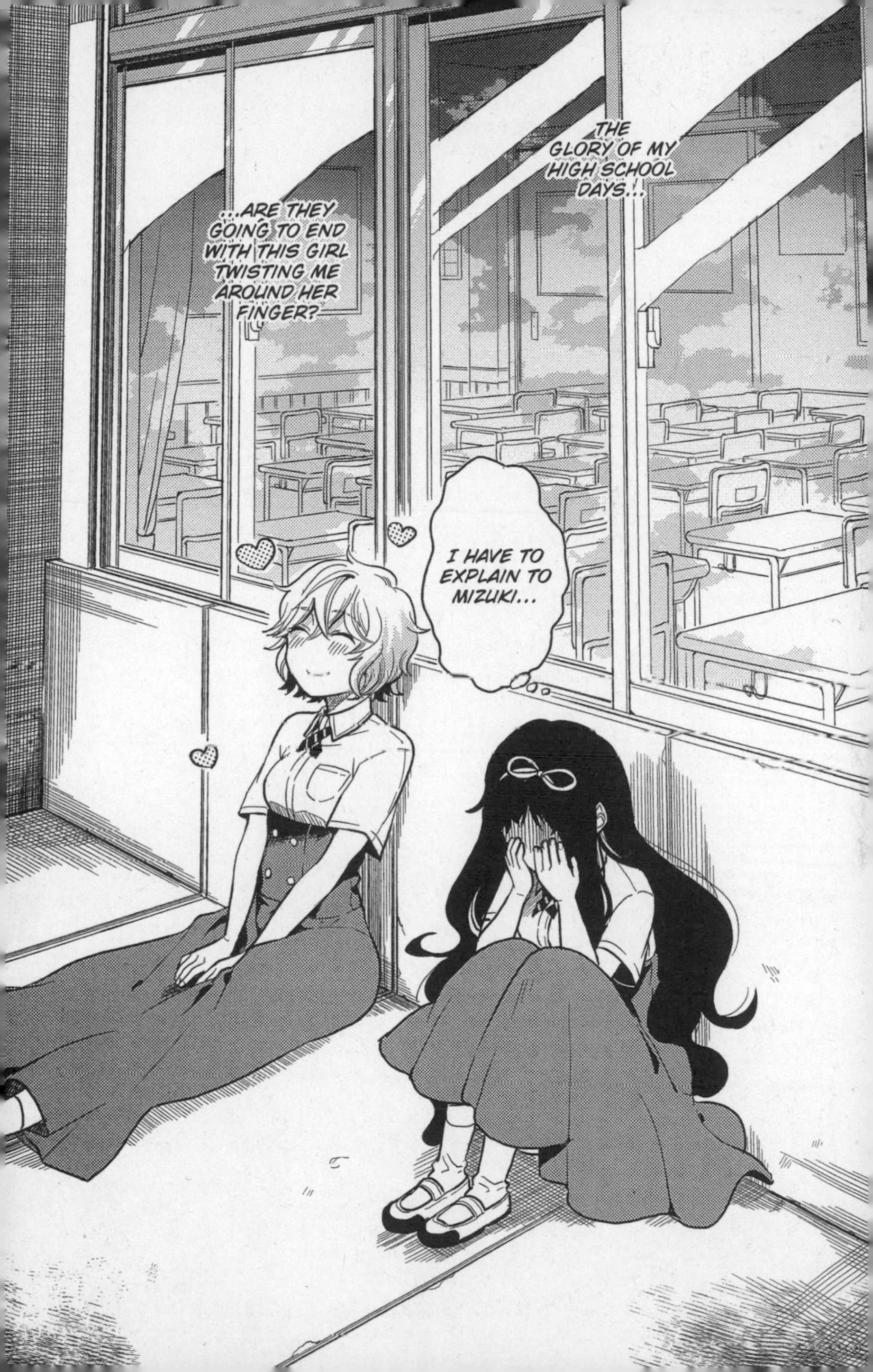
THE GLORY OF MY HIGH SCHOOL DAYS...
...ARE THEY GOING TO END WITH THIS GIRL TWISTING ME AROUND HER FINGER?
I HAVE TO EXPLAIN TO MIZUKI...

Break Time

YOUKO
FIRST-YEAR, CLASS C
BASKETBALL TEAM
GENTLE AND MILD

RISA
HER FRECKLES ARE HER BIG APPEAL.

KISS THEATER: WHAT'S BEHIND THE STORY!?

PEOPLE OTHER THAN THE MAIN CHARACTERS HAVE STORIES TOO. HERE, WE PRESENT THE "LITTLE LOVE" STORIES HAPPENING BEHIND THE SCENES.

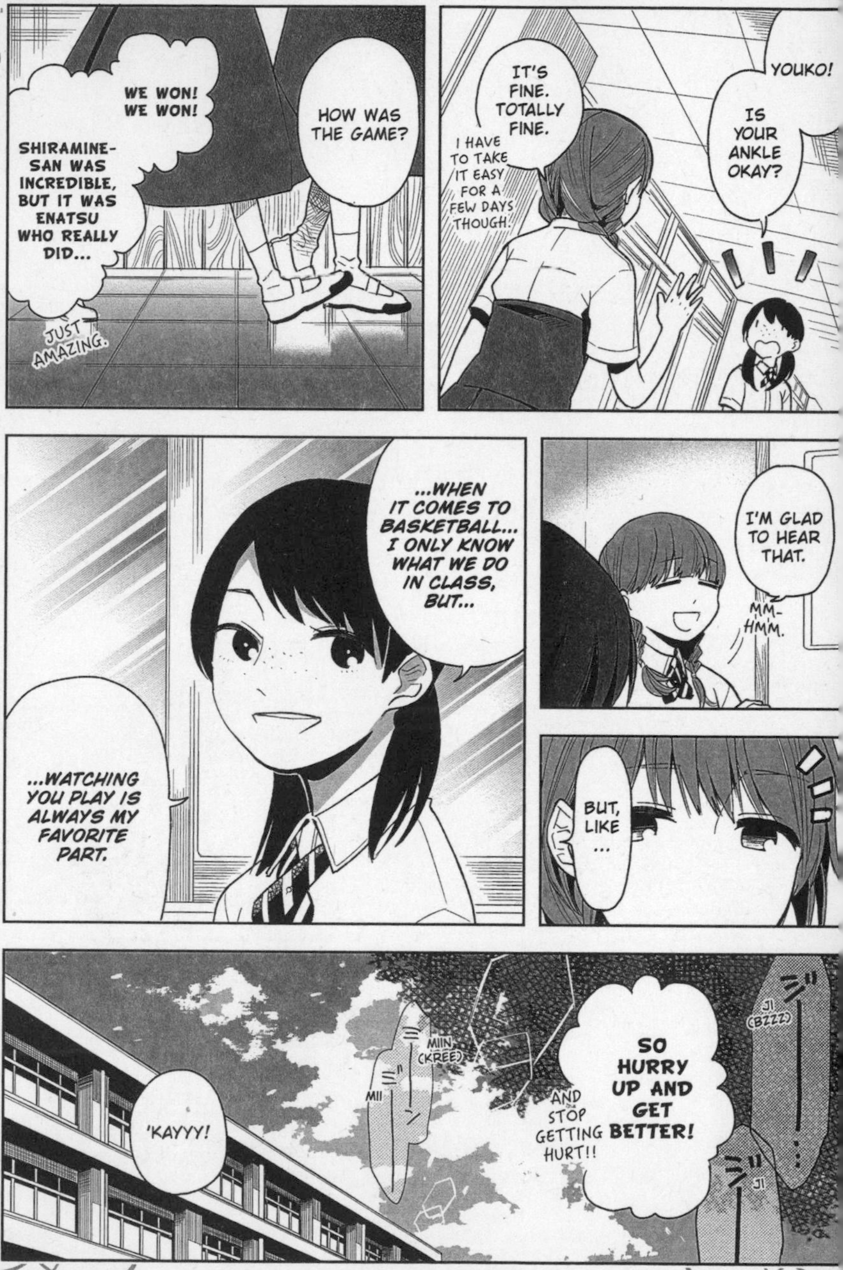
YOUKO!
IS YOUR ANKLE OKAY?
IT'S FINE. TOTALLY FINE.
I HAVE TO TAKE IT EASY FOR A FEW DAYS THOUGH.
HOW WAS THE GAME?
WE WON! WE WON!
SHIRAMINE-SAN WAS INCREDIBLE, BUT IT WAS ENATSU WHO REALLY DID...
JUST AMAZING.
I'M GLAD TO HEAR THAT.
MM-HMM.
BUT, LIKE...
...WHEN IT COMES TO BASKETBALL... I ONLY KNOW WHAT WE DO IN CLASS, BUT...
...WATCHING YOU PLAY IS ALWAYS MY FAVORITE PART.
JI (BZZZ)
JI
SO HURRY UP AND GET BETTER!
AND STOP GETTING HURT!!
MIIN (KREE)
MII
'KAYYY!

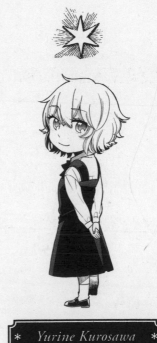

＊ *Yurine Kurosawa* ＊

Y u r i n e   K u r o s a w a

First-year student in the Seiran Academy High School. A so-called genius, she gets top grades with shockingly little effort compared to others. People have a tendency to keep their distance, and Kurosawa herself tends to reject people. She feigns sleep, but she actually does sleep a lot. The reason she chose Seiran for high school is because it's close to her house. She has a little sister, Sumire.

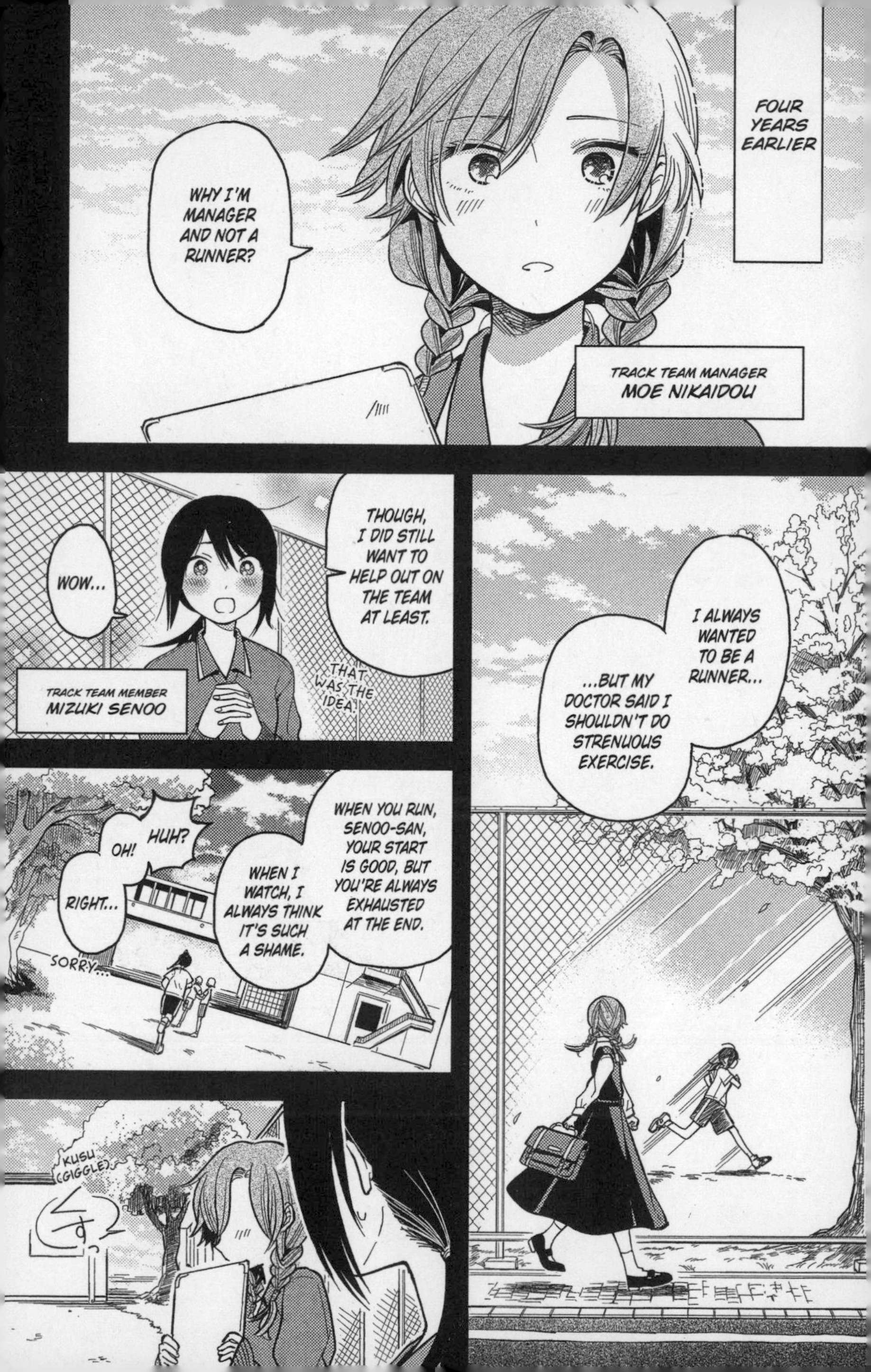
FOUR YEARS EARLIER
WHY I'M MANAGER AND NOT A RUNNER?
TRACK TEAM MANAGER
MOE NIKAIDOU
I ALWAYS WANTED TO BE A RUNNER...
...BUT MY DOCTOR SAID I SHOULDN'T DO STRENUOUS EXERCISE.
THOUGH, I DID STILL WANT TO HELP OUT ON THE TEAM AT LEAST.
THAT WAS THE IDEA.
WOW...
TRACK TEAM MEMBER
MIZUKI SENOO
WHEN YOU RUN, SENOO-SAN, YOUR START IS GOOD, BUT YOU'RE ALWAYS EXHAUSTED AT THE END.
WHEN I WATCH, I ALWAYS THINK IT'S SUCH A SHAME.
HUH?
OH!
RIGHT...
SORRY...
KUSU (GIGGLE)
くすっ

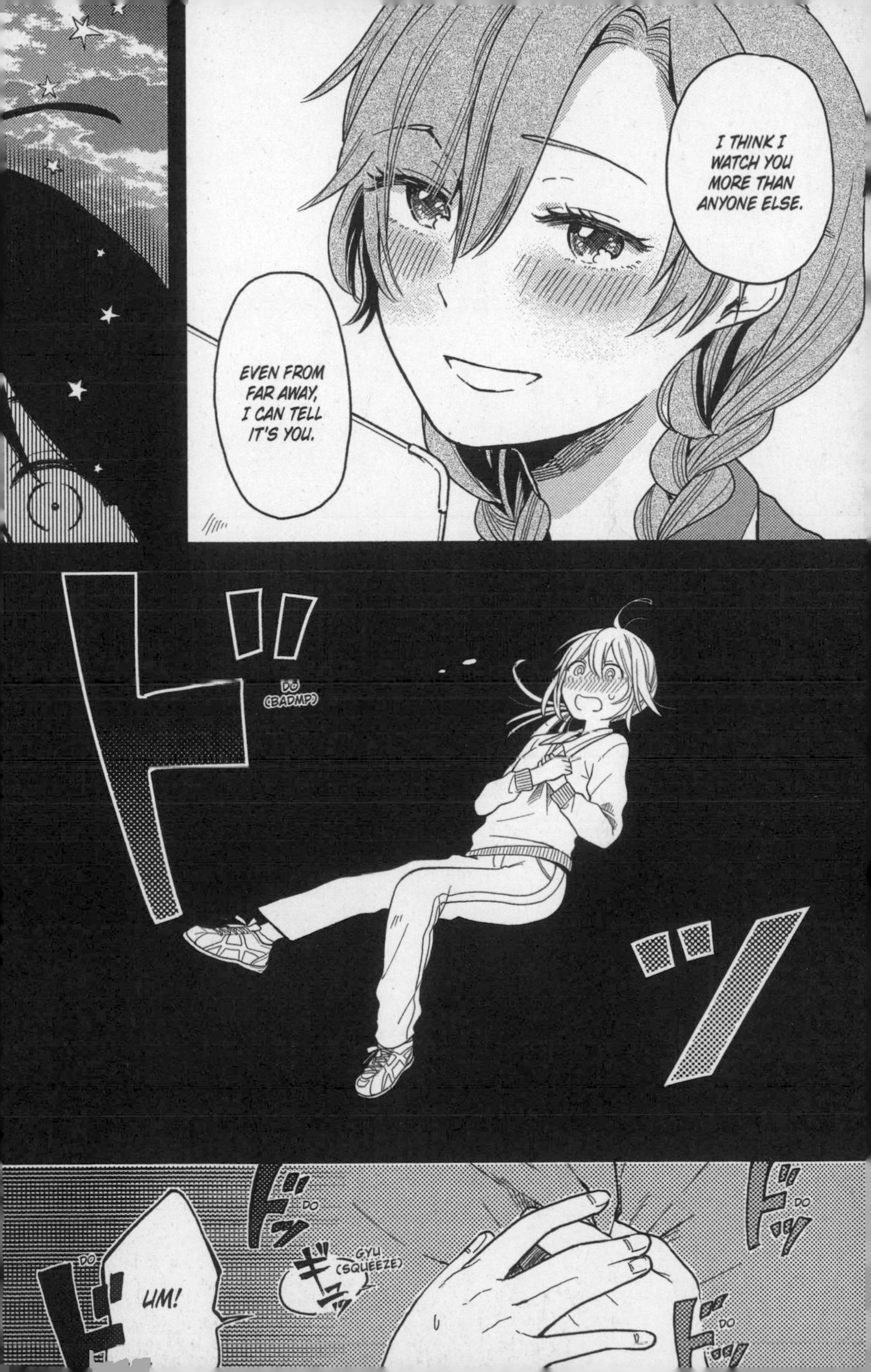
I THINK I WATCH YOU MORE THAN ANYONE ELSE.
EVEN FROM FAR AWAY, I CAN TELL IT'S YOU.
DO (BADMP)
DO
DO
DO
GYU (SQUEEZE)
DO
UM!

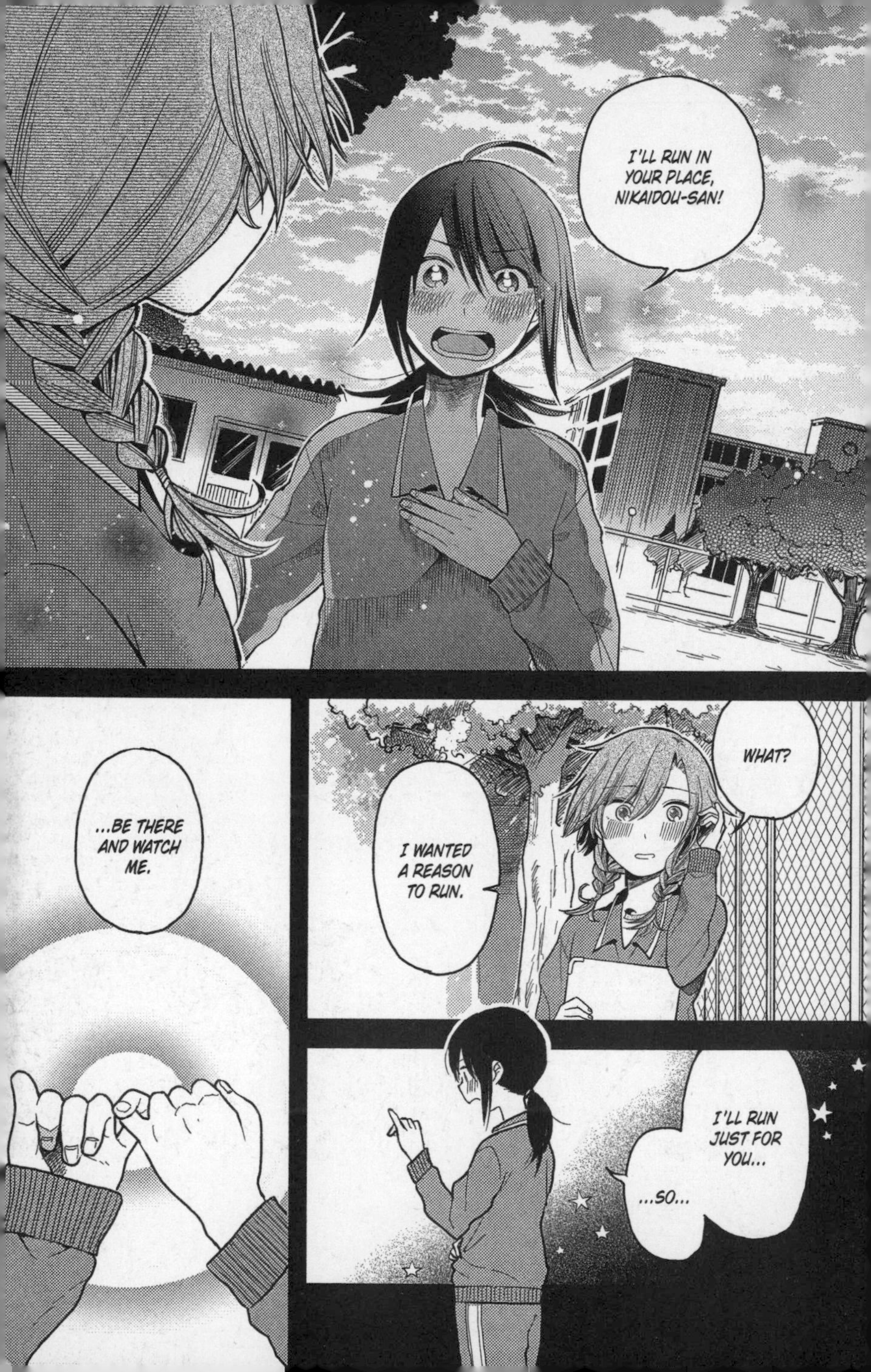
I'LL RUN IN YOUR PLACE, NIKAIDOU-SAN!
WHAT?
I WANTED A REASON TO RUN.
I'LL RUN JUST FOR YOU...
...SO...
...BE THERE AND WATCH ME.

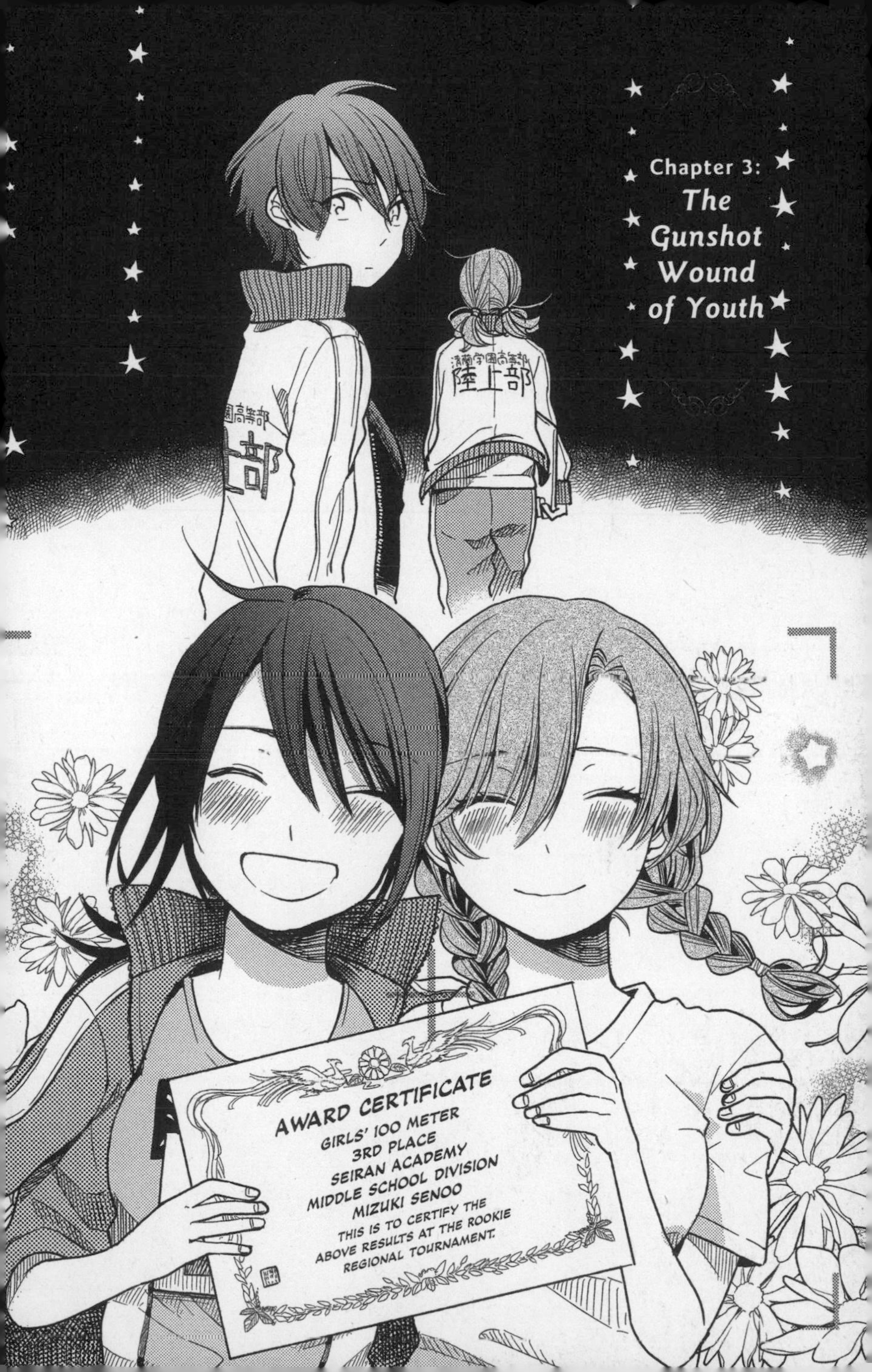
Chapter 3:
The Gunshot Wound of Youth
清蘭学園高等部
陸上部
AWARD CERTIFICATE
GIRLS' 100 METER
3RD PLACE
SEIRAN ACADEMY
MIDDLE SCHOOL DIVISION
MIZUKI SENOO
THIS IS TO CERTIFY THE ABOVE RESULTS AT THE ROOKIE REGIONAL TOURNAMENT.

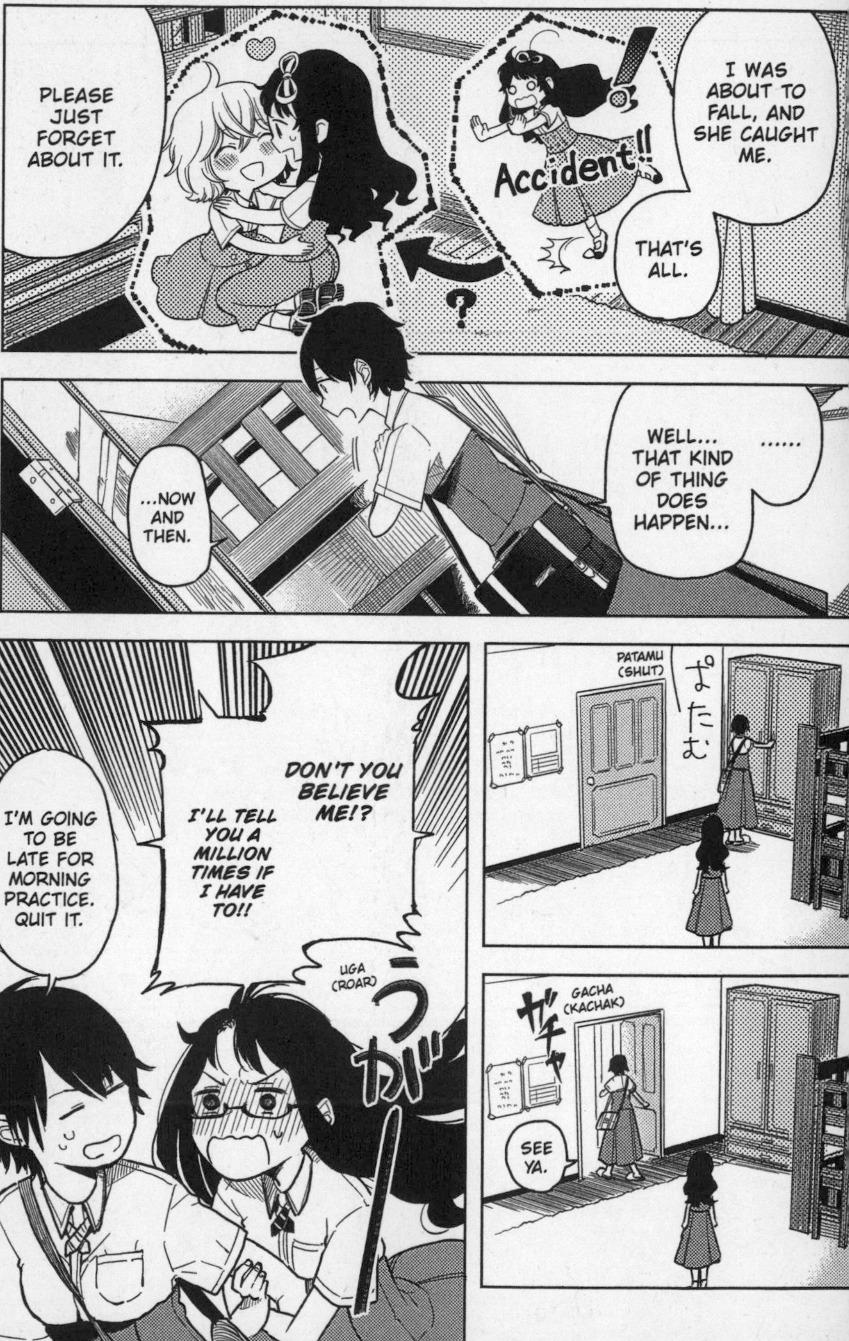
I WAS ABOUT TO FALL, AND SHE CAUGHT ME.
THAT'S ALL.
Accident!!
PLEASE JUST FORGET ABOUT IT.
......
WELL... THAT KIND OF THING DOES HAPPEN...
...NOW AND THEN.
ぱたむ
PATAMU (SHUT)
ガチャ
GACHA (KACHAK)
SEE YA.
DON'T YOU BELIEVE ME!?
I'LL TELL YOU A MILLION TIMES IF I HAVE TO!!
I'M GOING TO BE LATE FOR MORNING PRACTICE. QUIT IT.
うが
UGA (ROAR)

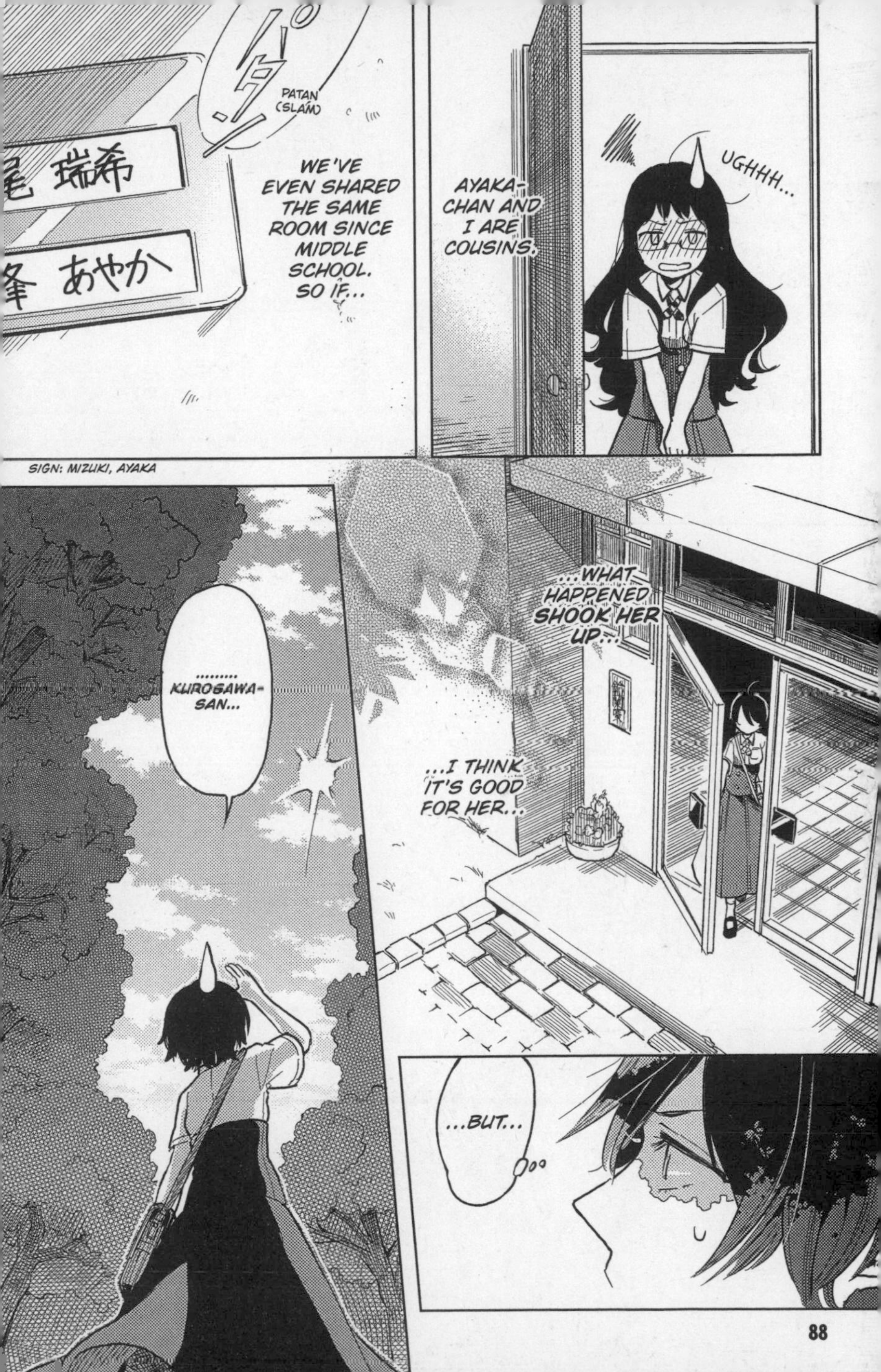
UGHHH...
AYAKA-CHAN AND I ARE COUSINS.
PATAN (SLAM)
WE'VE EVEN SHARED THE SAME ROOM SINCE MIDDLE SCHOOL. SO IF...
尾 瑞希
峰 あやか
SIGN: MIZUKI, AYAKA
...WHAT HAPPENED SHOOK HER UP...
...I THINK IT'S GOOD FOR HER...
...BUT...
.... KUROGAWA-SAN...

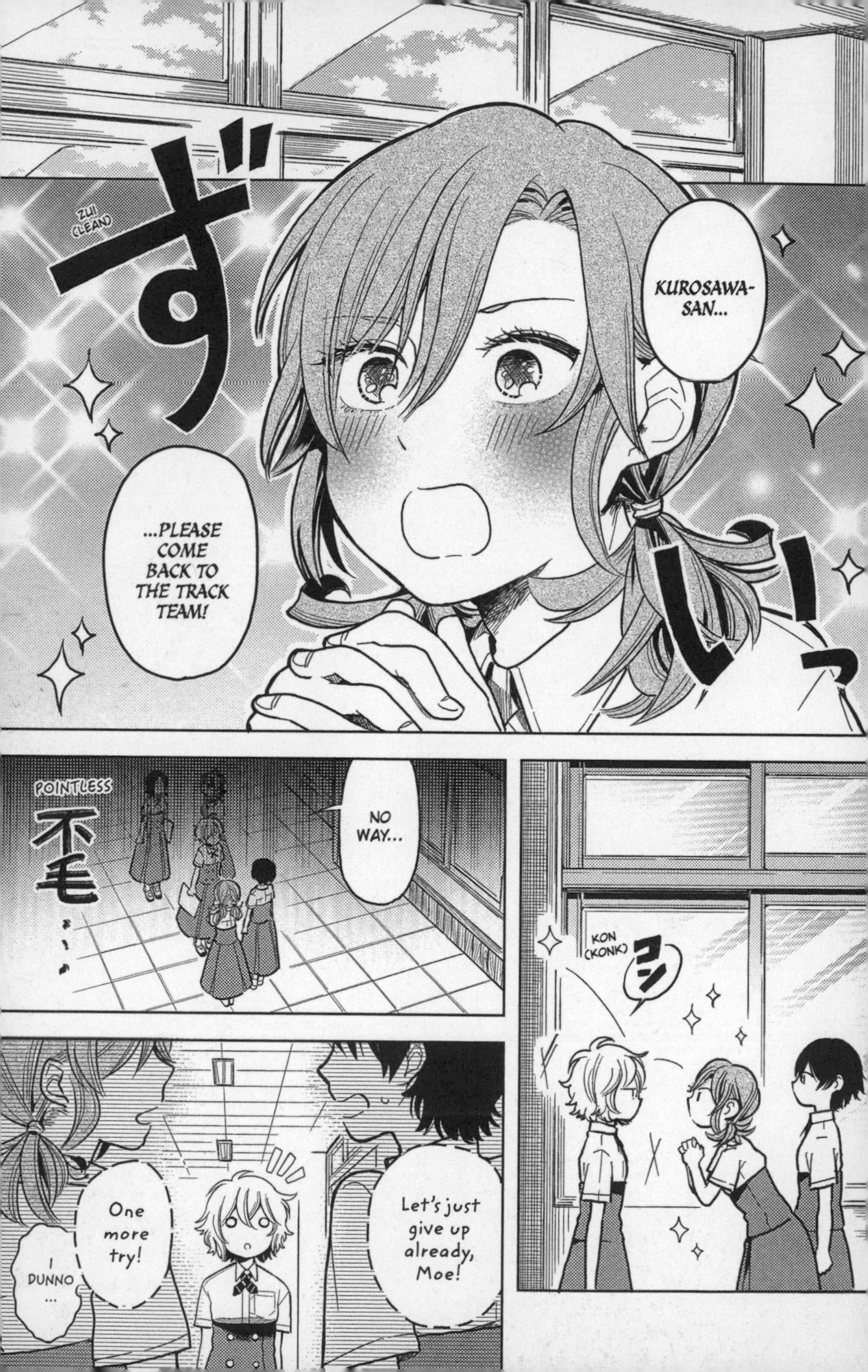
KUROSAWA-SAN...
ZUI (LEAN)
...PLEASE COME BACK TO THE TRACK TEAM!
KON (KONK)
コン
NO WAY...
POINTLESS
不毛
Let's just give up already, Moe!
One more try!
I DUNNO ...

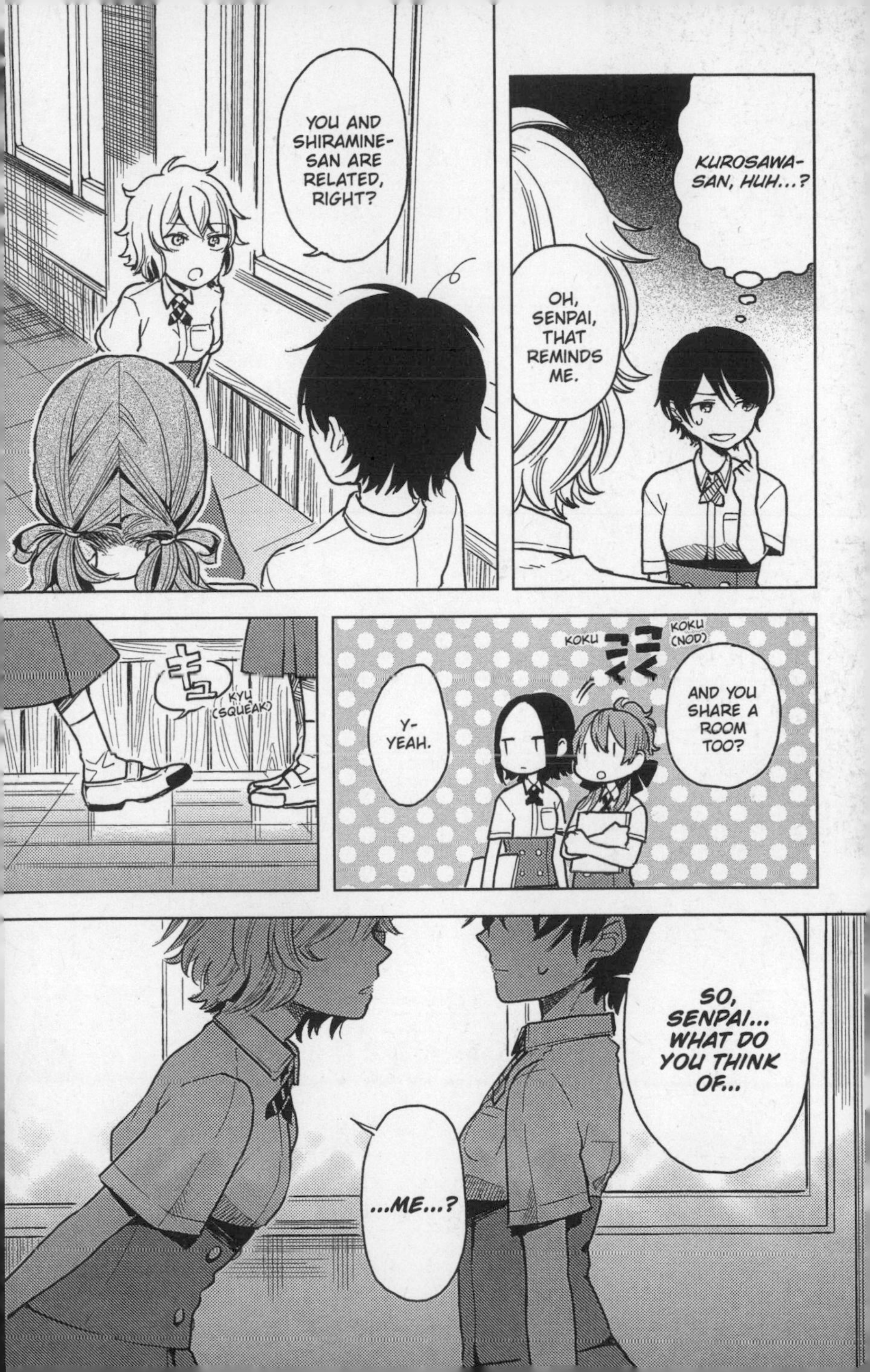
KUROSAWA-SAN, HUH...?
OH, SENPAI, THAT REMINDS ME.
YOU AND SHIRAMINE-SAN ARE RELATED, RIGHT?
こくこく
KOKU (NOD)
KOKU
AND YOU SHARE A ROOM TOO?
Y-YEAH.
キュ
KYU (SQUEAK)
SO, SENPAI... WHAT DO YOU THINK OF...
...ME...?

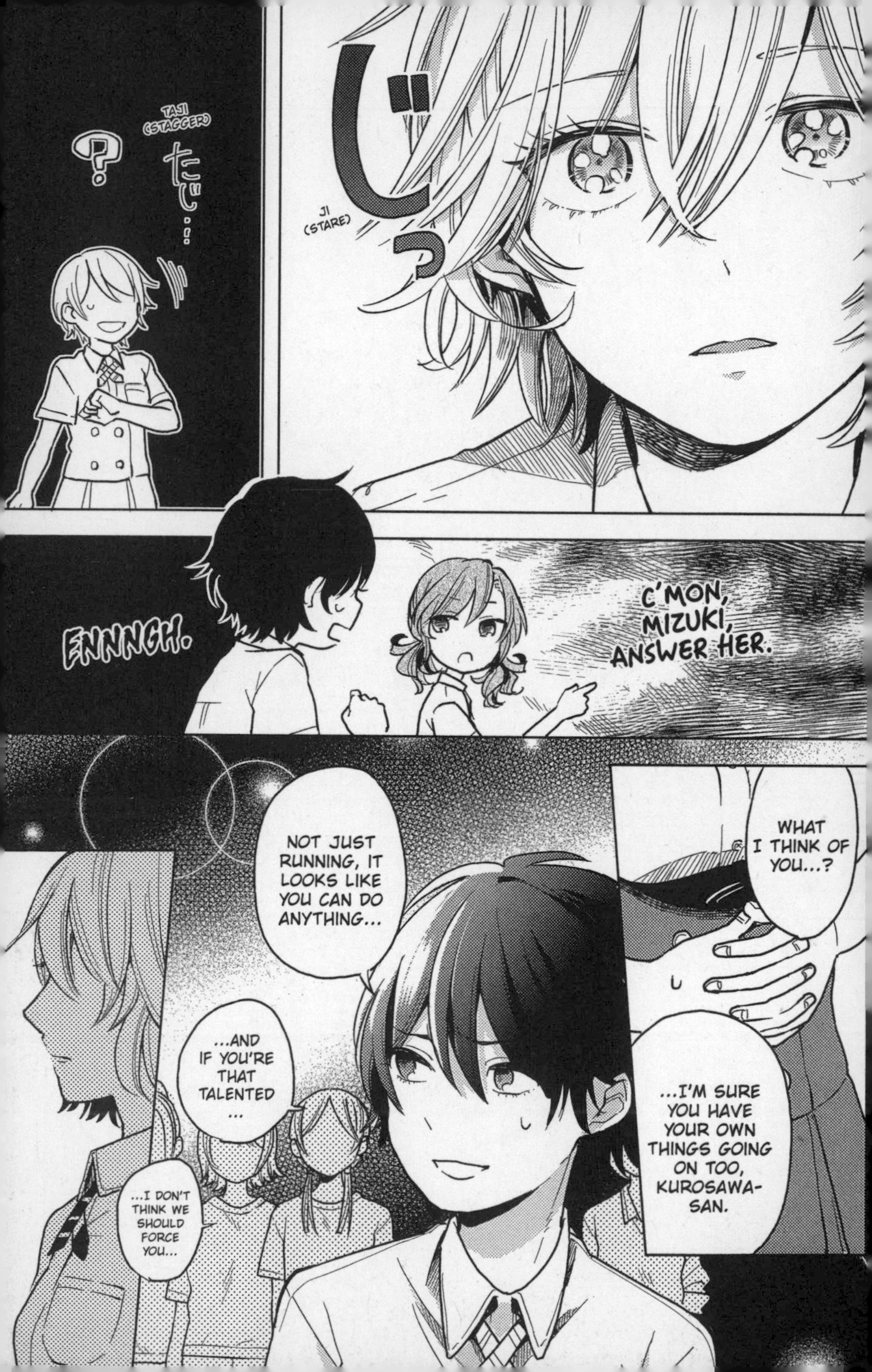
じっ
JI (STARE)
TAJI (STAGGER)
たじ…!!
?
C'MON, MIZUKI, ANSWER HER.
ENNNGH.
WHAT I THINK OF YOU...?
...I'M SURE YOU HAVE YOUR OWN THINGS GOING ON TOO, KUROSAWA-SAN.
NOT JUST RUNNING, IT LOOKS LIKE YOU CAN DO ANYTHING...
...AND IF YOU'RE THAT TALENTED...
...I DON'T THINK WE SHOULD FORCE YOU...

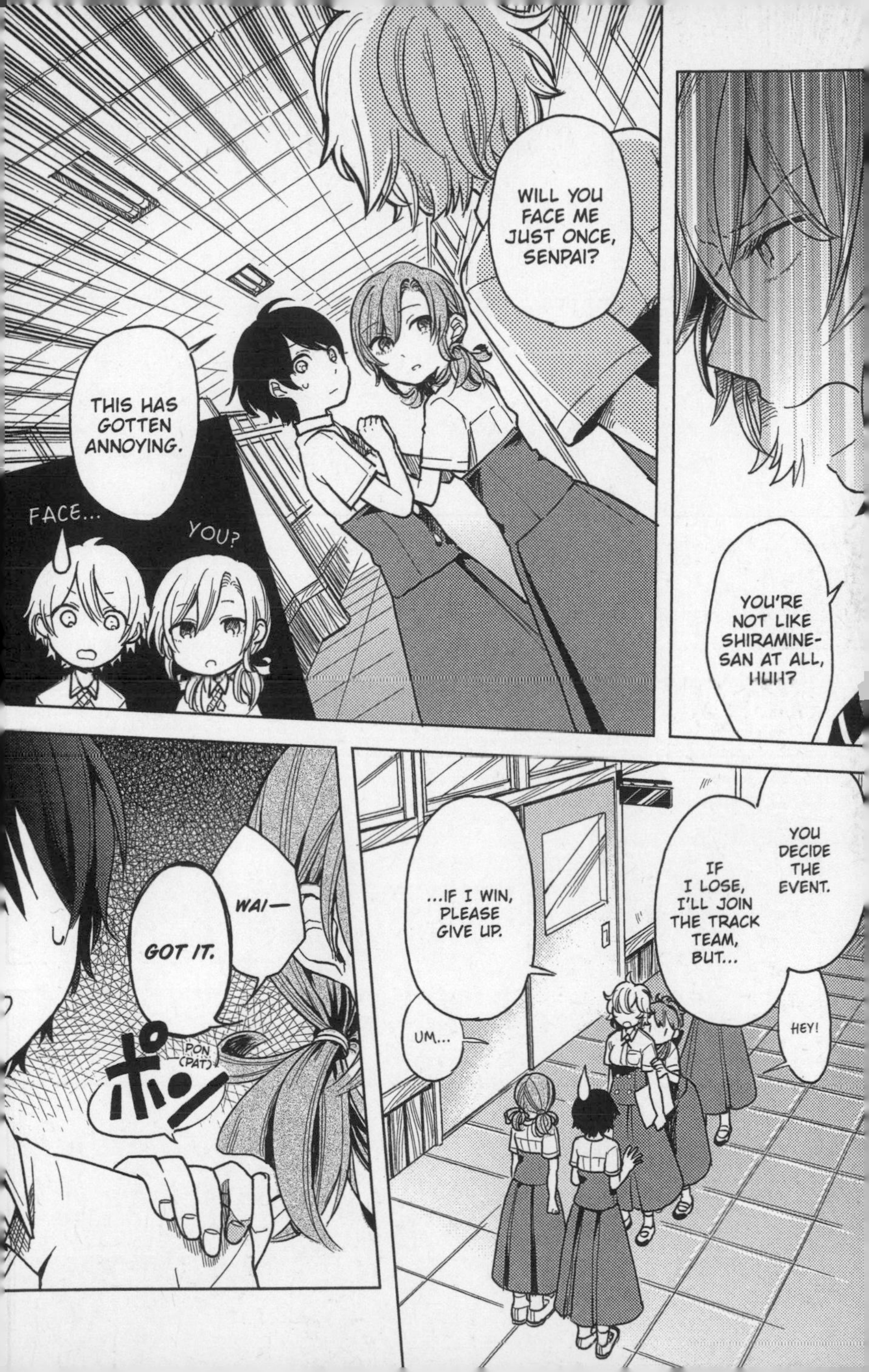
YOU'RE NOT LIKE SHIRAMINE-SAN AT ALL, HUH?
WILL YOU FACE ME JUST ONCE, SENPAI?
THIS HAS GOTTEN ANNOYING.
FACE...
YOU?
YOU DECIDE THE EVENT.
IF I LOSE, I'LL JOIN THE TRACK TEAM, BUT...
HEY!
...IF I WIN, PLEASE GIVE UP.
UM...
WAI—
GOT IT.
ポン
PON (PAT)

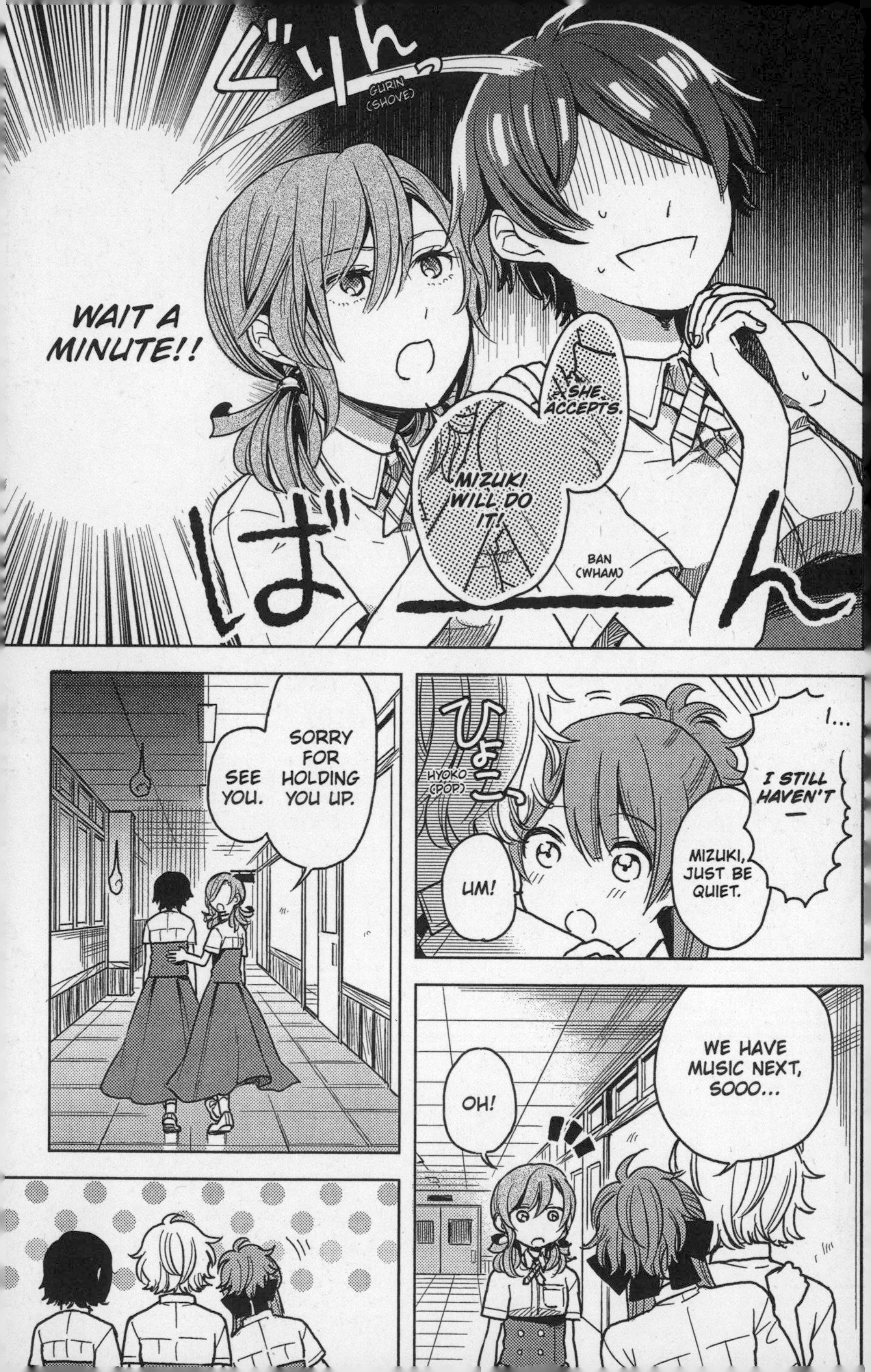
ぐりんっ
GURIN (SHOVE)
SHE ACCEPTS.
MIZUKI WILL DO IT!
WAIT A MINUTE!!
ばーーん
BAN (WHAM)
I...
I STILL HAVEN'T—
MIZUKI, JUST BE QUIET.
ひょこっ
HYOKO (POP)
UM!
WE HAVE MUSIC NEXT, SOOO...
OH!
SORRY FOR HOLDING YOU UP.
SEE YOU.

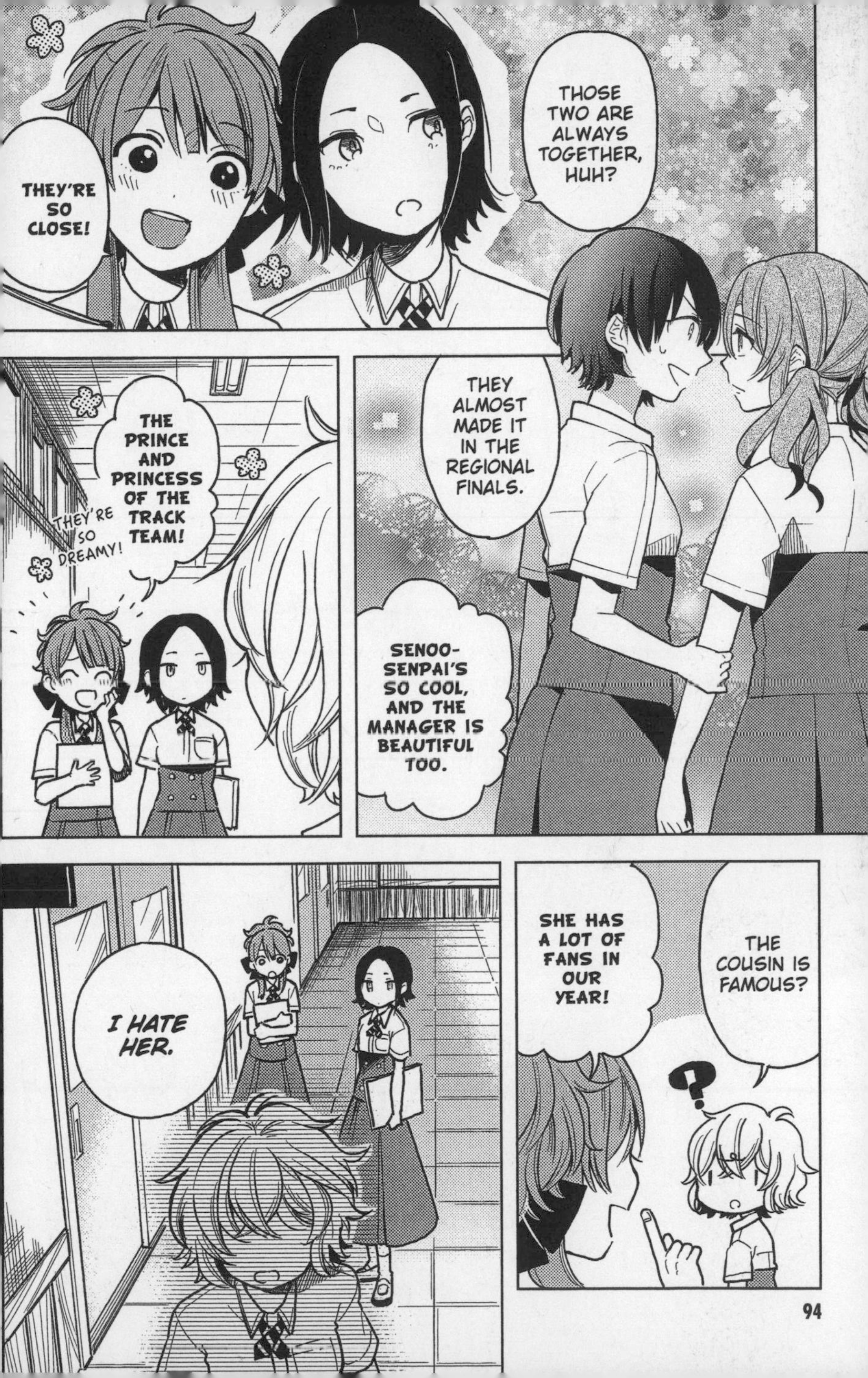
THOSE TWO ARE ALWAYS TOGETHER, HUH?
THEY'RE SO CLOSE!
THEY ALMOST MADE IT IN THE REGIONAL FINALS.
SENOO-SENPAI'S SO COOL, AND THE MANAGER IS BEAUTIFUL TOO.
THE PRINCE AND PRINCESS OF THE TRACK TEAM!
THEY'RE SO DREAMY!
THE COUSIN IS FAMOUS?
SHE HAS A LOT OF FANS IN OUR YEAR!
?
I HATE HER.

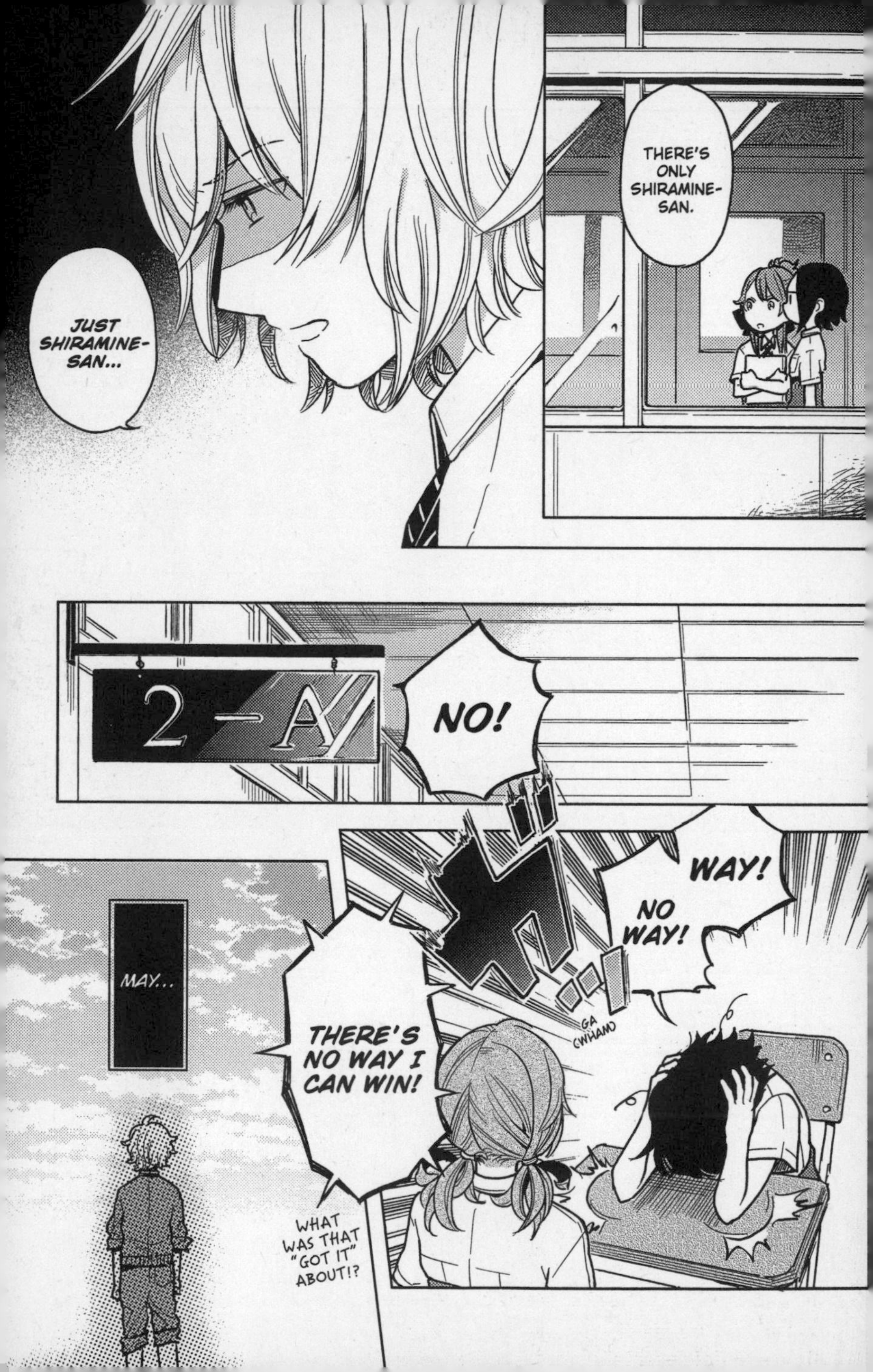
THERE'S ONLY SHIRAMINE-SAN.
JUST SHIRAMINE-SAN...
2-A
NO!
WAY!
NO WAY!
GA (WHAM)
THERE'S NO WAY I CAN WIN!
WHAT WAS THAT "GOT IT" ABOUT!?
MAY...

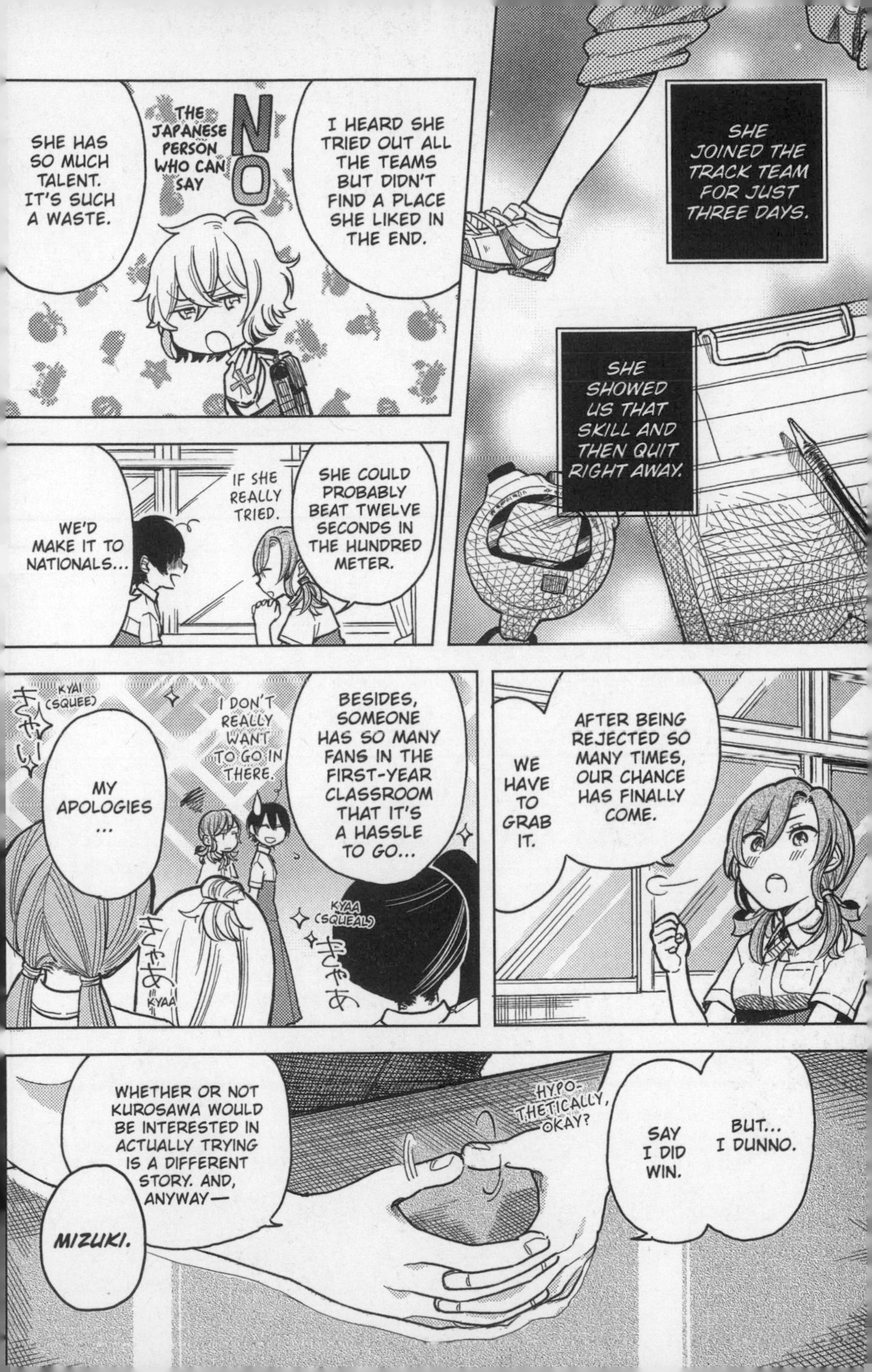
SHE JOINED THE TRACK TEAM FOR JUST THREE DAYS.
SHE SHOWED US THAT SKILL AND THEN QUIT RIGHT AWAY.
I HEARD SHE TRIED OUT ALL THE TEAMS BUT DIDN'T FIND A PLACE SHE LIKED IN THE END.
THE JAPANESE PERSON WHO CAN SAY NO
SHE HAS SO MUCH TALENT. IT'S SUCH A WASTE.
SHE COULD PROBABLY BEAT TWELVE SECONDS IN THE HUNDRED METER.
IF SHE REALLY TRIED.
WE'D MAKE IT TO NATIONALS...
AFTER BEING REJECTED SO MANY TIMES, OUR CHANCE HAS FINALLY COME.
WE HAVE TO GRAB IT.
BESIDES, SOMEONE HAS SO MANY FANS IN THE FIRST-YEAR CLASSROOM THAT IT'S A HASSLE TO GO...
I DON'T REALLY WANT TO GO IN THERE.
KYAI (SQUEE)
MY APOLOGIES ...
KYAA (SQUEAL)
KYAA
BUT... I DUNNO.
SAY I DID WIN.
HYPO-THETICALLY, OKAY?
WHETHER OR NOT KUROSAWA WOULD BE INTERESTED IN ACTUALLY TRYING IS A DIFFERENT STORY. AND, ANYWAY—
MIZUKI.

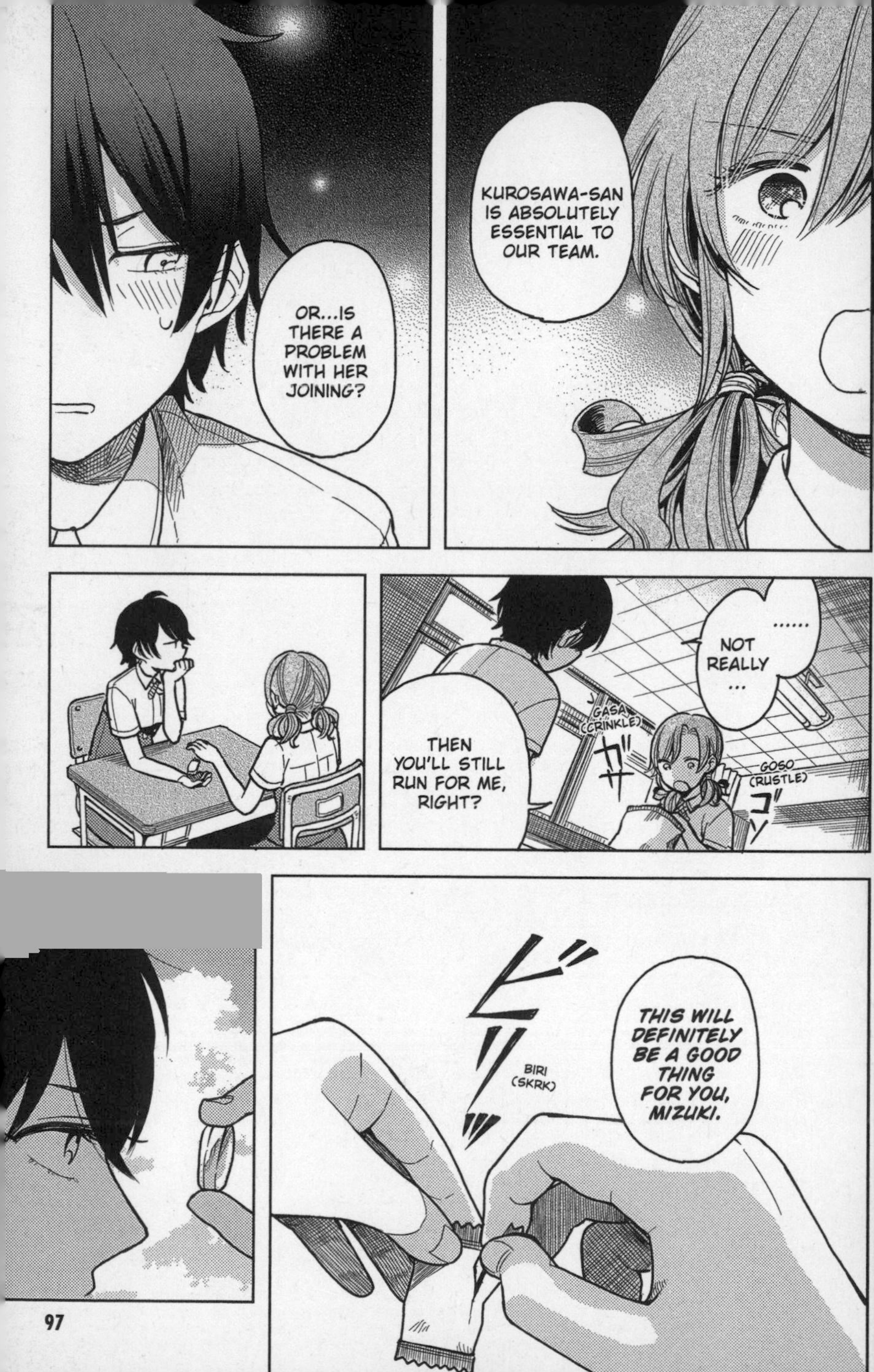
KUROSAWA-SAN IS ABSOLUTELY ESSENTIAL TO OUR TEAM.
OR...IS THERE A PROBLEM WITH HER JOINING?
......
NOT REALLY ...
GASA (CRINKLE)
GOSO (RUSTLE)
THEN YOU'LL STILL RUN FOR ME, RIGHT?
BIRI (SKRK)
THIS WILL DEFINITELY BE A GOOD THING FOR YOU, MIZUKI.

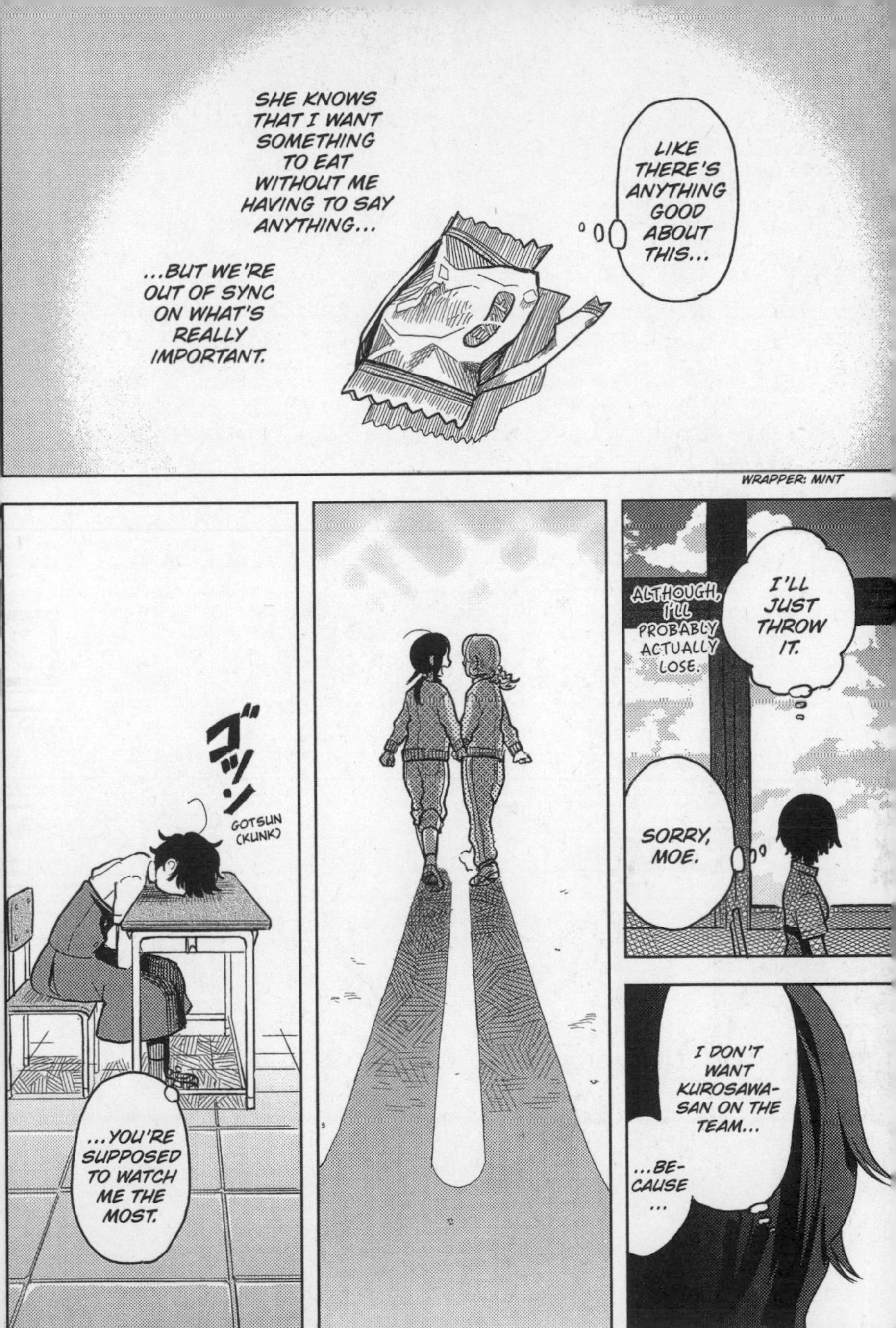
LIKE THERE'S ANYTHING GOOD ABOUT THIS...
SHE KNOWS THAT I WANT SOMETHING TO EAT WITHOUT ME HAVING TO SAY ANYTHING...
...BUT WE'RE OUT OF SYNC ON WHAT'S REALLY IMPORTANT.
WRAPPER: MINT
I'LL JUST THROW IT.
ALTHOUGH, I'LL PROBABLY ACTUALLY LOSE.
SORRY, MOE.
I DON'T WANT KUROSAWA-SAN ON THE TEAM...
...BE-CAUSE ...
ゴツン
GOTSUN (KUNK)
...YOU'RE SUPPOSED TO WATCH ME THE MOST.

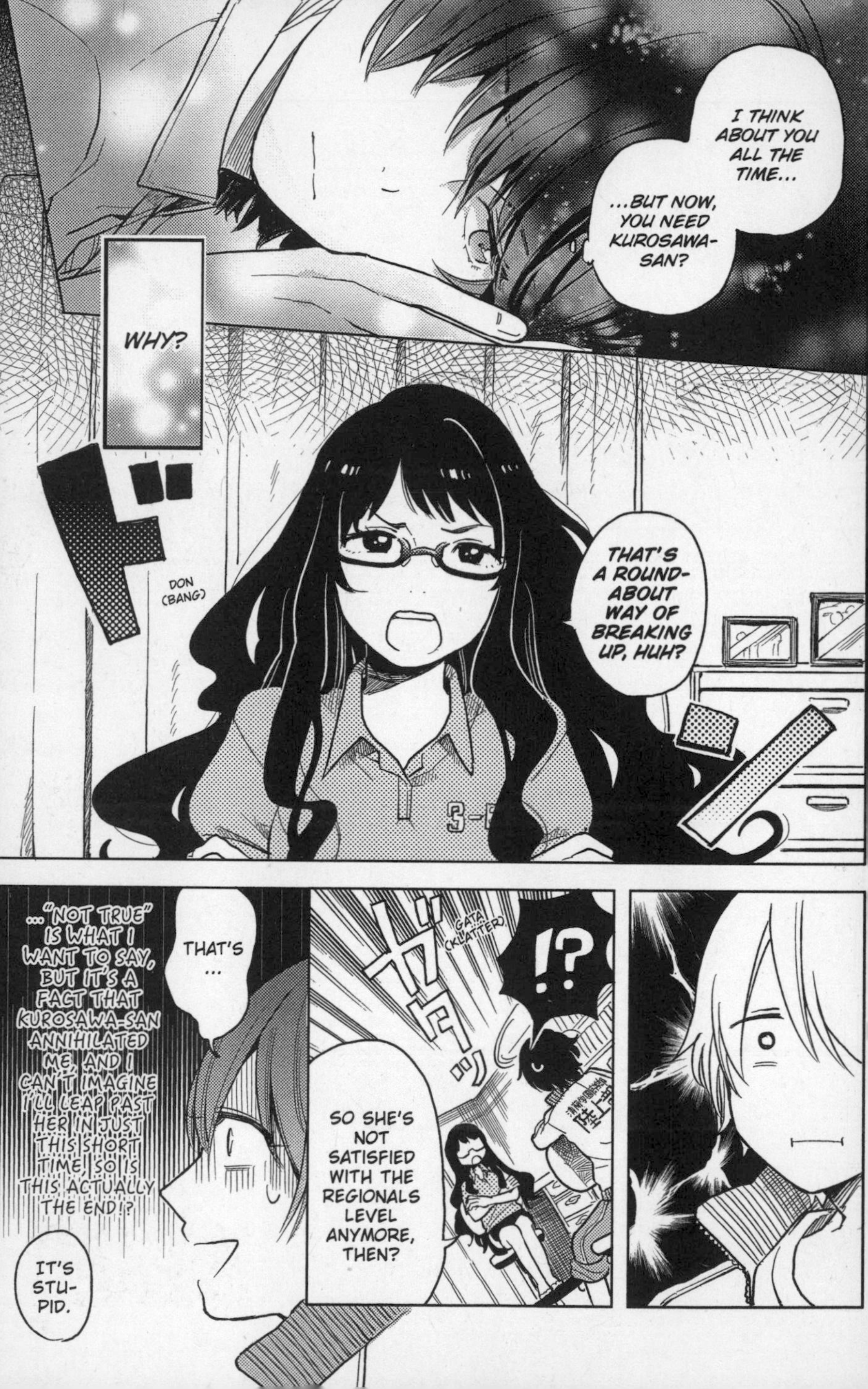
I THINK ABOUT YOU ALL THE TIME...
...BUT NOW, YOU NEED KUROSAWA-SAN?
WHY?
THAT'S A ROUND-ABOUT WAY OF BREAKING UP, HUH?
DON (BANG)
!?
GATA (KLATTER)
SO SHE'S NOT SATISFIED WITH THE REGIONALS LEVEL ANYMORE, THEN?
THAT'S ...
..."NOT TRUE" IS WHAT I WANT TO SAY, BUT IT'S A FACT THAT KUROSAWA-SAN ANNIHILATED ME, AND I CAN'T IMAGINE I'LL LEAP PAST HER IN JUST THIS SHORT TIME, SO IS THIS ACTUALLY THE END!?
IT'S STU-PID.

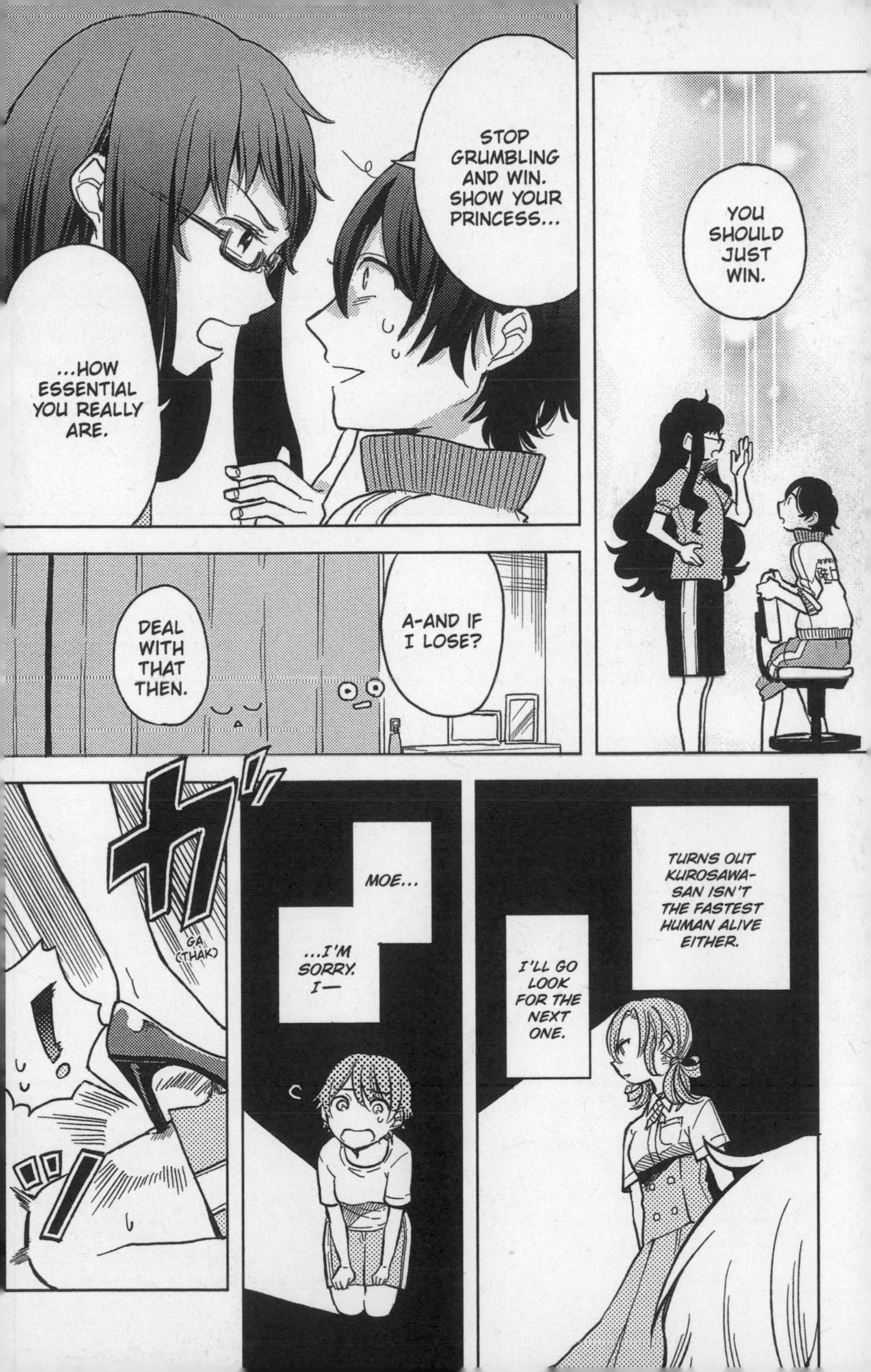
YOU SHOULD JUST WIN.
STOP GRUMBLING AND WIN. SHOW YOUR PRINCESS...
...HOW ESSENTIAL YOU REALLY ARE.
A-AND IF I LOSE?
DEAL WITH THAT THEN.
TURNS OUT KUROSAWA-SAN ISN'T THE FASTEST HUMAN ALIVE EITHER.
I'LL GO LOOK FOR THE NEXT ONE.
MOE...
...I'M SORRY. I—
GA (THAK)

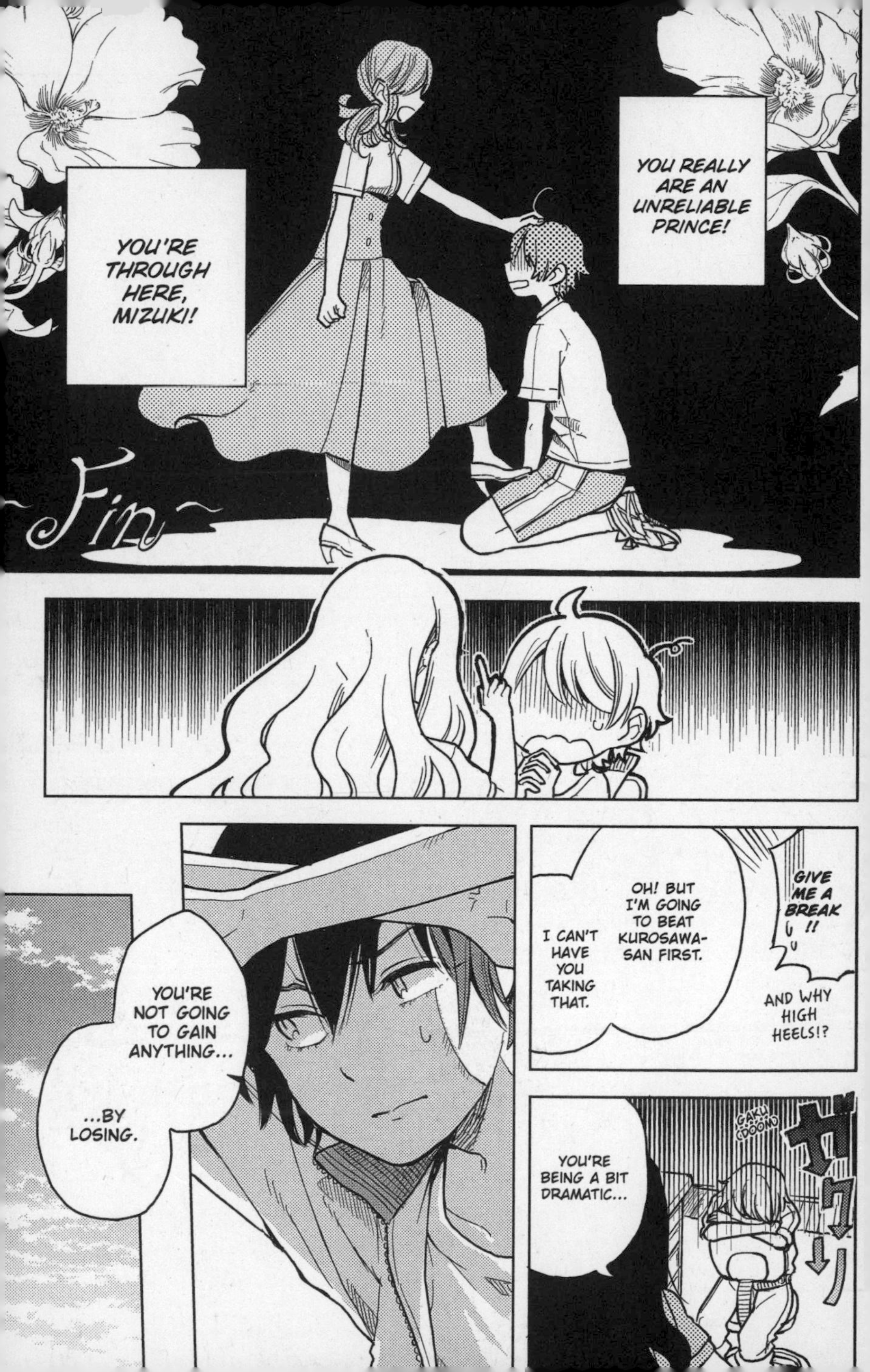
YOU REALLY ARE AN UNRELIABLE PRINCE!
YOU'RE THROUGH HERE, MIZUKI!
~Fin~
GIVE ME A BREAK!!
OH! BUT I'M GOING TO BEAT KUROSAWA-SAN FIRST.
I CAN'T HAVE YOU TAKING THAT.
AND WHY HIGH HEELS!?
GAKU (DOOM)
YOU'RE BEING A BIT DRAMATIC...
YOU'RE NOT GOING TO GAIN ANYTHING...
...BY LOSING.

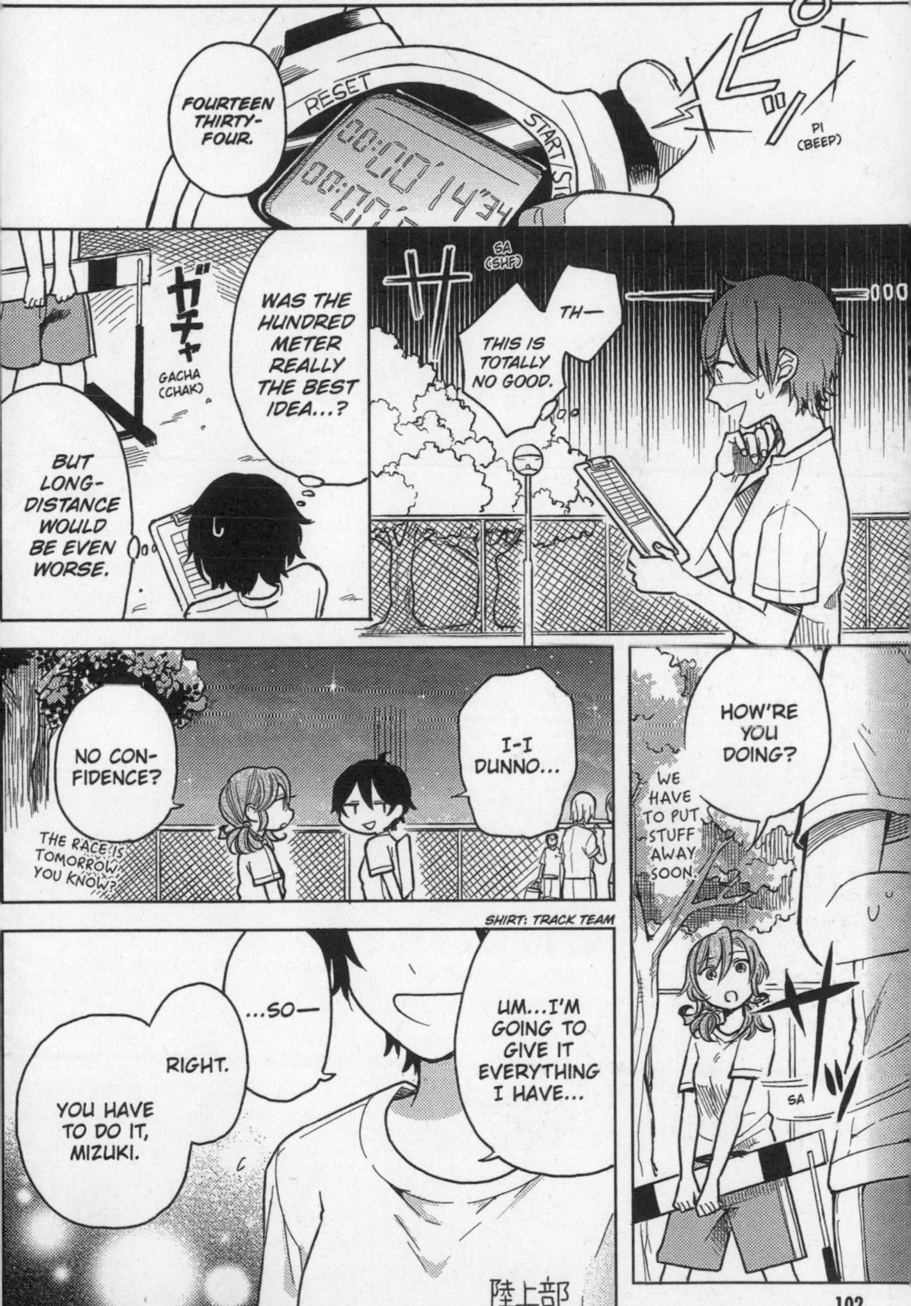
PI (BEEP)
FOURTEEN THIRTY-FOUR.
RESET
START/STOP
SA (SHF)
TH—
THIS IS TOTALLY NO GOOD.
WAS THE HUNDRED METER REALLY THE BEST IDEA...?
GACHA (CHAK)
BUT LONG-DISTANCE WOULD BE EVEN WORSE.
HOW'RE YOU DOING?
WE HAVE TO PUT STUFF AWAY SOON.
SA
I-I DUNNO...
NO CONFIDENCE?
THE RACE IS TOMORROW, YOU KNOW?
SHIRT: TRACK TEAM
UM...I'M GOING TO GIVE IT EVERYTHING I HAVE...
...SO—
RIGHT.
YOU HAVE TO DO IT, MIZUKI.
陸上部

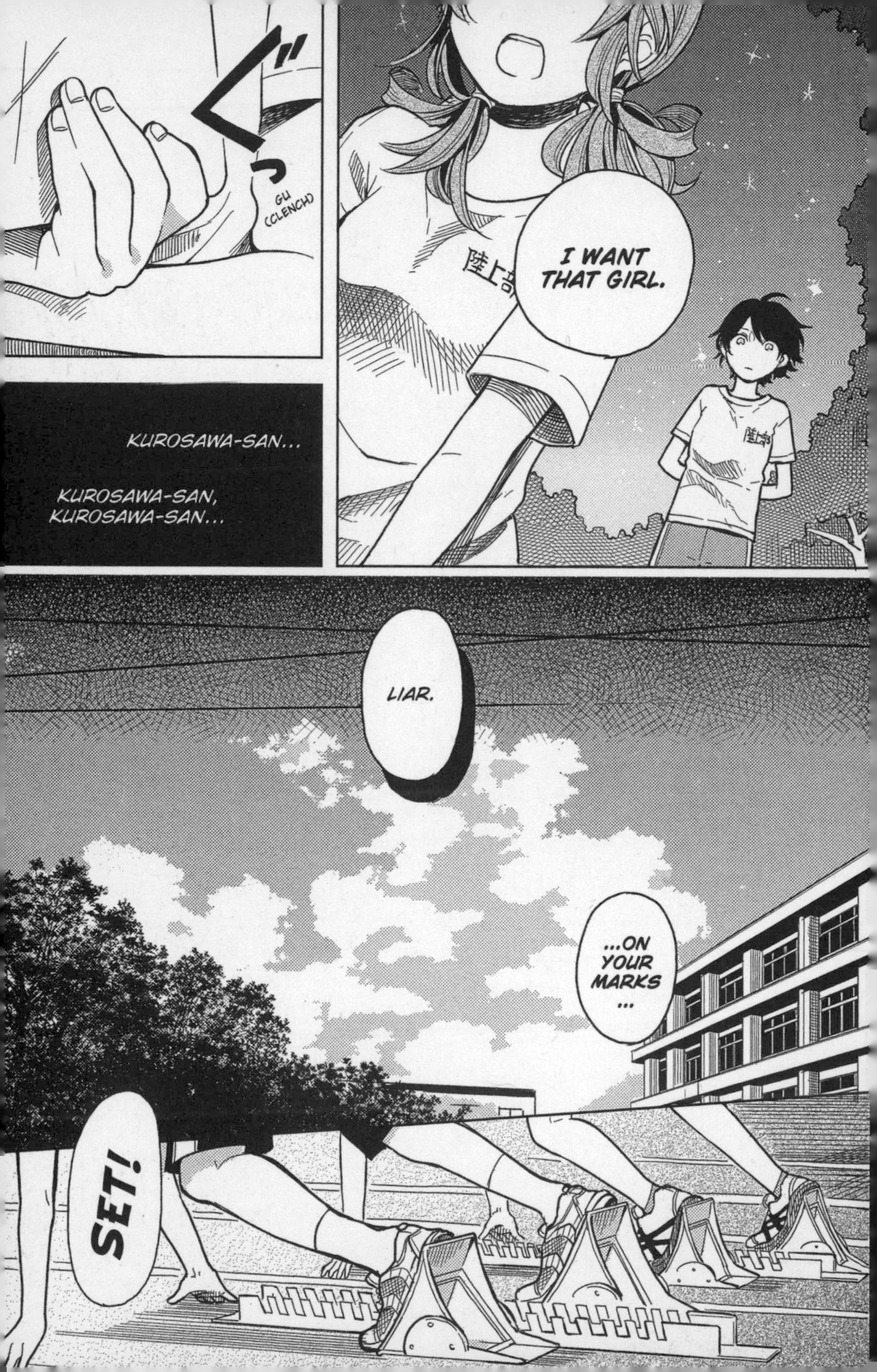
I WANT THAT GIRL.
ぐっ
GU (CLENCH)
KURASAWA-SAN...
KUROSAWA-SAN, KUROSAWA-SAN...
LIAR.
...ON YOUR MARKS...
SET!

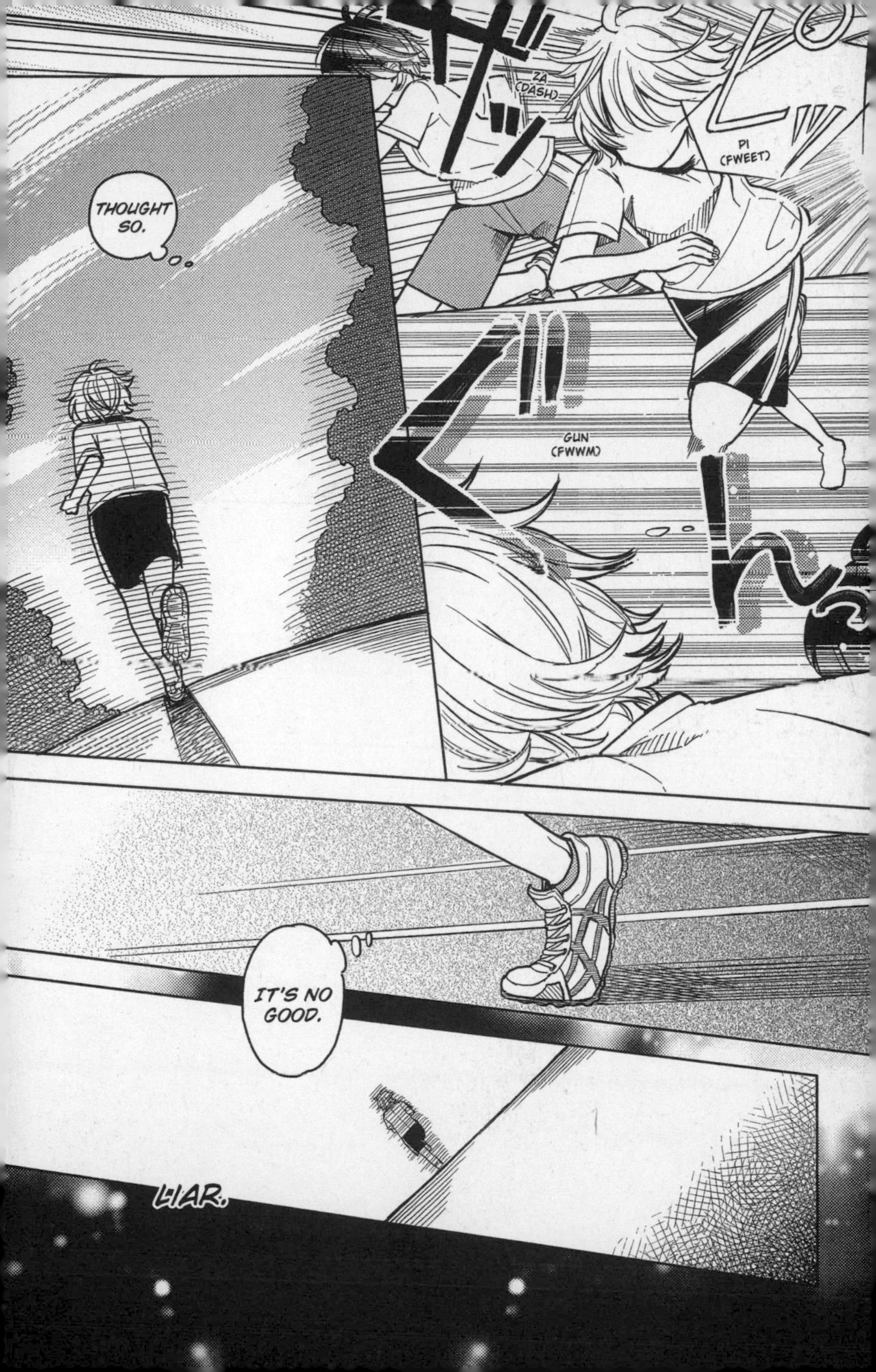
PI (FWEET)
ZA (DASH)
GUN (FWWM)
THOUGHT SO.
IT'S NO GOOD.
LIAR.

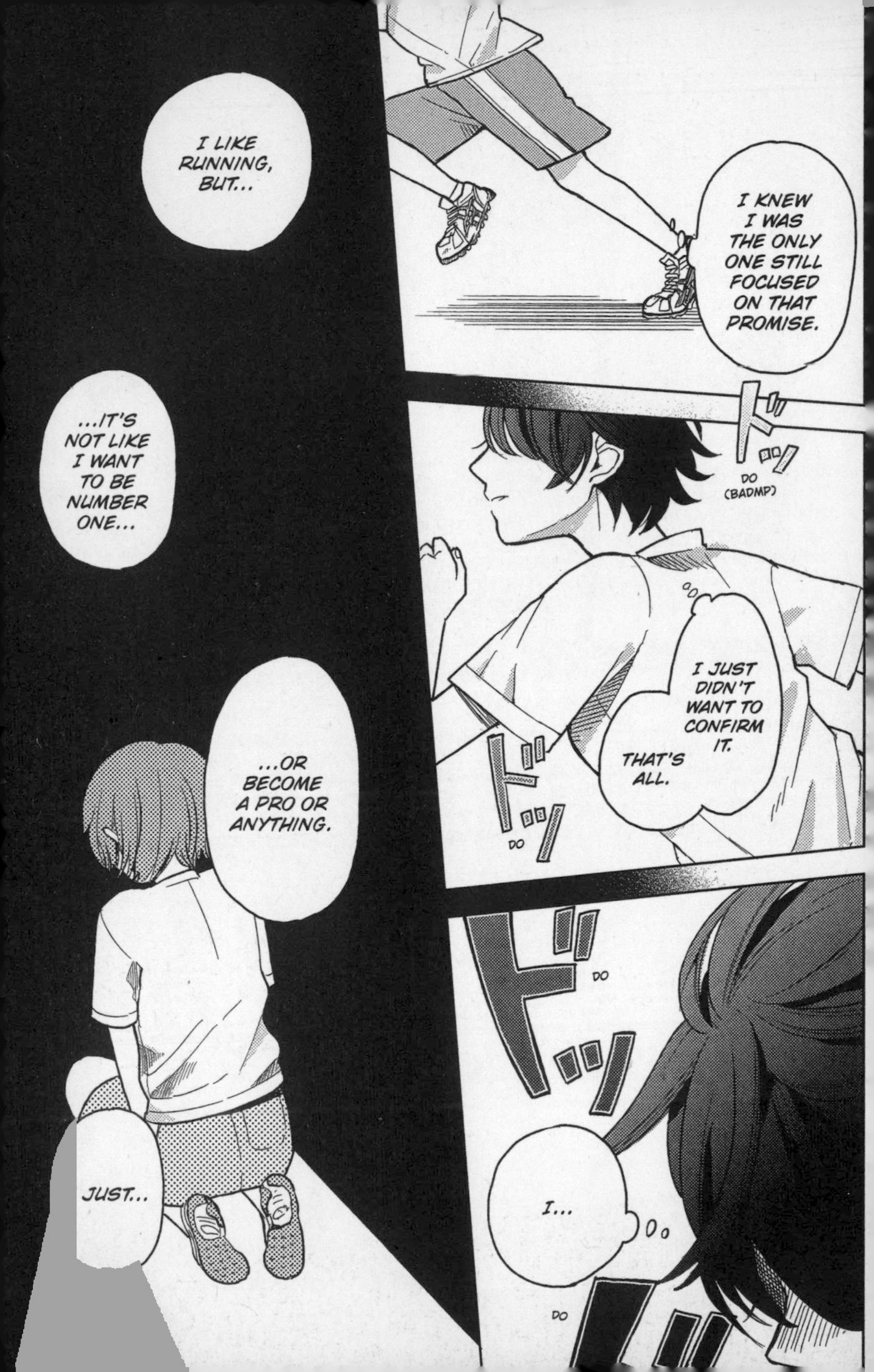
I KNEW I WAS THE ONLY ONE STILL FOCUSED ON THAT PROMISE.
ドッ
DO (BADMP)
I JUST DIDN'T WANT TO CONFIRM IT.
THAT'S ALL.
ドッ
DO
ドッ
DO
I...
DO
I LIKE RUNNING, BUT...
...IT'S NOT LIKE I WANT TO BE NUMBER ONE...
...OR BECOME A PRO OR ANYTHING.
JUST...

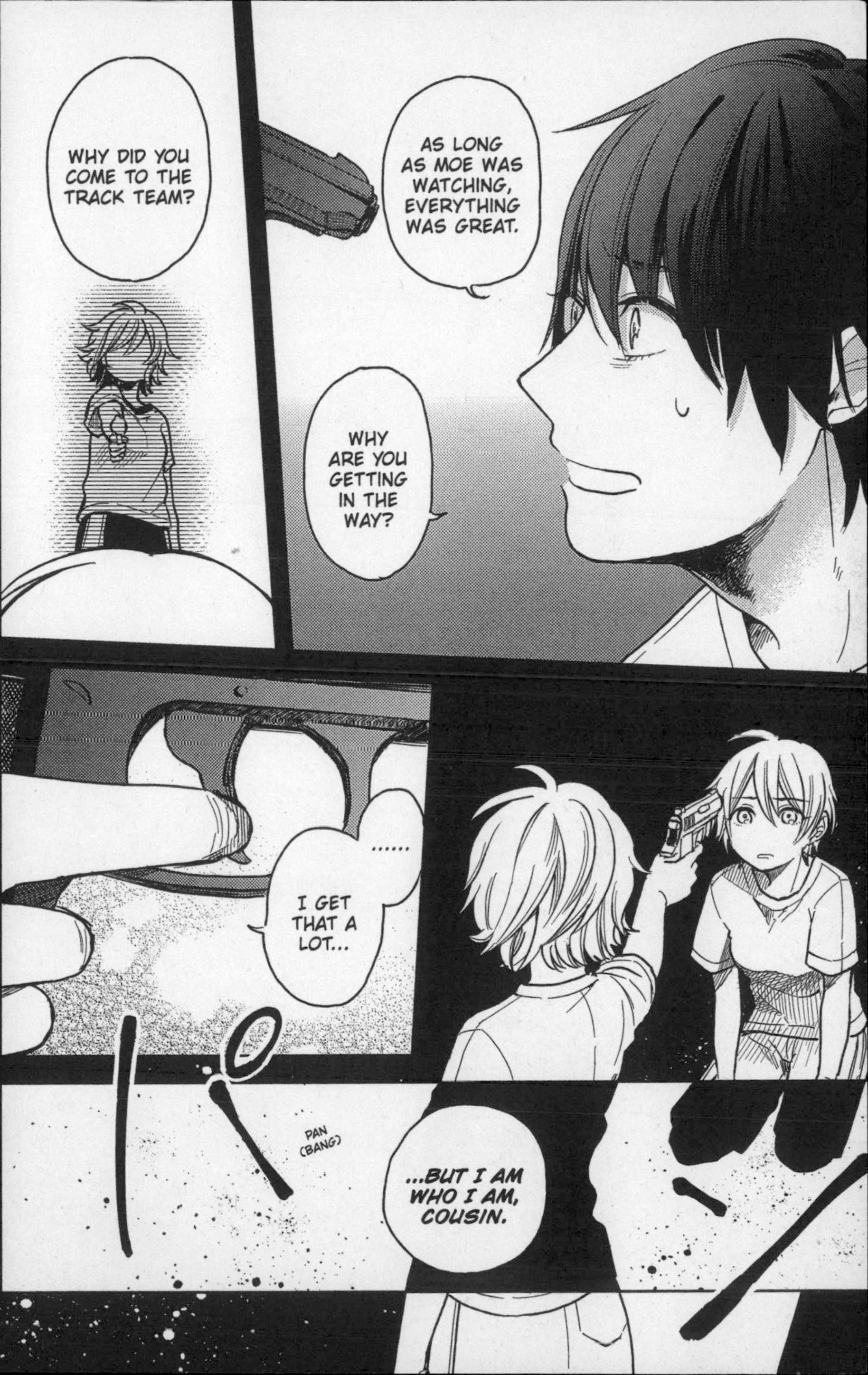
AS LONG AS MOE WAS WATCHING, EVERYTHING WAS GREAT.
WHY ARE YOU GETTING IN THE WAY?
WHY DID YOU COME TO THE TRACK TEAM?
......
I GET THAT A LOT...
PAN (BANG)
...BUT I AM WHO I AM, COUSIN.

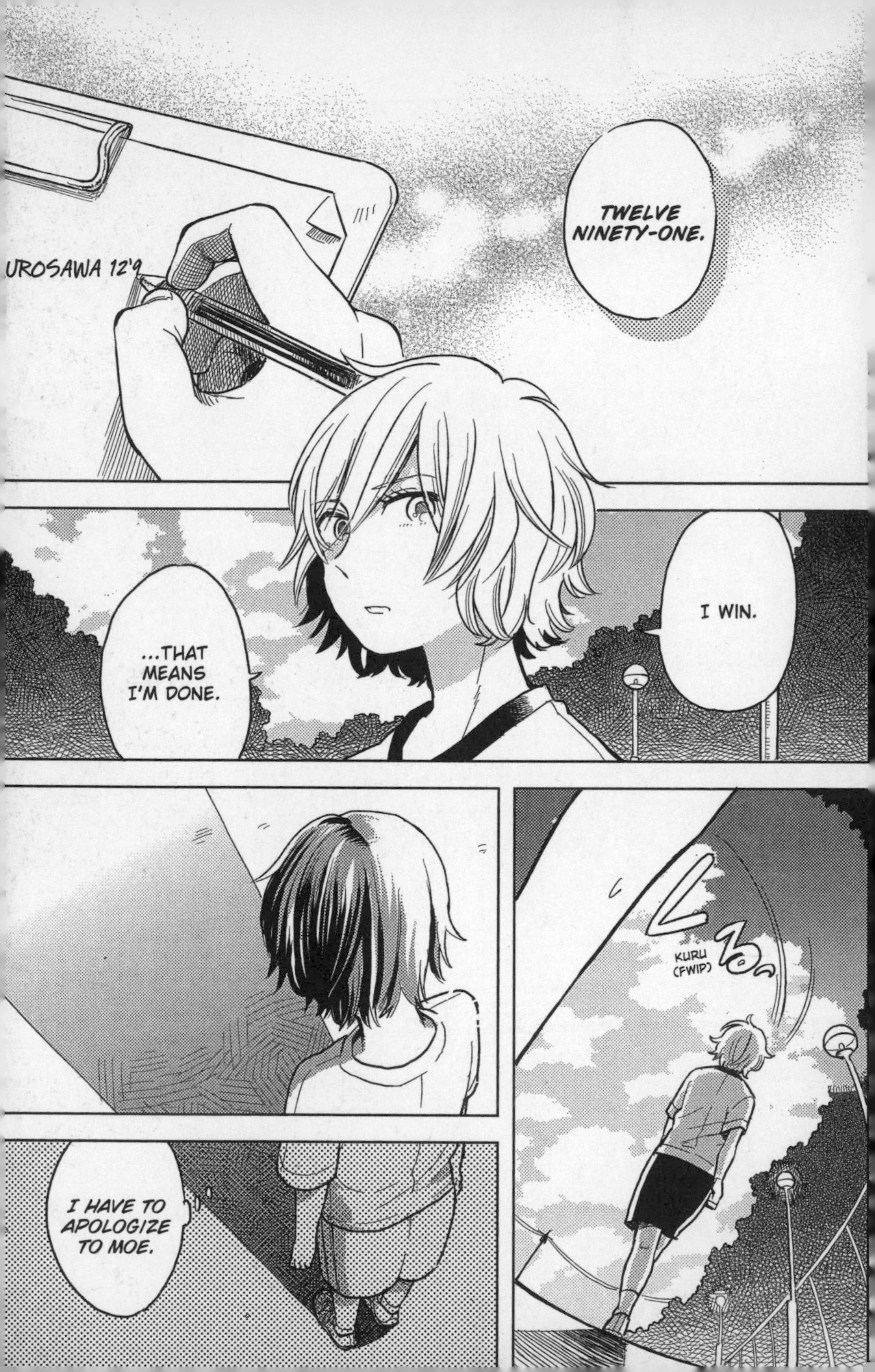
TWELVE NINETY-ONE.
UROSAWA 12'9
I WIN.
...THAT MEANS I'M DONE.
KURU (FWIP)
I HAVE TO APOLOGIZE TO MOE.

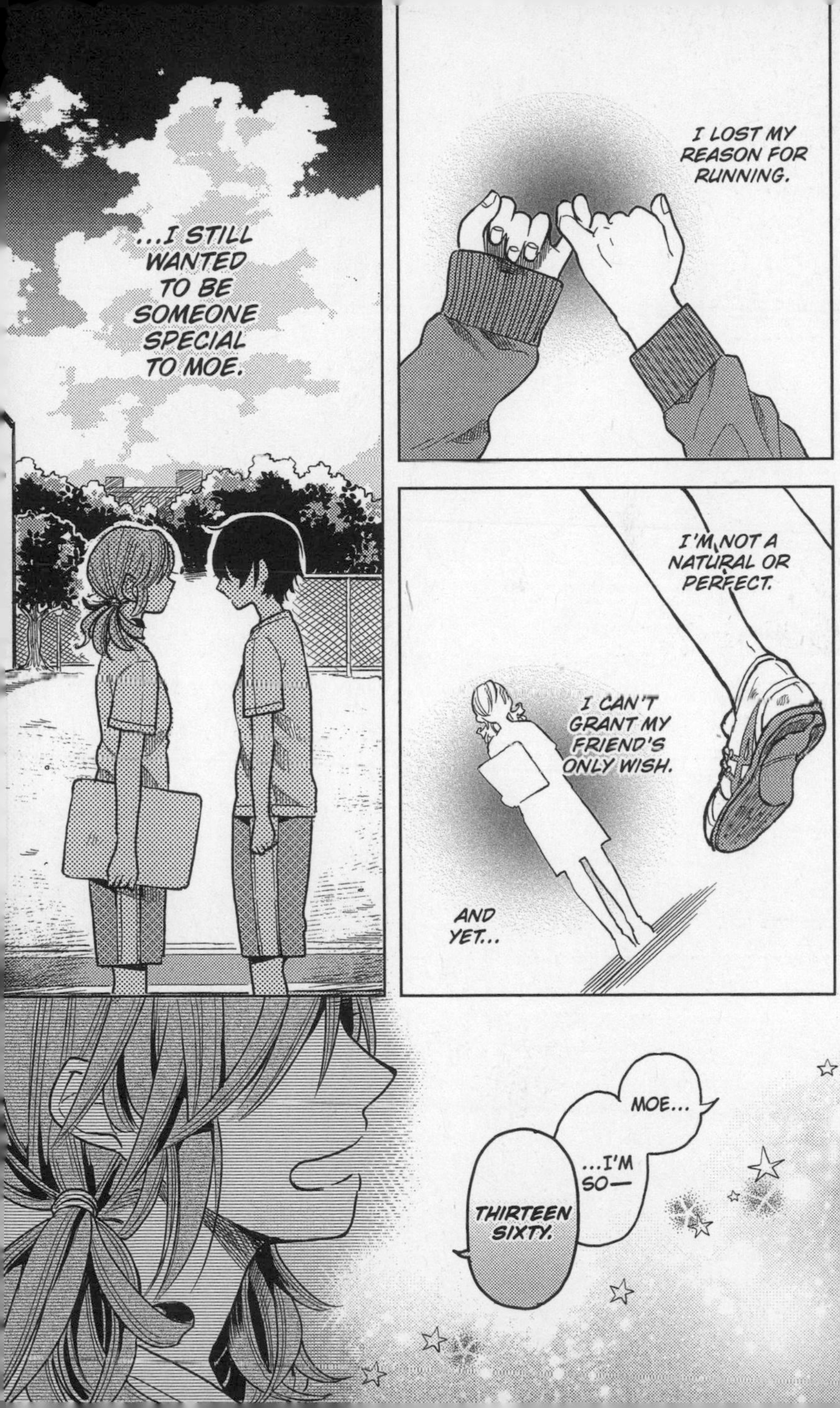
I LOST MY REASON FOR RUNNING.
I'M NOT A NATURAL OR PERFECT.
I CAN'T GRANT MY FRIEND'S ONLY WISH.
AND YET...
...I STILL WANTED TO BE SOMEONE SPECIAL TO MOE.
MOE...
...I'M SO—
THIRTEEN SIXTY.

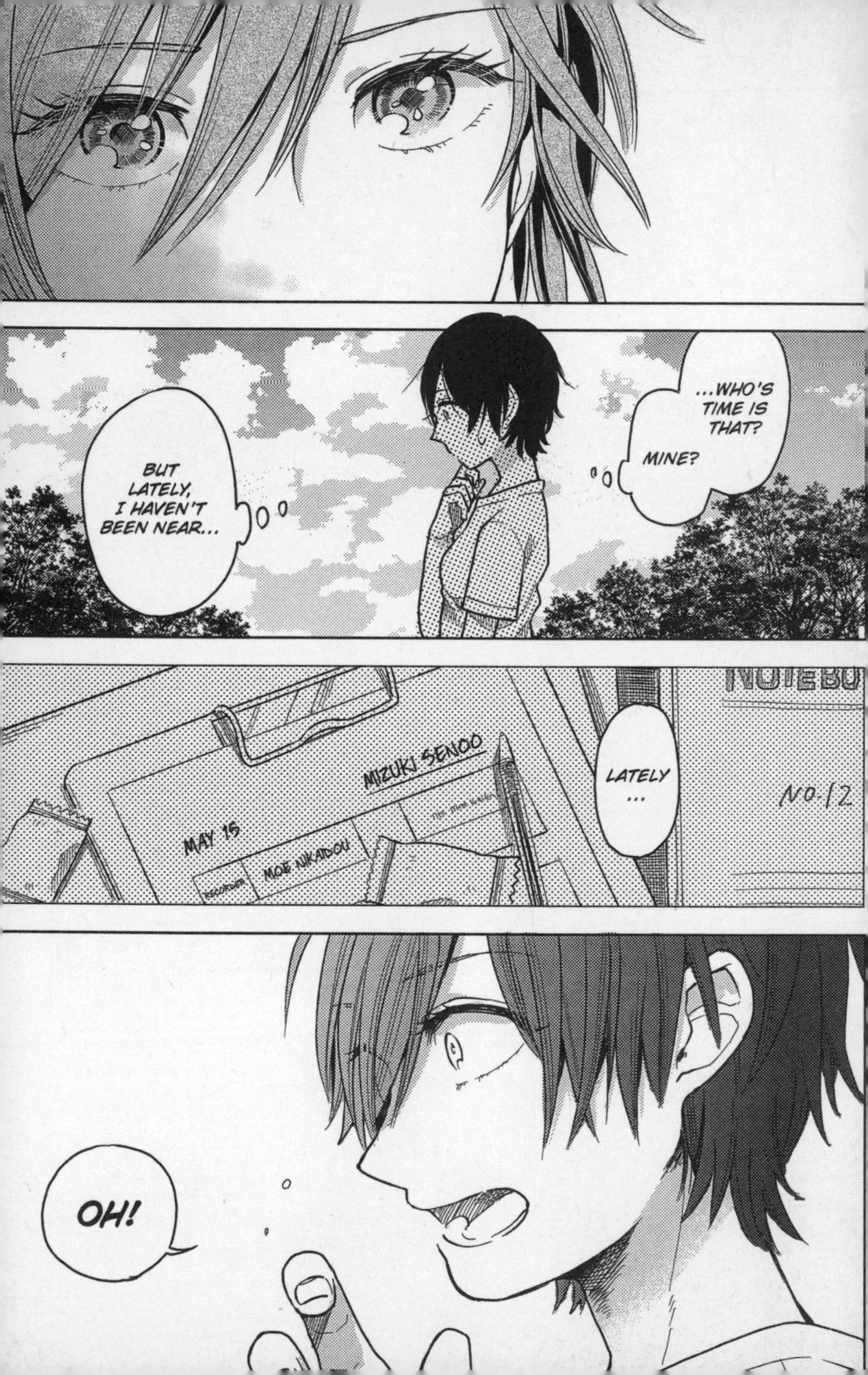

...WHO'S TIME IS THAT?
MINE?
BUT LATELY, I HAVEN'T BEEN NEAR...
NO.12
LATELY ...
MIZUKI SENOO
MAY 15
MOE NIKAIDOU
OH!

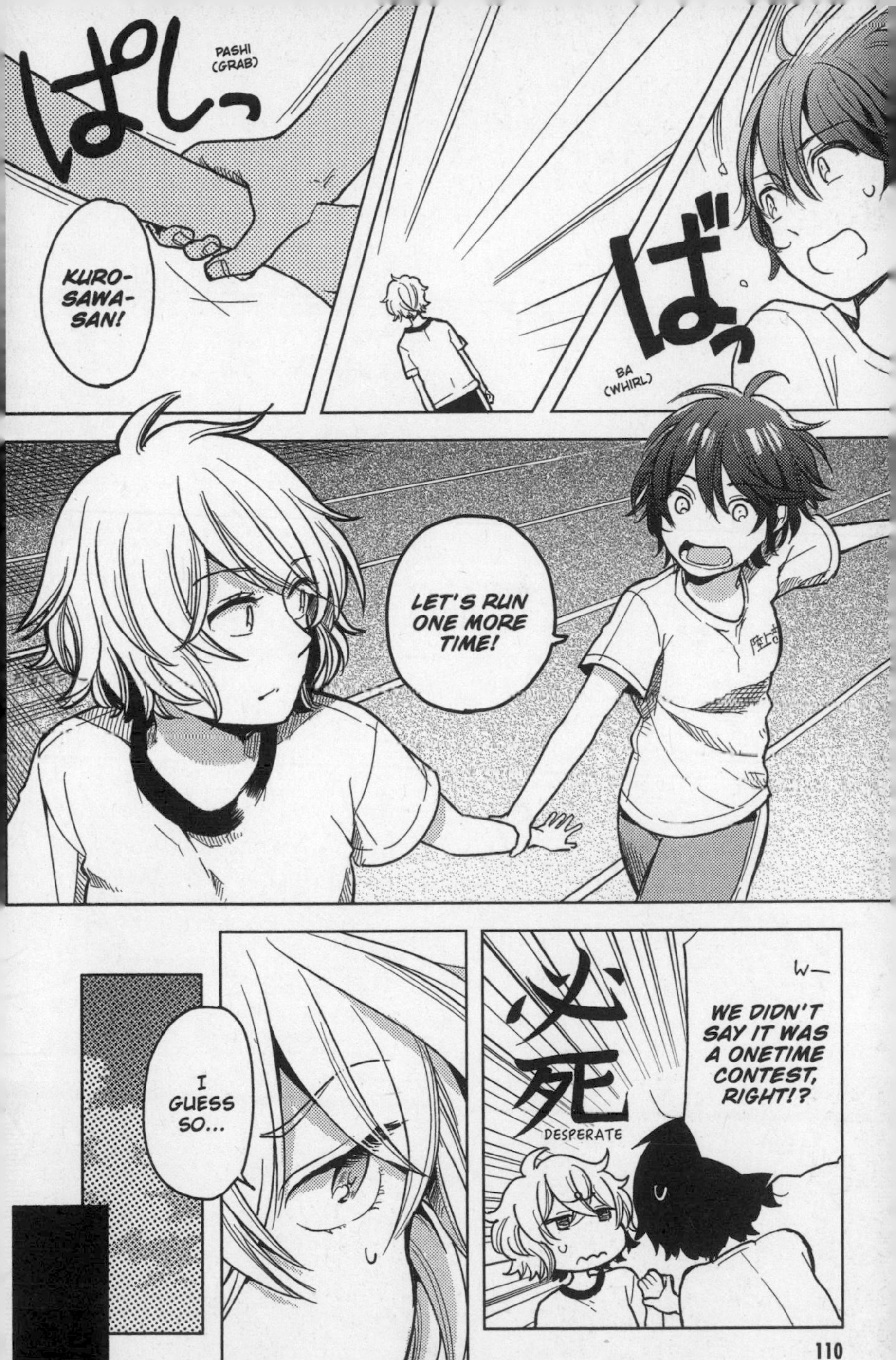
ばっ
BA
(WHIRL)
ぱしっ
PASHI
(GRAB)
KURO-SAWA-SAN!
LET'S RUN ONE MORE TIME!
必死
DESPERATE
W—
WE DIDN'T SAY IT WAS A ONETIME CONTEST, RIGHT!?
I GUESS SO...

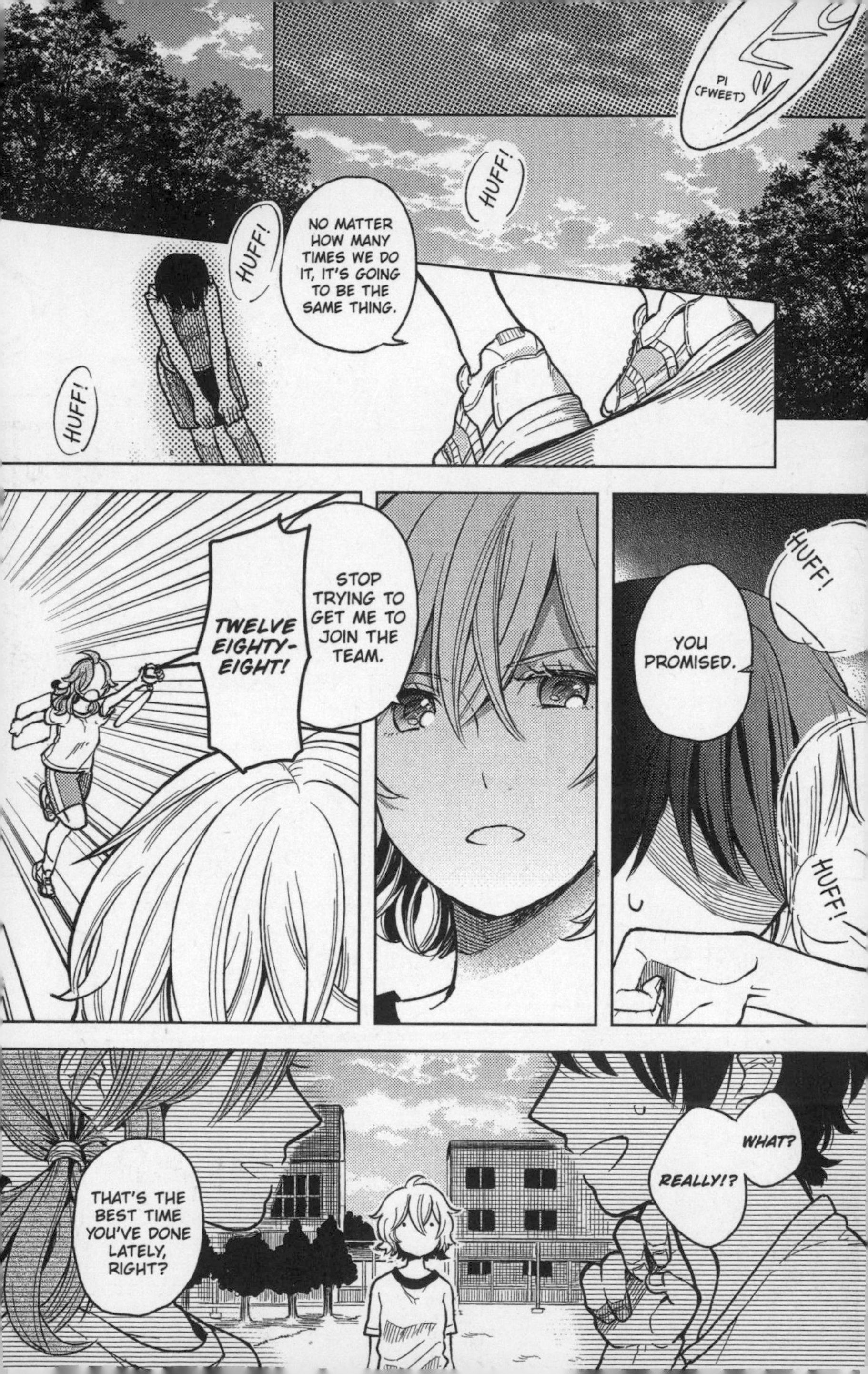
PI (FWEET)
HUFF!
NO MATTER HOW MANY TIMES WE DO IT, IT'S GOING TO BE THE SAME THING.
HUFF!
HUFF!
HUFF!
YOU PROMISED.
HUFF!
STOP TRYING TO GET ME TO JOIN THE TEAM.
TWELVE EIGHTY-EIGHT!
WHAT?
REALLY!?
THAT'S THE BEST TIME YOU'VE DONE LATELY, RIGHT?

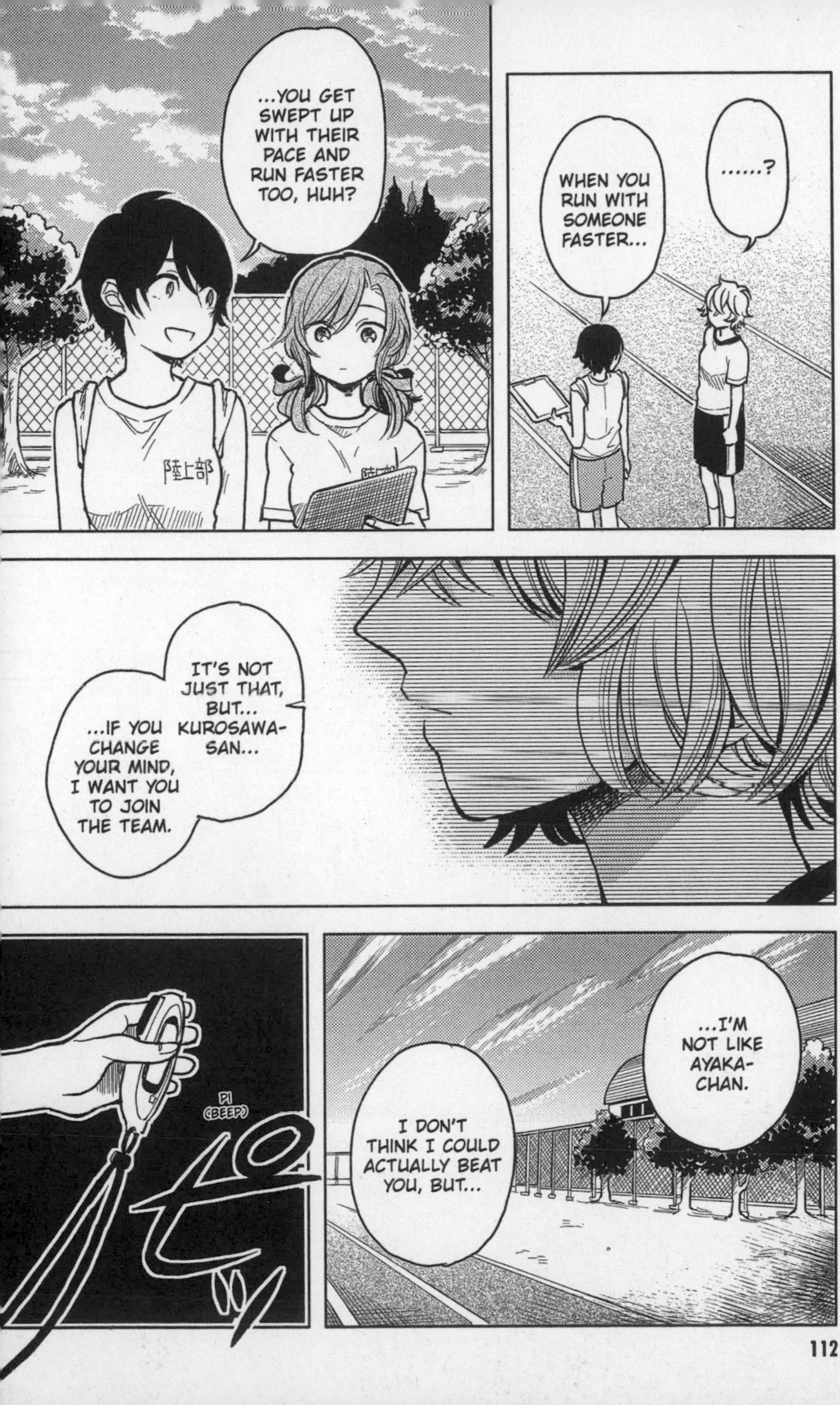
......?
WHEN YOU RUN WITH SOMEONE FASTER...
...YOU GET SWEPT UP WITH THEIR PACE AND RUN FASTER TOO, HUH?
IT'S NOT JUST THAT, BUT... KUROSAWA-SAN...
...IF YOU CHANGE YOUR MIND, I WANT YOU TO JOIN THE TEAM.
...I'M NOT LIKE AYAKA-CHAN.
I DON'T THINK I COULD ACTUALLY BEAT YOU, BUT...
PI (BEEP)

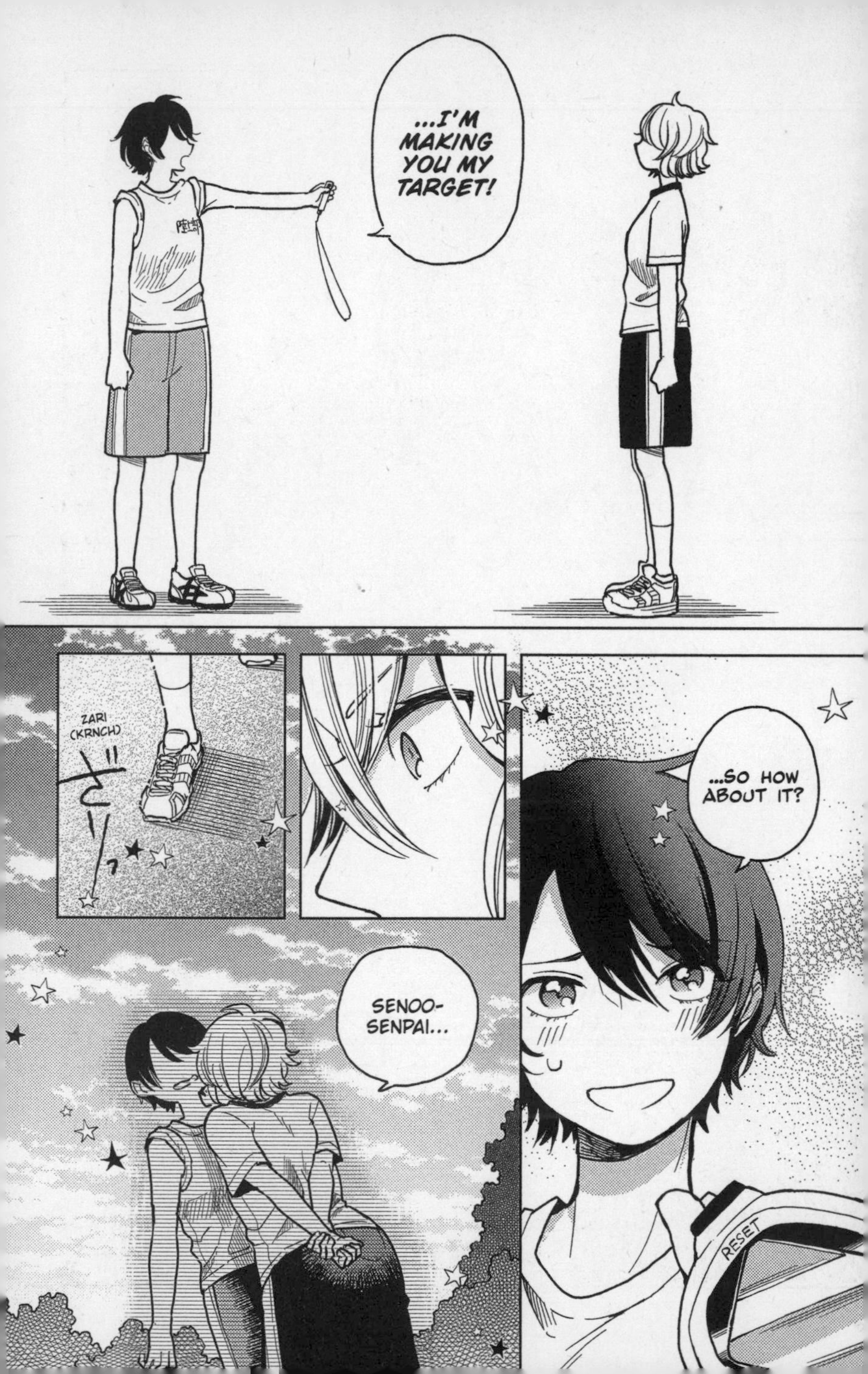
...I'M MAKING YOU MY TARGET!
...SO HOW ABOUT IT?
RESET
ZARI (KRNCH)
SENOO-SENPAI...

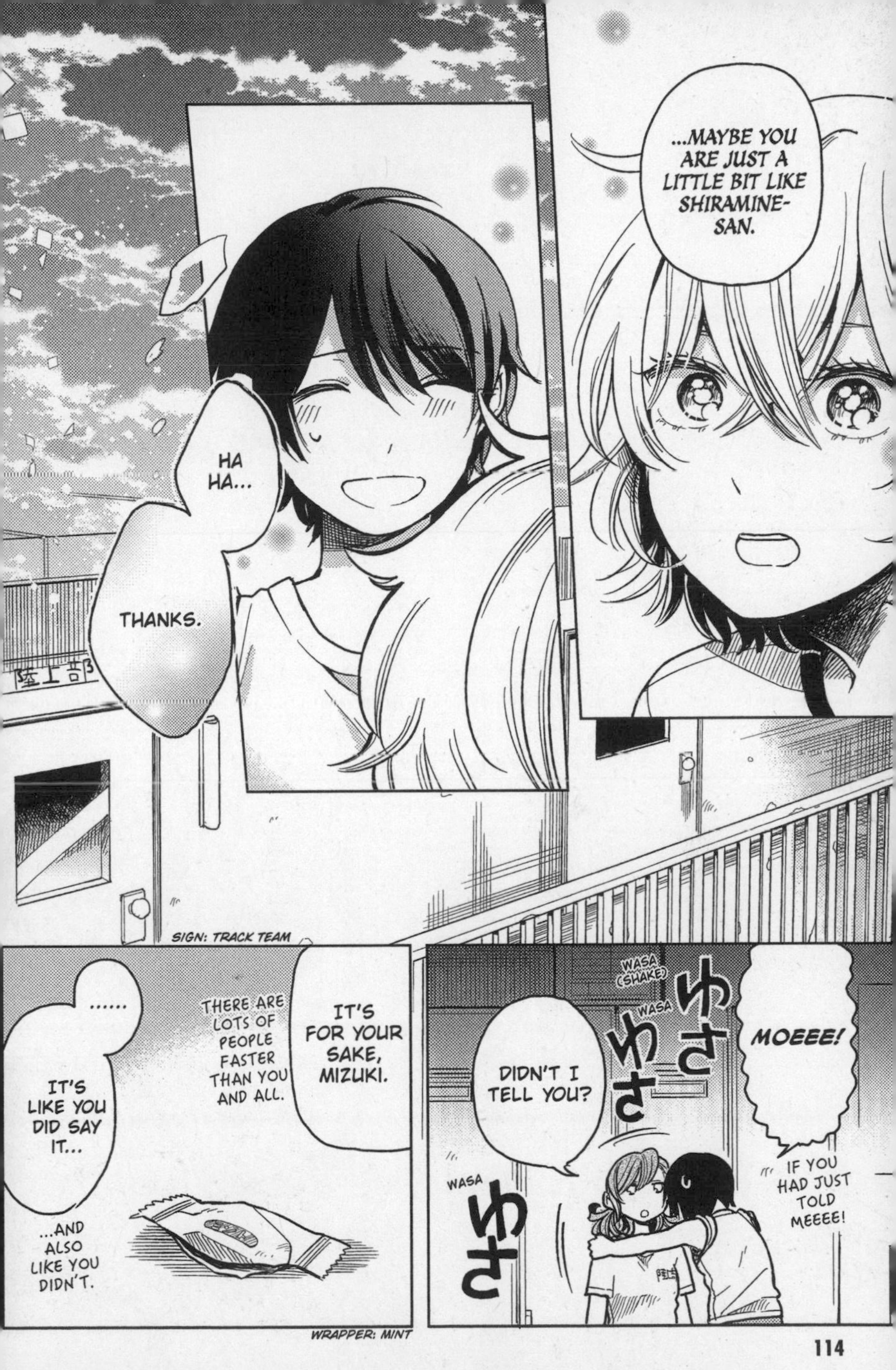
...MAYBE YOU ARE JUST A LITTLE BIT LIKE SHIRAMINE-SAN.
HA HA...
THANKS.
陸上部
SIGN: TRACK TEAM
MOEEE!
WASA (SHAKE)
ゆさ
WASA
ゆさ
DIDN'T I TELL YOU?
IF YOU HAD JUST TOLD MEEEE!
WASA
ゆさ
IT'S FOR YOUR SAKE, MIZUKI.
THERE ARE LOTS OF PEOPLE FASTER THAN YOU AND ALL.
......
IT'S LIKE YOU DID SAY IT...
...AND ALSO LIKE YOU DIDN'T.
WRAPPER: MINT

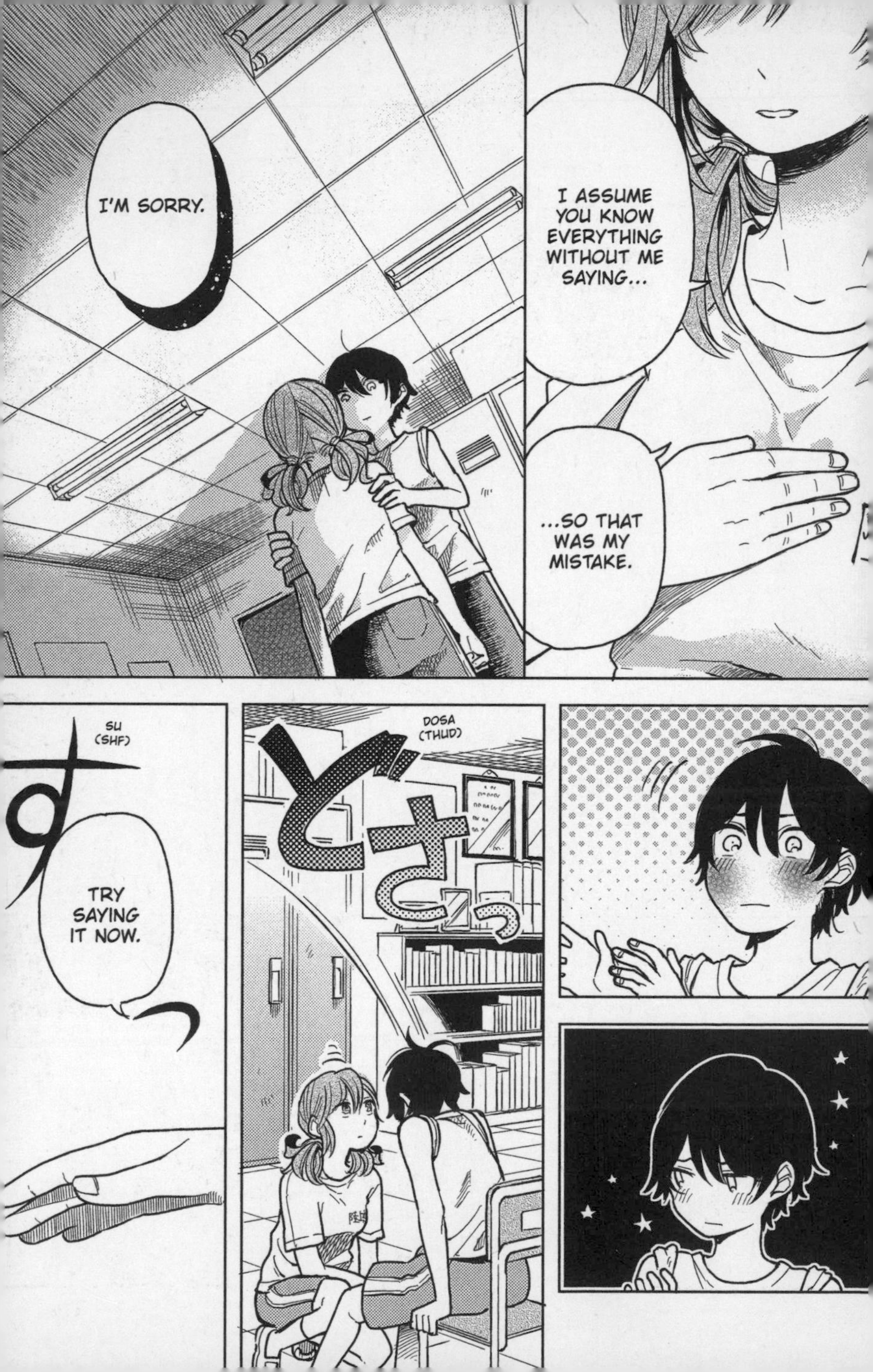
I ASSUME YOU KNOW EVERYTHING WITHOUT ME SAYING...
...SO THAT WAS MY MISTAKE.
I'M SORRY.
DOSA (THUD)
どさっ
SU (SHF)
す
TRY SAYING IT NOW.

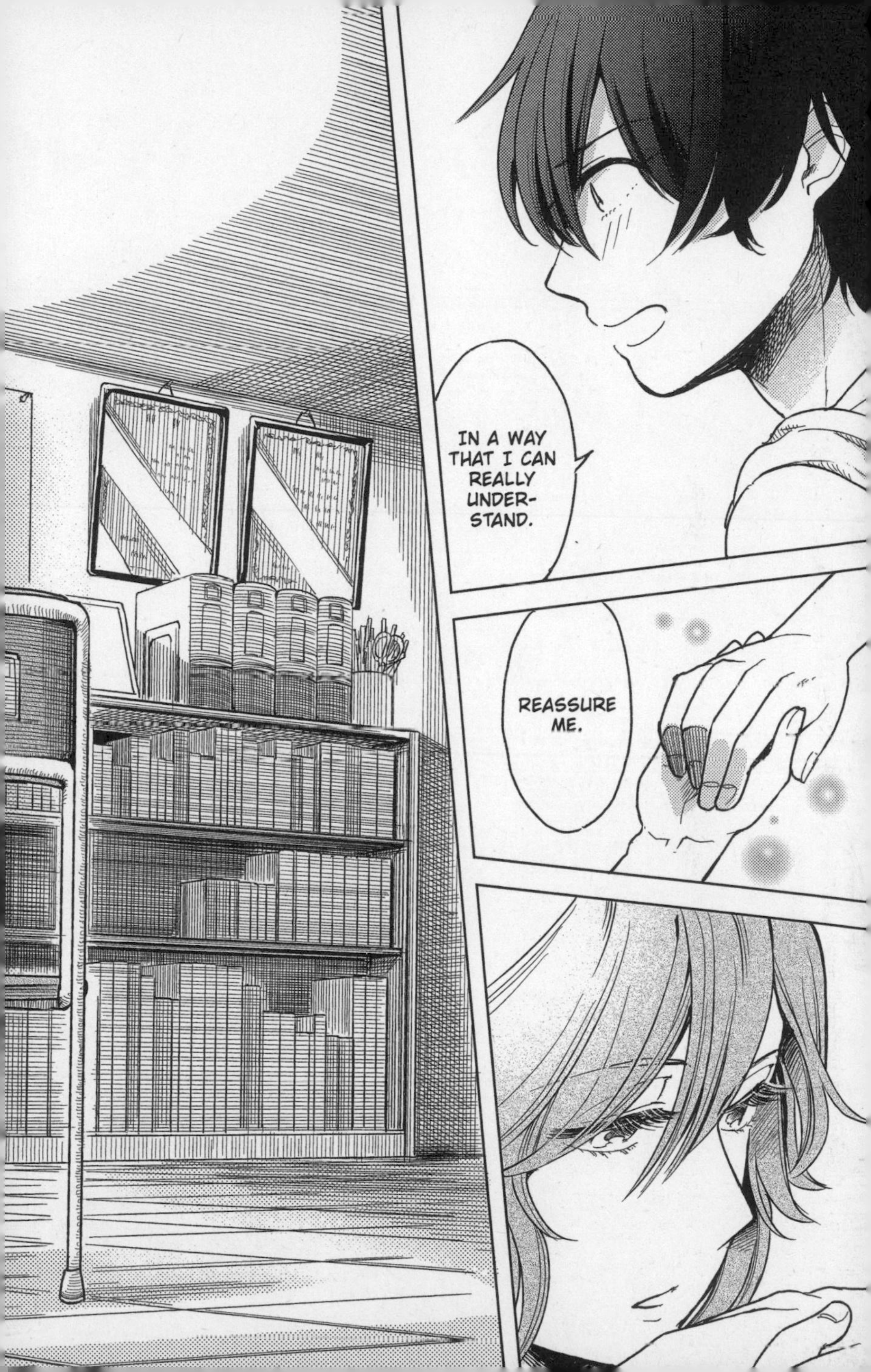
IN A WAY THAT I CAN REALLY UNDER-STAND.
REASSURE ME.

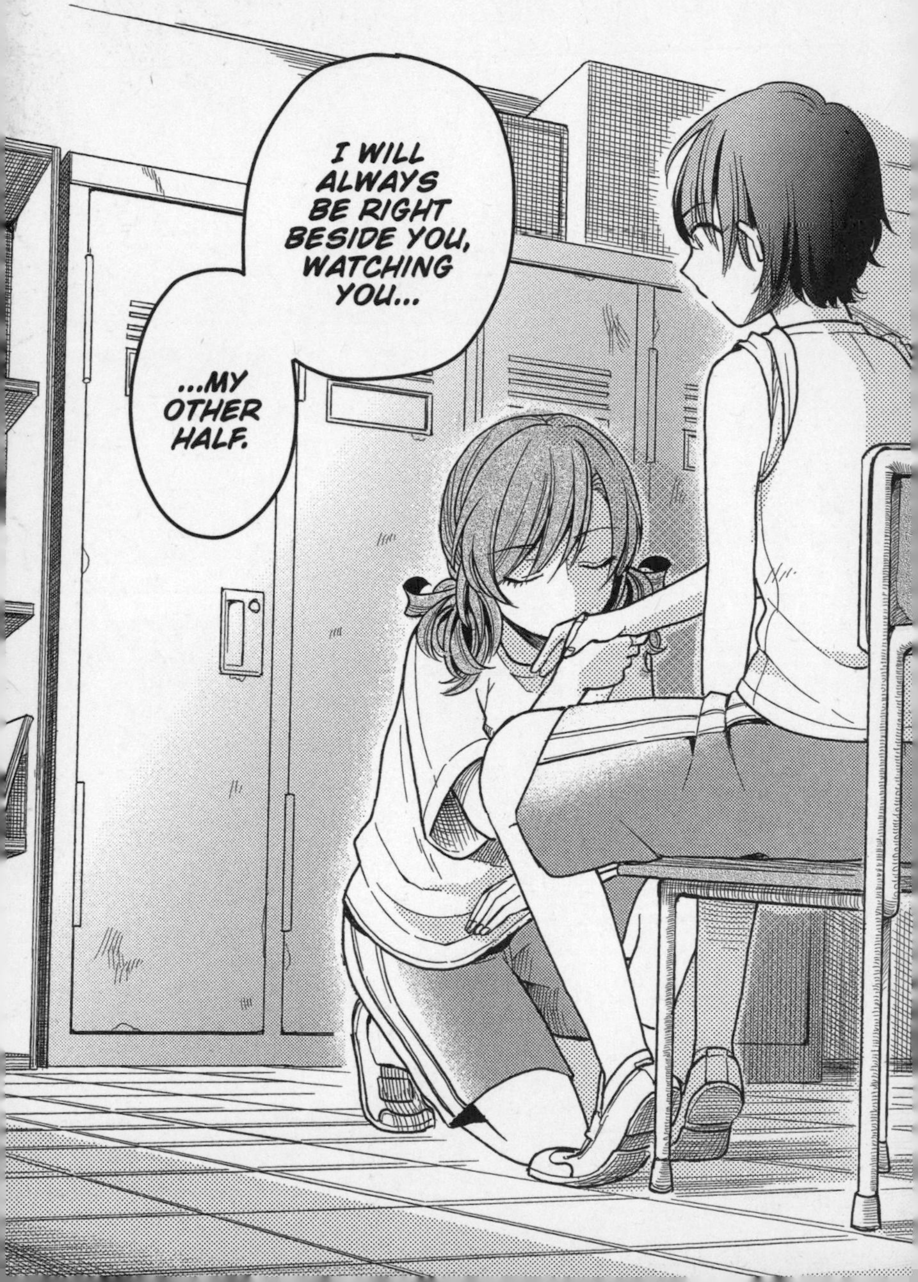
I WILL ALWAYS BE RIGHT BESIDE YOU, WATCHING YOU...
...MY OTHER HALF.

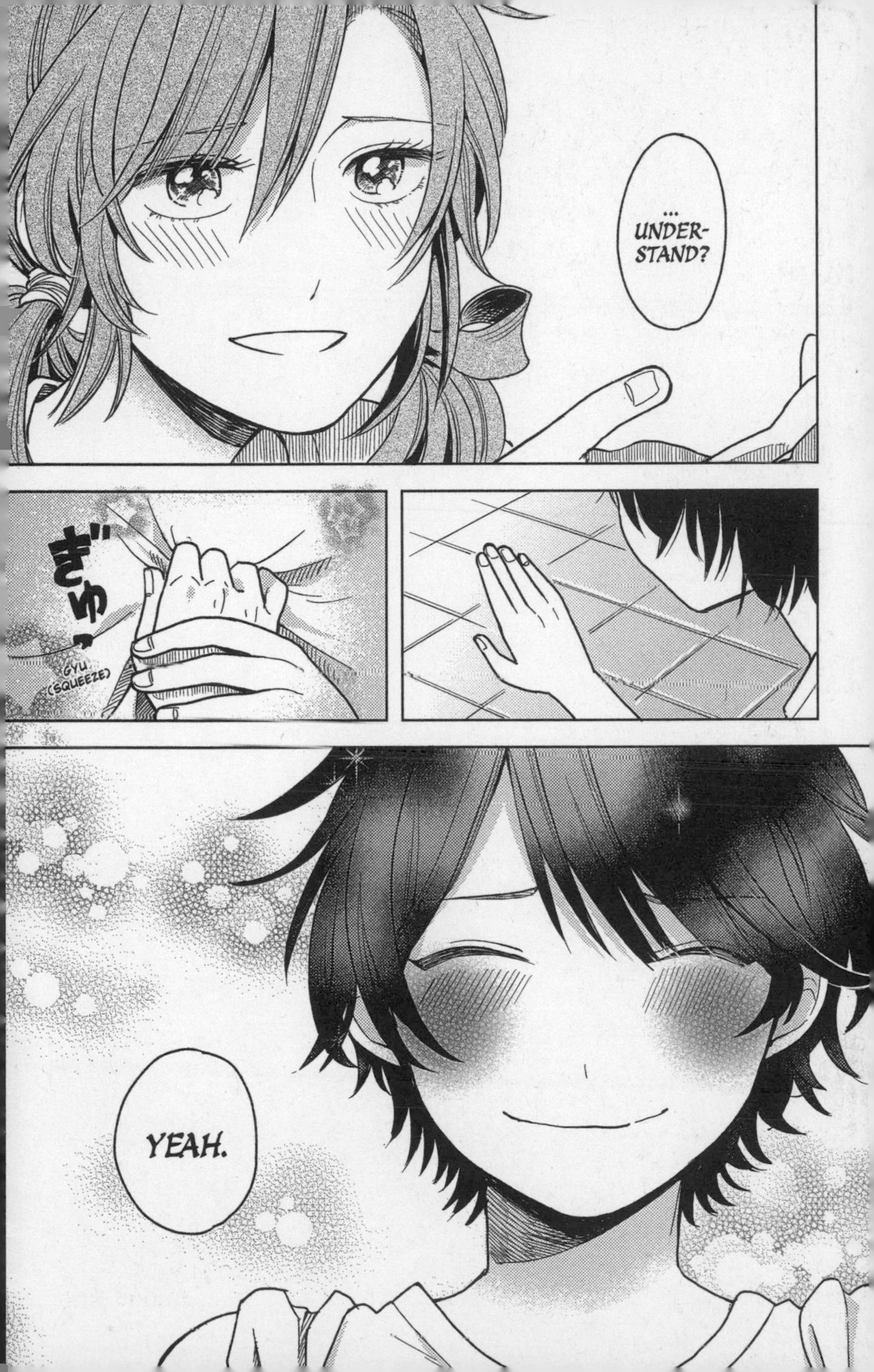
...UNDER-STAND?
ぎゅっ
GYU (SQUEEZE)
YEAH.

KISS THEATER: WHAT'S BEHIND THE STORY!?

PEOPLE OTHER THAN THE MAIN CHARACTERS HAVE STORIES TOO. HERE, WE PRESENT THE "LITTLE LOVE" STORIES HAPPENING BEHIND THE SCENES.

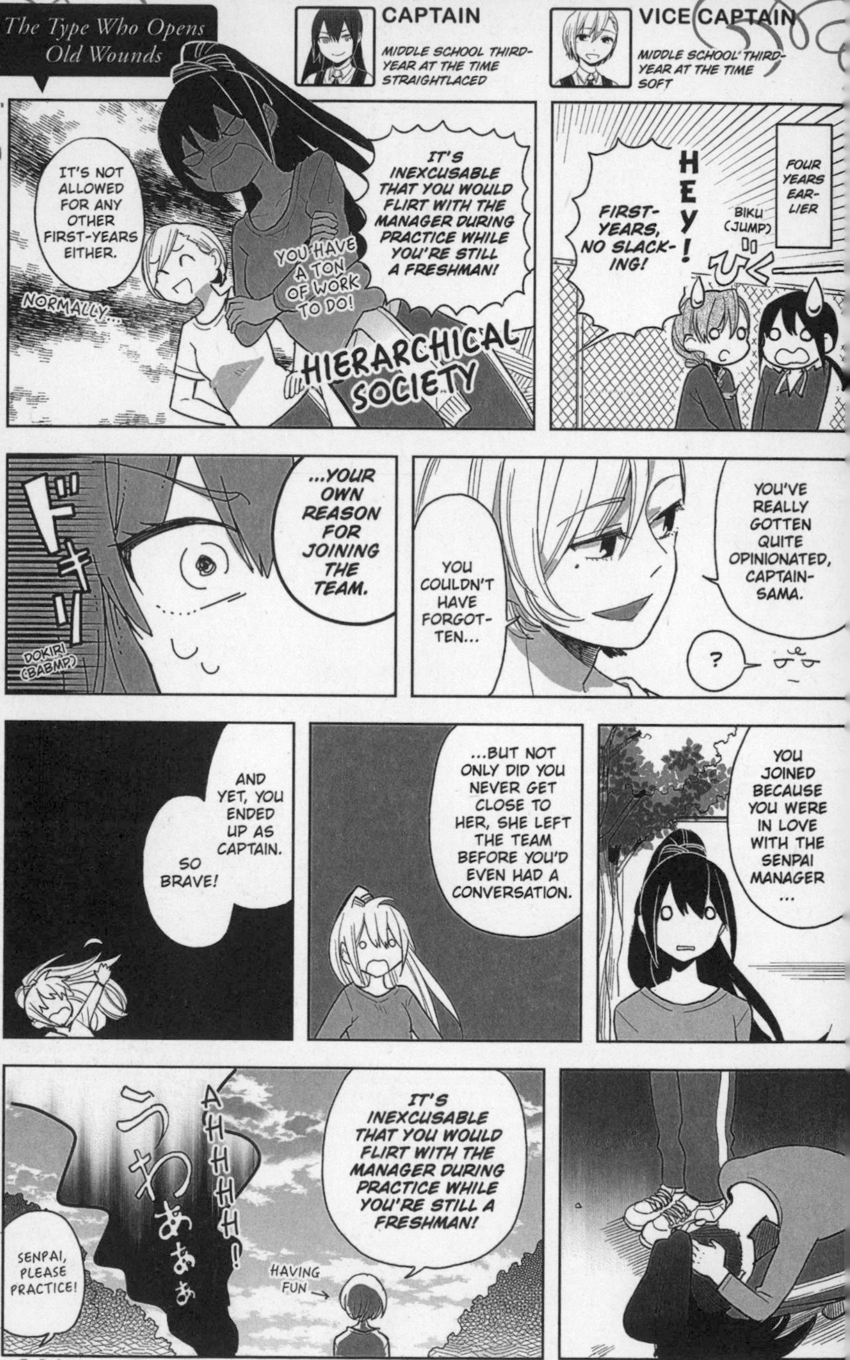
The Type Who Opens Old Wounds
VICE CAPTAIN
MIDDLE SCHOOL THIRD-YEAR AT THE TIME SOFT
CAPTAIN
MIDDLE SCHOOL THIRD-YEAR AT THE TIME STRAIGHTLACED
FOUR YEARS EARLIER
HEY!
FIRST-YEARS, NO SLACKING!
BIKU (JUMP)
IT'S INEXCUSABLE THAT YOU WOULD FLIRT WITH THE MANAGER DURING PRACTICE WHILE YOU'RE STILL A FRESHMAN!
YOU HAVE A TON OF WORK TO DO!
HIERARCHICAL SOCIETY
IT'S NOT ALLOWED FOR ANY OTHER FIRST-YEARS EITHER.
NORMALLY...
YOU'VE REALLY GOTTEN QUITE OPINIONATED, CAPTAIN-SAMA.
?
YOU COULDN'T HAVE FORGOTTEN...
...YOUR OWN REASON FOR JOINING THE TEAM.
DOKIRI (BABMP)
YOU JOINED BECAUSE YOU WERE IN LOVE WITH THE SENPAI MANAGER...
...BUT NOT ONLY DID YOU NEVER GET CLOSE TO HER, SHE LEFT THE TEAM BEFORE YOU'D EVEN HAD A CONVERSATION.
AND YET, YOU ENDED UP AS CAPTAIN.
SO BRAVE!
IT'S INEXCUSABLE THAT YOU WOULD FLIRT WITH THE MANAGER DURING PRACTICE WHILE YOU'RE STILL A FRESHMAN!
HAVING FUN
AHHHHH!
うわあああ
SENPAI, PLEASE PRACTICE!

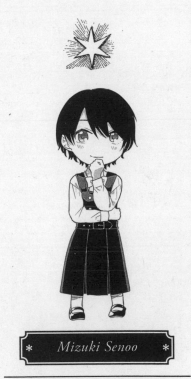

Mizuki Senoo

Mizuki Senoo

Second-year at the Seiran Academy High School.
Short-distance runner on the Track team. Because
of her boyish appearance and that she is pretty
good at track, she has more than a few students
who look up to her, but she herself is timid and gets
anxious over things she blows out of proportion.
She is Ayaka Shiramine's cousin and childhood
friend; the two are like sisters.

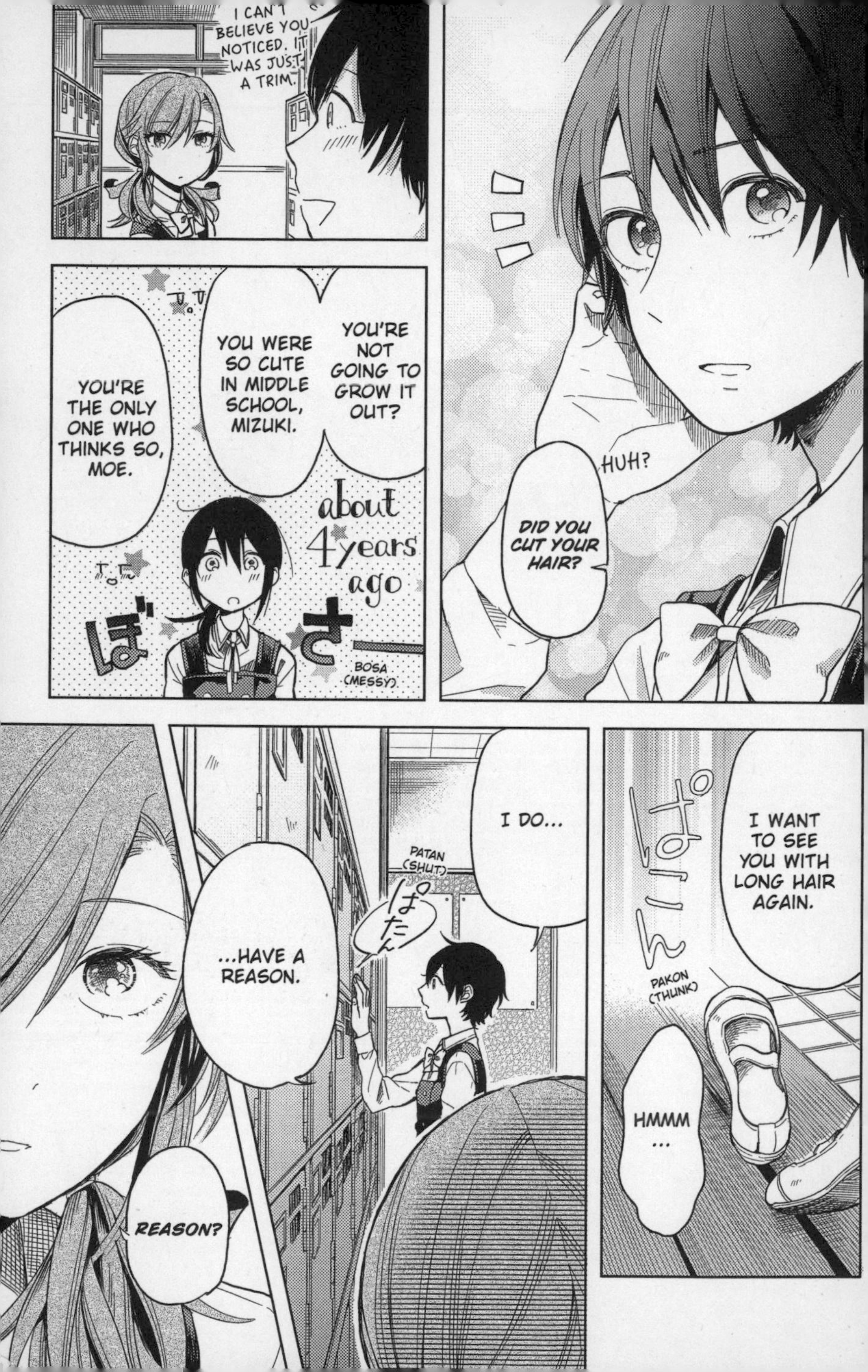
HUH?
DID YOU CUT YOUR HAIR?
I CAN'T BELIEVE YOU NOTICED. IT WAS JUST A TRIM.
YOU'RE NOT GOING TO GROW IT OUT?
YOU WERE SO CUTE IN MIDDLE SCHOOL, MIZUKI.
YOU'RE THE ONLY ONE WHO THINKS SO, MOE.
about 4 years ago
ぼさー
BOSA (MESSY)
I WANT TO SEE YOU WITH LONG HAIR AGAIN.
ぱこん
PAKON (THUNK)
HMMM ...
I DO...
ぱたん
PATAN (SHUT)
...HAVE A REASON.
REASON?

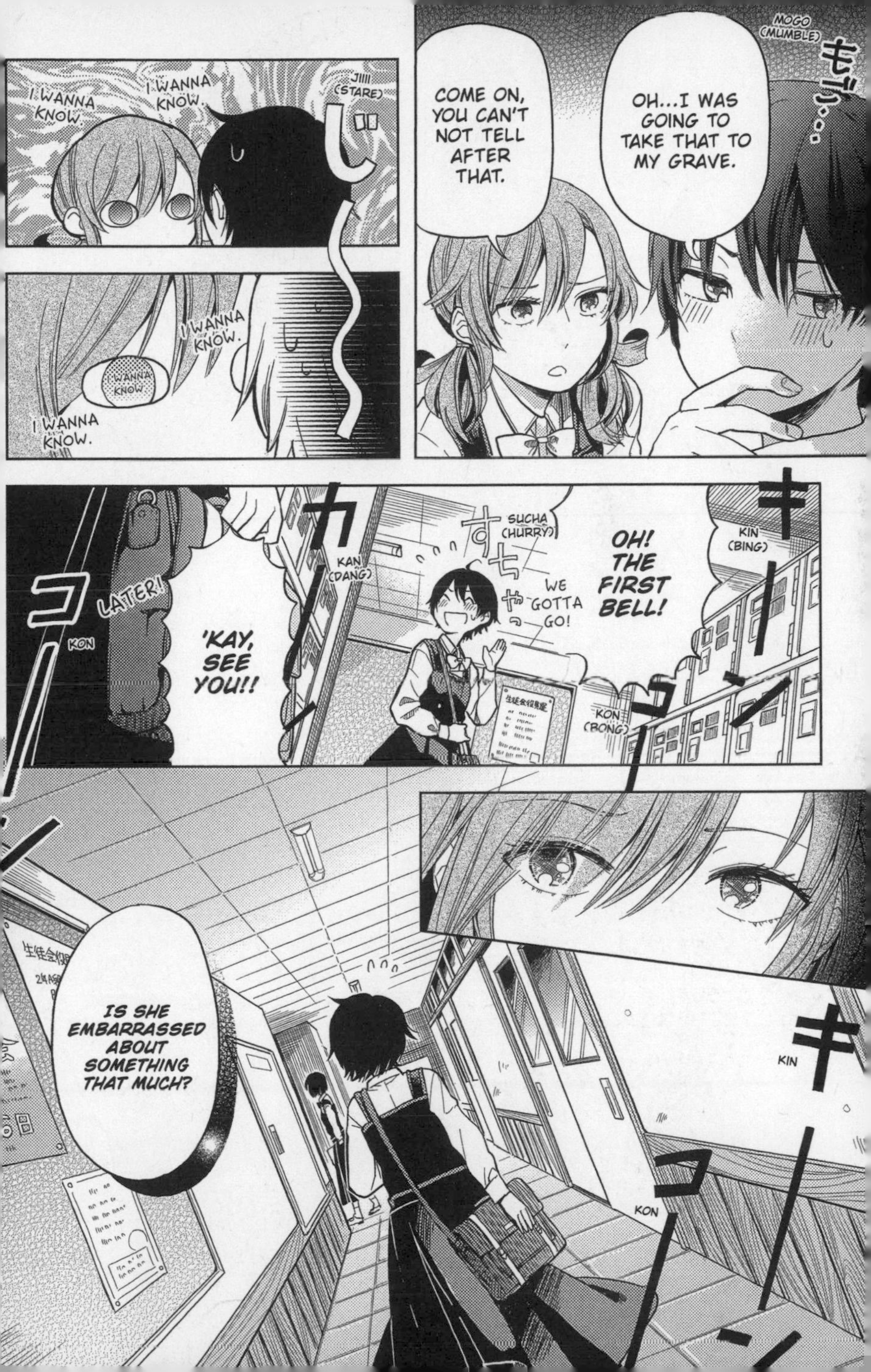
MOGO (MUMBLE)
OH...I WAS GOING TO TAKE THAT TO MY GRAVE.
COME ON, YOU CAN'T NOT TELL AFTER THAT.
JIIII (STARE)
I WANNA KNOW.
I WANNA KNOW.
I WANNA KNOW.
I WANNA KNOW
I WANNA KNOW.
KIN (BING)
KON (BONG)
OH! THE FIRST BELL!
SUCHA (HURRY)
WE GOTTA GO!
KAN (DANG)
'KAY, SEE YOU!!
LATER!
KON
KIN
KON
IS SHE EMBARRASSED ABOUT SOMETHING THAT MUCH?

Chapter 4: *The Secret of My Girl*

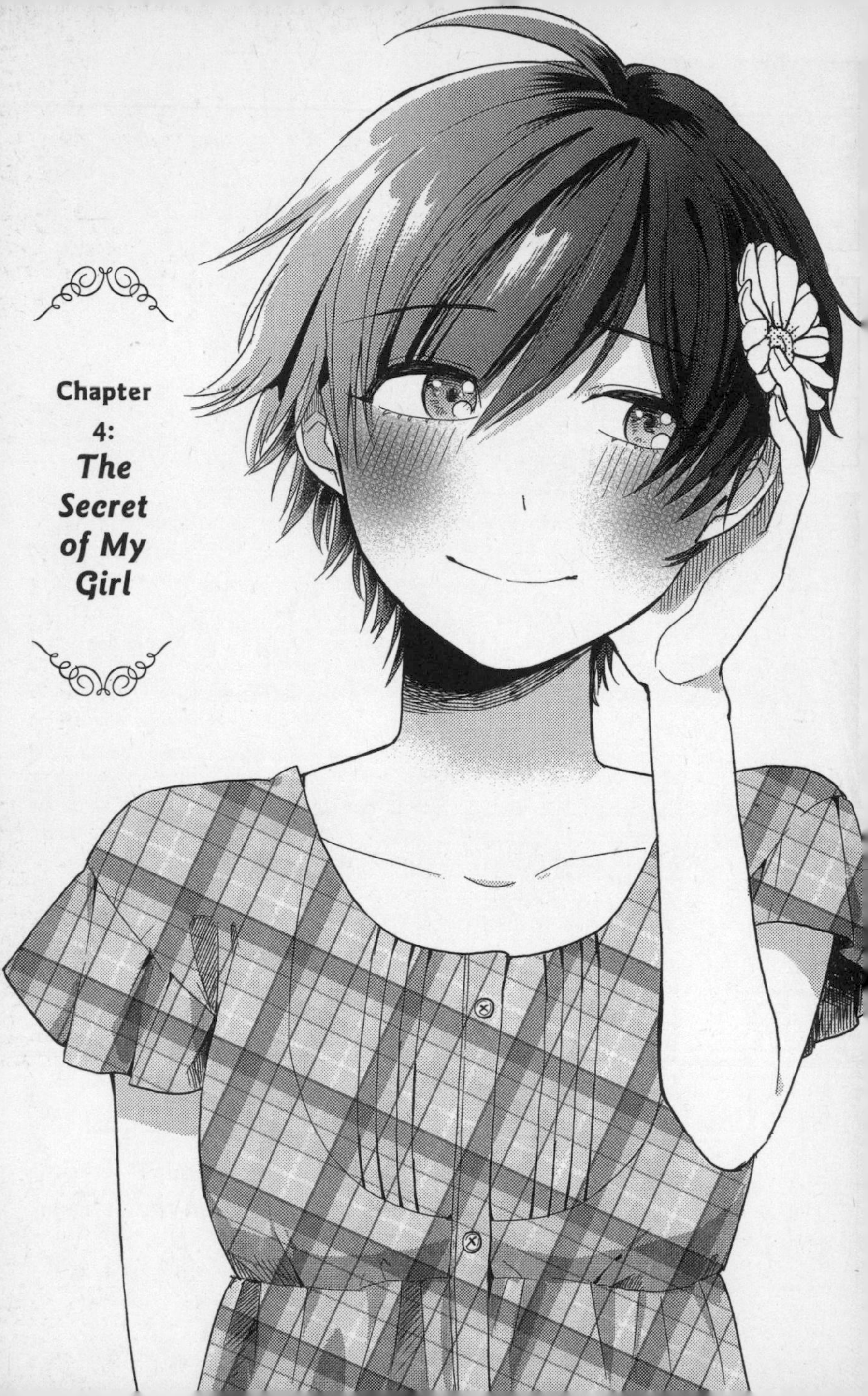

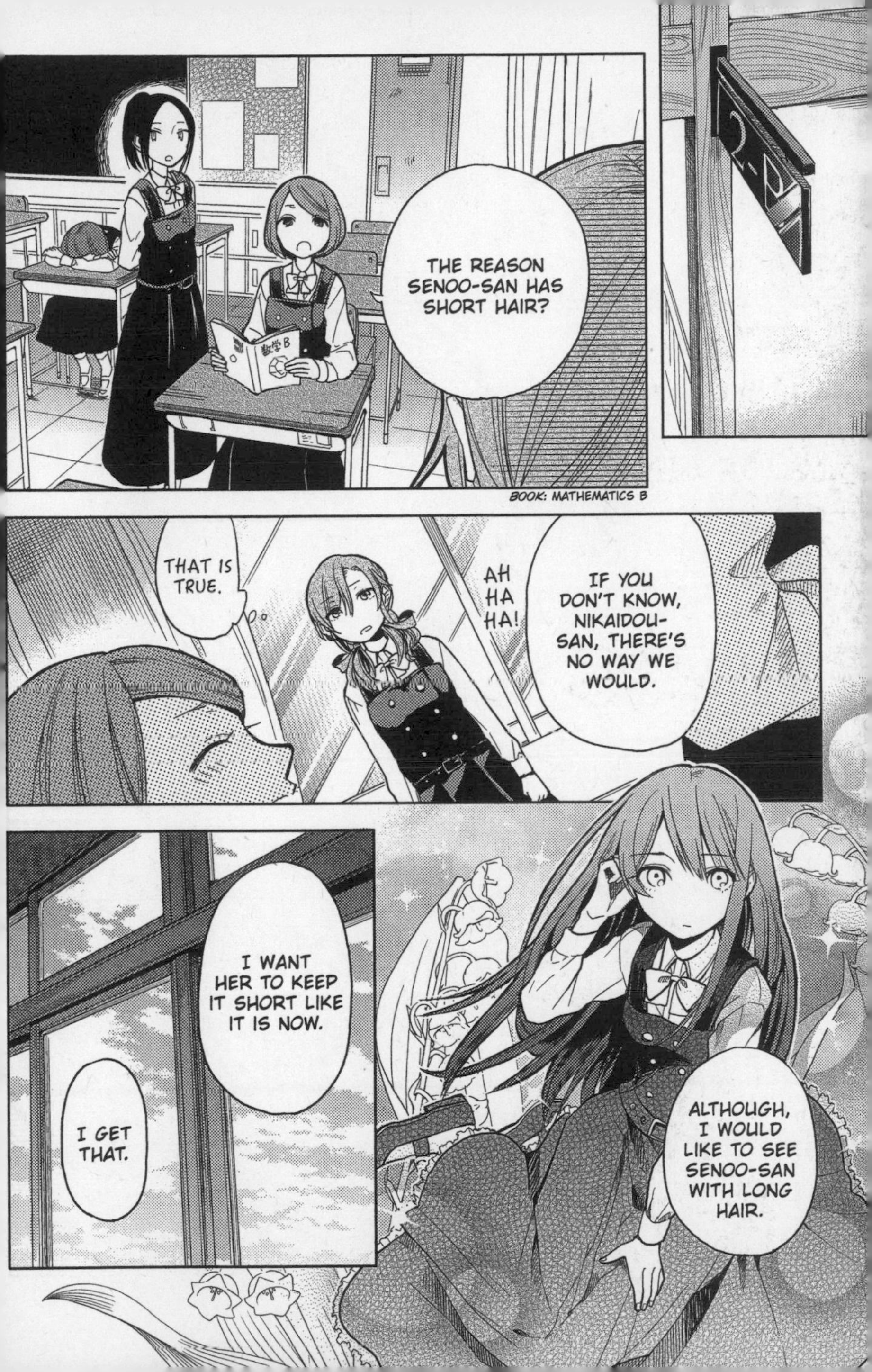
THE REASON SENOO-SAN HAS SHORT HAIR?
数学B
IF YOU DON'T KNOW, NIKAIDOU-SAN, THERE'S NO WAY WE WOULD.
AH HA HA!
THAT IS TRUE.
I WANT HER TO KEEP IT SHORT LIKE IT IS NOW.
I GET THAT.
ALTHOUGH, I WOULD LIKE TO SEE SENOO-SAN WITH LONG HAIR.
BOOK: MATHEMATICS B

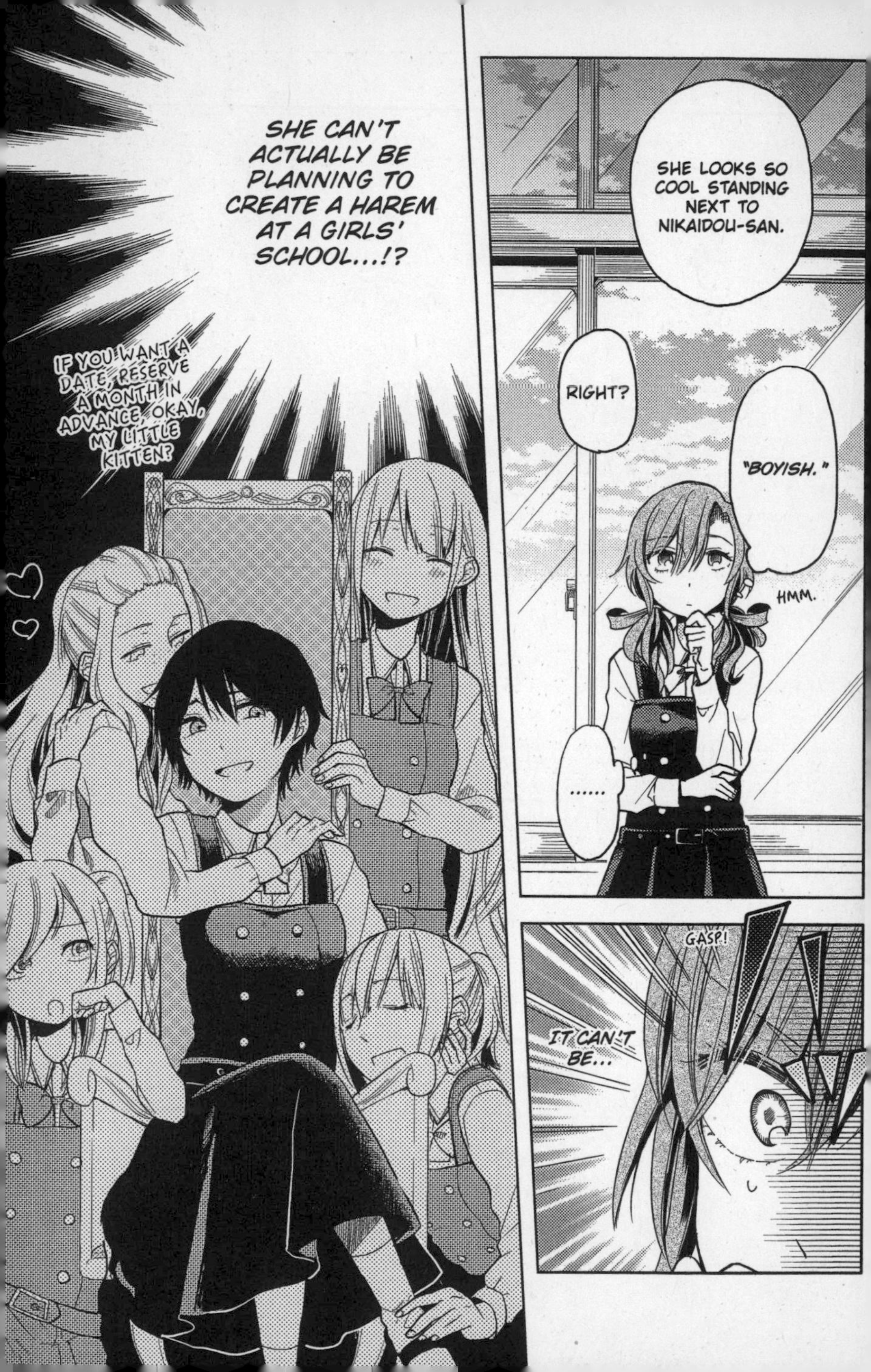
SHE LOOKS SO COOL STANDING NEXT TO NIKAIDOU-SAN.
"BOYISH."
RIGHT?
HMM.
......
GASP!
IT CAN'T BE...
SHE CAN'T ACTUALLY BE PLANNING TO CREATE A HAREM AT A GIRLS' SCHOOL...!?
IF YOU WANT A DATE, RESERVE A MONTH IN ADVANCE, OKAY, MY LITTLE KITTEN?

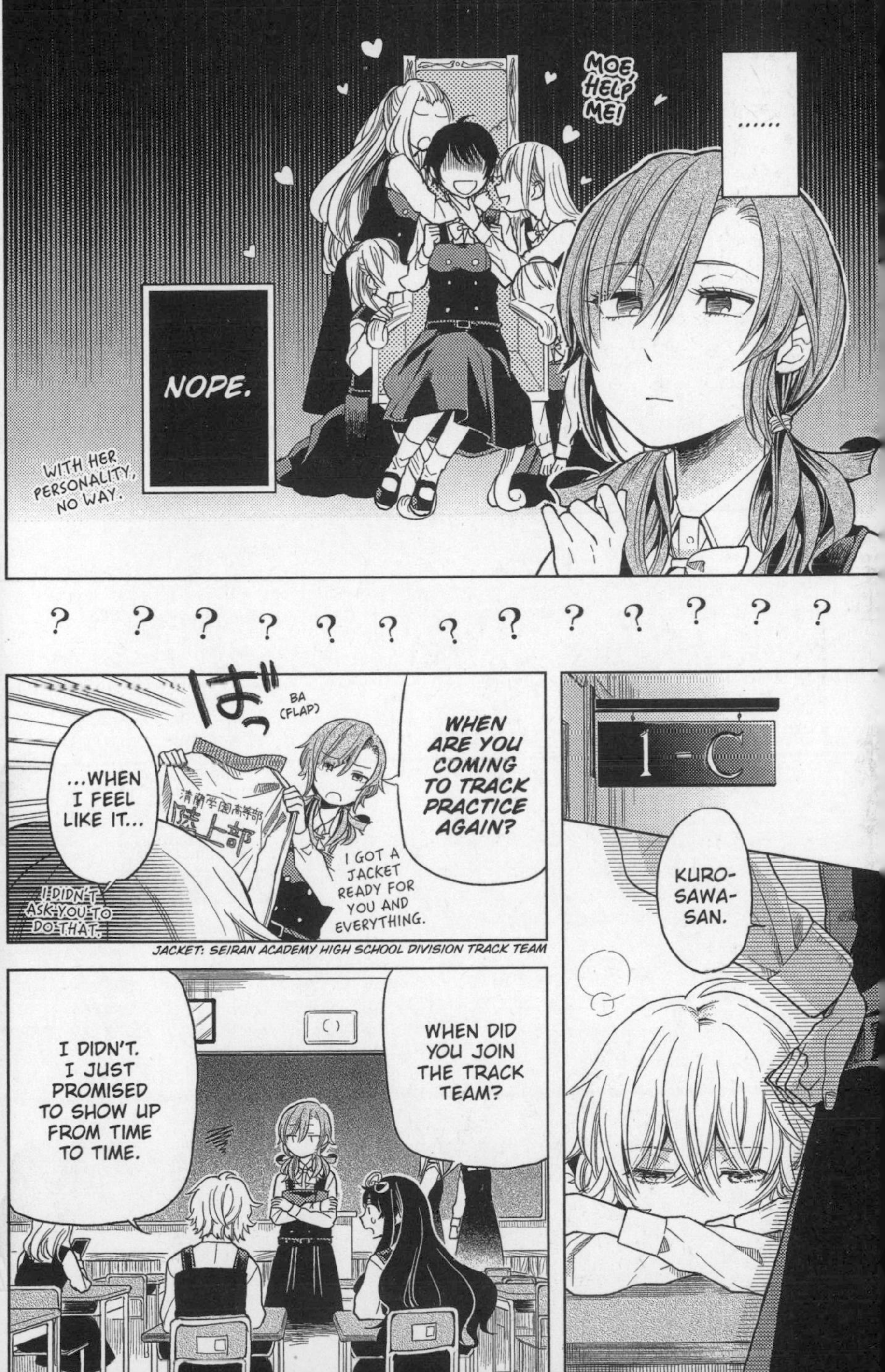
......
MOE, HELP ME!
NOPE.
WITH HER PERSONALITY, NO WAY.
? ? ? ? ? ? ? ? ? ? ? ? ?
1-C
KURO-SAWA-SAN.
WHEN ARE YOU COMING TO TRACK PRACTICE AGAIN?
I GOT A JACKET READY FOR YOU AND EVERYTHING.
ばっ
BA (FLAP)
清蘭学園高等部 陸上部
...WHEN I FEEL LIKE IT...
I DIDN'T ASK YOU TO DO THAT.
JACKET: SEIRAN ACADEMY HIGH SCHOOL DIVISION TRACK TEAM
WHEN DID YOU JOIN THE TRACK TEAM?
I DIDN'T. I JUST PROMISED TO SHOW UP FROM TIME TO TIME.

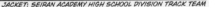

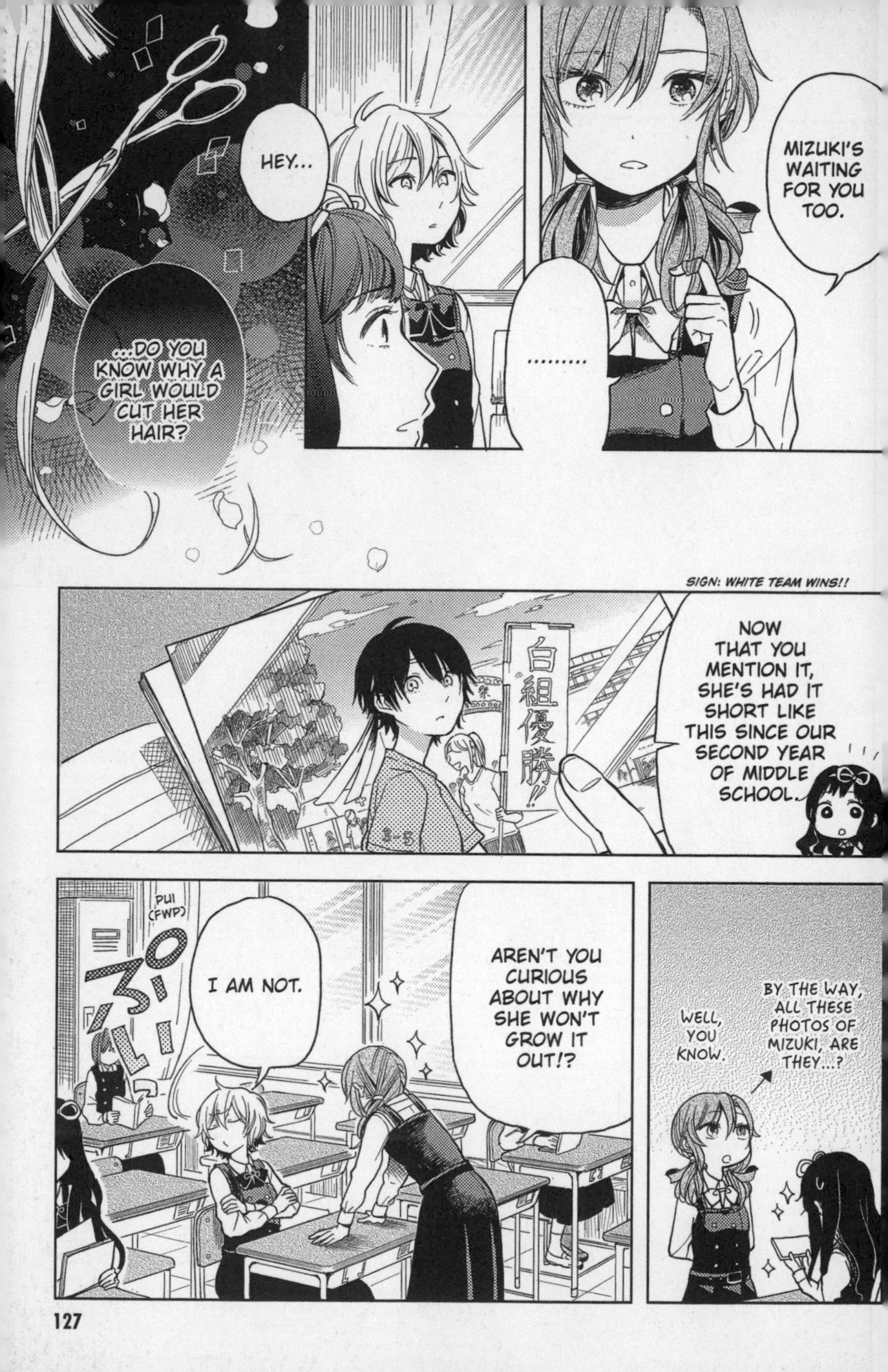
MIZUKI'S WAITING FOR YOU TOO.
....
HEY...
...DO YOU KNOW WHY A GIRL WOULD CUT HER HAIR?
SIGN: WHITE TEAM WINS!!
白組優勝!!
NOW THAT YOU MENTION IT, SHE'S HAD IT SHORT LIKE THIS SINCE OUR SECOND YEAR OF MIDDLE SCHOOL.
BY THE WAY, ALL THESE PHOTOS OF MIZUKI, ARE THEY...?
WELL, YOU KNOW.
AREN'T YOU CURIOUS ABOUT WHY SHE WON'T GROW IT OUT!?
I AM NOT.
ぷい
PUI (FWP)

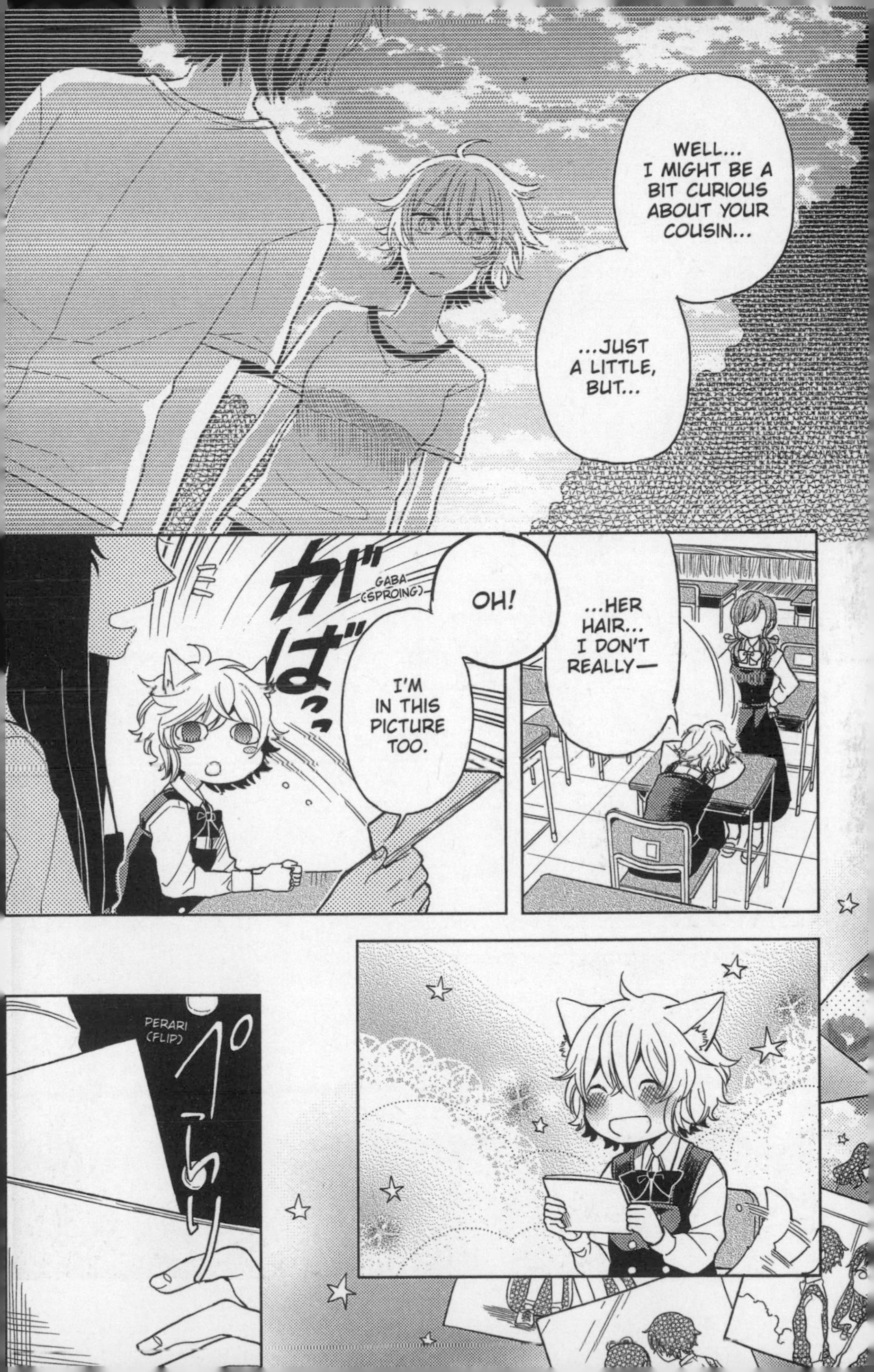
WELL... I MIGHT BE A BIT CURIOUS ABOUT YOUR COUSIN...
...JUST A LITTLE, BUT...
...HER HAIR... I DON'T REALLY—
GABA (SPROING)
OH!
I'M IN THIS PICTURE TOO.
PERARI (FLIP)

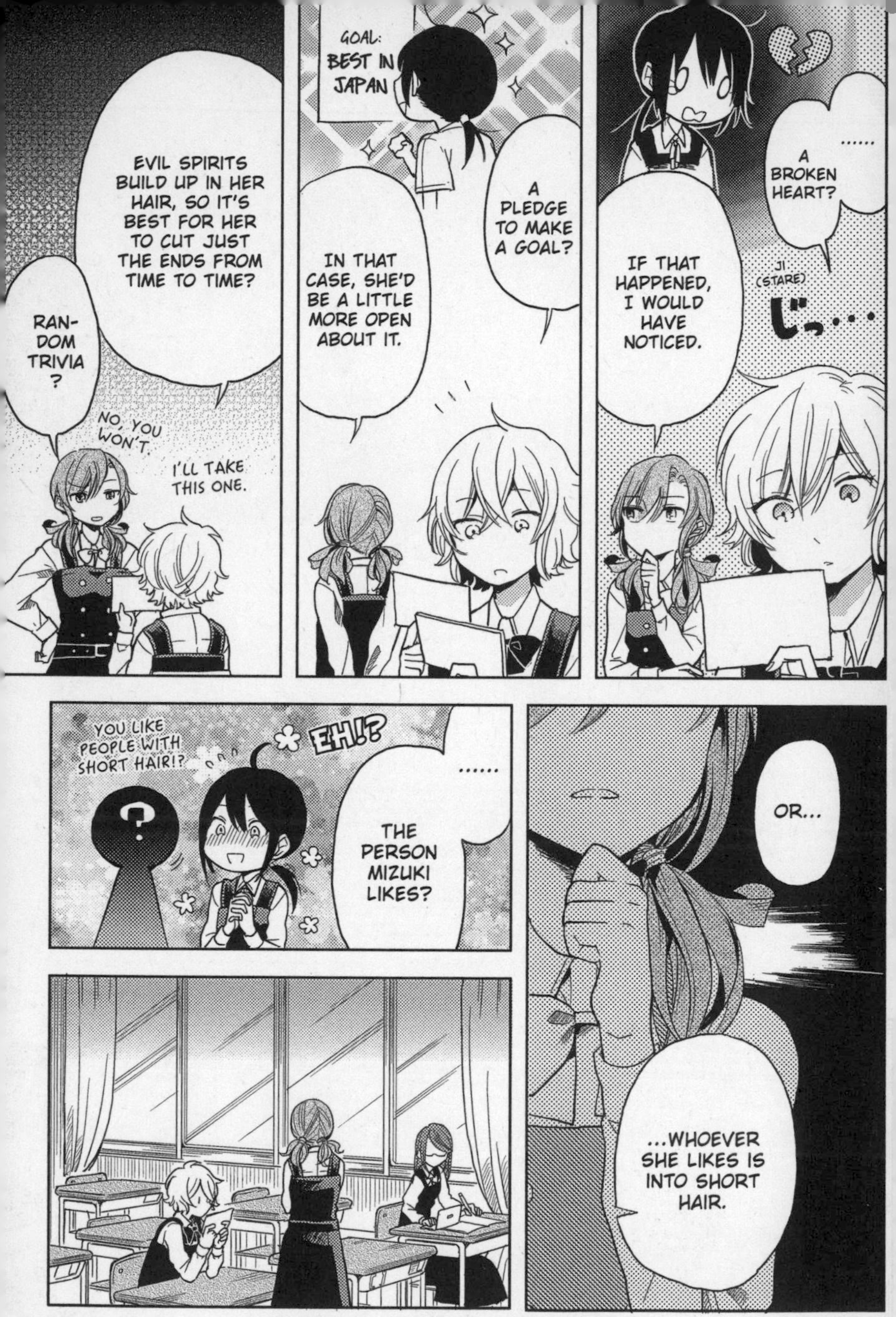
......
A BROKEN HEART?
JI (STARE)
じっ…
IF THAT HAPPENED, I WOULD HAVE NOTICED.
GOAL: BEST IN JAPAN
A PLEDGE TO MAKE A GOAL?
IN THAT CASE, SHE'D BE A LITTLE MORE OPEN ABOUT IT.
EVIL SPIRITS BUILD UP IN HER HAIR, SO IT'S BEST FOR HER TO CUT JUST THE ENDS FROM TIME TO TIME?
RAN-DOM TRIVIA?
NO, YOU WON'T.
I'LL TAKE THIS ONE.
OR...
...WHOEVER SHE LIKES IS INTO SHORT HAIR.
......
THE PERSON MIZUKI LIKES?
EH!?
YOU LIKE PEOPLE WITH SHORT HAIR!?

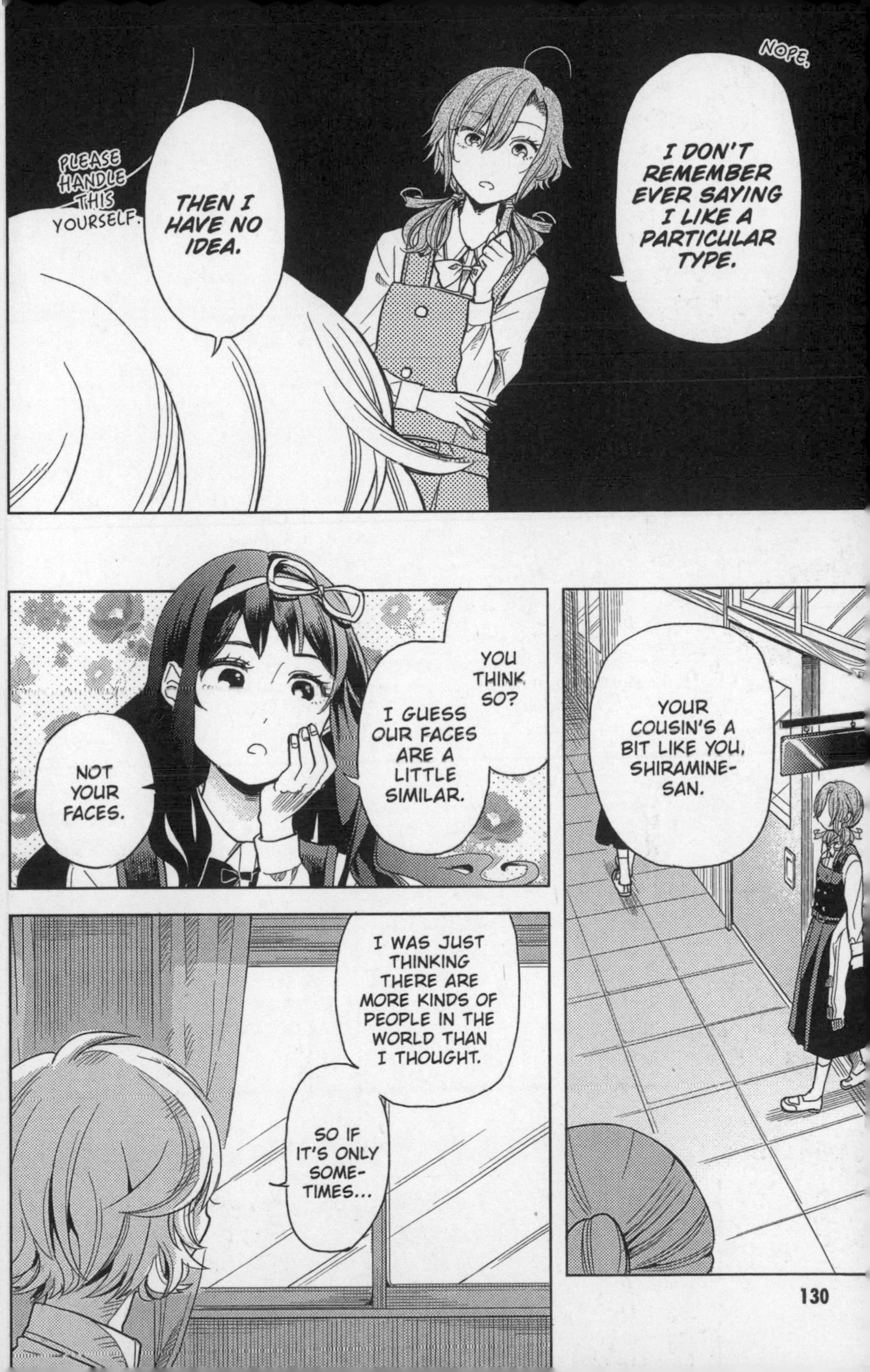
NOPE.
I DON'T REMEMBER EVER SAYING I LIKE A PARTICULAR TYPE.
THEN I HAVE NO IDEA.
PLEASE HANDLE THIS YOURSELF.
YOUR COUSIN'S A BIT LIKE YOU, SHIRAMINE-SAN.
YOU THINK SO?
I GUESS OUR FACES ARE A LITTLE SIMILAR.
NOT YOUR FACES.
I WAS JUST THINKING THERE ARE MORE KINDS OF PEOPLE IN THE WORLD THAN I THOUGHT.
SO IF IT'S ONLY SOME-TIMES...

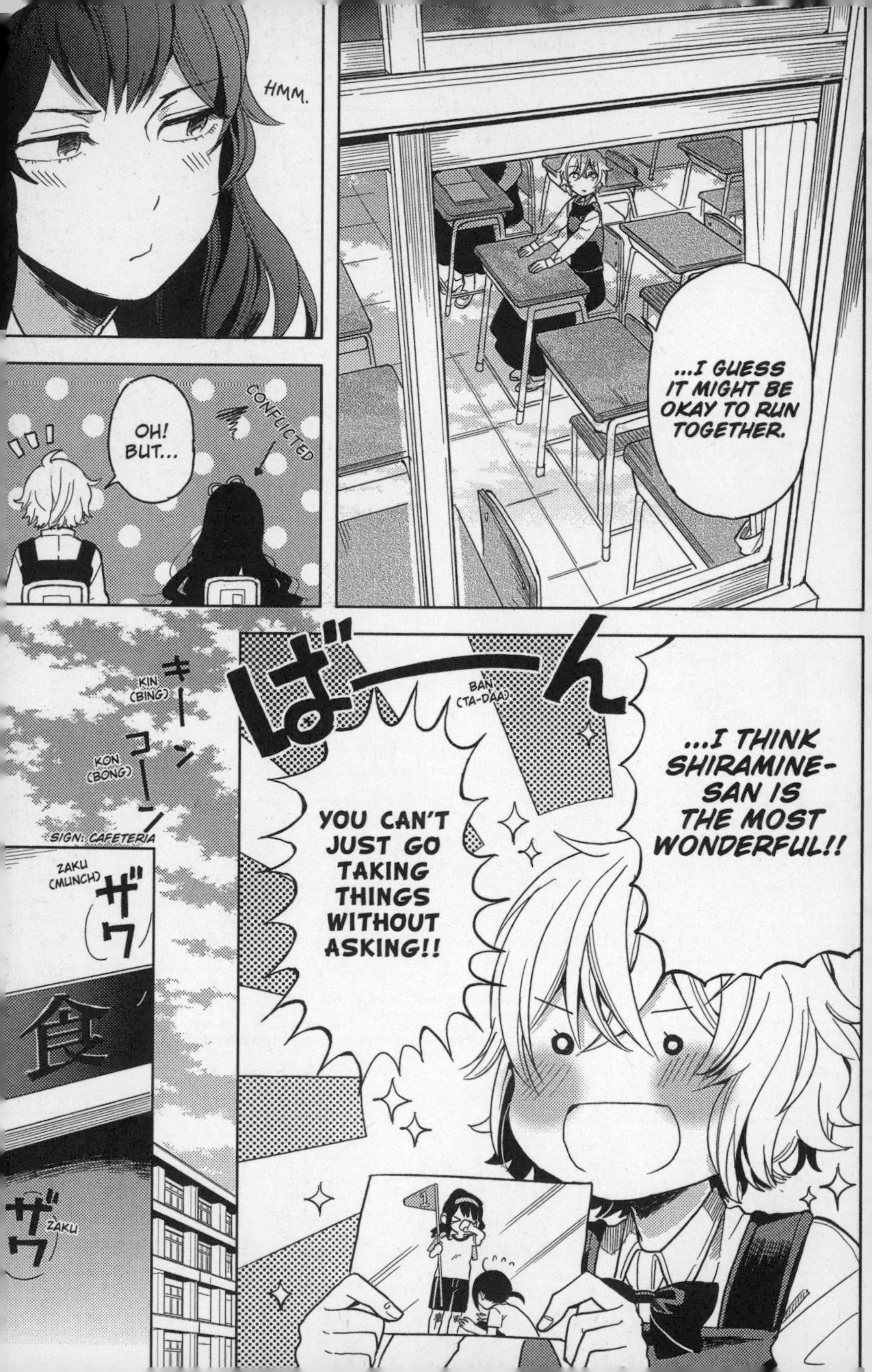
...I GUESS IT MIGHT BE OKAY TO RUN TOGETHER.
HMM.
OH! BUT...
CONFLICTED
ばーーん
BAN (TA-DAA)
...I THINK SHIRAMINE-SAN IS THE MOST WONDERFUL!!
YOU CAN'T JUST GO TAKING THINGS WITHOUT ASKING!!
キーン
KIN (BING)
コーン
KON (BONG)
SIGN: CAFETERIA
食
ザク
ZAKU (MUNCH)
ザク
ZAKU

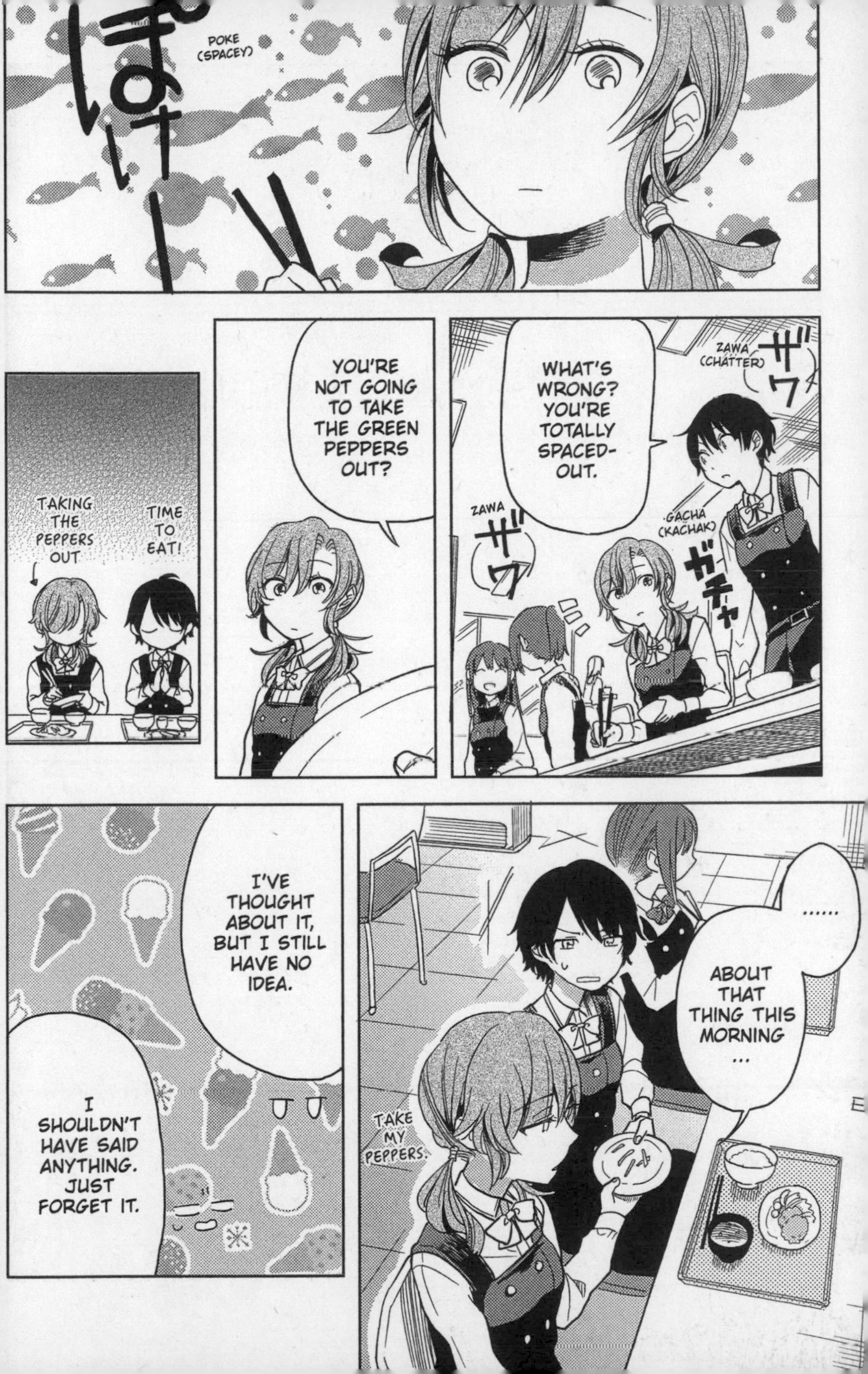
ぽけー
POKE (SPACEY)
ZAWA (CHATTER)
ザワ
WHAT'S WRONG? YOU'RE TOTALLY SPACED-OUT.
ZAWA
ザワ
GACHA (KACHAK)
ガチャ
YOU'RE NOT GOING TO TAKE THE GREEN PEPPERS OUT?
TIME TO EAT!
TAKING THE PEPPERS OUT
......
ABOUT THAT THING THIS MORNING ...
TAKE MY PEPPERS.
I'VE THOUGHT ABOUT IT, BUT I STILL HAVE NO IDEA.
I SHOULDN'T HAVE SAID ANYTHING. JUST FORGET IT.

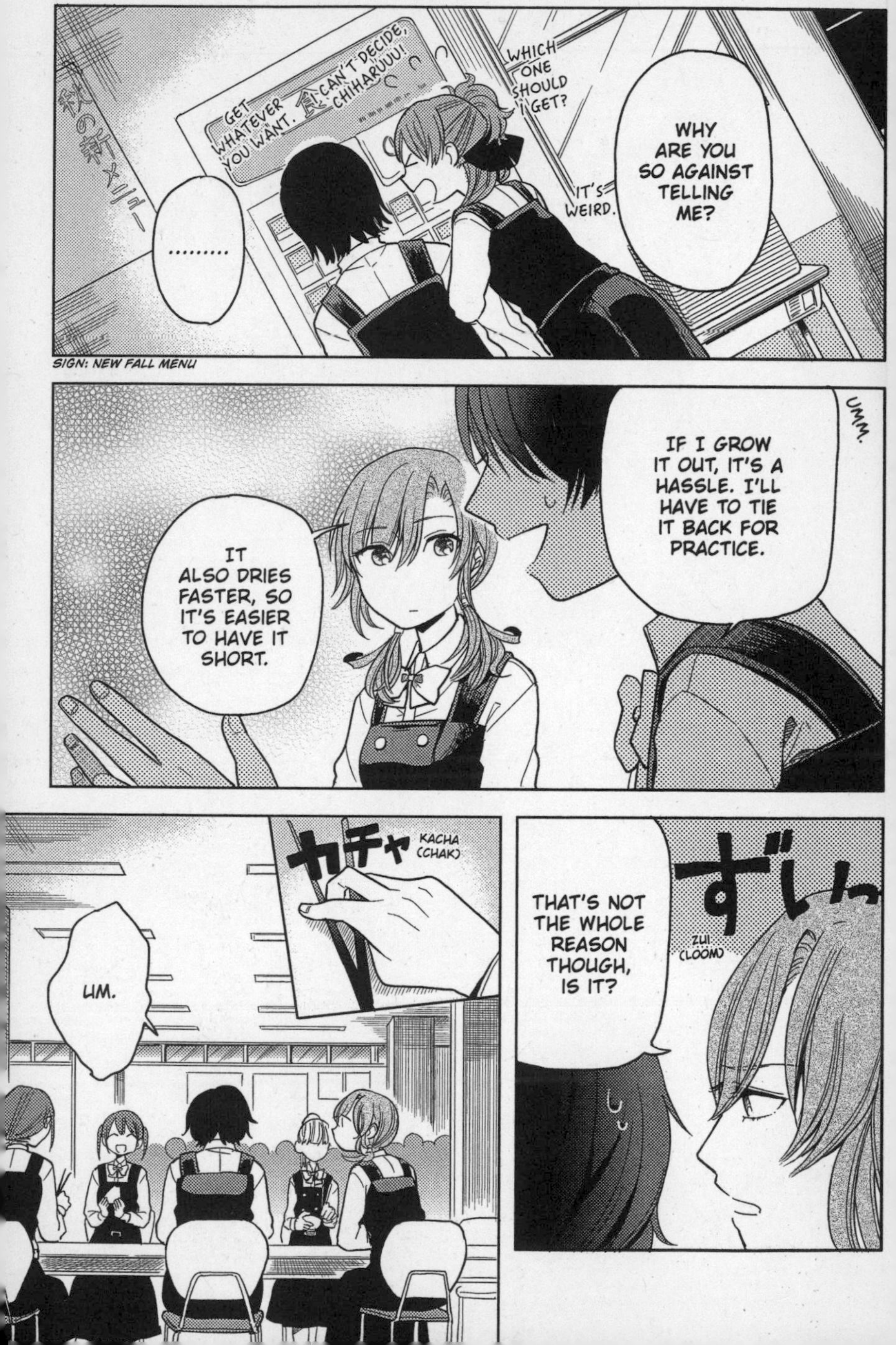
WHY ARE YOU SO AGAINST TELLING ME?
IT'S WEIRD.
WHICH ONE SHOULD I GET?
CAN'T DECIDE, CHIHARUUU!
GET WHATEVER YOU WANT.
秋の新メニュー
食
....
SIGN: NEW FALL MENU
UMM.
IF I GROW IT OUT, IT'S A HASSLE. I'LL HAVE TO TIE IT BACK FOR PRACTICE.
IT ALSO DRIES FASTER, SO IT'S EASIER TO HAVE IT SHORT.
ずいっ
ZUI (LOOM)
THAT'S NOT THE WHOLE REASON THOUGH, IS IT?
カチャ
KACHA (CHAK)
UM.

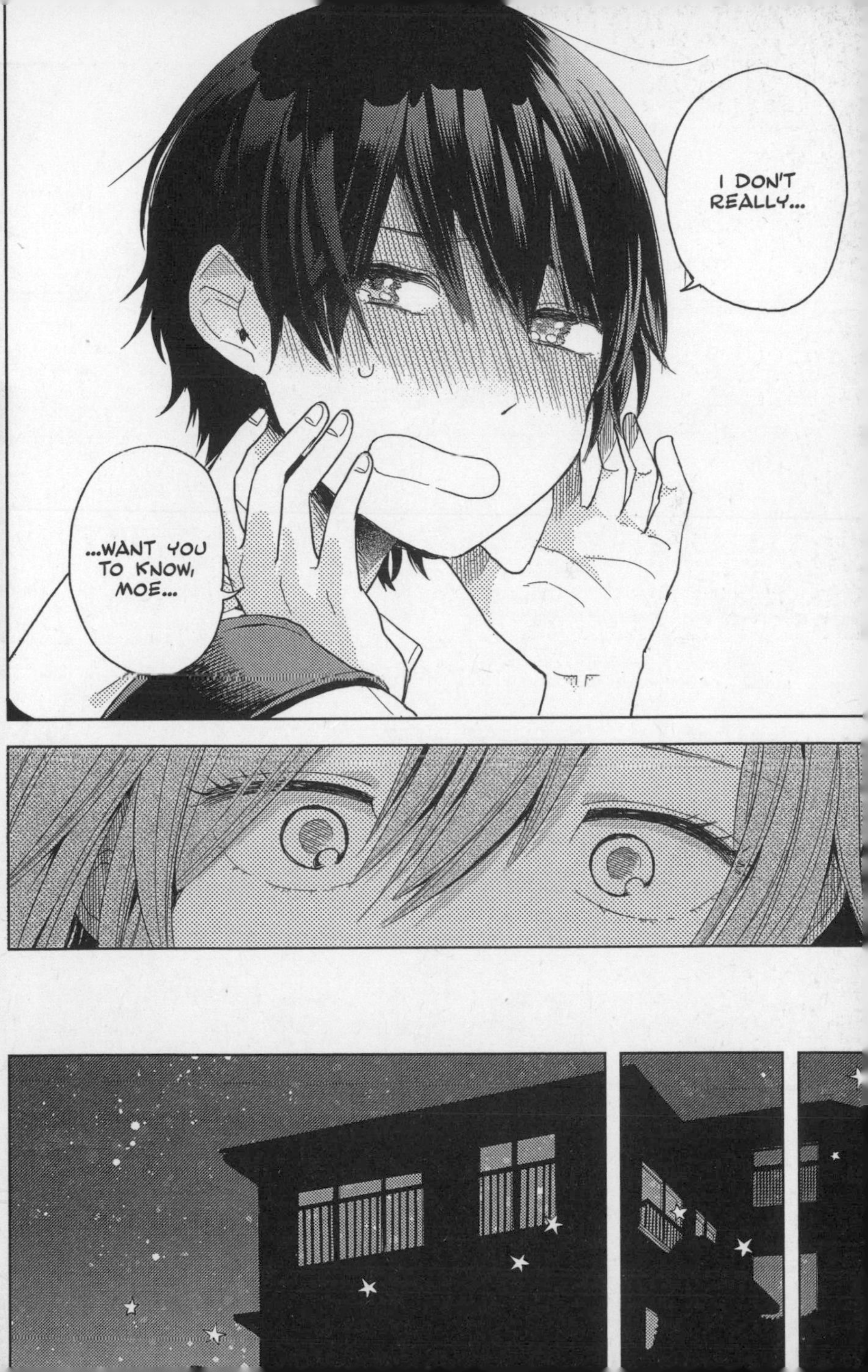
I DON'T REALLY...
...WANT YOU TO KNOW, MOE...

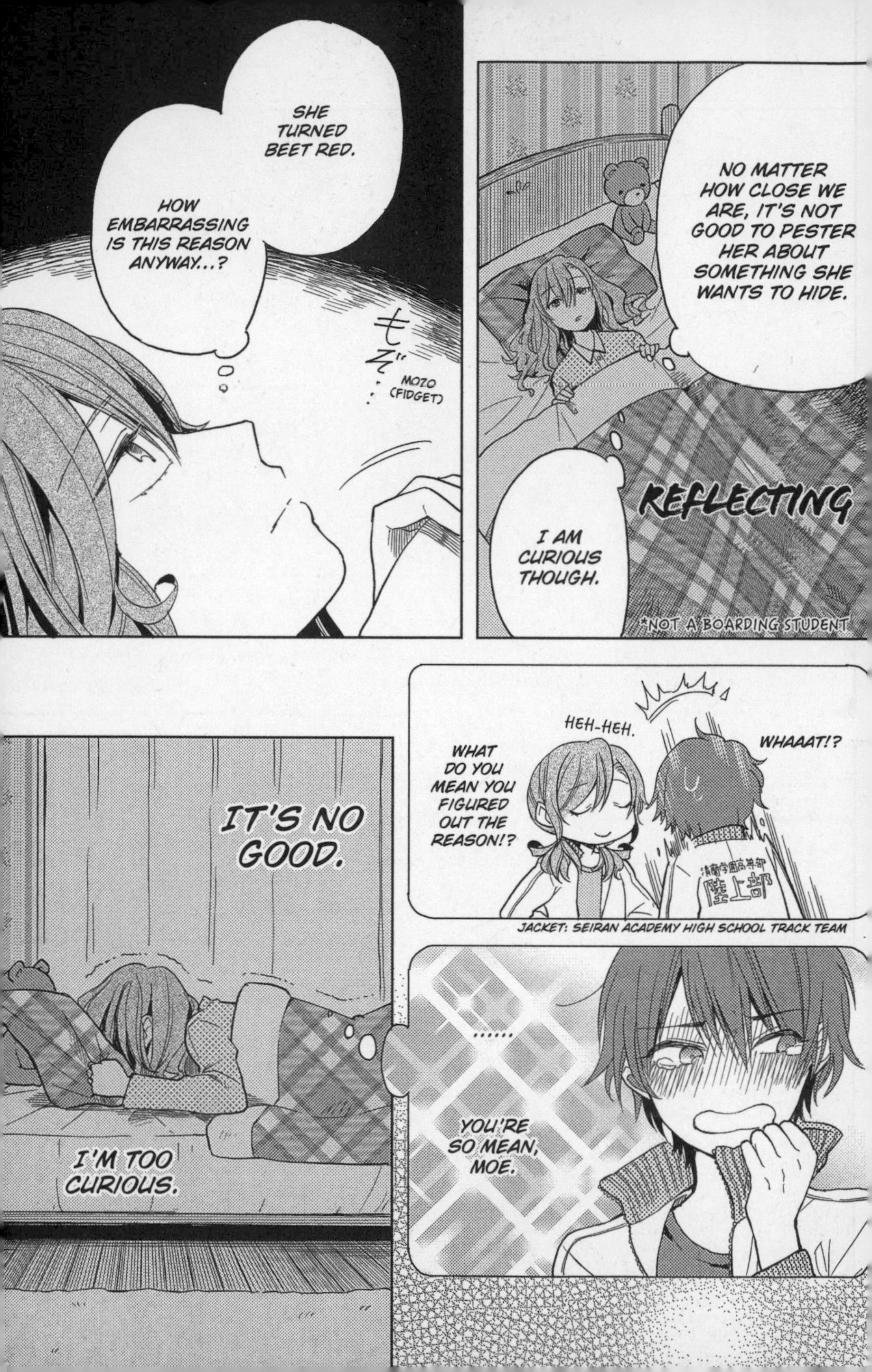
NO MATTER HOW CLOSE WE ARE, IT'S NOT GOOD TO PESTER HER ABOUT SOMETHING SHE WANTS TO HIDE.
REFLECTING
I AM CURIOUS THOUGH.
*NOT A BOARDING STUDENT
SHE TURNED BEET RED.
HOW EMBARRASSING IS THIS REASON ANYWAY...?
もぞ
MOZO (FIDGET)
WHAAAT!?
HEH-HEH.
WHAT DO YOU MEAN YOU FIGURED OUT THE REASON!?
陸上部
JACKET: SEIRAN ACADEMY HIGH SCHOOL TRACK TEAM
......
YOU'RE SO MEAN, MOE.
IT'S NO GOOD.
I'M TOO CURIOUS.

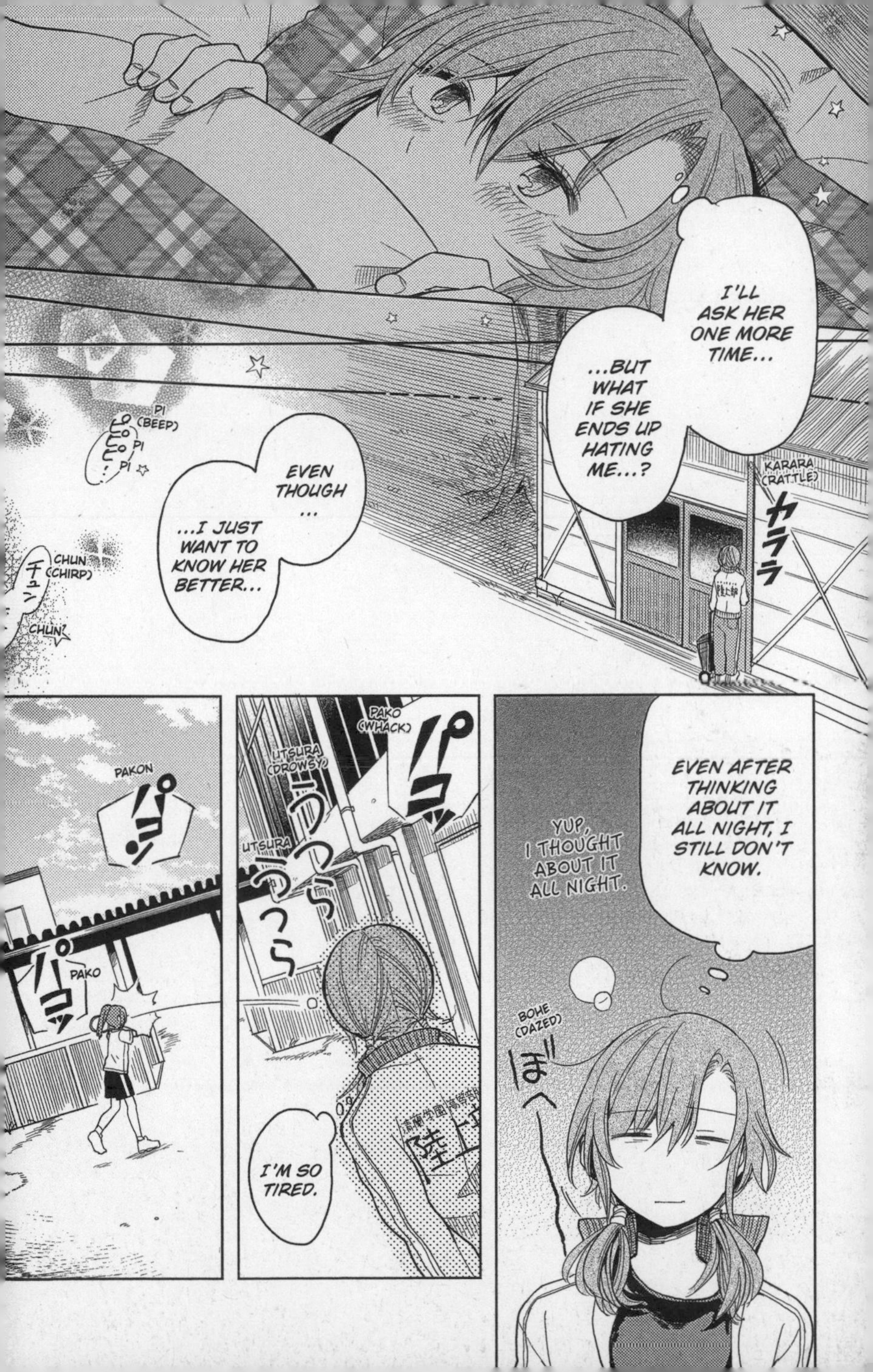
I'LL ASK HER ONE MORE TIME...
...BUT WHAT IF SHE ENDS UP HATING ME...?
KARARA (RATTLE)
カララ
EVEN THOUGH ...
...I JUST WANT TO KNOW HER BETTER...
PI (BEEP) PI PI
CHUN (CHIRP)
CHUN
EVEN AFTER THINKING ABOUT IT ALL NIGHT, I STILL DON'T KNOW.
YUP, I THOUGHT ABOUT IT ALL NIGHT.
BOHE (DAZED)
ぼへ
PAKO (WHACK)
UTSURA (DROWSY)
UTSURA
I'M SO TIRED.
PAKON
PAKO

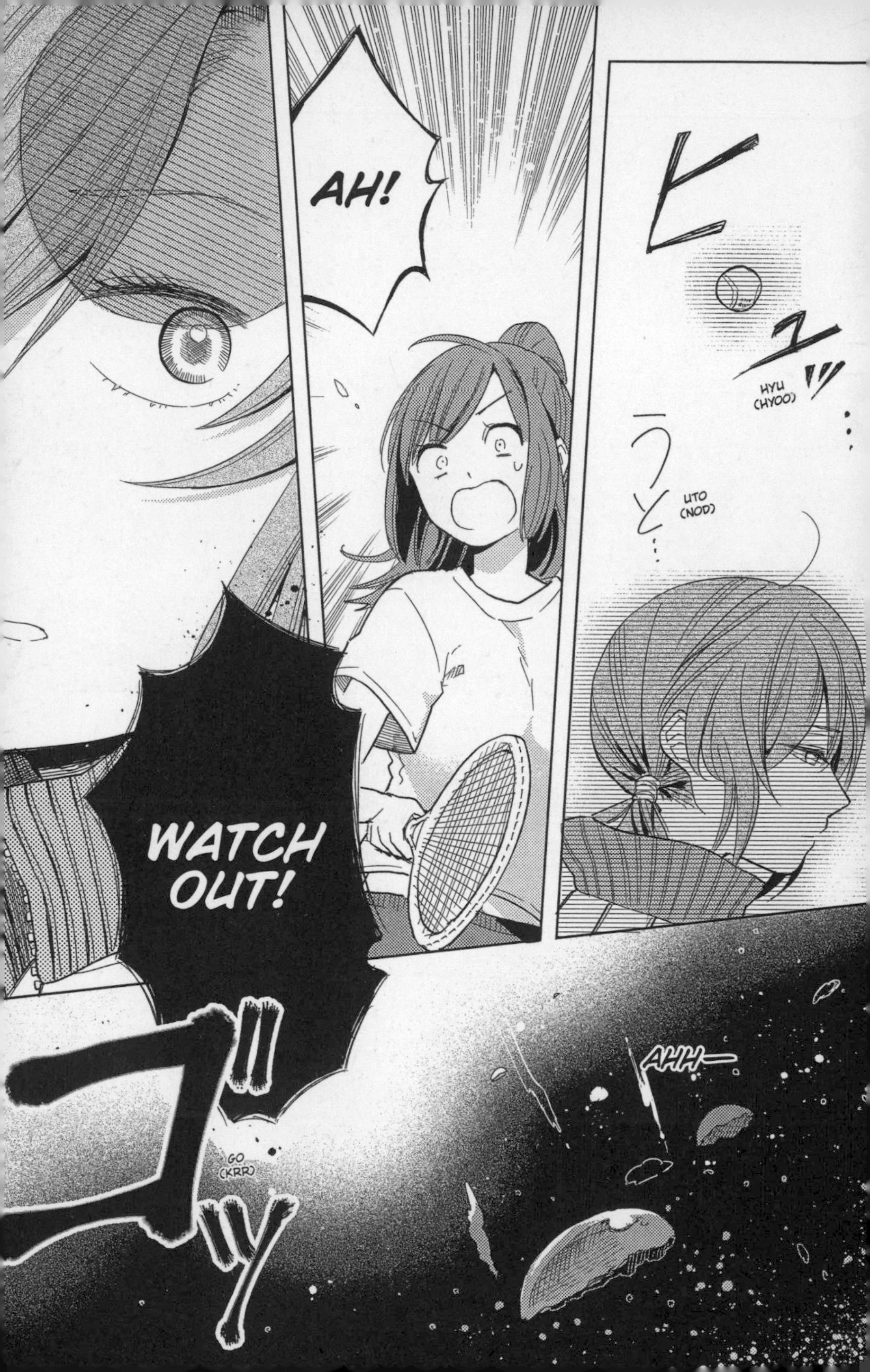
HYU (HYOO)
UTO (NOD)
AH!
WATCH OUT!
AHH—
GO (KRR)

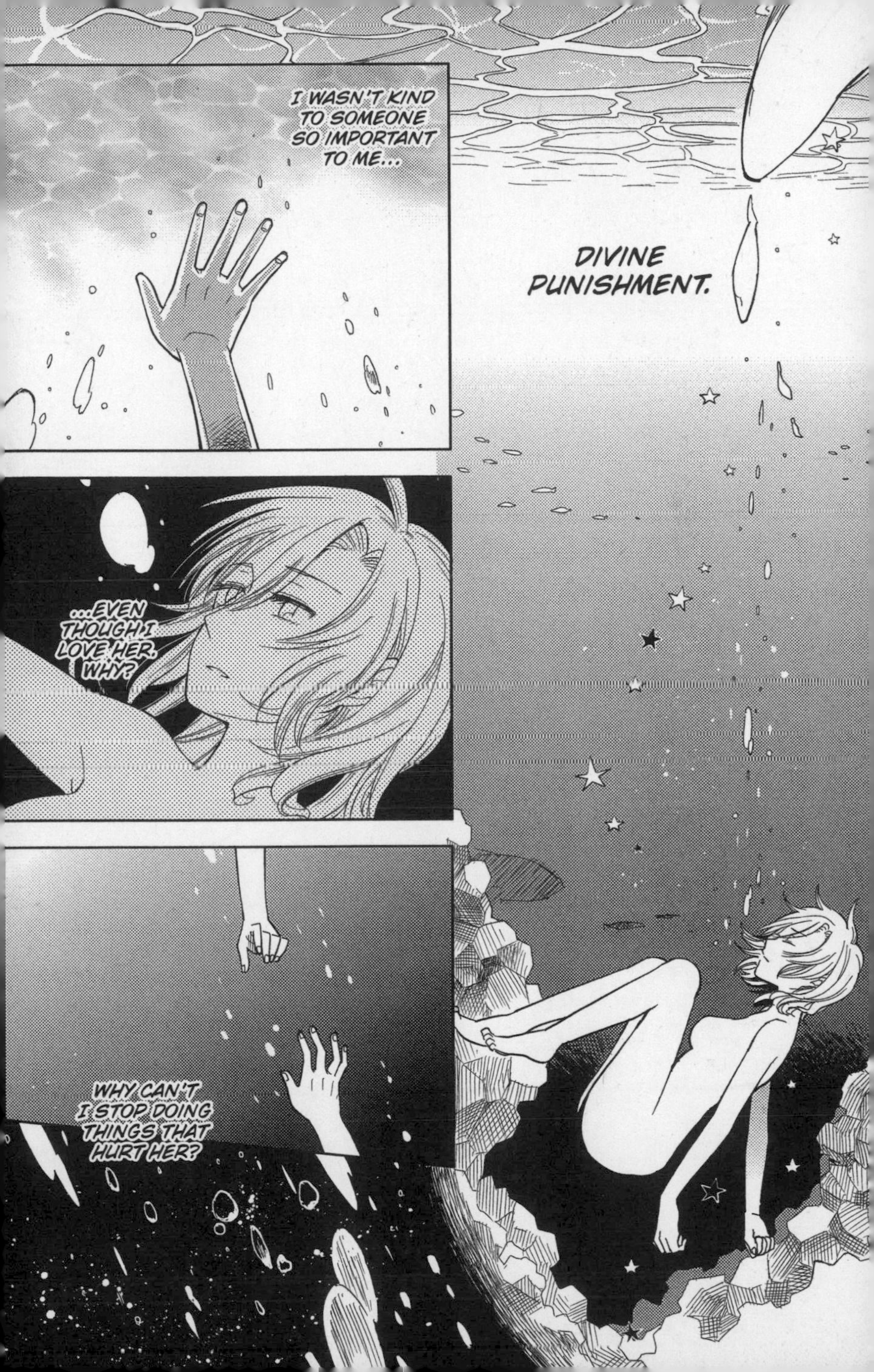
DIVINE PUNISHMENT.
I WASN'T KIND TO SOMEONE SO IMPORTANT TO ME...
...EVEN THOUGH I LOVE HER. WHY?
WHY CAN'T I STOP DOING THINGS THAT HURT HER?

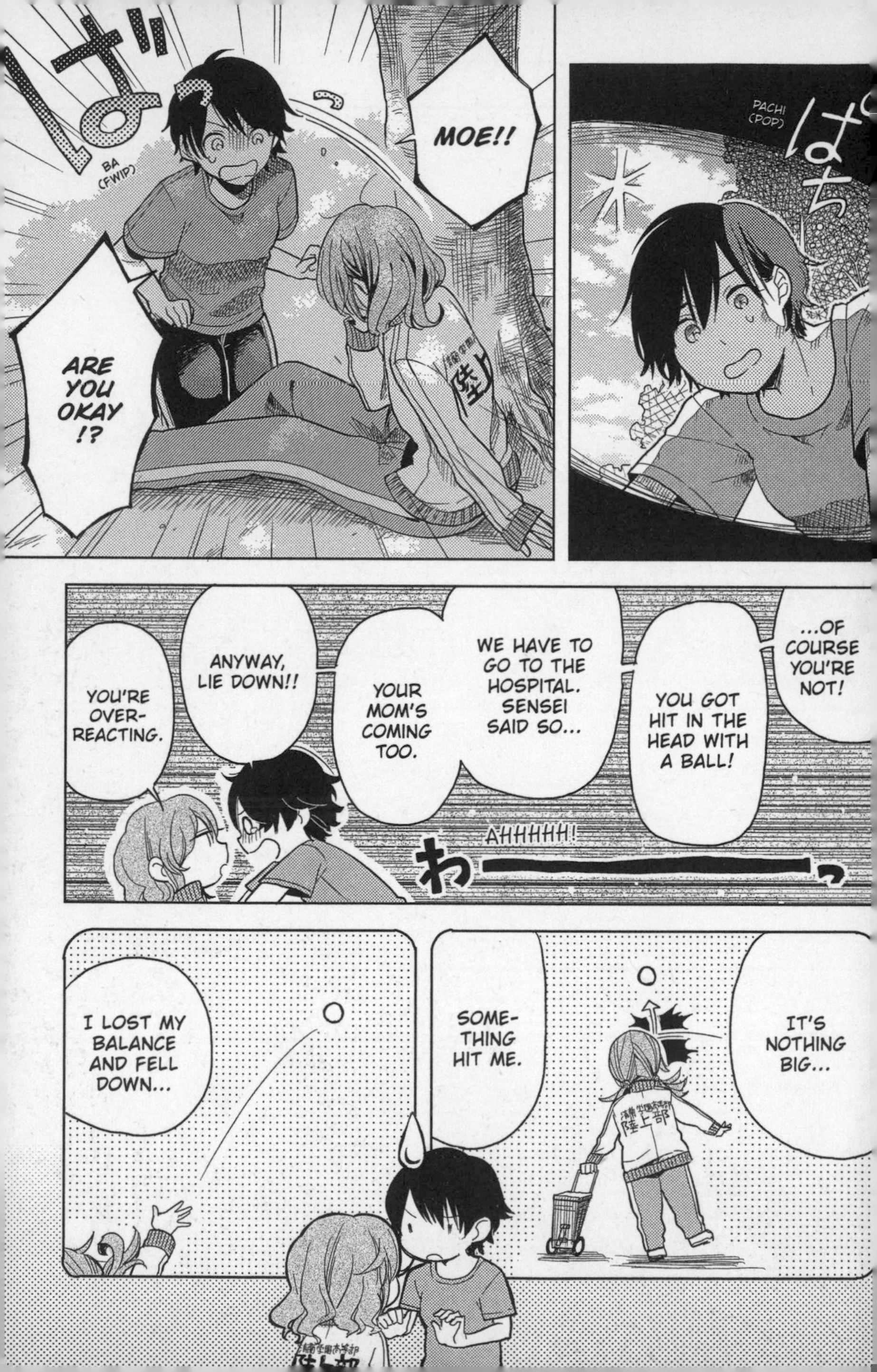
PACHI (POP)
MOE!!
BA (FWIP)
ARE YOU OKAY!?
...OF COURSE YOU'RE NOT!
YOU GOT HIT IN THE HEAD WITH A BALL!
WE HAVE TO GO TO THE HOSPITAL. SENSEI SAID SO...
YOUR MOM'S COMING TOO.
ANYWAY, LIE DOWN!!
AHHHHH!
YOU'RE OVER-REACTING.
IT'S NOTHING BIG...
SOME-THING HIT ME.
I LOST MY BALANCE AND FELL DOWN...

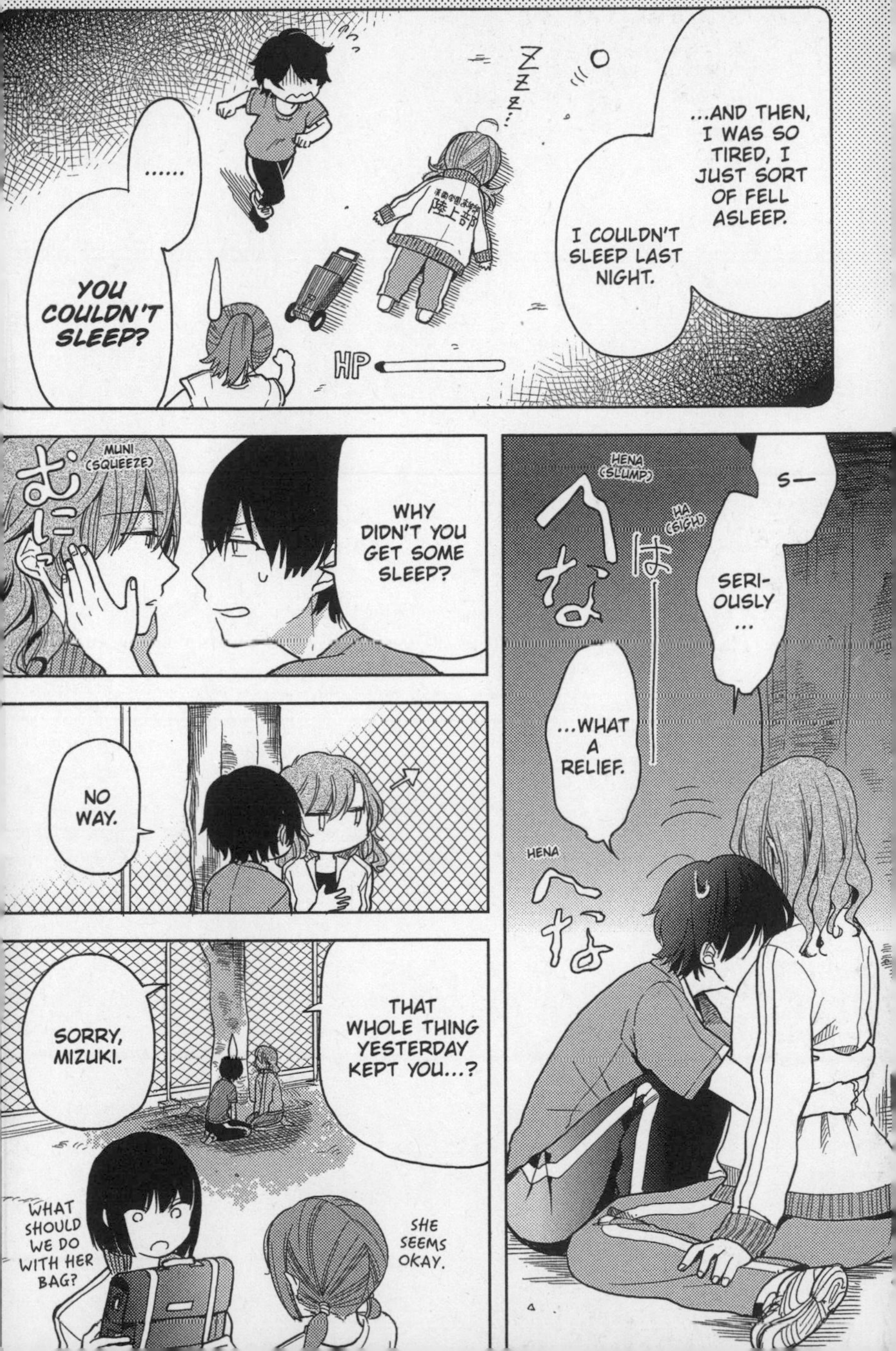
I COULDN'T SLEEP LAST NIGHT.
...AND THEN, I WAS SO TIRED, I JUST SORT OF FELL ASLEEP.
ZZZ...
陸上部
HP
......
YOU COULDN'T SLEEP?
S—
SERI-OUSLY...
HENA (SLUMP)
へな
HA (SIGH)
はー
...WHAT A RELIEF.
HENA
へな
MUNI (SQUEEZE)
むに
WHY DIDN'T YOU GET SOME SLEEP?
NO WAY.
THAT WHOLE THING YESTERDAY KEPT YOU...?
SORRY, MIZUKI.
SHE SEEMS OKAY.
WHAT SHOULD WE DO WITH HER BAG?

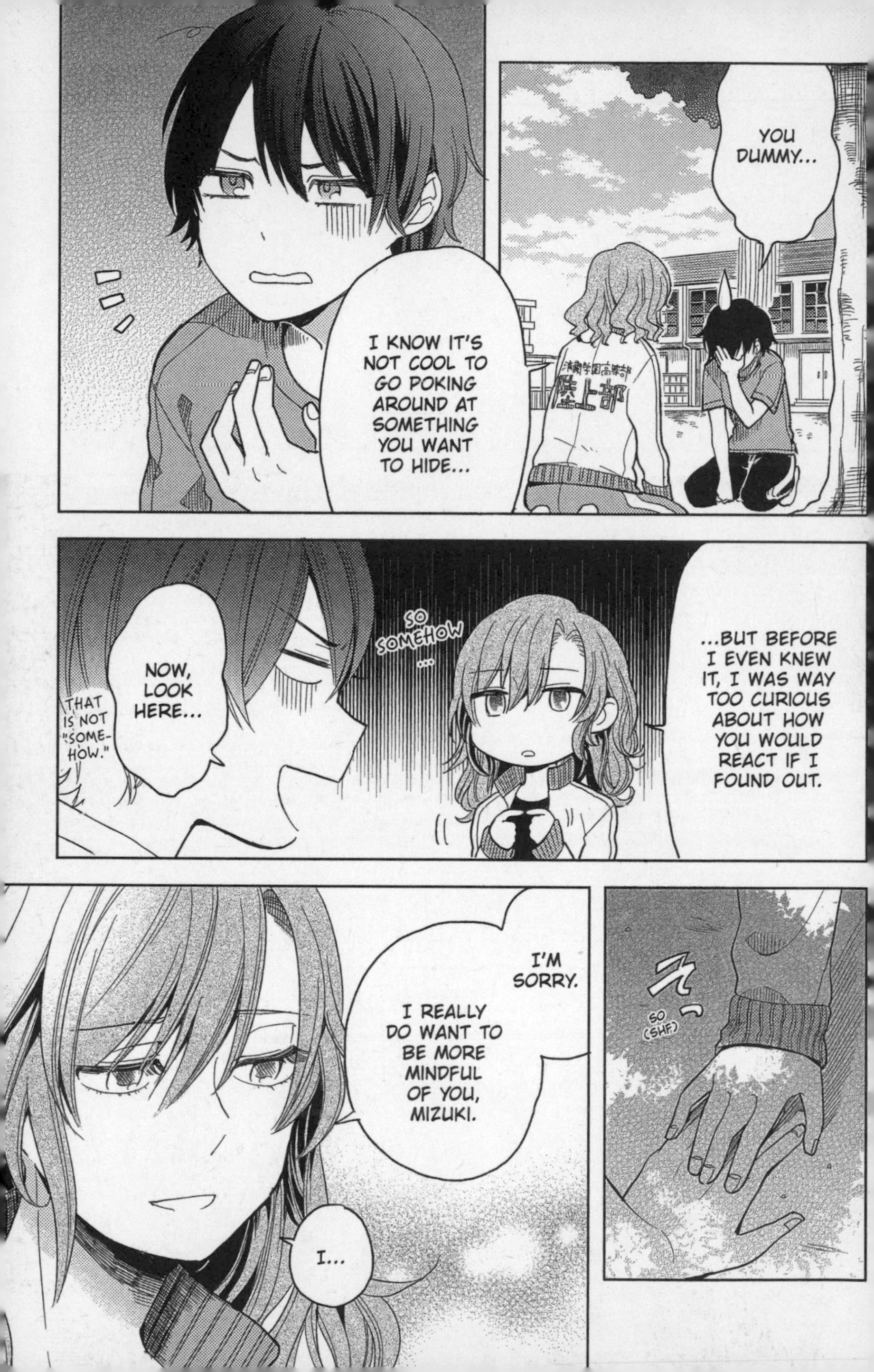
YOU DUMMY...
I KNOW IT'S NOT COOL TO GO POKING AROUND AT SOMETHING YOU WANT TO HIDE...
...BUT BEFORE I EVEN KNEW IT, I WAS WAY TOO CURIOUS ABOUT HOW YOU WOULD REACT IF I FOUND OUT.
SO SOMEHOW...
NOW, LOOK HERE...
THAT IS NOT "SOME-HOW."
SO (SHF)
I'M SORRY.
I REALLY DO WANT TO BE MORE MINDFUL OF YOU, MIZUKI.
I...

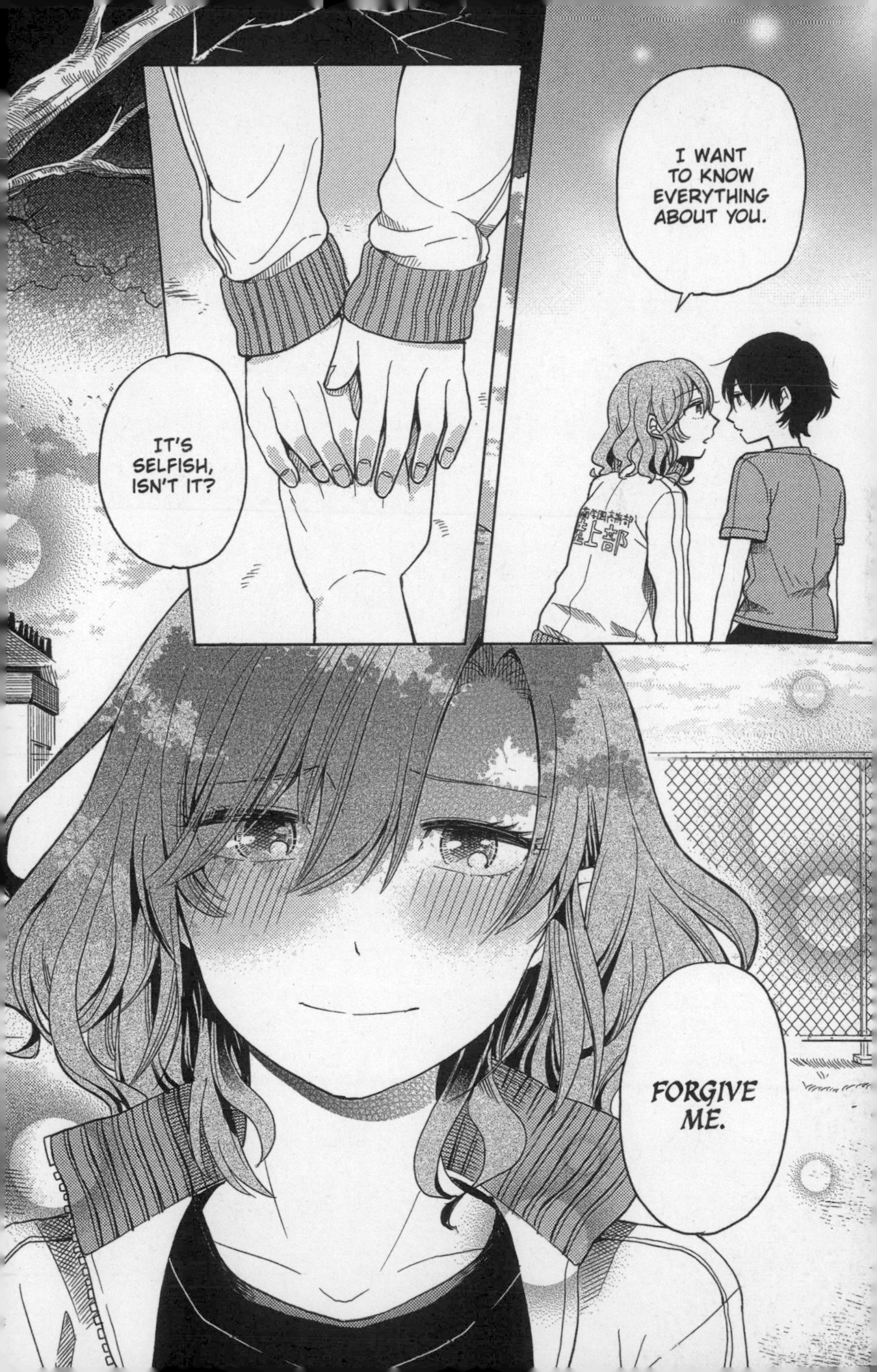
I WANT TO KNOW EVERYTHING ABOUT YOU.
IT'S SELFISH, ISN'T IT?
FORGIVE ME.

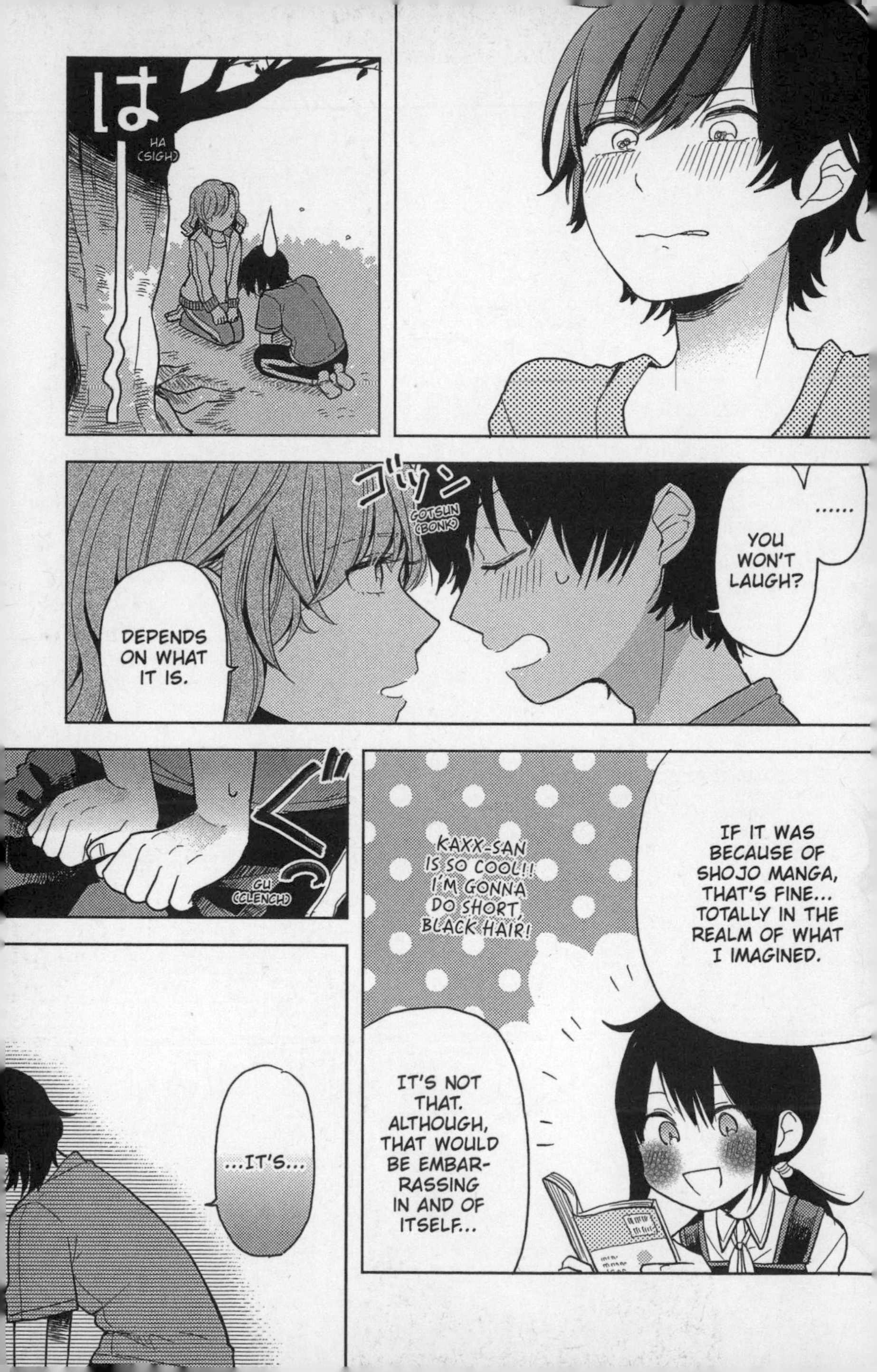

は
HA (SIGH)
......
YOU WON'T LAUGH?
ゴツン
GOTSUN (BONK)
DEPENDS ON WHAT IT IS.
IF IT WAS BECAUSE OF SHOJO MANGA, THAT'S FINE... TOTALLY IN THE REALM OF WHAT I IMAGINED.
KAXX-SAN IS SO COOL!! I'M GONNA DO SHORT, BLACK HAIR!
IT'S NOT THAT. ALTHOUGH, THAT WOULD BE EMBARRASSING IN AND OF ITSELF...
ぐっ
GU (CLENCH)
...IT'S...

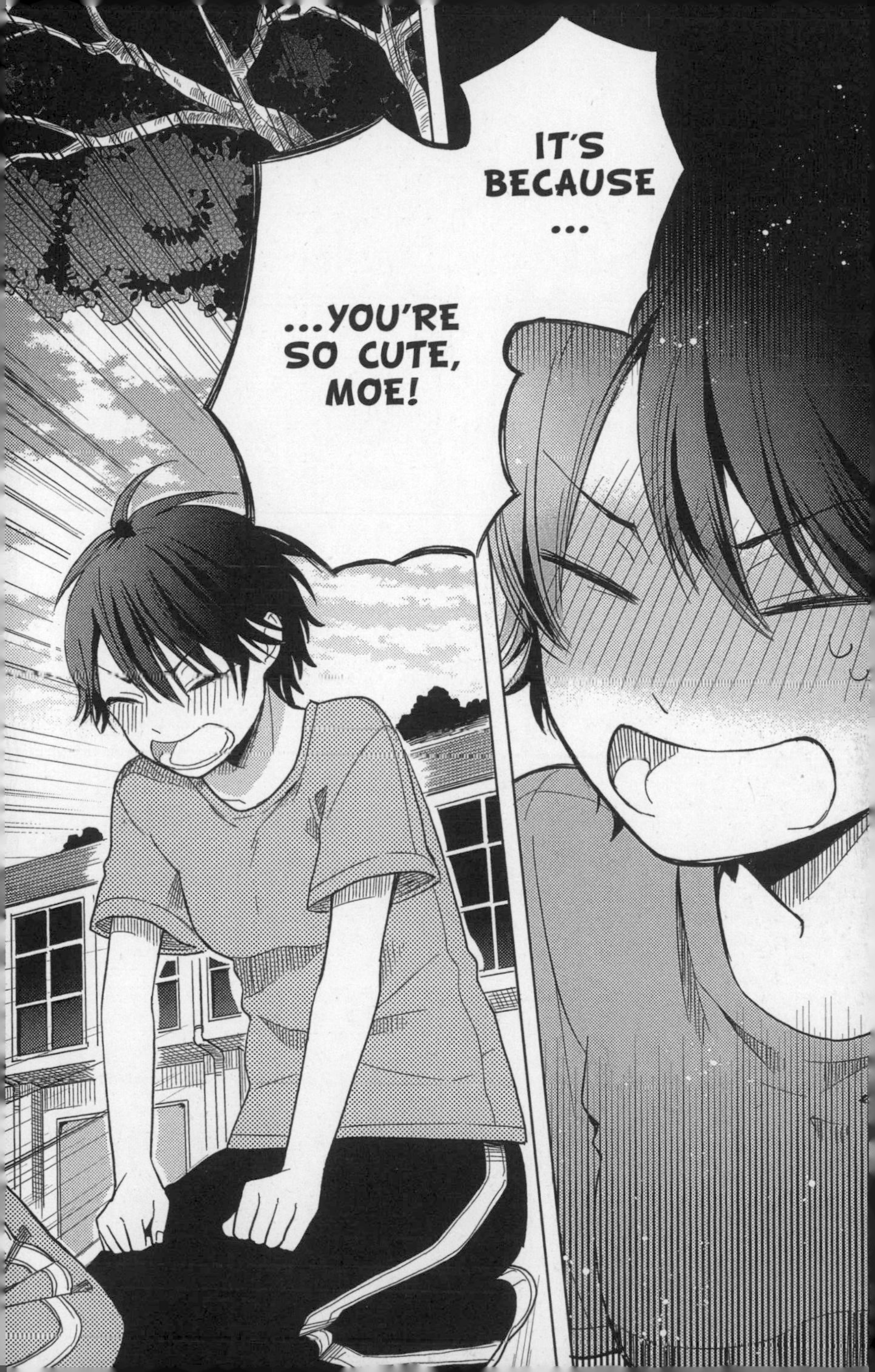
IT'S BECAUSE ...
...YOU'RE SO CUTE, MOE!

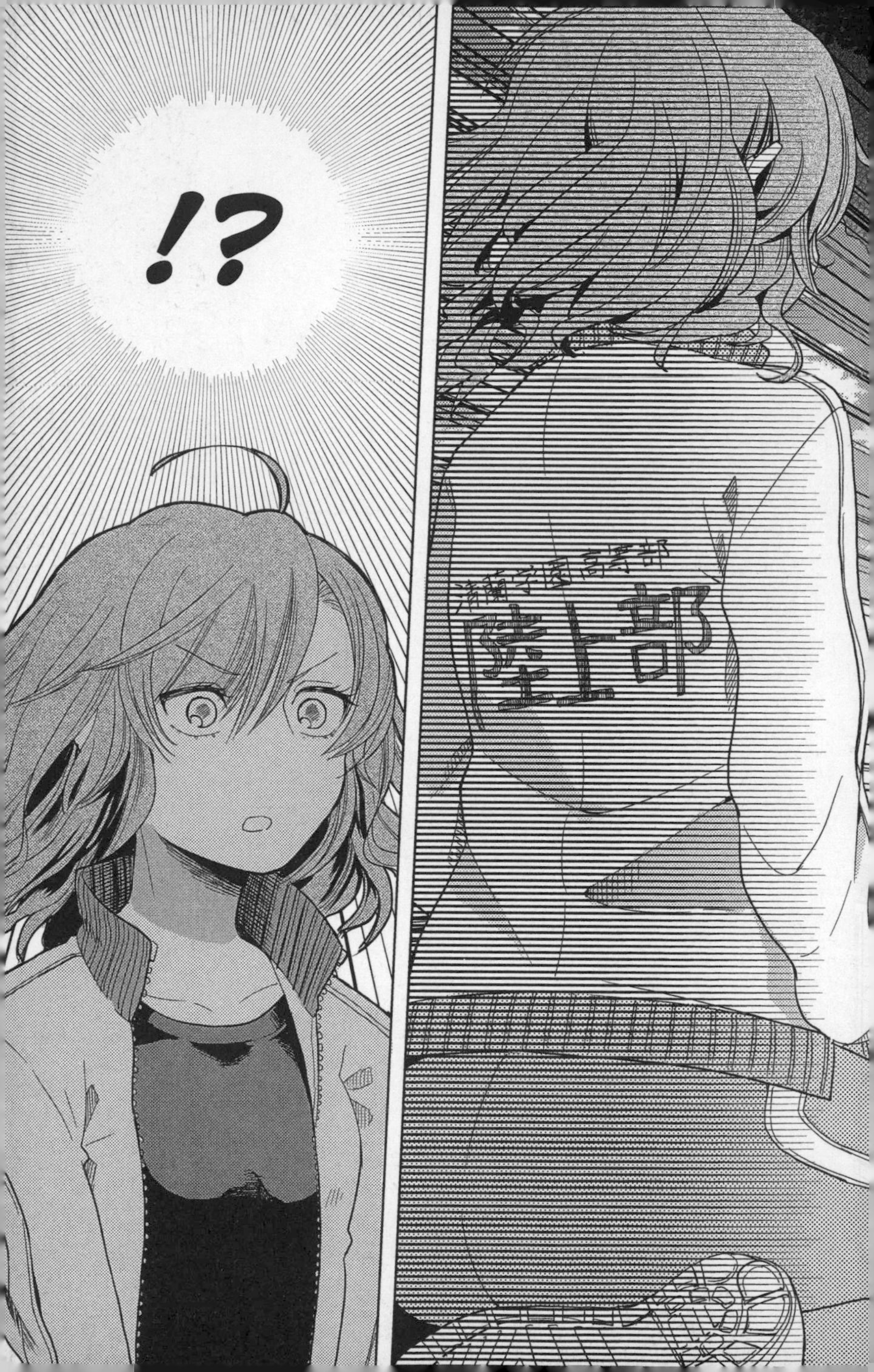
陸上部
!?

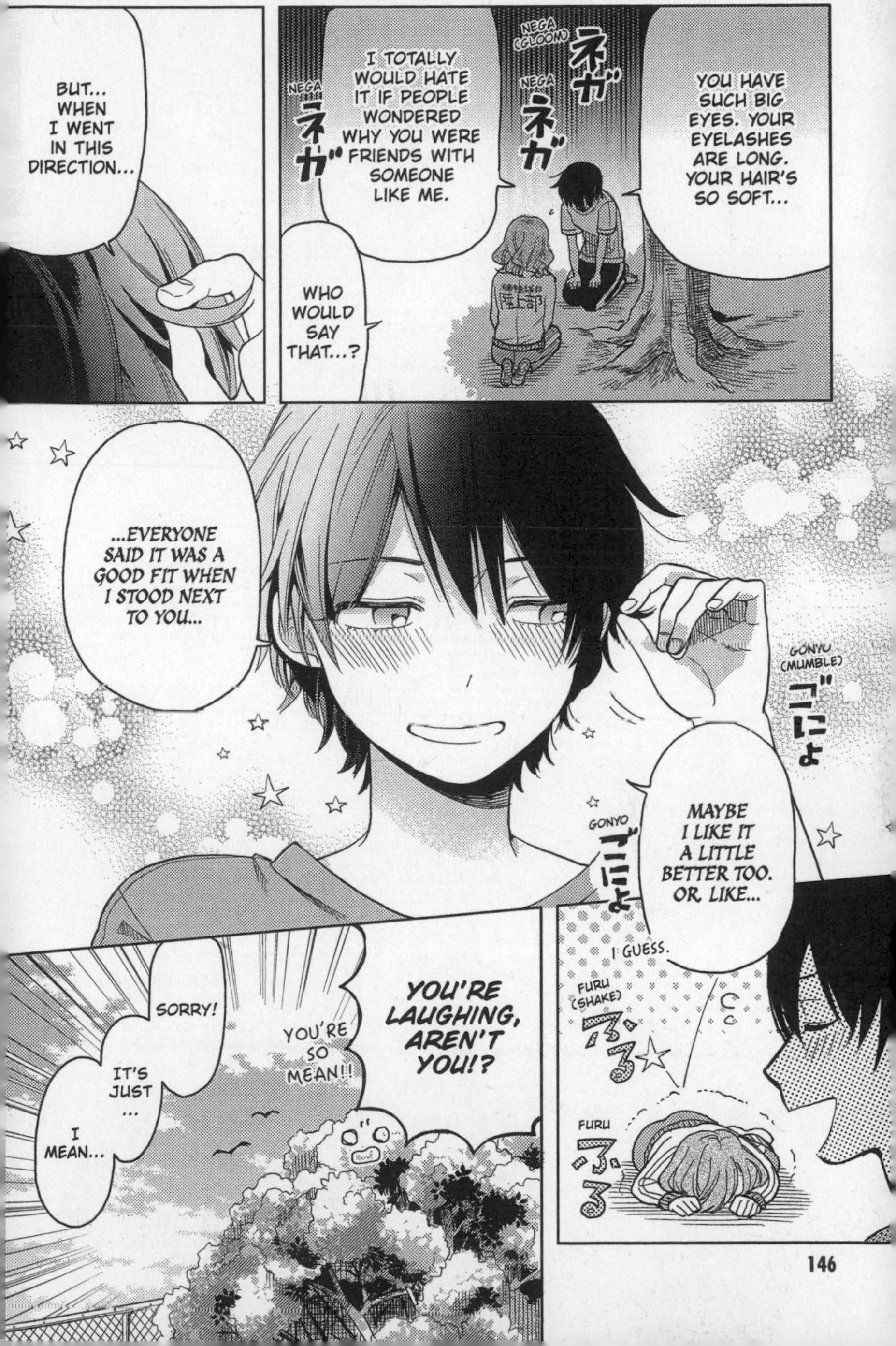
YOU HAVE SUCH BIG EYES. YOUR EYELASHES ARE LONG. YOUR HAIR'S SO SOFT...
NEGA (GLOOM) ネガ
NEGA ネガ
I TOTALLY WOULD HATE IT IF PEOPLE WONDERED WHY YOU WERE FRIENDS WITH SOMEONE LIKE ME.
NEGA ネガ
WHO WOULD SAY THAT...?
BUT... WHEN I WENT IN THIS DIRECTION...
...EVERYONE SAID IT WAS A GOOD FIT WHEN I STOOD NEXT TO YOU...
GONYU (MUMBLE) ごにょ
MAYBE I LIKE IT A LITTLE BETTER TOO. OR LIKE...
GONYO ごにょ
I GUESS.
FURU (SHAKE) ふる
FURU ふる
YOU'RE LAUGHING, AREN'T YOU!?
YOU'RE SO MEAN!!
SORRY!
IT'S JUST...
I MEAN...

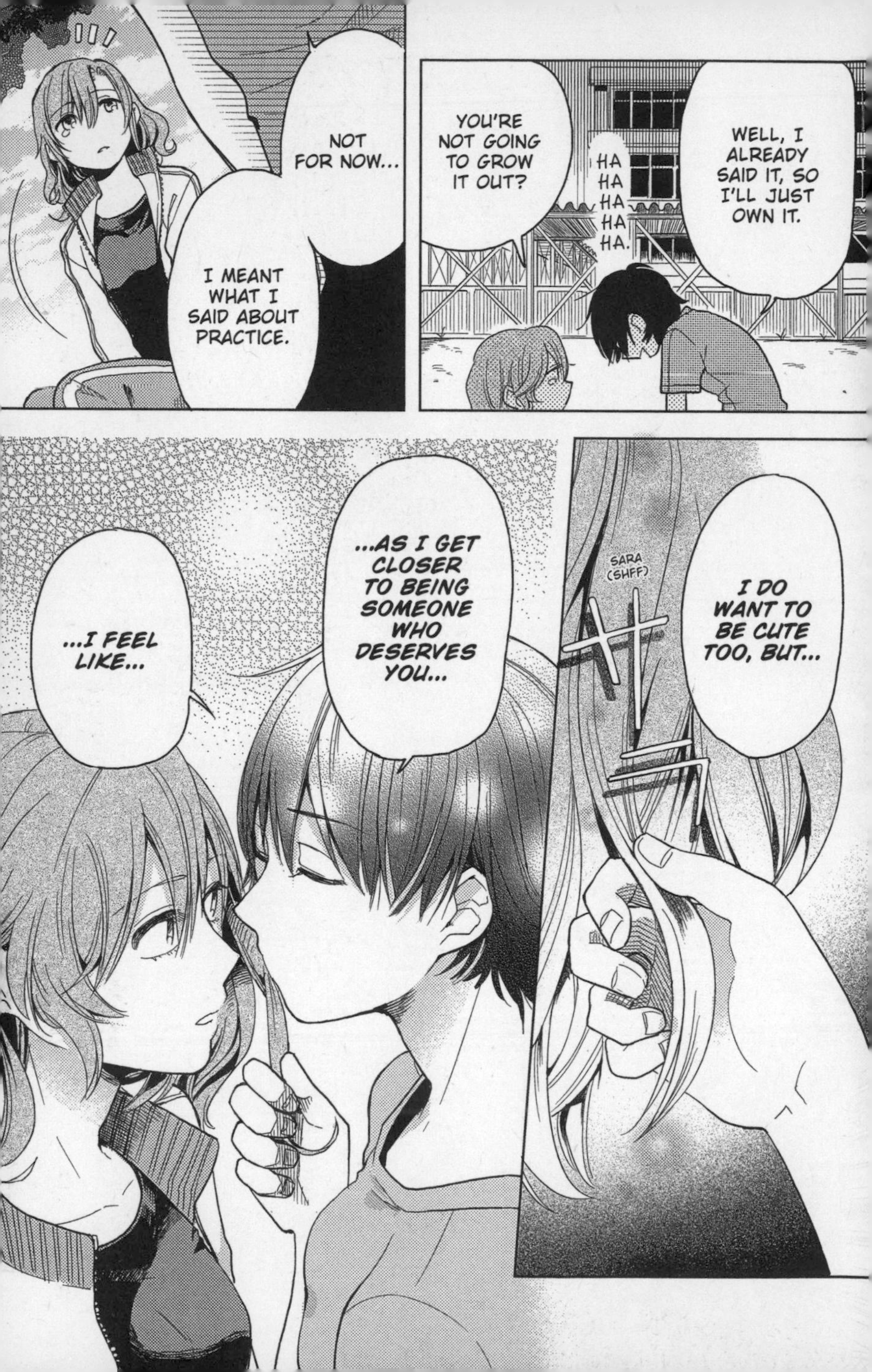
WELL, I ALREADY SAID IT, SO I'LL JUST OWN IT.
HA HA HA HA HA.
YOU'RE NOT GOING TO GROW IT OUT?
NOT FOR NOW...
I MEANT WHAT I SAID ABOUT PRACTICE.
SARA (SHFF)
I DO WANT TO BE CUTE TOO, BUT...
...AS I GET CLOSER TO BEING SOMEONE WHO DESERVES YOU...
...I FEEL LIKE...

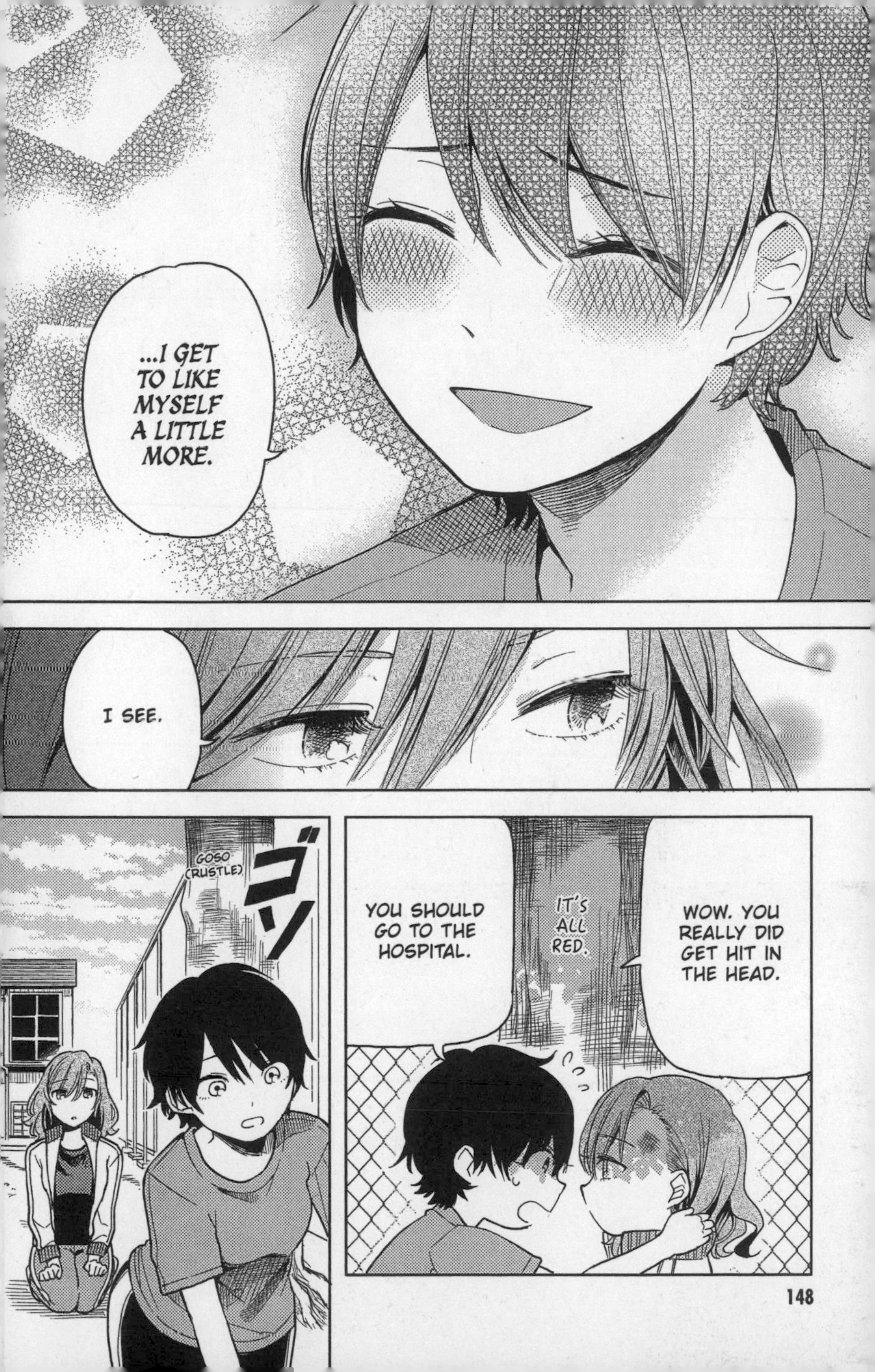
...I GET TO LIKE MYSELF A LITTLE MORE.
I SEE.
WOW. YOU REALLY DID GET HIT IN THE HEAD.
IT'S ALL RED.
YOU SHOULD GO TO THE HOSPITAL.
ゴソ
GOSO (RUSTLE)

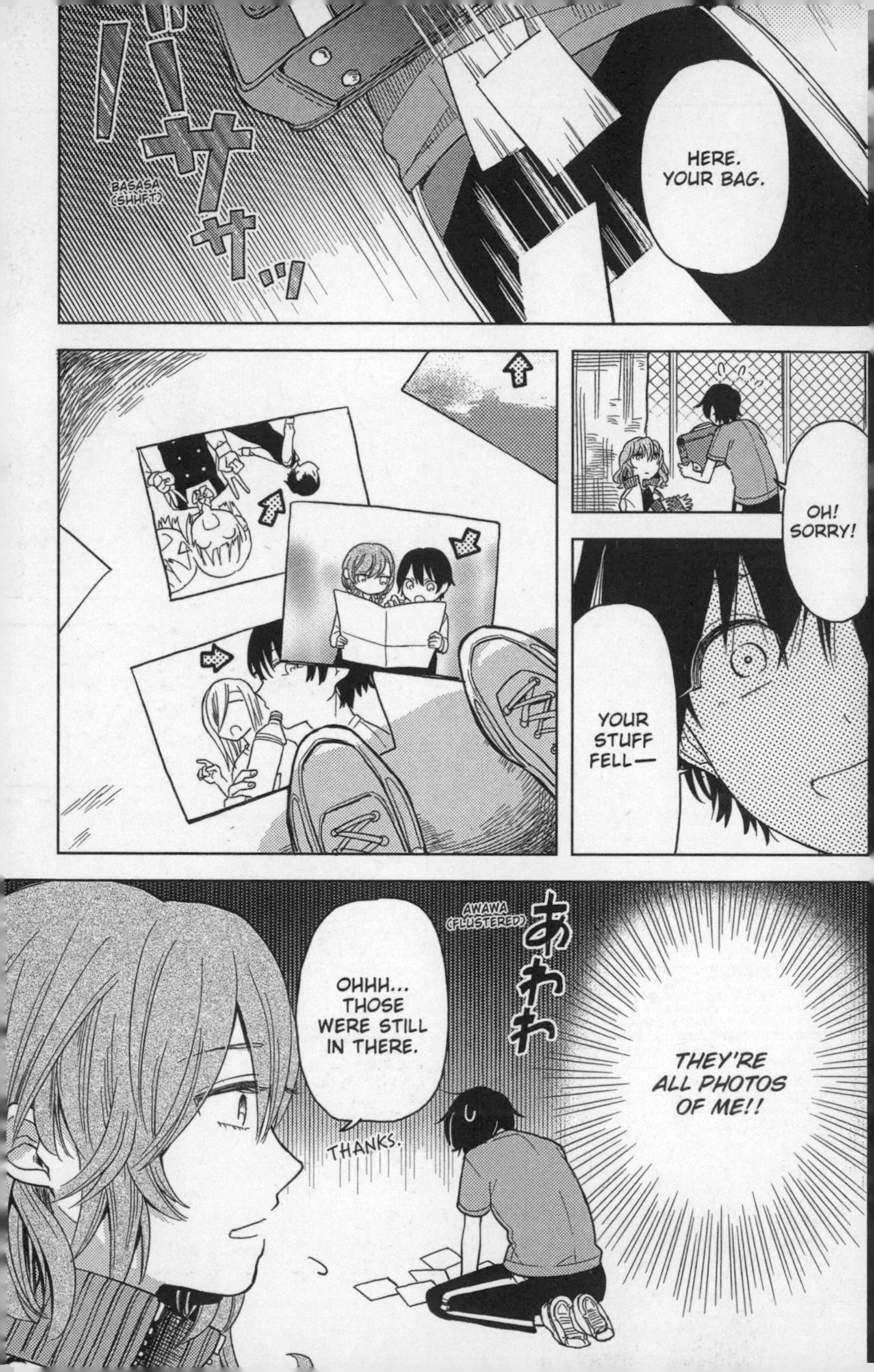
HERE. YOUR BAG.
BASASA (SHHFT)
OH! SORRY!
YOUR STUFF FELL—
THEY'RE ALL PHOTOS OF ME!!
AWAWA (FLUSTERED)
OHHH... THOSE WERE STILL IN THERE.
THANKS.

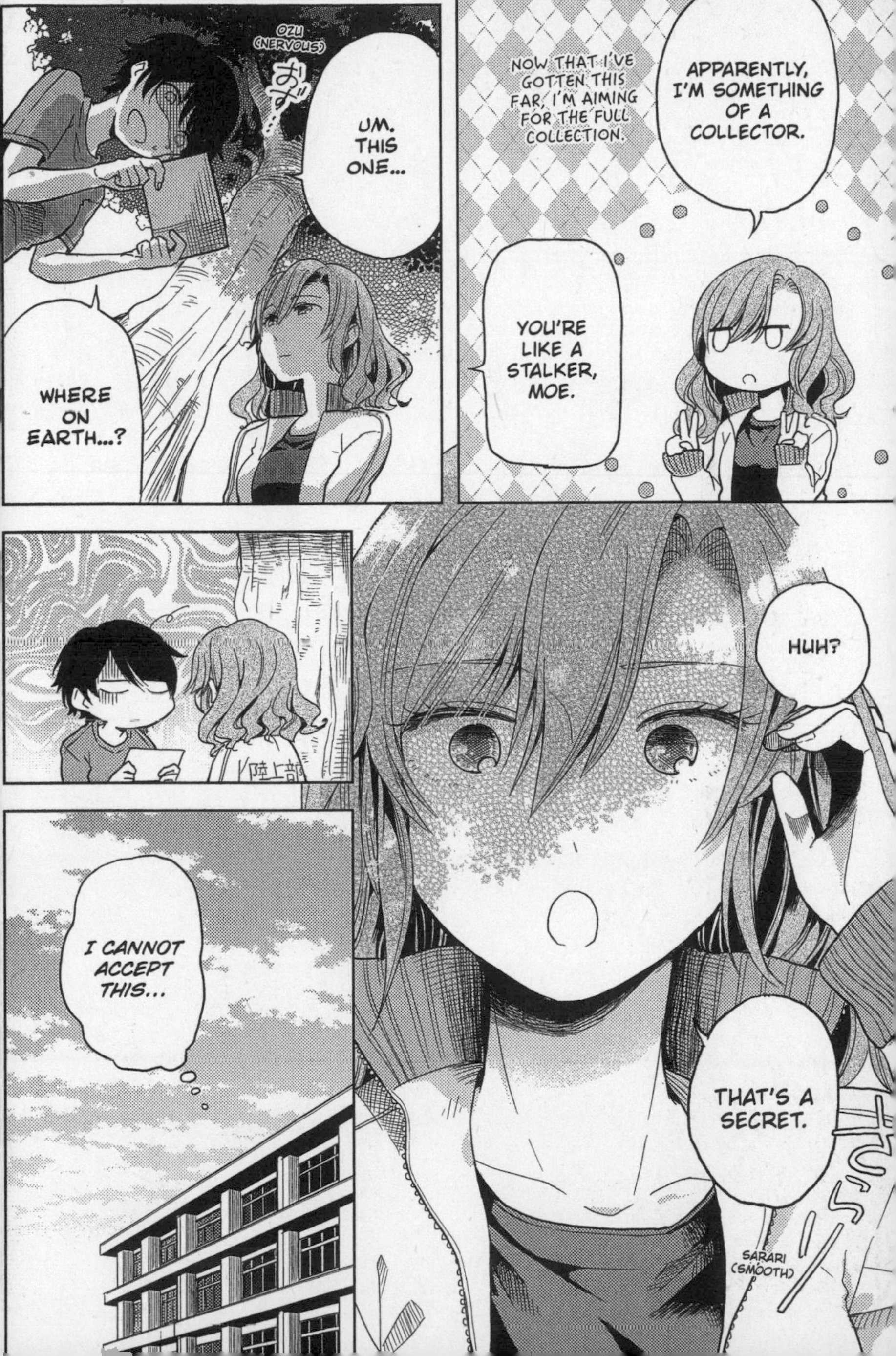
APPARENTLY, I'M SOMETHING OF A COLLECTOR.
NOW THAT I'VE GOTTEN THIS FAR, I'M AIMING FOR THE FULL COLLECTION.
YOU'RE LIKE A STALKER, MOE.
OZU (NERVOUS)
UM. THIS ONE...
WHERE ON EARTH...?
HUH?
THAT'S A SECRET.
SARARI (SMOOTH)
陸上部
I CANNOT ACCEPT THIS...

When It Rains, It Pours

RURI
FIRST-YEAR, CLASS D
TRACK TEAM ALTERNATE
BROUGHT UP LIKE A PRINCESS
AND CALM, BUT A BIT CHILDISH

YAKUMO
FIRST-YEAR, CLASS A
SHORT-DISTANCE RUNNER
THE OLDEST OF FIVE CHILDREN,
SHE IS GENTLE TO THE CORE

KISS THEATER: WHAT'S BEHIND THE STORY!?

PEOPLE OTHER THAN THE MAIN CHARACTERS HAVE STORIES TOO. HERE, WE PRESENT THE "LITTLE LOVE" STORIES HAPPENING BEHIND THE SCENES.

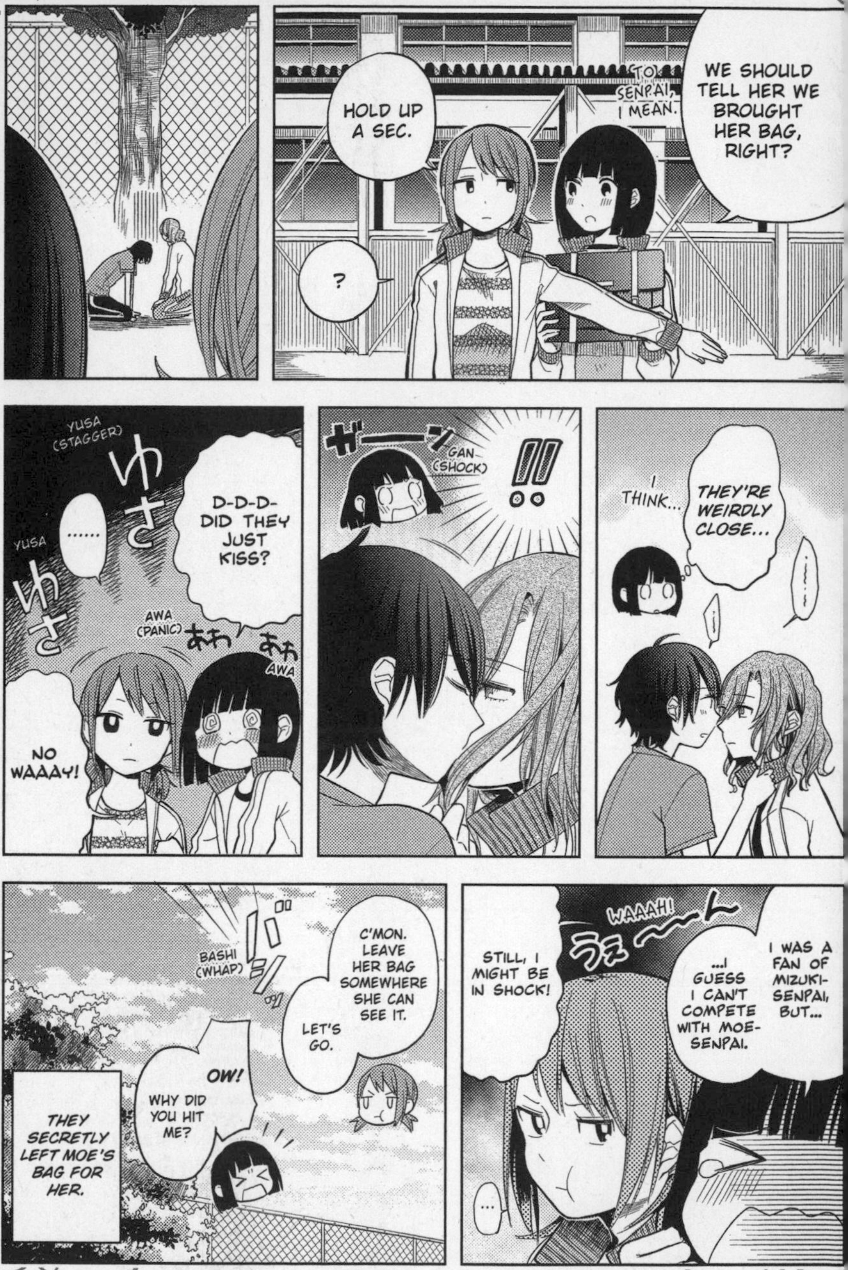
WE SHOULD TELL HER WE BROUGHT HER BAG, RIGHT?
TO SENPAI, I MEAN.
HOLD UP A SEC.
?
THEY'RE WEIRDLY CLOSE...
I THINK...
ガーーン
GAN (SHOCK)
!!
ゆさ
YUSA (STAGGER)
D-D-D-DID THEY JUST KISS?
ゆさ
YUSA
......
あわ
AWA (PANIC)
あわ
AWA
NO WAAAY!
I WAS A FAN OF MIZUKI-SENPAI, BUT...
...I GUESS I CAN'T COMPETE WITH MOE-SENPAI.
うぇ〜〜ん
WAAAH!
STILL, I MIGHT BE IN SHOCK!
...
C'MON. LEAVE HER BAG SOMEWHERE SHE CAN SEE IT.
LET'S GO.
バシッ
BASHI (WHAP)
OW!
WHY DID YOU HIT ME?
THEY SECRETLY LEFT MOE'S BAG FOR HER.

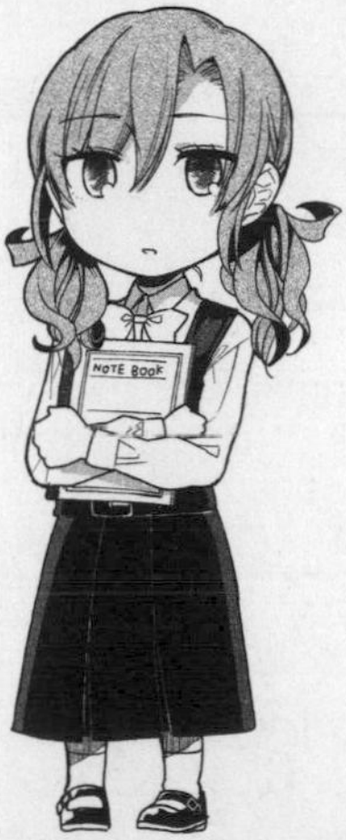
NOTE BOOK

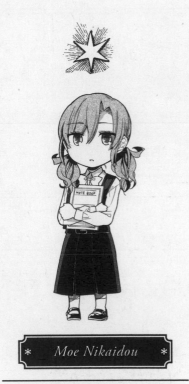

* Moe Nikaidou *

Moe Nikaidou

Second-year at the Seiran Academy High School. Manager of the Track team. It's hard to tell from her expression, but she's more positive and passionate than pretty much anyone else. She adores Mizuki. She collects both important and unimportant things related to her object of interest. She hates green peppers. She has a cat and an older brother.

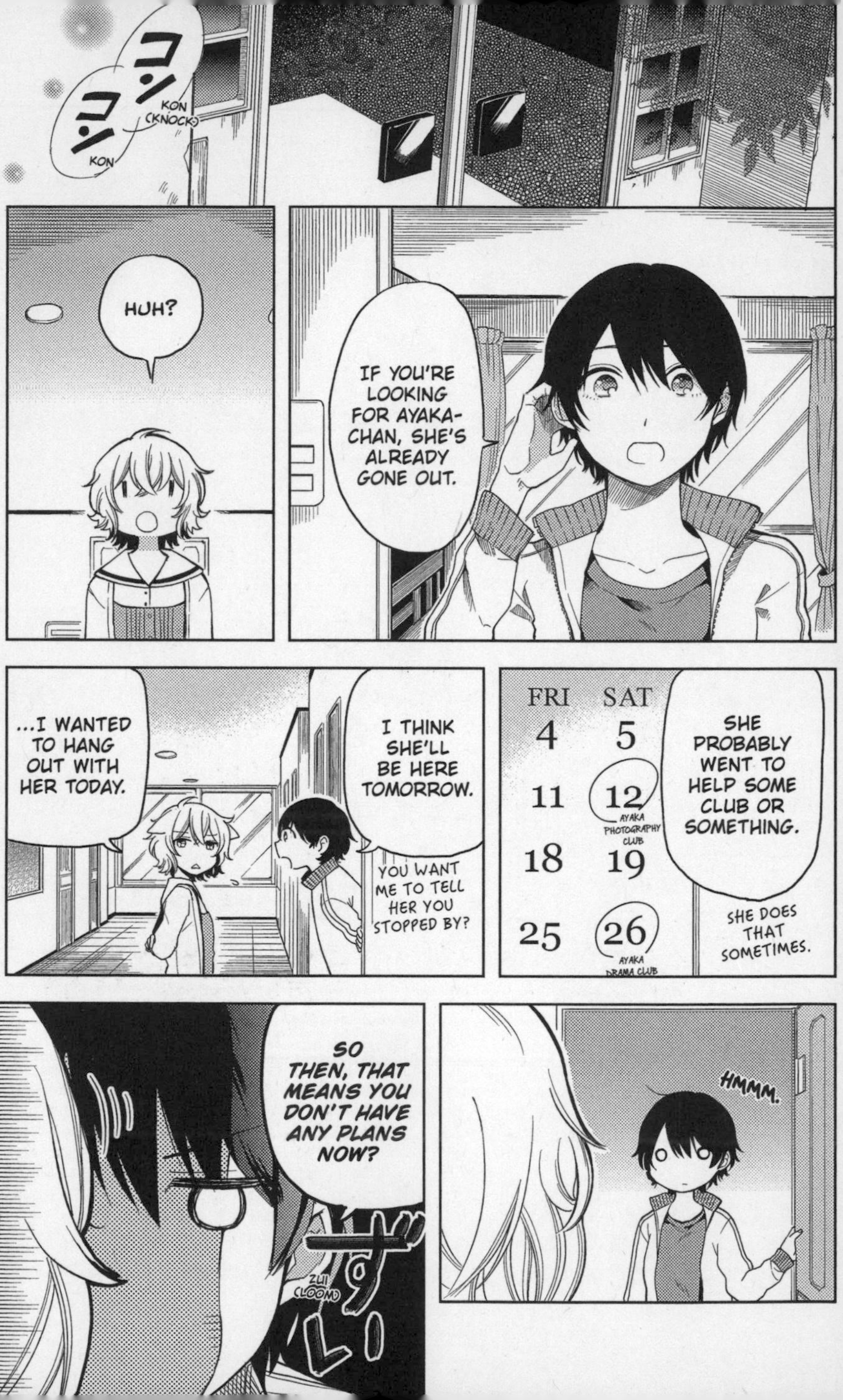
コン
コン
KON (KNOCK)
KON
IF YOU'RE LOOKING FOR AYAKA-CHAN, SHE'S ALREADY GONE OUT.
HUH?
FRI SAT
4 5
11 12
AYAKA PHOTOGRAPHY CLUB
18 19
25 26
AYAKA DRAMA CLUB
SHE PROBABLY WENT TO HELP SOME CLUB OR SOMETHING.
SHE DOES THAT SOMETIMES.
I THINK SHE'LL BE HERE TOMORROW.
YOU WANT ME TO TELL HER YOU STOPPED BY?
...I WANTED TO HANG OUT WITH HER TODAY.
HMMM.
SO THEN, THAT MEANS YOU DON'T HAVE ANY PLANS NOW?
ずい
ZUI (LOOM)

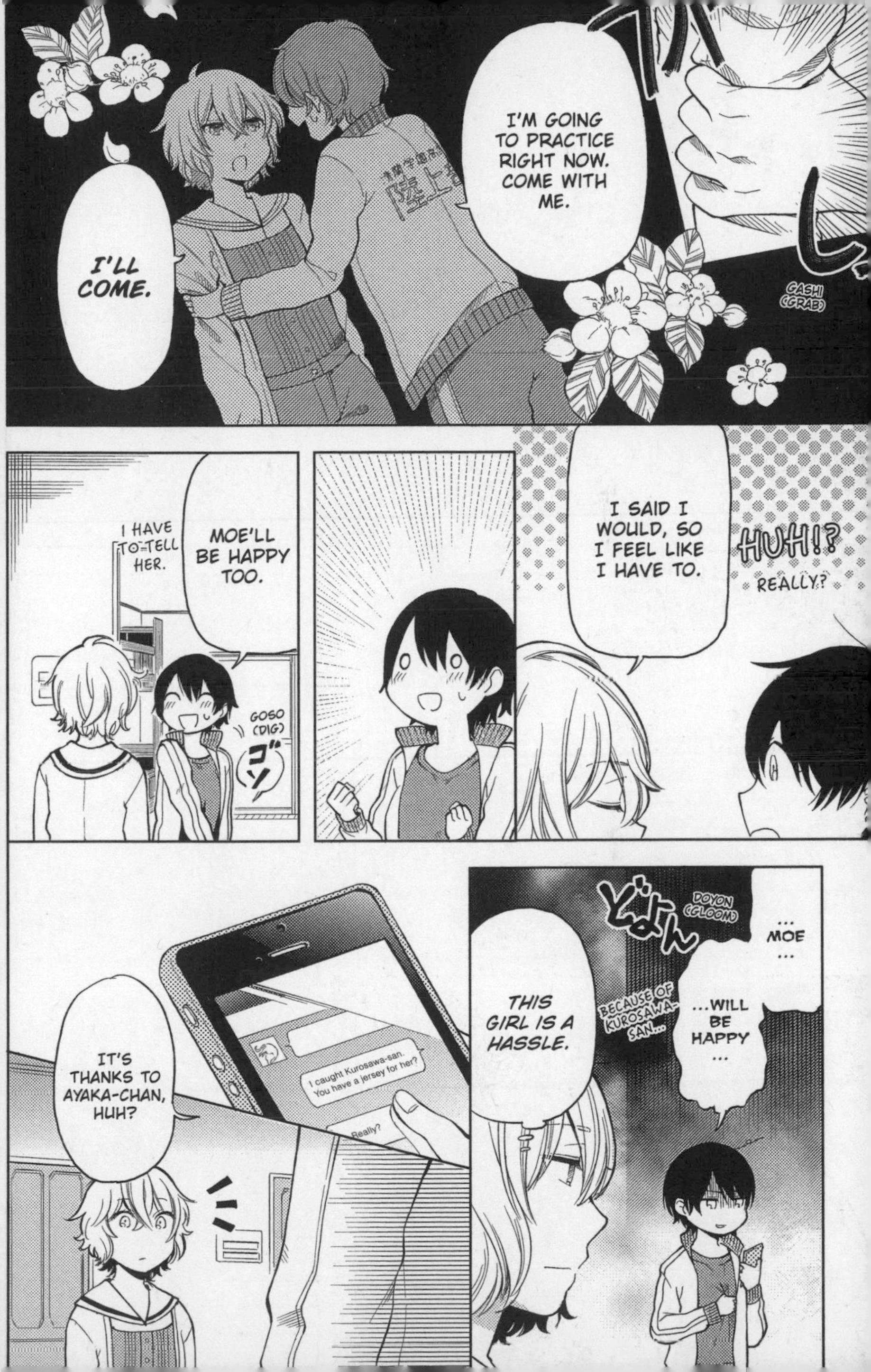
GASHI (GRAB)
I'M GOING TO PRACTICE RIGHT NOW. COME WITH ME.
I'LL COME.
HUH!?
REALLY?
I SAID I WOULD, SO I FEEL LIKE I HAVE TO.
MOE'LL BE HAPPY TOO.
I HAVE TO TELL HER.
GOSO (DIG)
DOYON (GLOOM)
... MOE ...
...WILL BE HAPPY ...
BECAUSE OF KUROSAWA-SAN...
THIS GIRL IS A HASSLE.
I caught Kurosawa-san. You have a jersey for her?
Really?
IT'S THANKS TO AYAKA-CHAN, HUH?

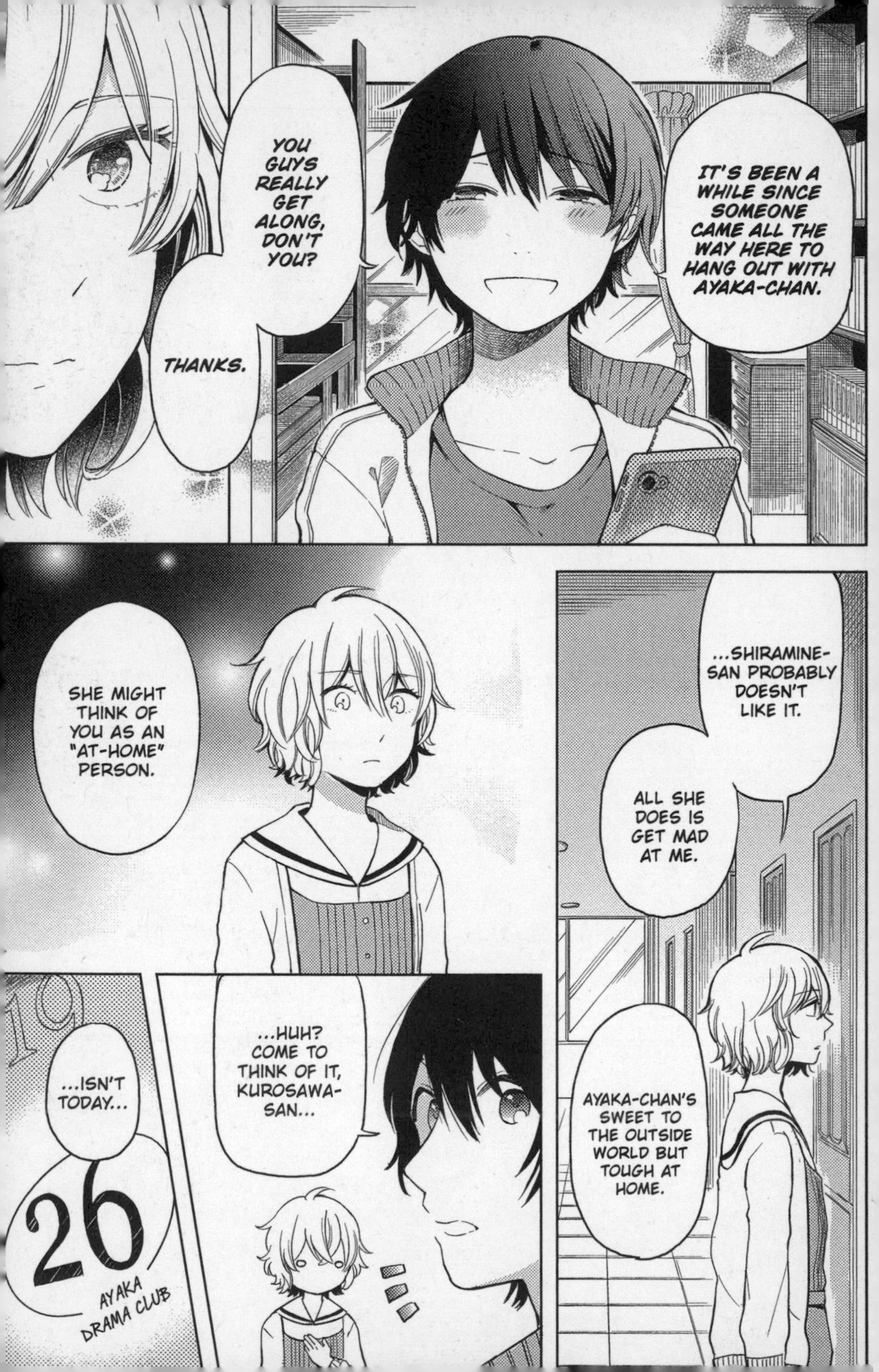
IT'S BEEN A WHILE SINCE SOMEONE CAME ALL THE WAY HERE TO HANG OUT WITH AYAKA-CHAN.
YOU GUYS REALLY GET ALONG, DON'T YOU?
THANKS.
...SHIRAMINE-SAN PROBABLY DOESN'T LIKE IT.
ALL SHE DOES IS GET MAD AT ME.
AYAKA-CHAN'S SWEET TO THE OUTSIDE WORLD BUT TOUGH AT HOME.
SHE MIGHT THINK OF YOU AS AN "AT-HOME" PERSON.
...HUH? COME TO THINK OF IT, KUROSAWA-SAN...
...ISN'T TODAY...
26
AYAKA DRAMA CLUB

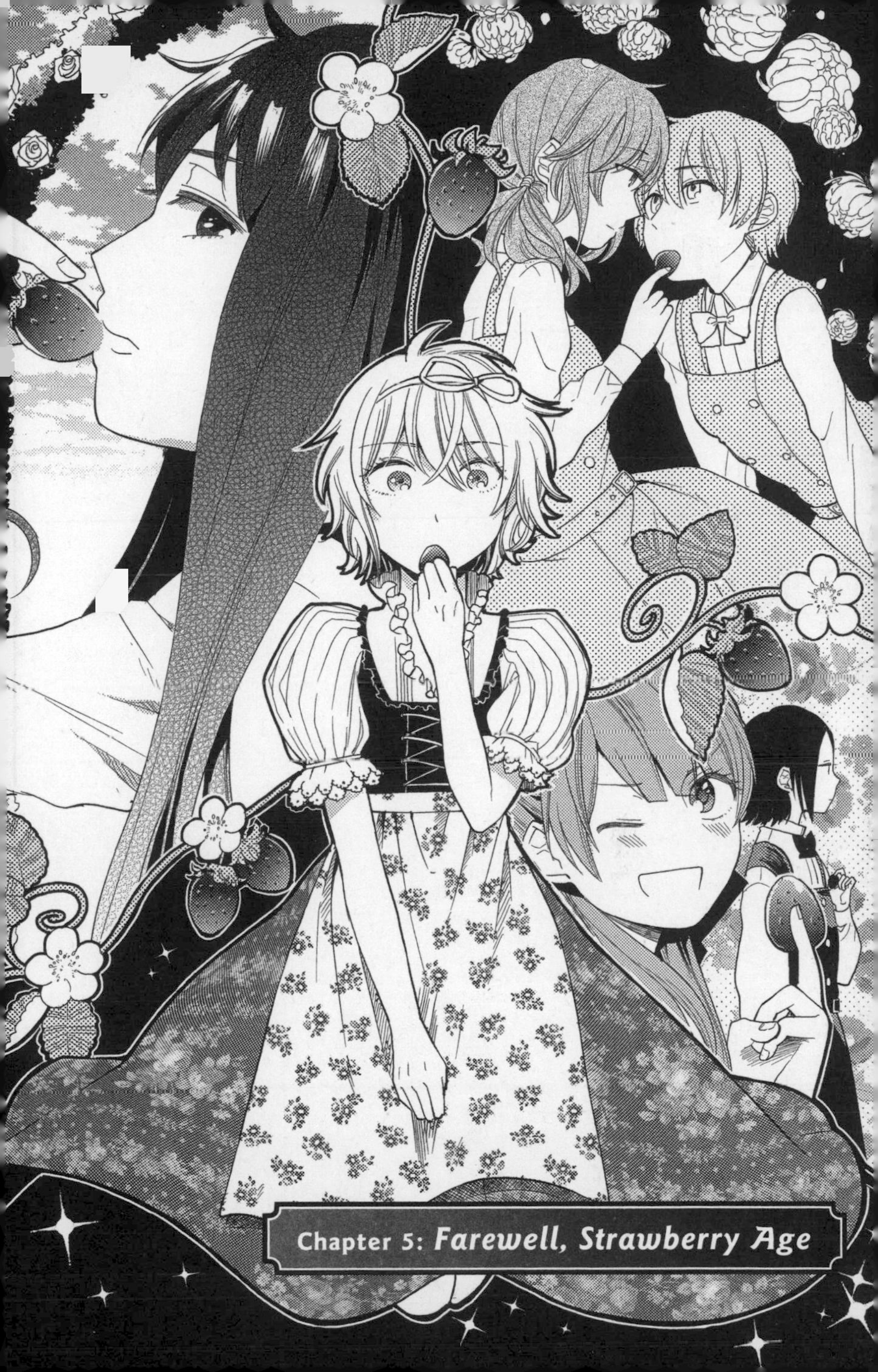
Chapter 5: Farewell, Strawberry Age

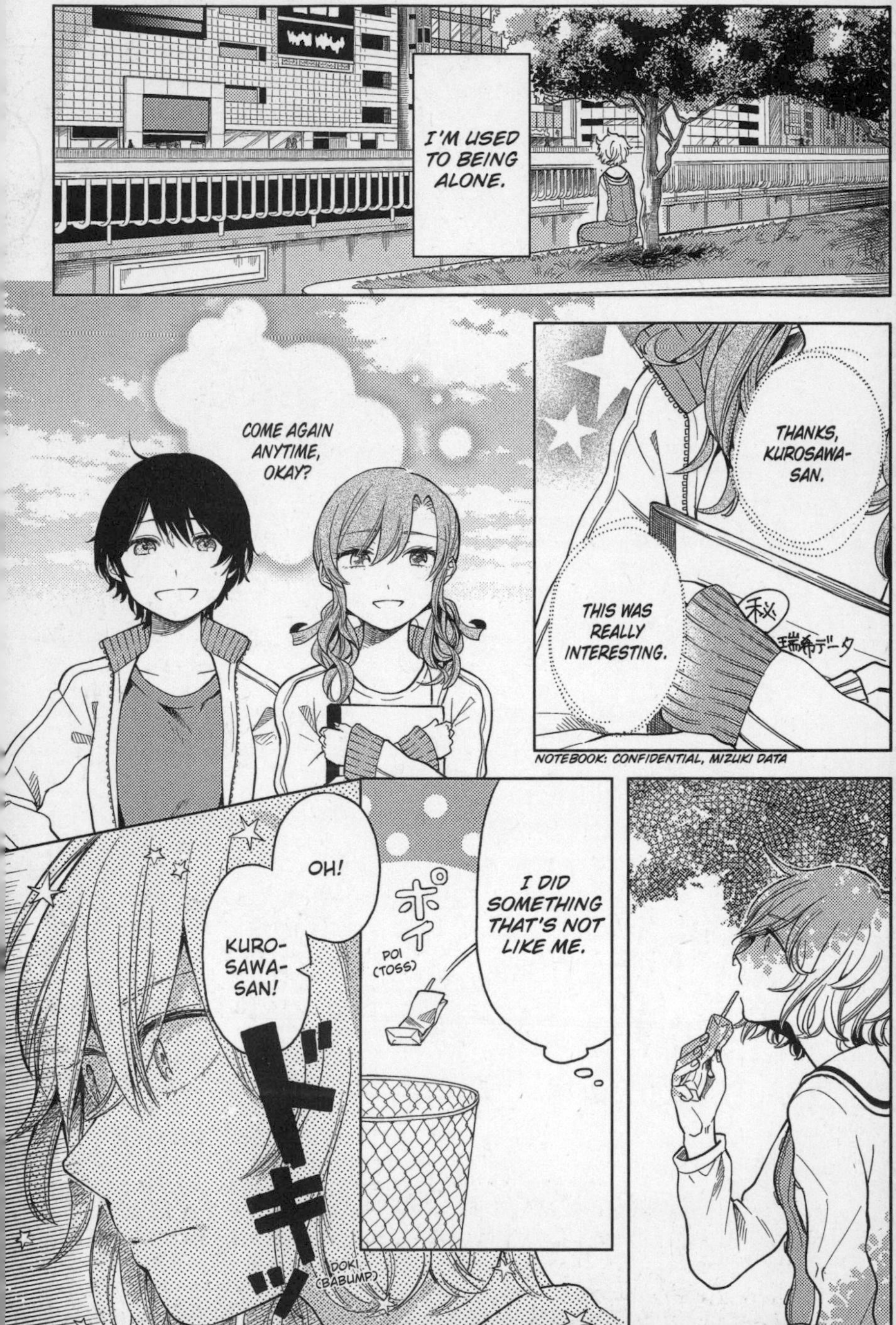
I'M USED TO BEING ALONE.
THANKS, KUROSAWA-SAN.
THIS WAS REALLY INTERESTING.
秘
瑞希データ
NOTEBOOK: CONFIDENTIAL, MIZUKI DATA
COME AGAIN ANYTIME, OKAY?
I DID SOMETHING THAT'S NOT LIKE ME.
ポイ
POI (TOSS)
OH!
KURO-SAWA-SAN!
ドキッ
DOKI (BABUMP)

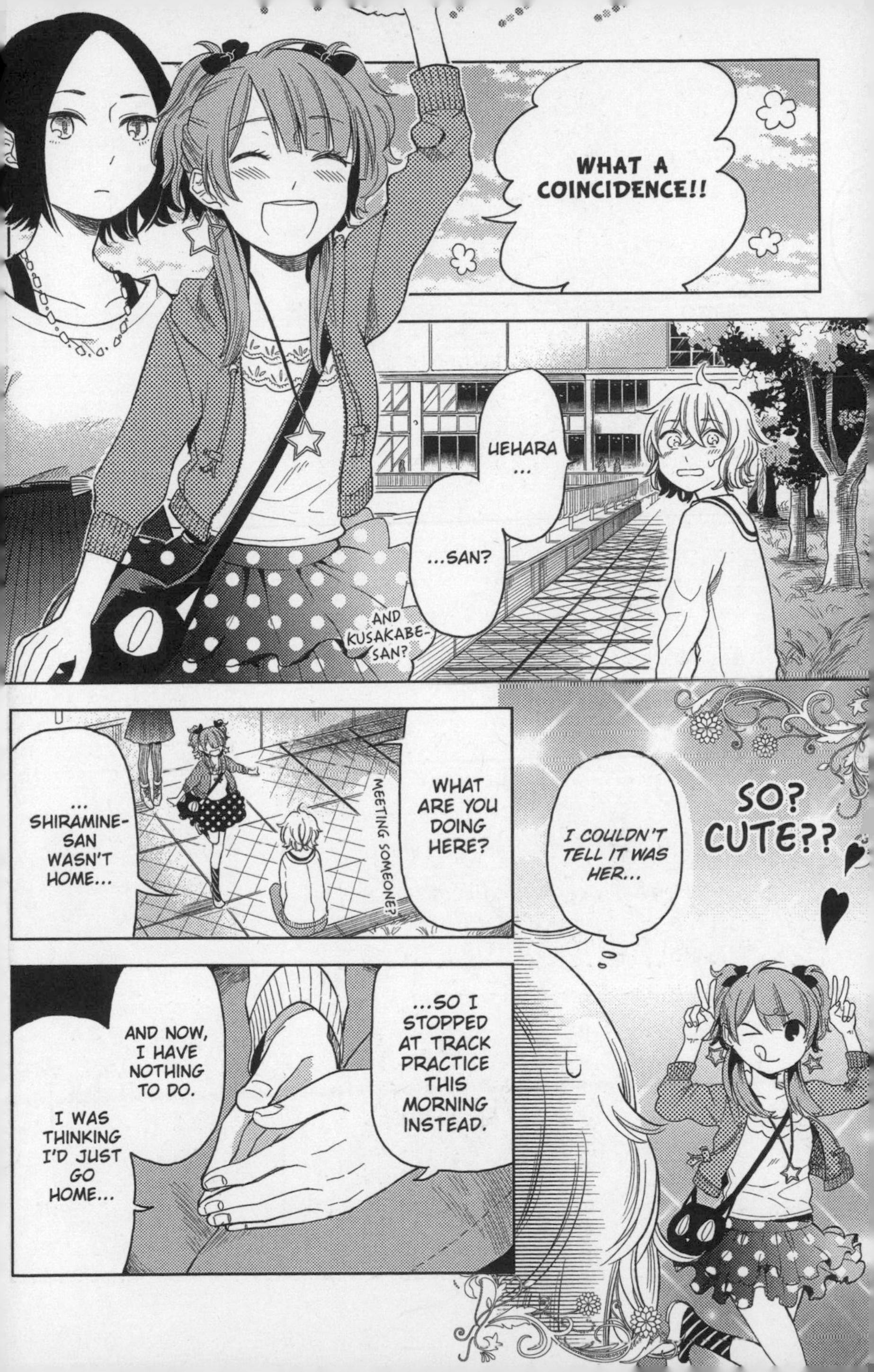
WHAT A COINCIDENCE!!
UEHARA ...
...SAN?
AND KUSAKABE-SAN?
SO? CUTE??
I COULDN'T TELL IT WAS HER...
WHAT ARE YOU DOING HERE?
MEETING SOMEONE?
... SHIRAMINE-SAN WASN'T HOME...
...SO I STOPPED AT TRACK PRACTICE THIS MORNING INSTEAD.
AND NOW, I HAVE NOTHING TO DO.
I WAS THINKING I'D JUST GO HOME...

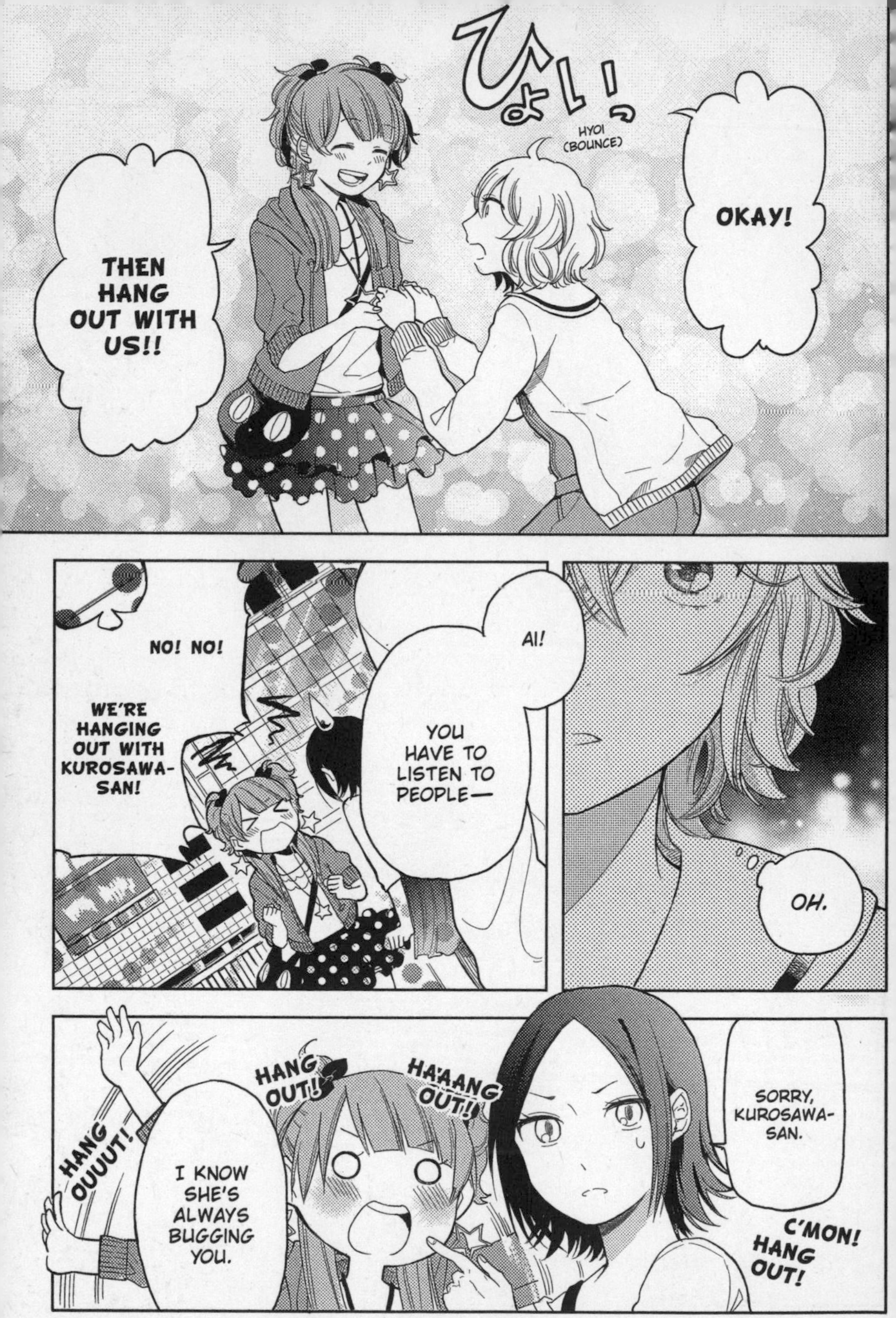
ひょいっ
HYOI (BOUNCE)
OKAY!
THEN HANG OUT WITH US!!
OH.
AI!
YOU HAVE TO LISTEN TO PEOPLE—
NO! NO!
WE'RE HANGING OUT WITH KUROSAWA-SAN!
SORRY, KUROSAWA-SAN.
C'MON! HANG OUT!
HA'AANG OUT!
HANG OUT!
I KNOW SHE'S ALWAYS BUGGING YOU.
HANG OUUUT!

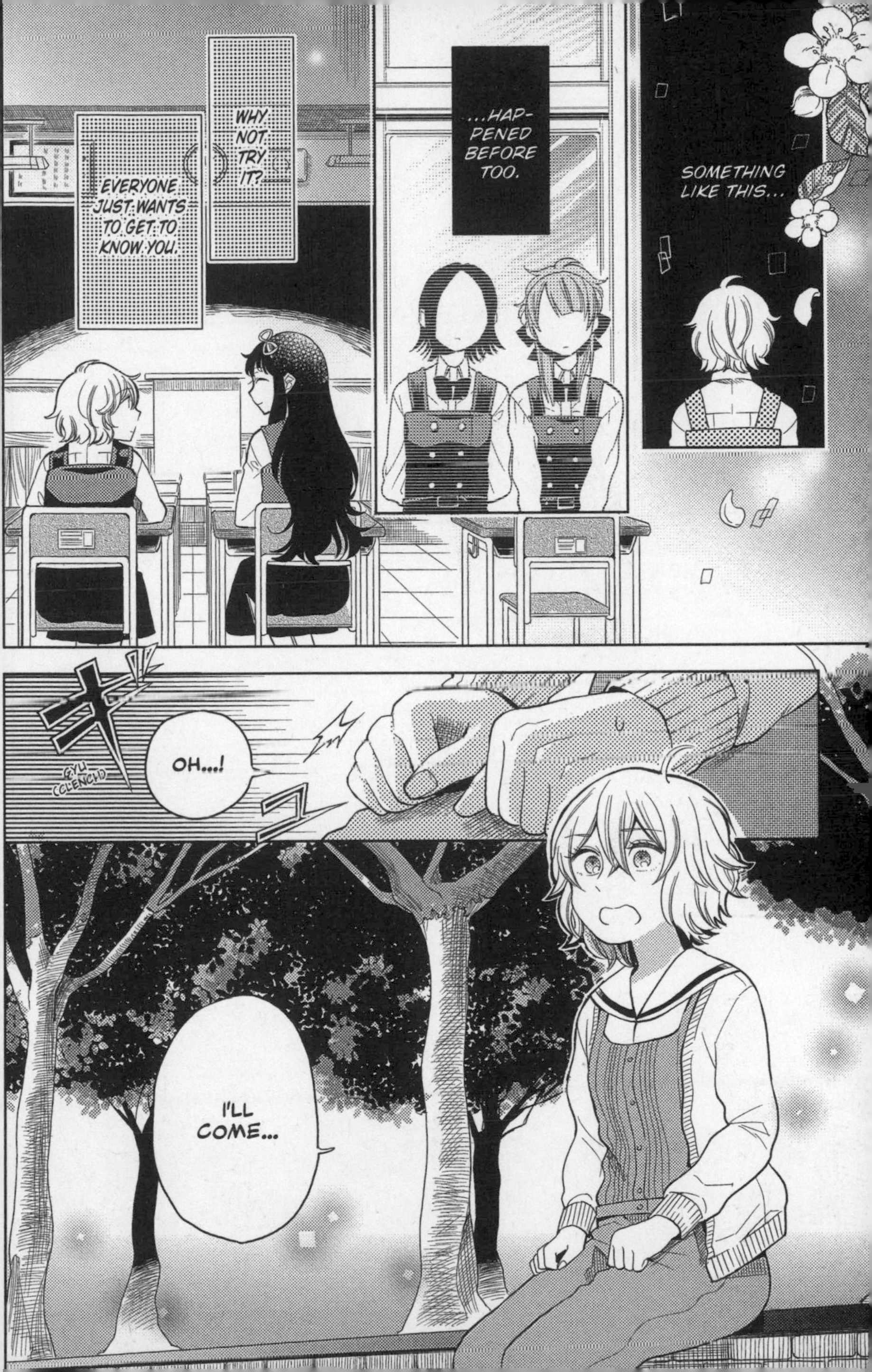
SOMETHING LIKE THIS...
...HAP-PENED BEFORE TOO.
WHY NOT TRY IT?
EVERYONE JUST WANTS TO GET TO KNOW YOU.
OH...!
GYU (CLENCH)
I'LL COME...

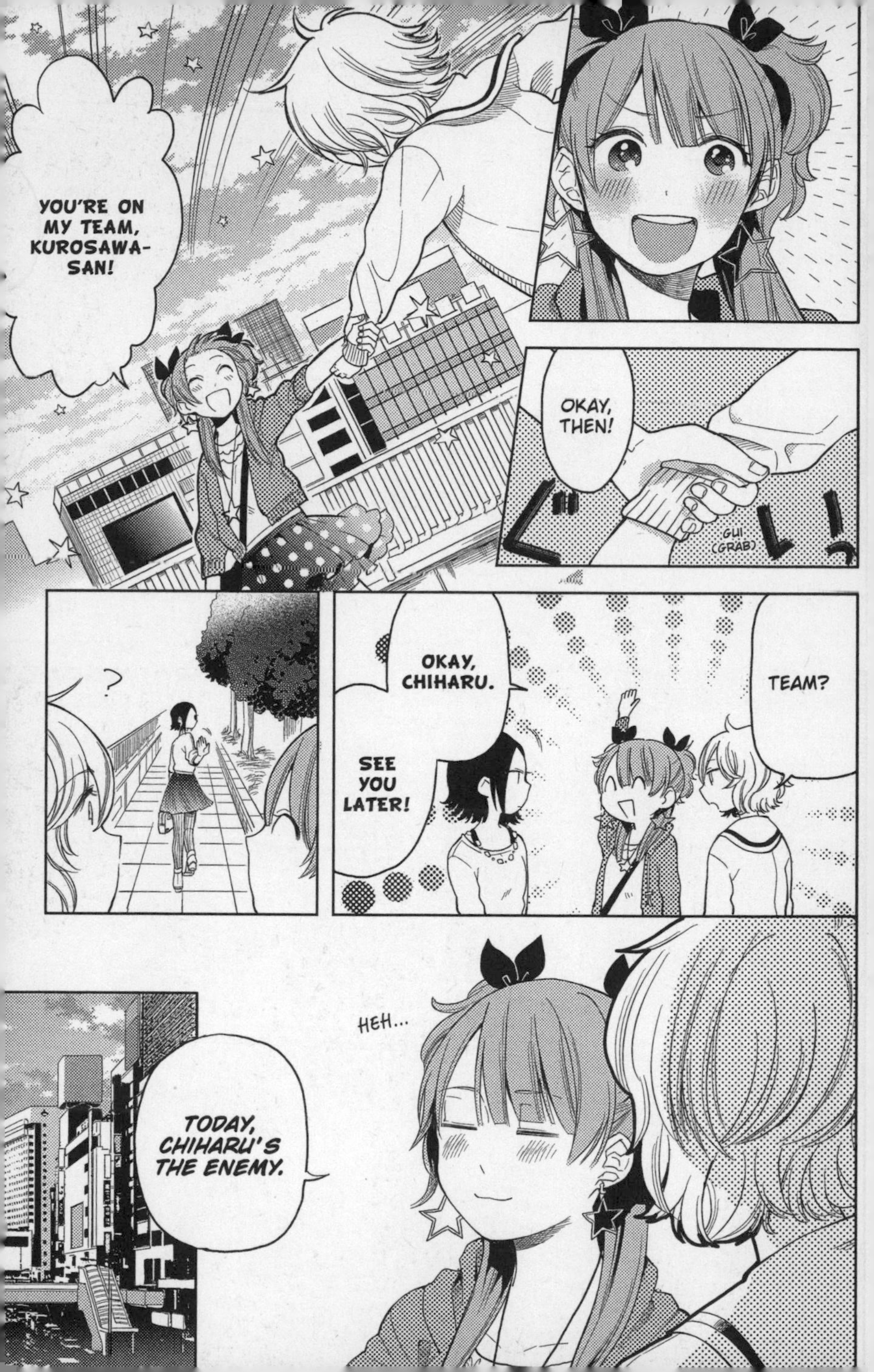

OKAY, THEN!
GUI (GRAB)
YOU'RE ON MY TEAM, KUROSAWA-SAN!
TEAM?
OKAY, CHIHARU.
SEE YOU LATER!
?
HEH...
TODAY, CHIHARU'S THE ENEMY.

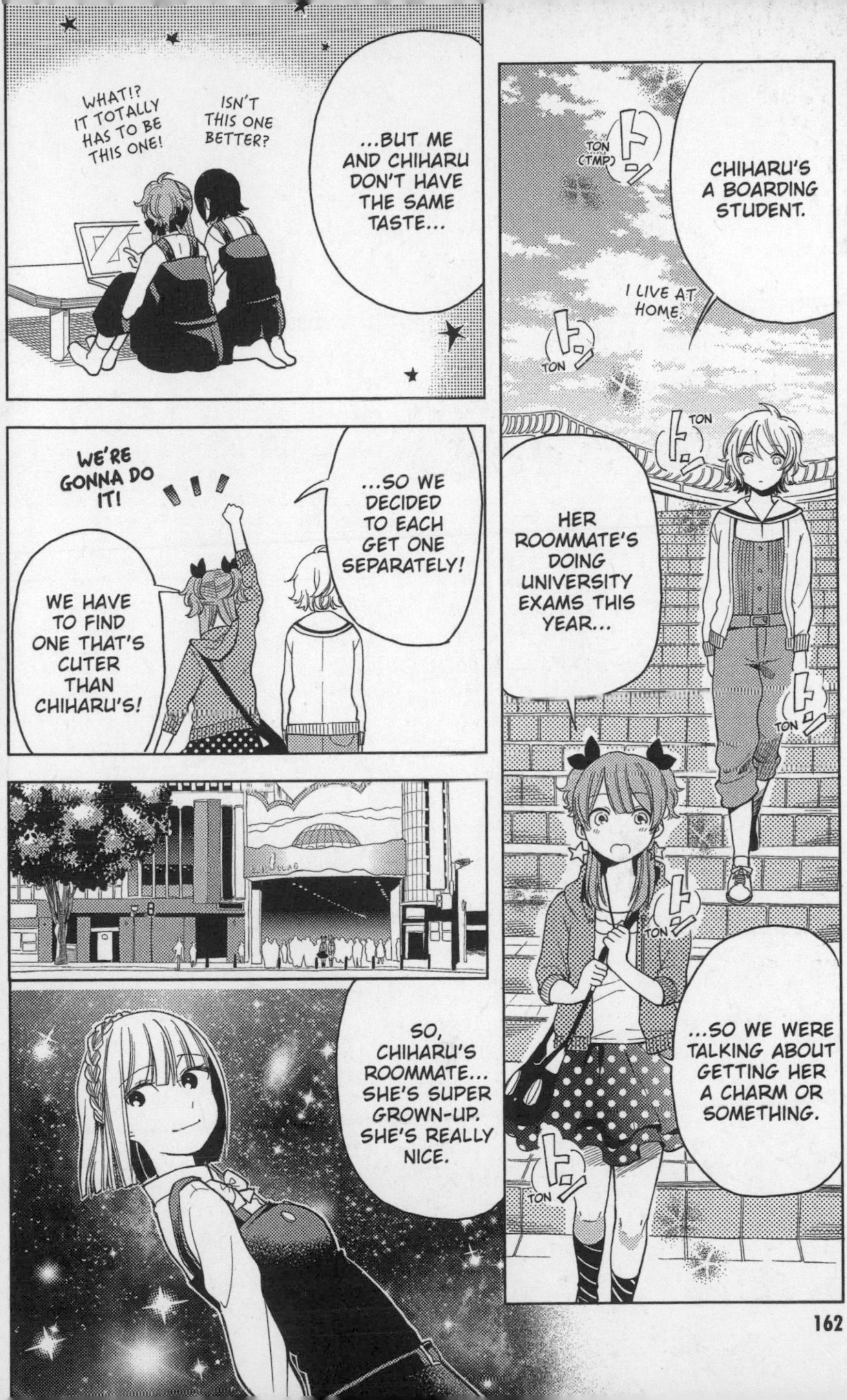
TON (TMP)
CHIHARU'S A BOARDING STUDENT.
I LIVE AT HOME.
TON
TON
HER ROOMMATE'S DOING UNIVERSITY EXAMS THIS YEAR...
TON
TON
...SO WE WERE TALKING ABOUT GETTING HER A CHARM OR SOMETHING.
TON
...BUT ME AND CHIHARU DON'T HAVE THE SAME TASTE...
ISN'T THIS ONE BETTER?
WHAT!? IT TOTALLY HAS TO BE THIS ONE!
...SO WE DECIDED TO EACH GET ONE SEPARATELY!
WE'RE GONNA DO IT!
WE HAVE TO FIND ONE THAT'S CUTER THAN CHIHARU'S!
SO, CHIHARU'S ROOMMATE... SHE'S SUPER GROWN-UP. SHE'S REALLY NICE.

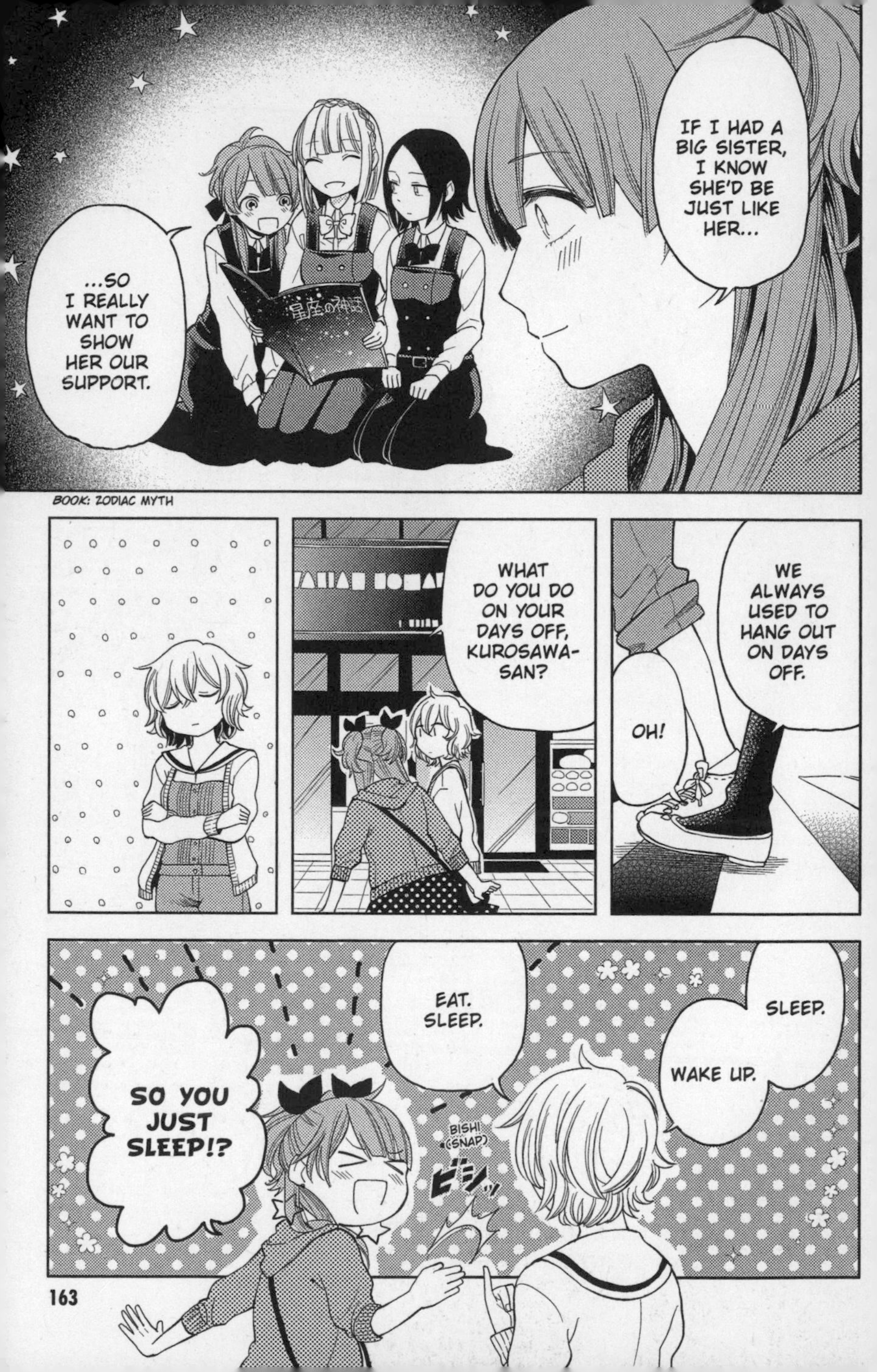
IF I HAD A BIG SISTER, I KNOW SHE'D BE JUST LIKE HER...
...SO I REALLY WANT TO SHOW HER OUR SUPPORT.
星座の神話
BOOK: ZODIAC MYTH
WE ALWAYS USED TO HANG OUT ON DAYS OFF.
OH!
WHAT DO YOU DO ON YOUR DAYS OFF, KUROSAWA-SAN?
SLEEP.
WAKE UP.
EAT. SLEEP.
BISHI (SNAP)
SO YOU JUST SLEEP!?

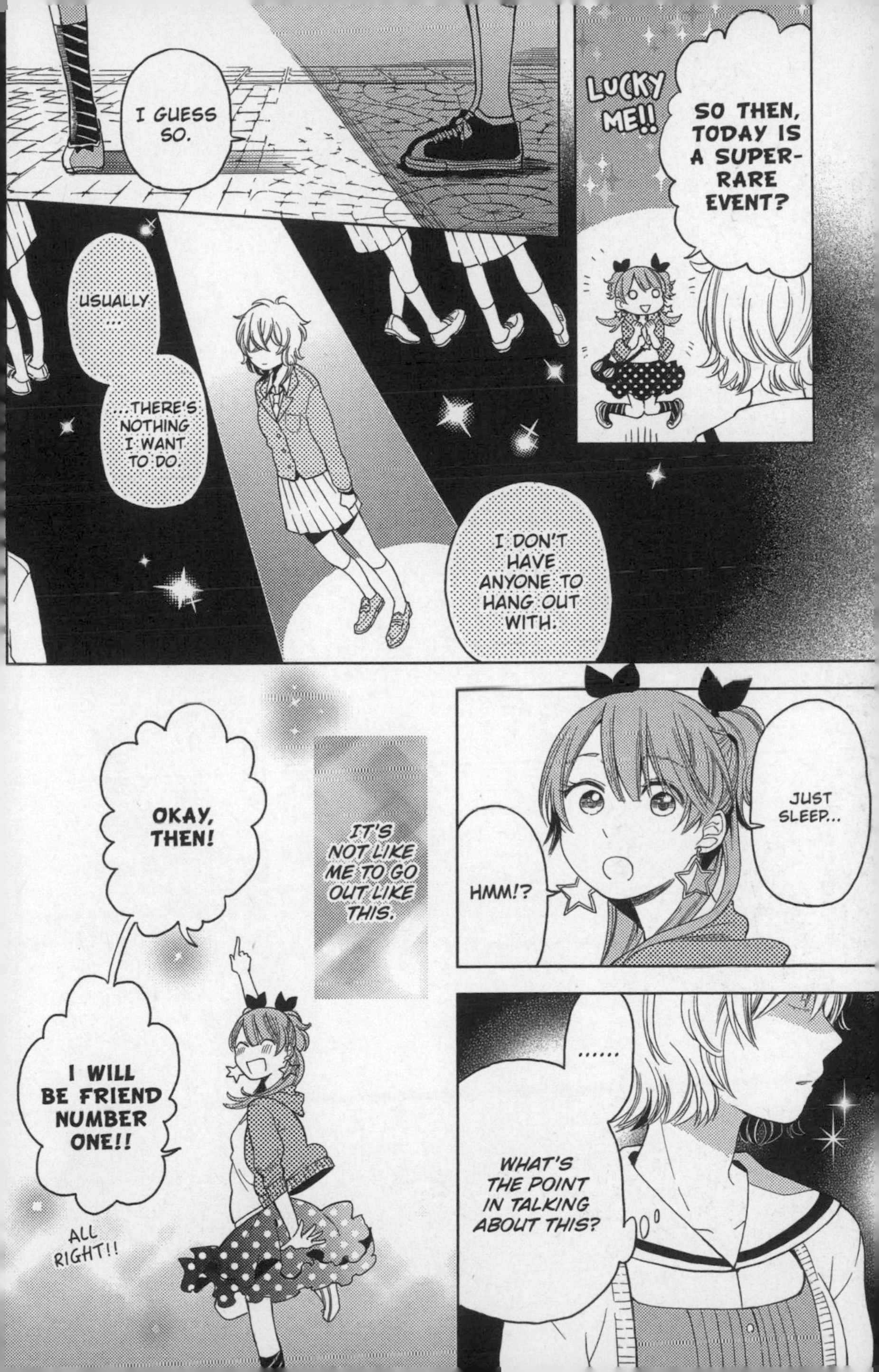
SO THEN, TODAY IS A SUPER-RARE EVENT?
LUCKY ME!!
I GUESS SO.
USUALLY...
...THERE'S NOTHING I WANT TO DO.
I DON'T HAVE ANYONE TO HANG OUT WITH.
JUST SLEEP...
HMM!?
......
WHAT'S THE POINT IN TALKING ABOUT THIS?
IT'S NOT LIKE ME TO GO OUT LIKE THIS.
OKAY, THEN!
I WILL BE FRIEND NUMBER ONE!!
ALL RIGHT!!

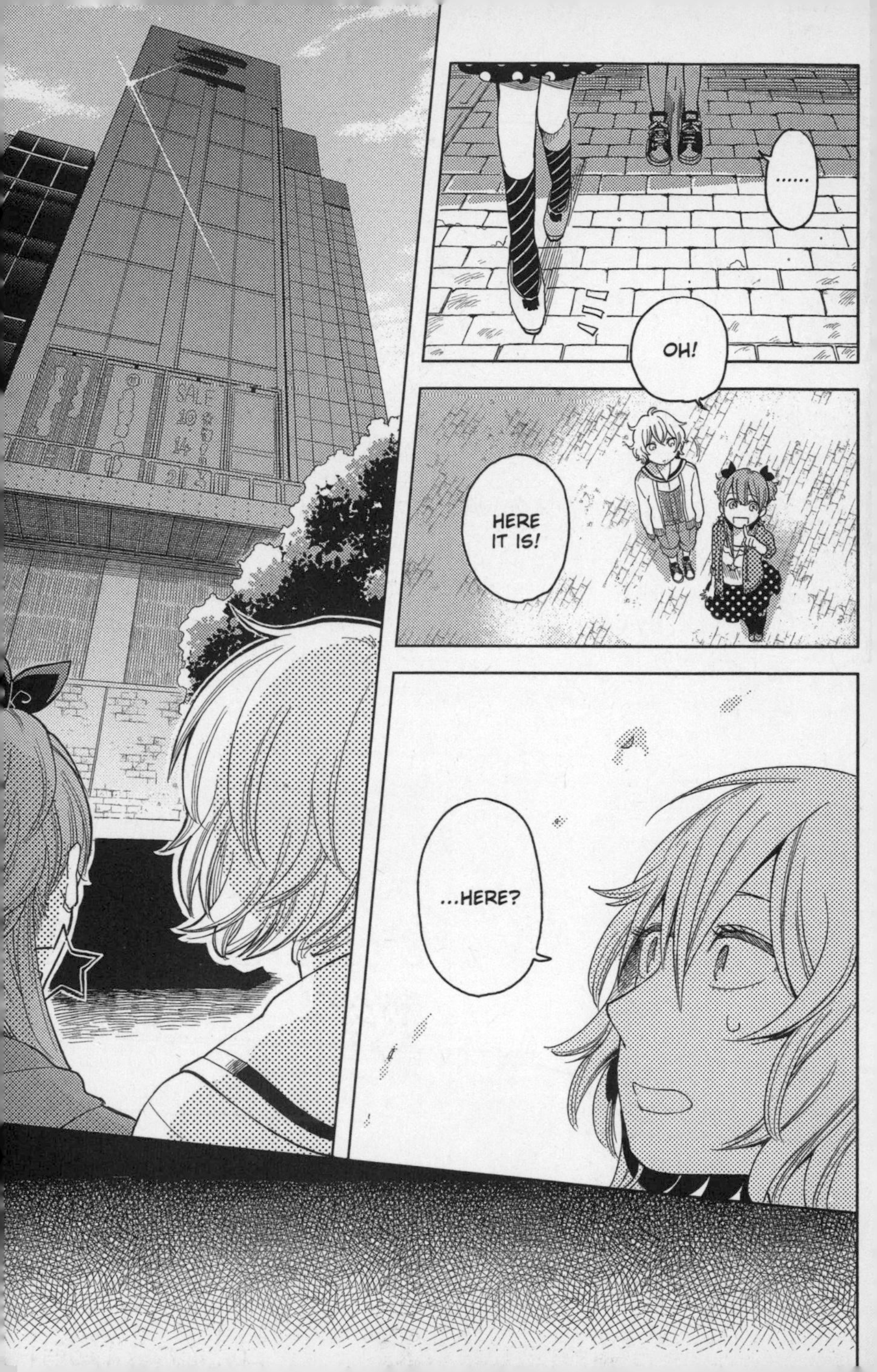
......
OH!
HERE IT IS!
...HERE?

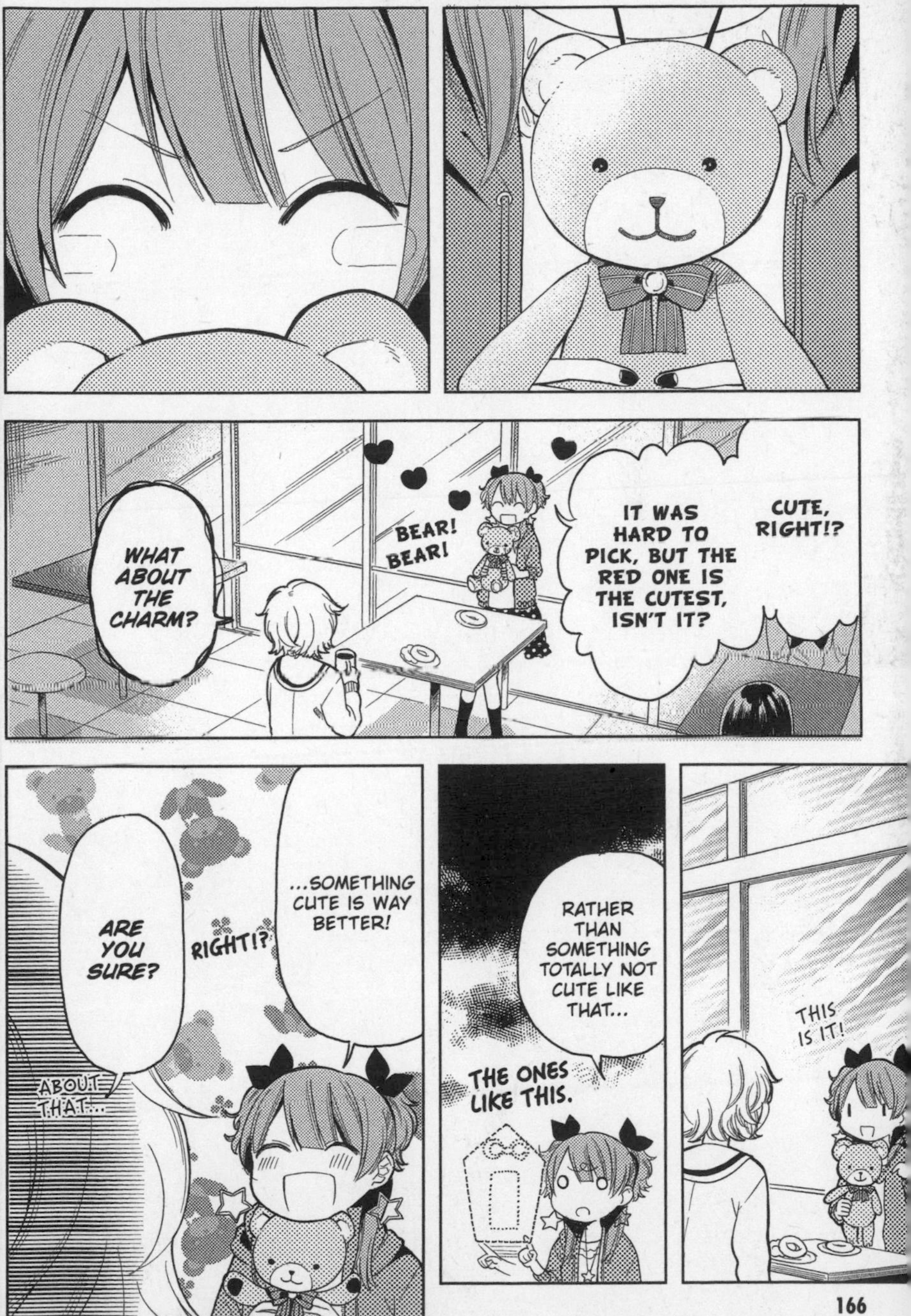
CUTE, RIGHT!?
IT WAS HARD TO PICK, BUT THE RED ONE IS THE CUTEST, ISN'T IT?
BEAR! BEAR!
WHAT ABOUT THE CHARM?
THIS IS IT!
RATHER THAN SOMETHING TOTALLY NOT CUTE LIKE THAT...
THE ONES LIKE THIS.
...SOMETHING CUTE IS WAY BETTER!
RIGHT!?
ARE YOU SURE?
ABOUT THAT...

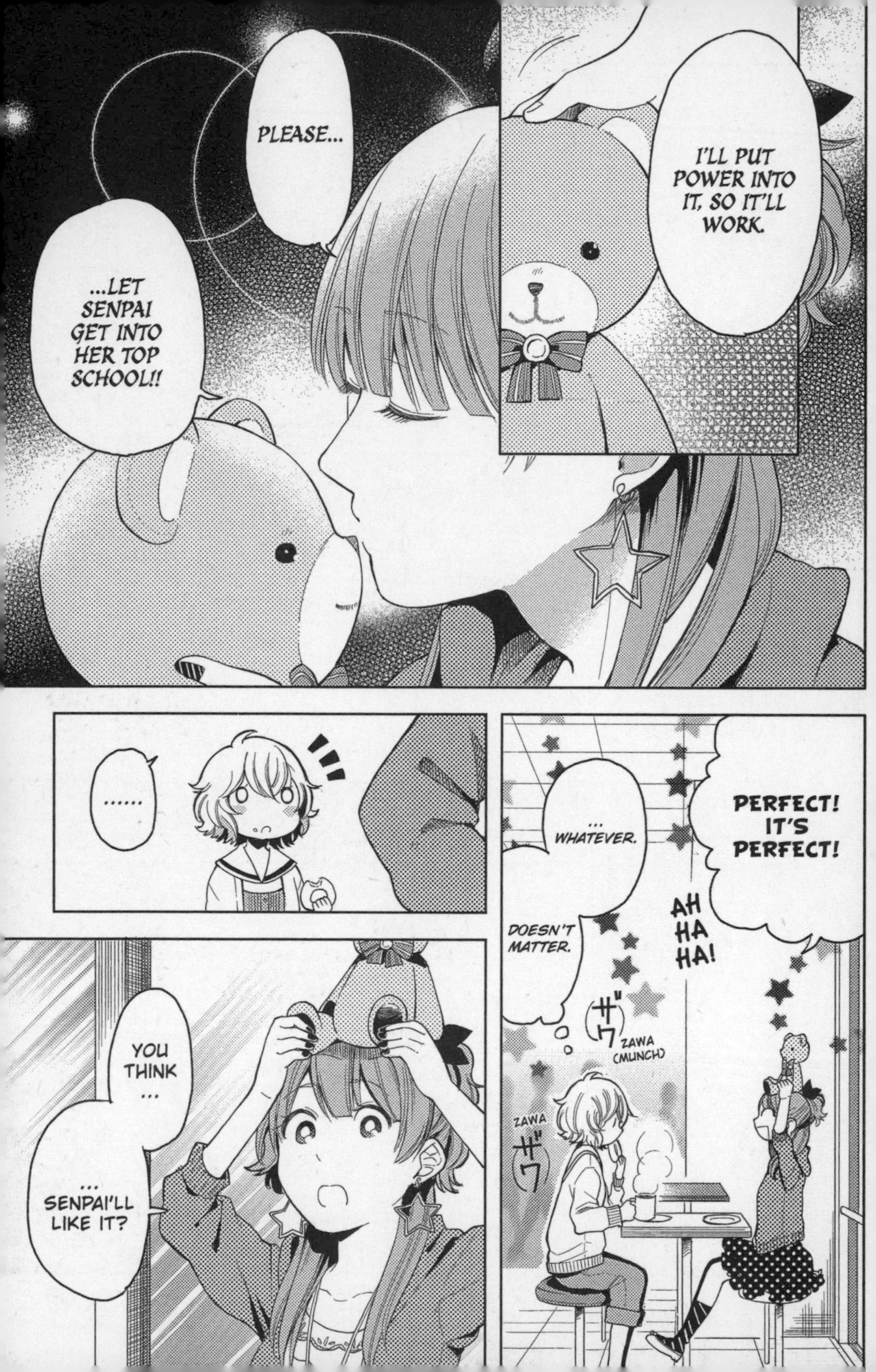
I'LL PUT POWER INTO IT, SO IT'LL WORK.
PLEASE...
...LET SENPAI GET INTO HER TOP SCHOOL!!
PERFECT! IT'S PERFECT!
AH HA HA!
... WHATEVER.
DOESN'T MATTER.
ザワ
ZAWA (MUNCH)
ZAWA
ザワ
......
YOU THINK ...
... SENPAI'LL LIKE IT?

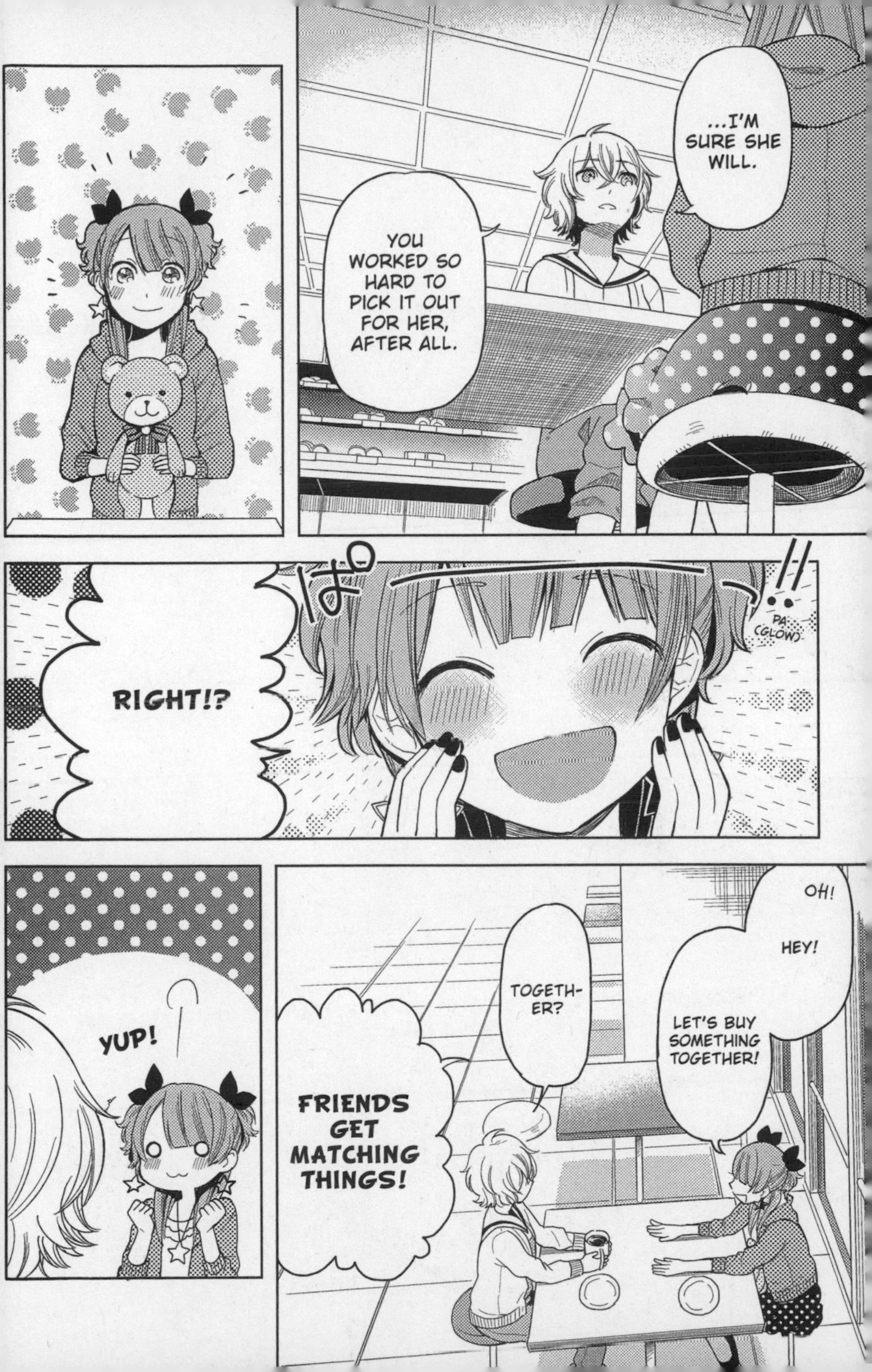
...I'M SURE SHE WILL.
YOU WORKED SO HARD TO PICK IT OUT FOR HER, AFTER ALL.
PA (GLOW)
RIGHT!?
OH!
HEY!
LET'S BUY SOMETHING TOGETHER!
TOGETH-ER?
FRIENDS GET MATCHING THINGS!
YUP!

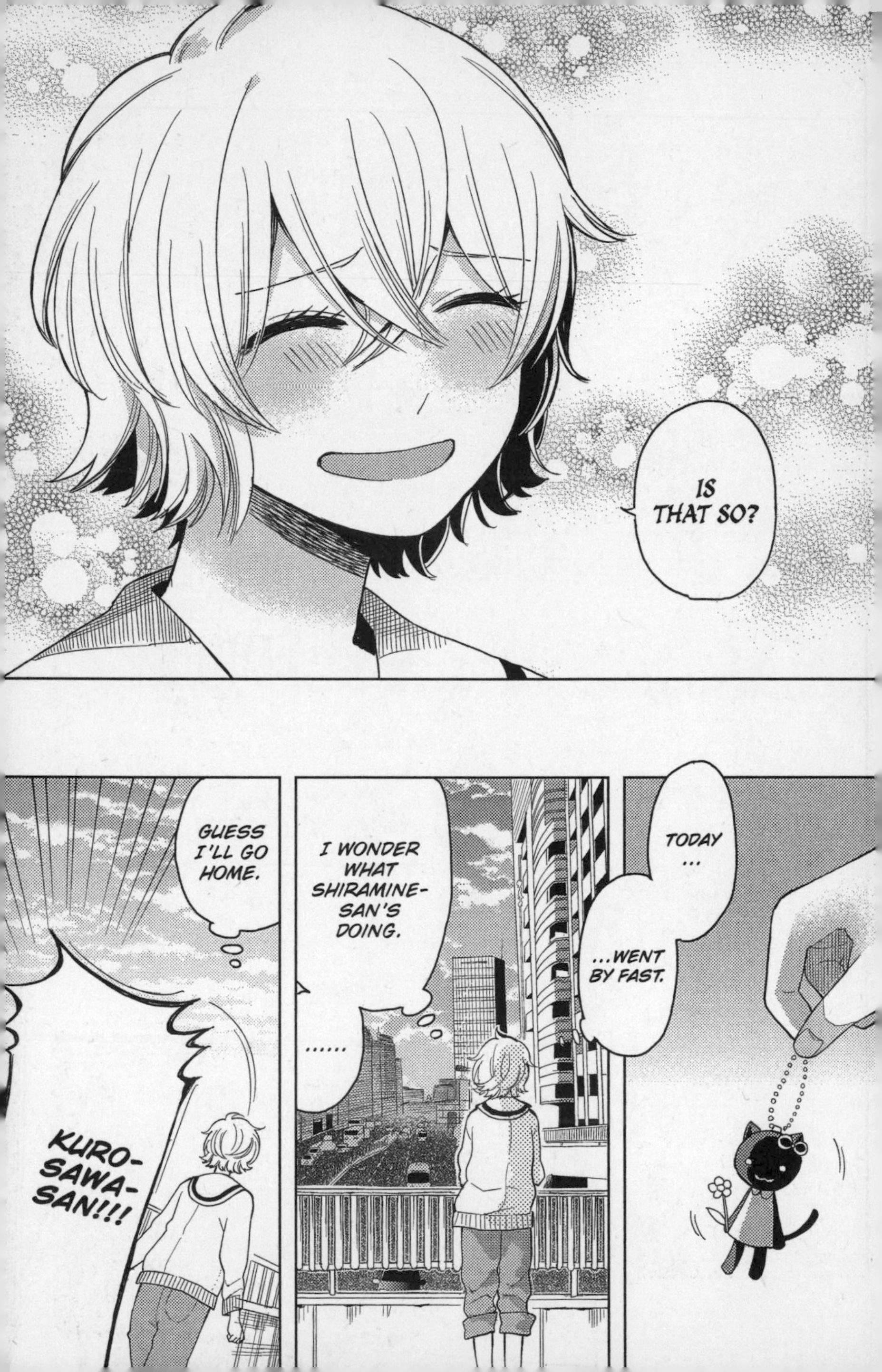
IS THAT SO?
TODAY ...
...WENT BY FAST.
I WONDER WHAT SHIRAMINE-SAN'S DOING.
......
GUESS I'LL GO HOME.
KURO-SAWA-SAN!!!

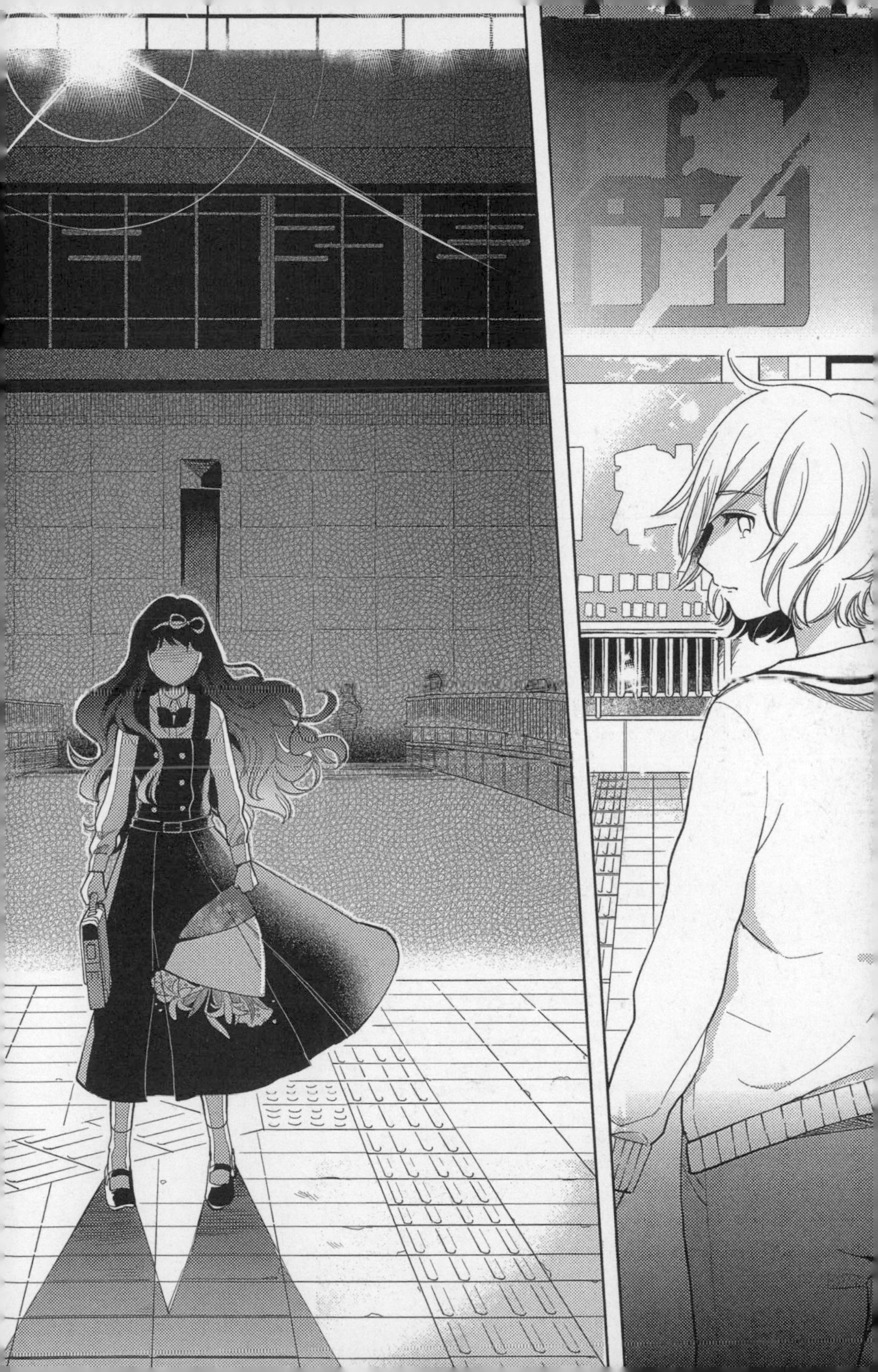

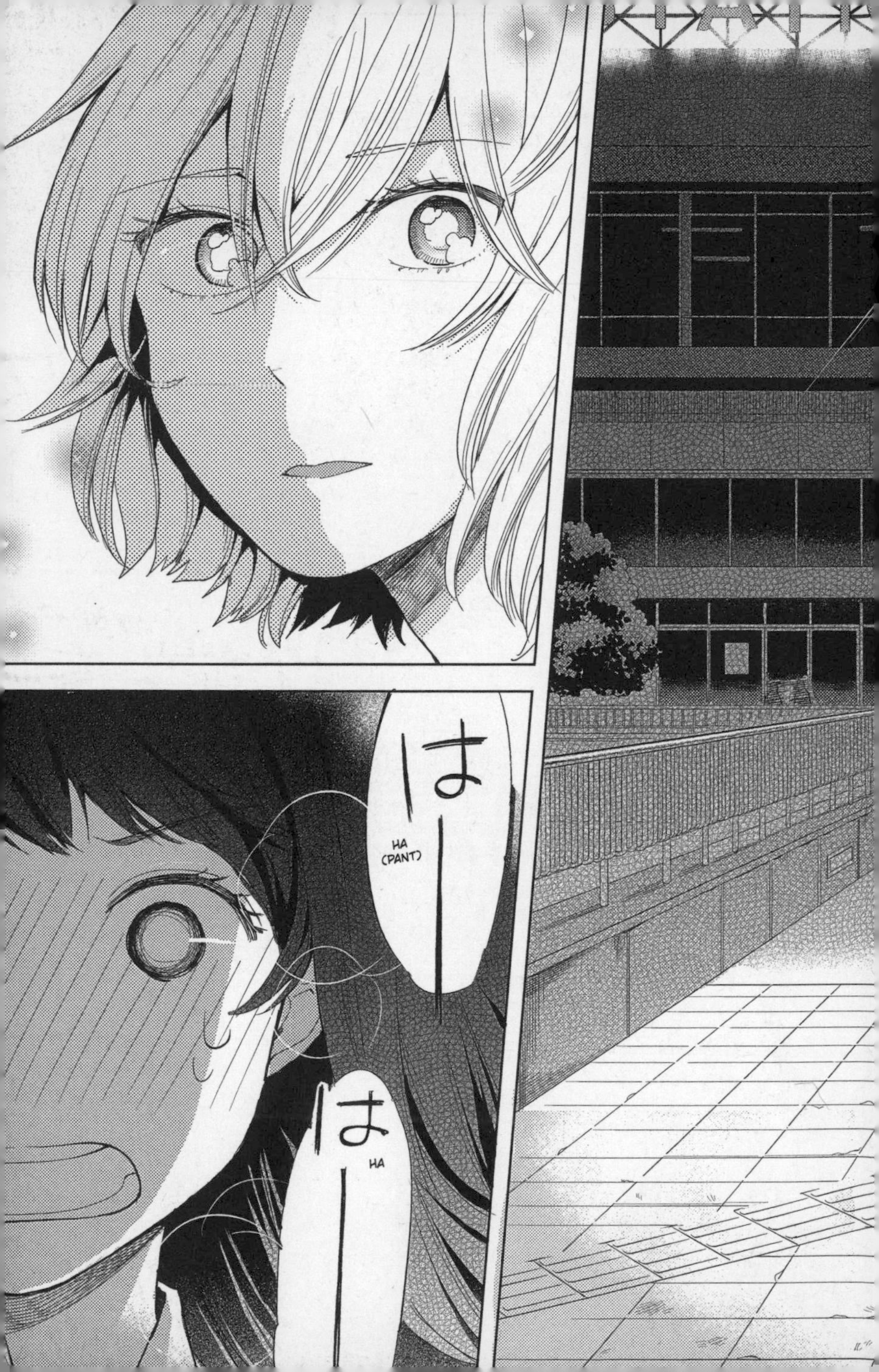
はー
HA (PANT)
はー
HA

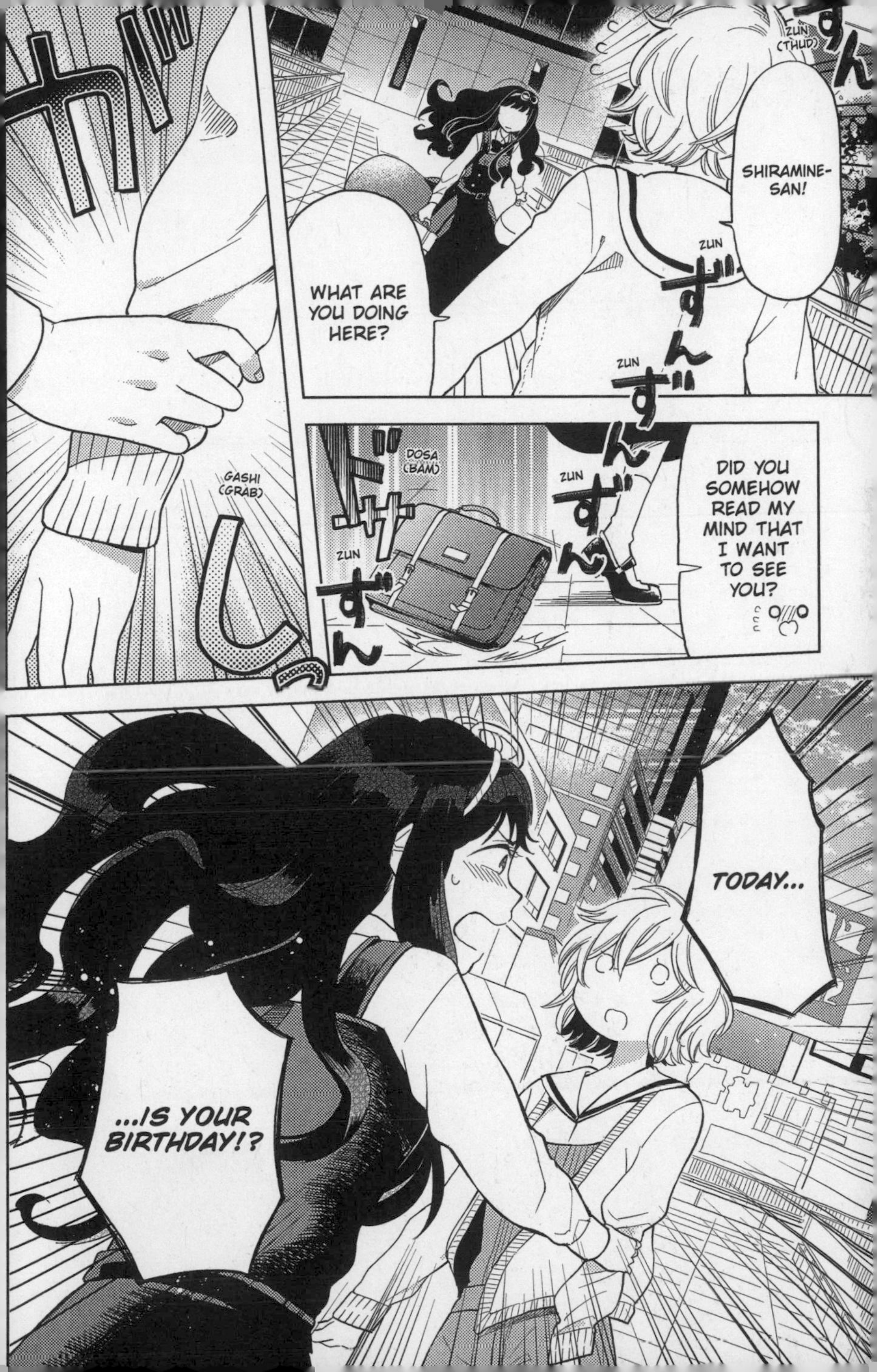
ZUN (THUD)
SHIRAMINE-SAN!
WHAT ARE YOU DOING HERE?
ZUN
ZUN
DID YOU SOMEHOW READ MY MIND THAT I WANT TO SEE YOU?
ZUN
DOSA (BAM)
ZUN
GASHI (GRAB)
TODAY...
...IS YOUR BIRTHDAY!?

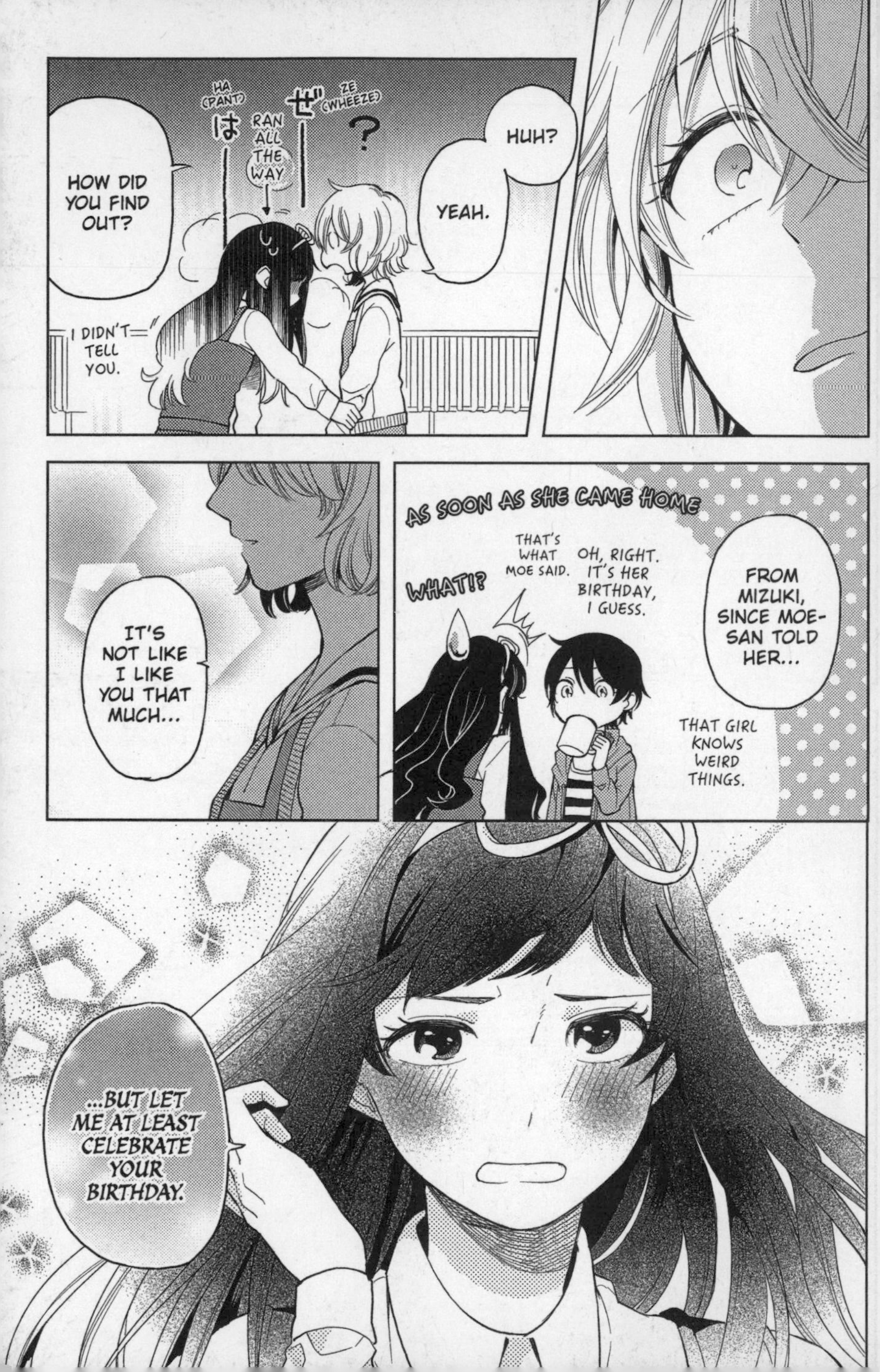
HUH?
YEAH.
ZE (WHEEZE)
ぜー
?
RAN ALL THE WAY
HA (PANT)
はー
HOW DID YOU FIND OUT?
I DIDN'T TELL YOU.
FROM MIZUKI, SINCE MOE-SAN TOLD HER...
THAT GIRL KNOWS WEIRD THINGS.
AS SOON AS SHE CAME HOME
OH, RIGHT. IT'S HER BIRTHDAY, I GUESS.
THAT'S WHAT MOE SAID.
WHAT!?
IT'S NOT LIKE I LIKE YOU THAT MUCH...
...BUT LET ME AT LEAST CELEBRATE YOUR BIRTHDAY.

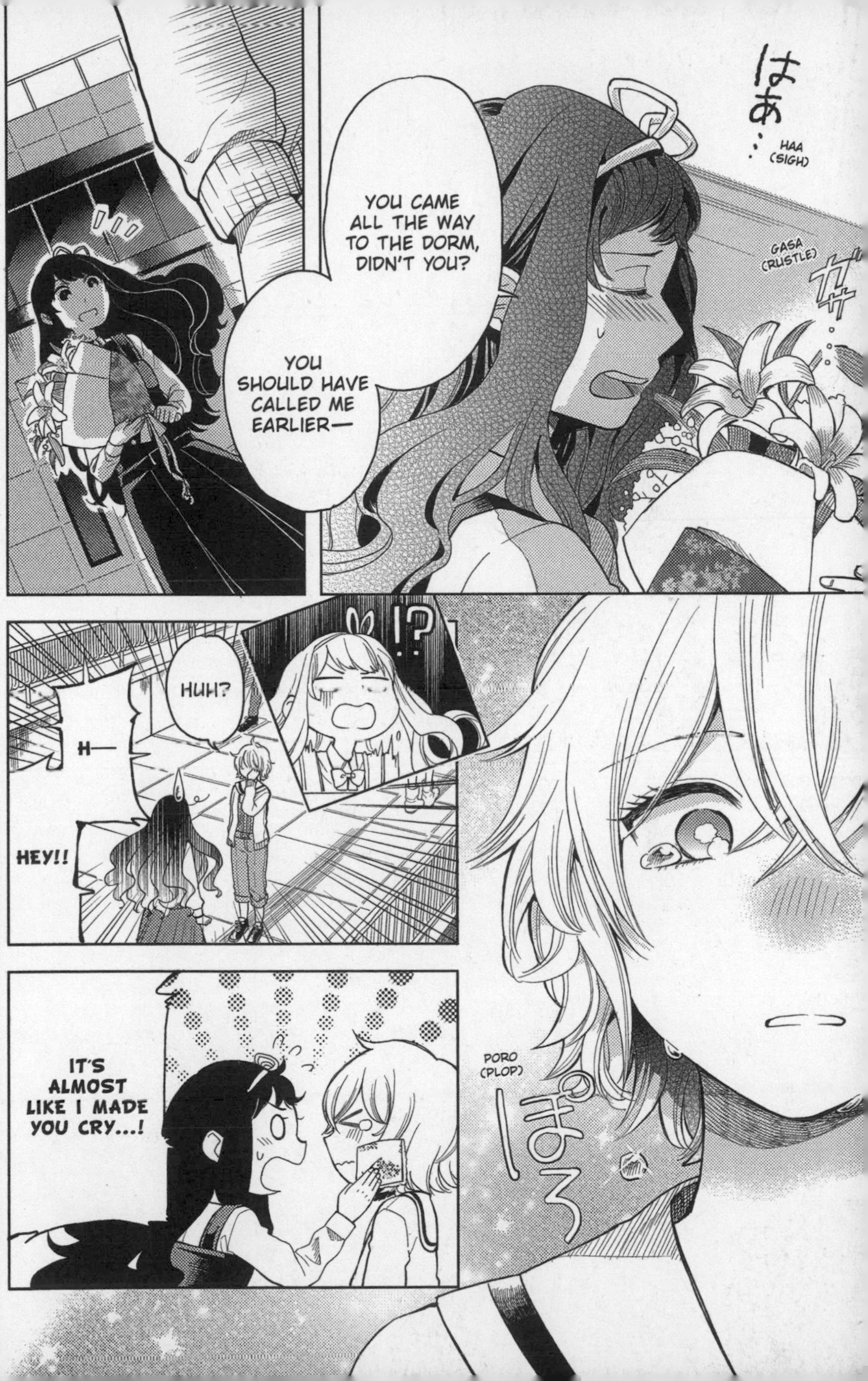
はあ…
HAA (SIGH)
GASA (RUSTLE)
ガサ…
YOU CAME ALL THE WAY TO THE DORM, DIDN'T YOU?
YOU SHOULD HAVE CALLED ME EARLIER—
ぽろ
PORO (PLOP)
!?
HUH?
H—
HEY!!
IT'S ALMOST LIKE I MADE YOU CRY...!

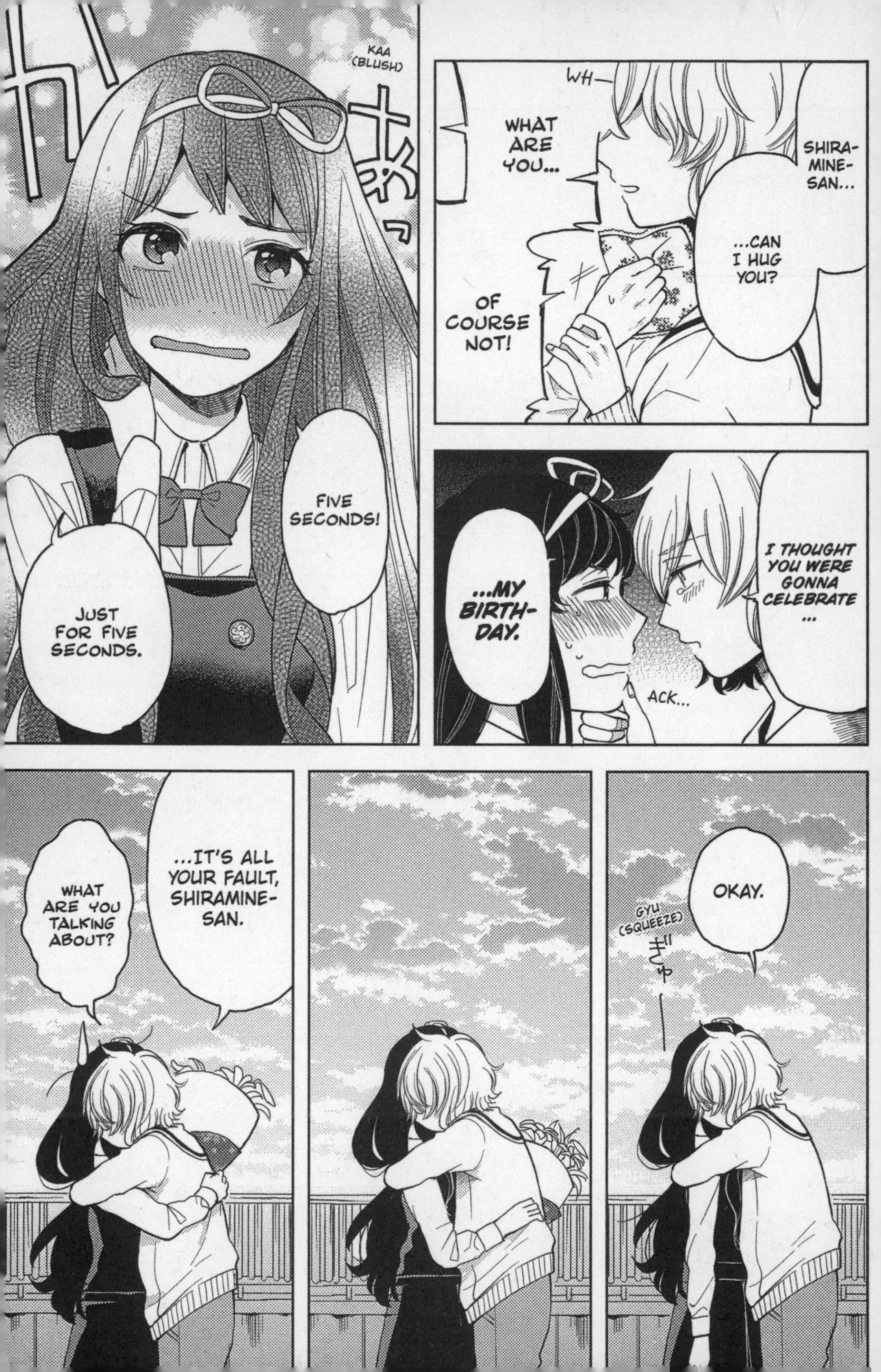
SHIRA-MINE-SAN...
...CAN I HUG YOU?
WH—
WHAT ARE YOU...
OF COURSE NOT!
I THOUGHT YOU WERE GONNA CELEBRATE ...
...MY BIRTH-DAY.
ACK...
KAA (BLUSH)
FIVE SECONDS!
JUST FOR FIVE SECONDS.
OKAY.
GYU (SQUEEZE)
...IT'S ALL YOUR FAULT, SHIRAMINE-SAN.
WHAT ARE YOU TALKING ABOUT?

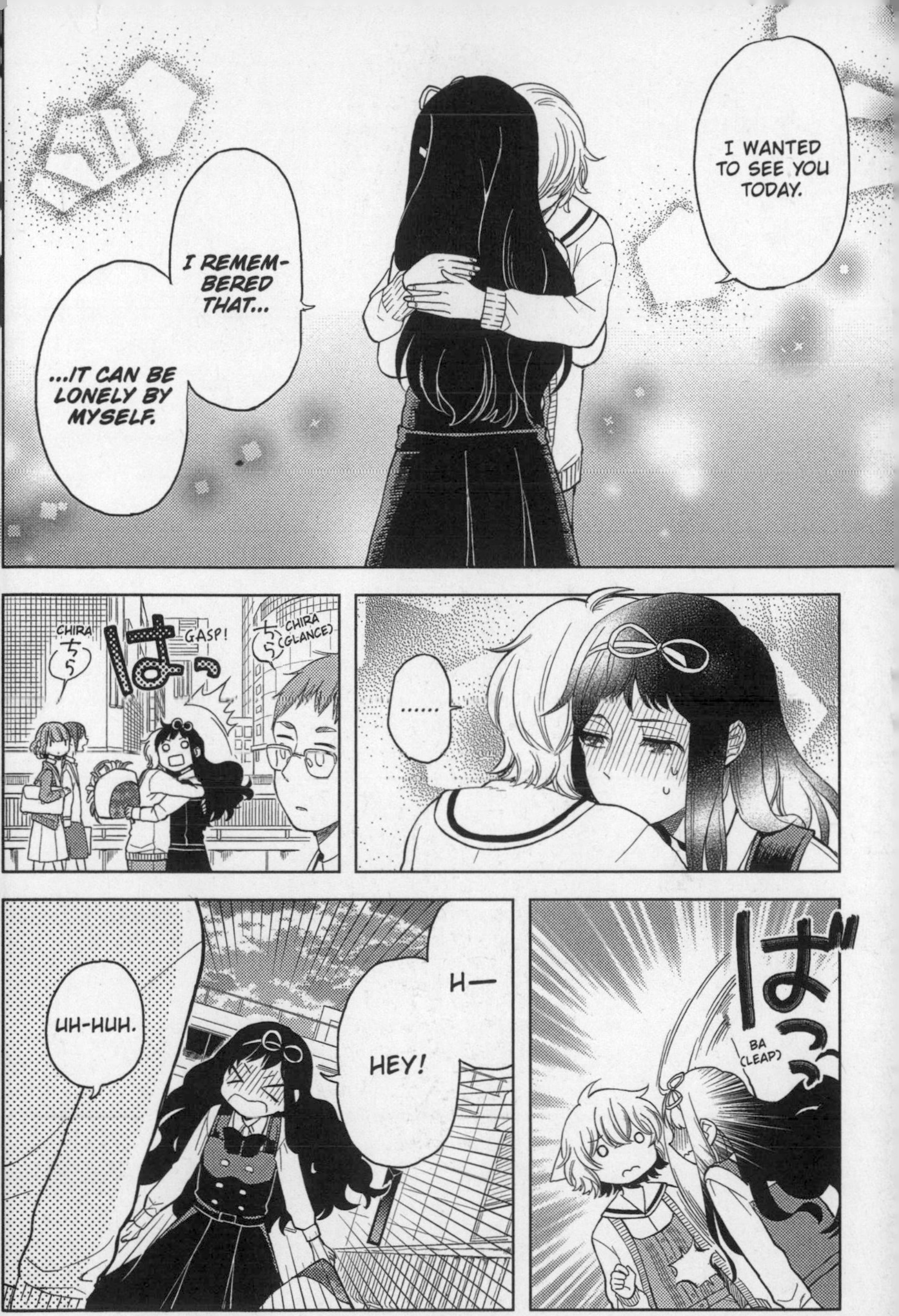
I WANTED TO SEE YOU TODAY.
I REMEMBERED THAT...
...IT CAN BE LONELY BY MYSELF.
......
ちら
CHIRA (GLANCE)
はっ
GASP!
ちら
CHIRA
ばっ
BA (LEAP)
H—
HEY!
UH-HUH.

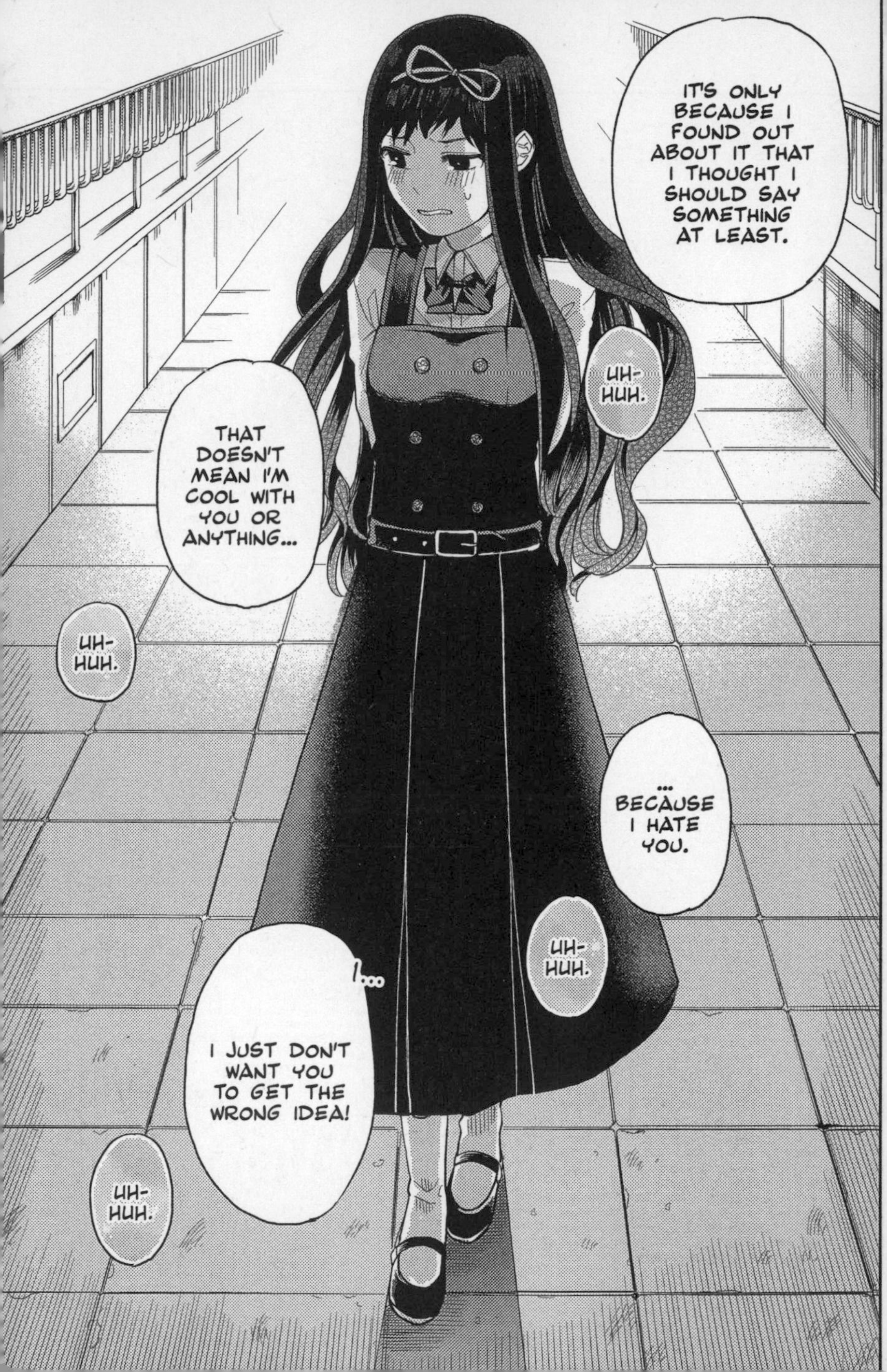
IT'S ONLY BECAUSE I FOUND OUT ABOUT IT THAT I THOUGHT I SHOULD SAY SOMETHING AT LEAST.
UH-HUH.
THAT DOESN'T MEAN I'M COOL WITH YOU OR ANYTHING...
UH-HUH.
...BECAUSE I HATE YOU.
UH-HUH.
I...
I JUST DON'T WANT YOU TO GET THE WRONG IDEA!
UH-HUH.

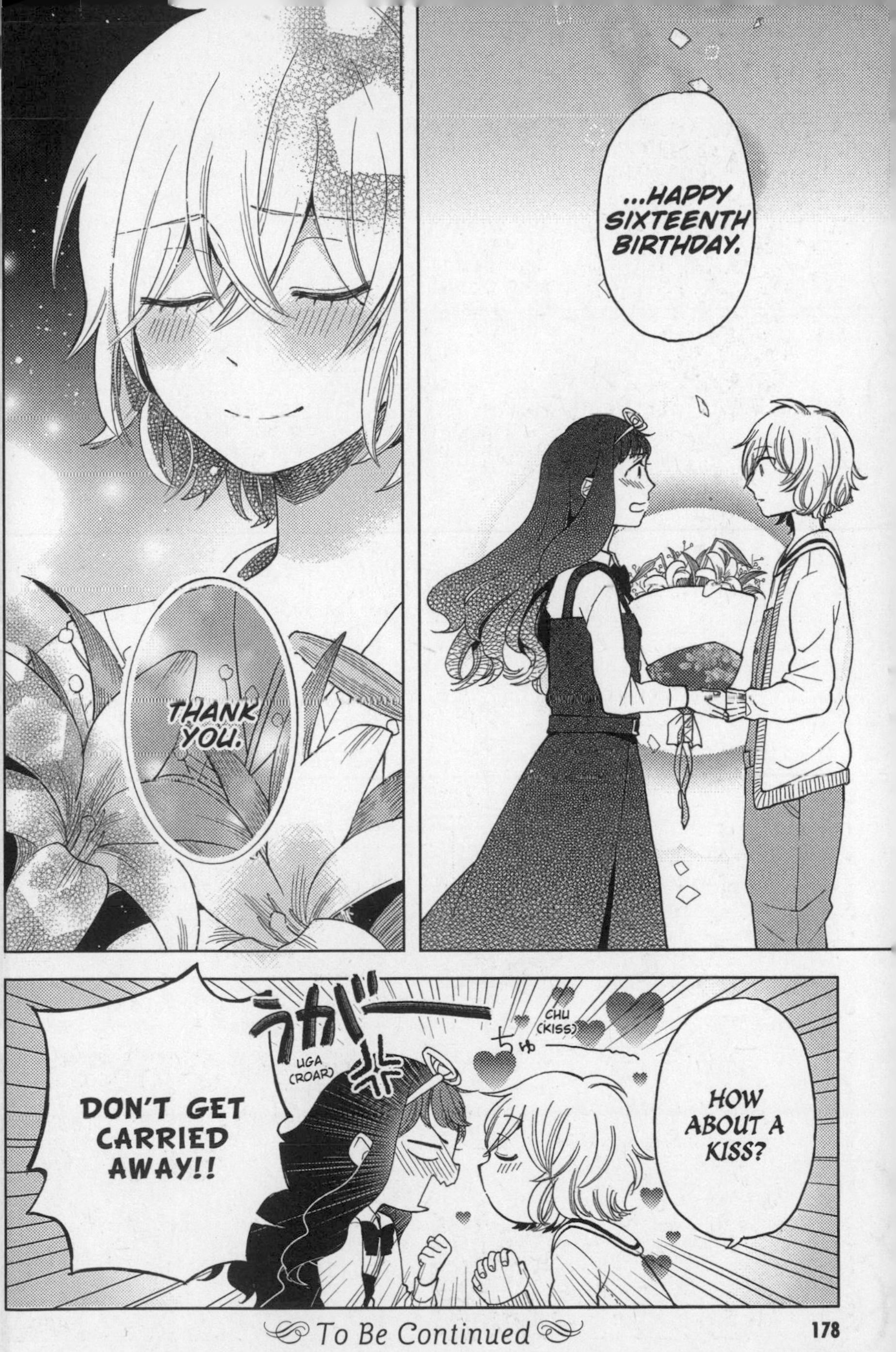
...HAPPY SIXTEENTH BIRTHDAY.
THANK YOU.
HOW ABOUT A KISS?
CHU (KISS)
UGA (ROAR)
DON'T GET CARRIED AWAY!!

To Be Continued

Even After the Dreaming Stage

NENE
25 YEARS OLD. HIGH SCHOOL INSTRUCTOR. SHE SEEMS NICE, SO SHE'S POPULAR WITH STUDENTS.

CHIHIRO
26 YEARS OLD. CITY HALL EMPLOYEE. SHE'S BEEN WRAPPED AROUND NENE'S FINGER SINCE THEY WERE IN HIGH SCHOOL.

KISS THEATER: WHAT'S BEHIND THE STORY!?

✶ PEOPLE OTHER THAN THE MAIN CHARACTERS HAVE STORIES TOO. HERE, WE PRESENT THE "LITTLE LOVE" STORIES HAPPENING BEHIND THE SCENES.

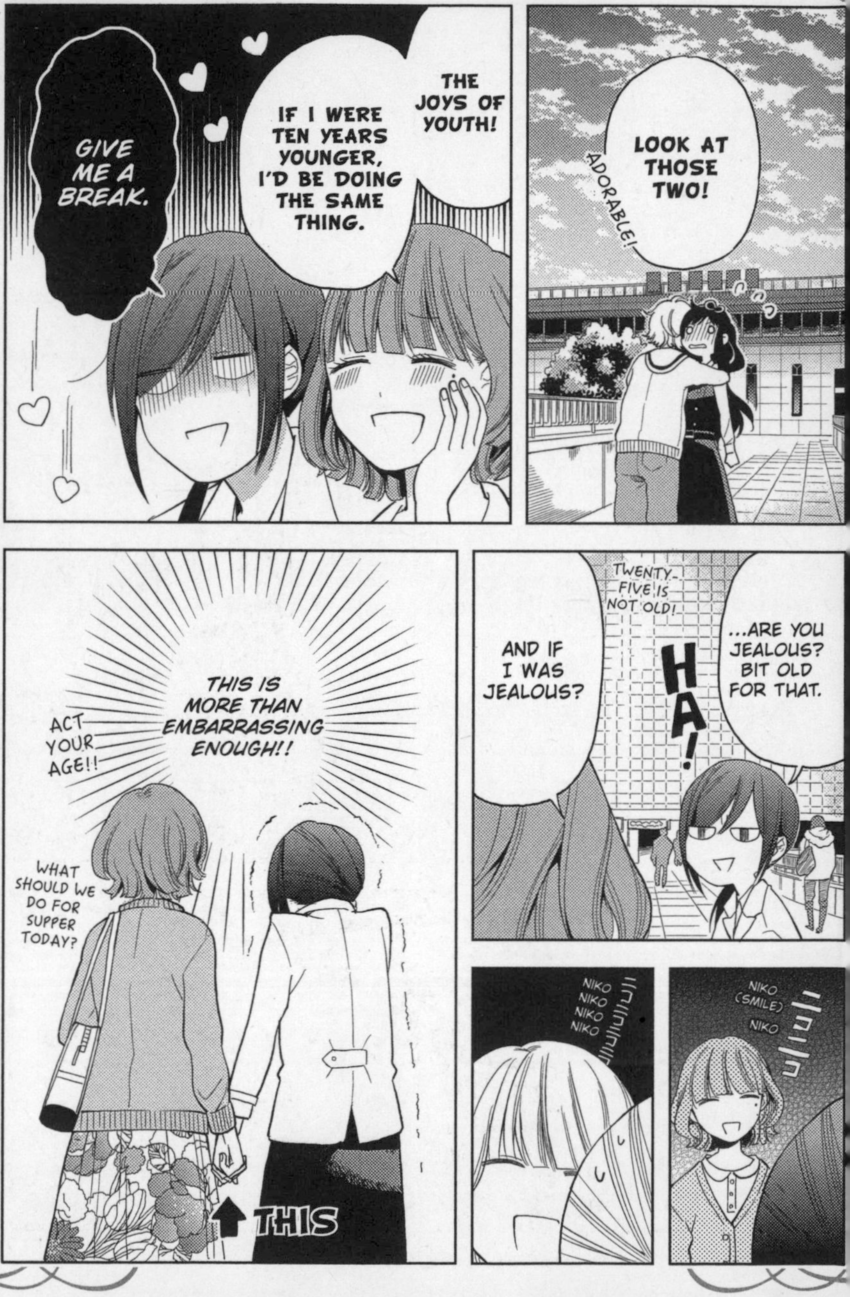
LOOK AT THOSE TWO!
ADORABLE!
THE JOYS OF YOUTH!
IF I WERE TEN YEARS YOUNGER, I'D BE DOING THE SAME THING.
GIVE ME A BREAK.
...ARE YOU JEALOUS? BIT OLD FOR THAT.
HA!
TWENTY-FIVE IS NOT OLD!
AND IF I WAS JEALOUS?
NIKO (SMILE) NIKO
NIKO NIKO NIKO NIKO
THIS IS MORE THAN EMBARRASSING ENOUGH!!
ACT YOUR AGE!!
WHAT SHOULD WE DO FOR SUPPER TODAY?
THIS

KISS THEATER ✳ SHIRA-KURO LATER

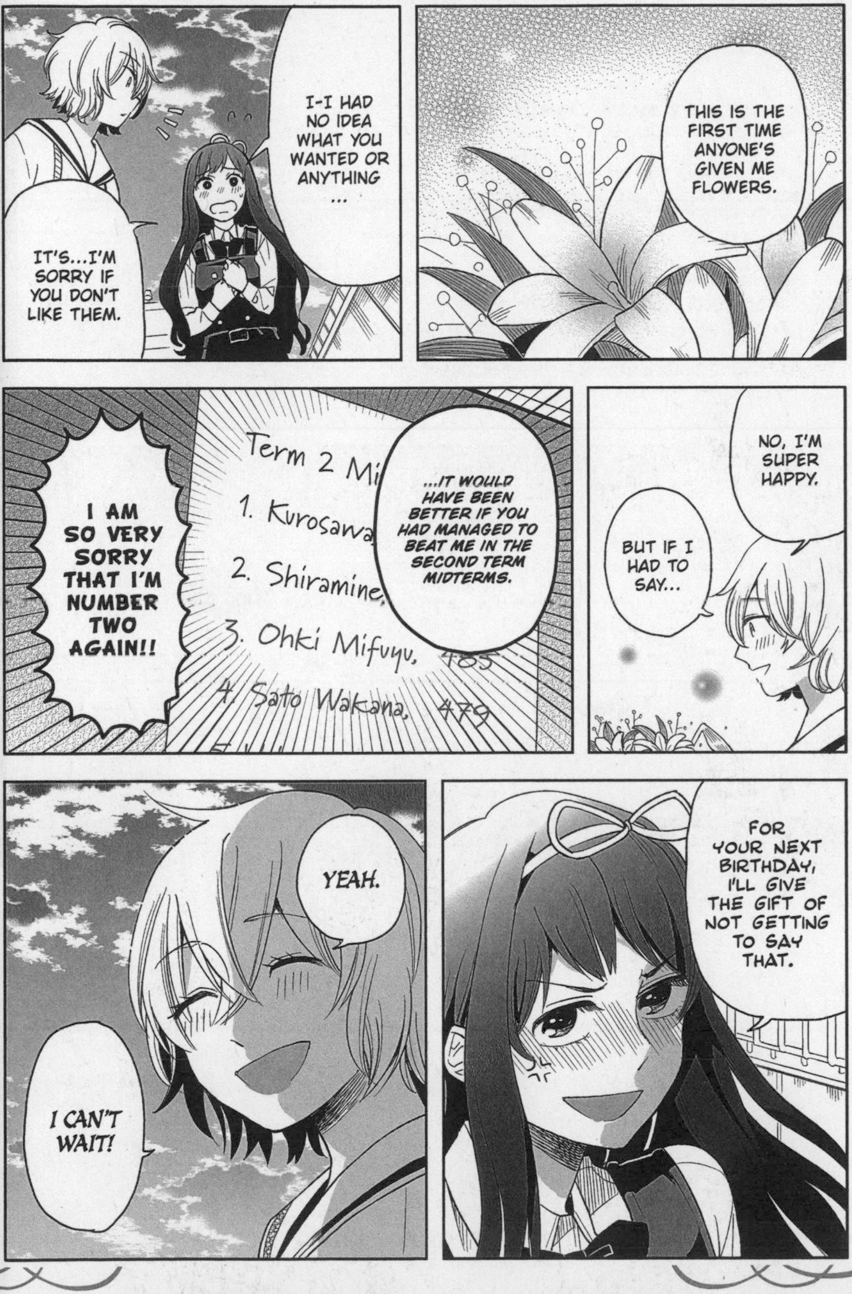
THIS IS THE FIRST TIME ANYONE'S GIVEN ME FLOWERS.
I-I HAD NO IDEA WHAT YOU WANTED OR ANYTHING ...
IT'S...I'M SORRY IF YOU DON'T LIKE THEM.
NO, I'M SUPER HAPPY.
BUT IF I HAD TO SAY...
...IT WOULD HAVE BEEN BETTER IF YOU HAD MANAGED TO BEAT ME IN THE SECOND TERM MIDTERMS.
Term 2 Mi
1. Kurosawa
2. Shiramine,
3. Ohki Mifuyu, 485
4. Sato Wakana, 479
I AM SO VERY SORRY THAT I'M NUMBER TWO AGAIN!!
FOR YOUR NEXT BIRTHDAY, I'LL GIVE THE GIFT OF NOT GETTING TO SAY THAT.
YEAH.
I CAN'T WAIT!

THIS IS A DEEP-SEA FISH.

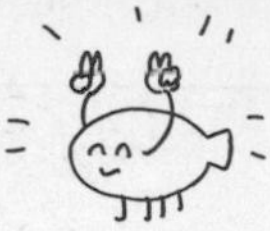

AFTERWORD

HI THERE, NICE TO MEET YOU. MY NAME IS CANNO.
THANK YOU SO MUCH FOR PICKING UP *KISS AND WHITE LILY FOR MY DEAREST GIRL*!

WHEN MY EDITOR CAME TO ME WITH THIS, I THOUGHT IT MIGHT BE SOME KIND OF NEW TRICK (SORRY), BUT I'M REALLY DELIGHTED THAT WE WERE ABLE TO PUT OUT THE BOOK LIKE THIS. WRITING THE AFTERWORD TO A FULL VOLUME HAS BEEN A SECRET DREAM. AND IT CAME TRUE. HOORAY!

TO MY EDITOR; EVERYONE IN THE ALIVE EDITORIAL DIVISION; THE DESIGNER, SEKI-SAN; ALL THE PEOPLE INVOLVED IN THE PRODUCTION OF THIS BOOK; AND ALL OF MY FAMILY AND FRIENDS WHO SUPPORTED ME, I HONESTLY CAN'T THANK YOU ENOUGH. THANK YOU SO MUCH!

I'M SO HAPPY THAT YOU'VE READ THIS FAR. THANK YOU!!
I HOPE TO SEE YOU AGAIN IN VOLUME 2...

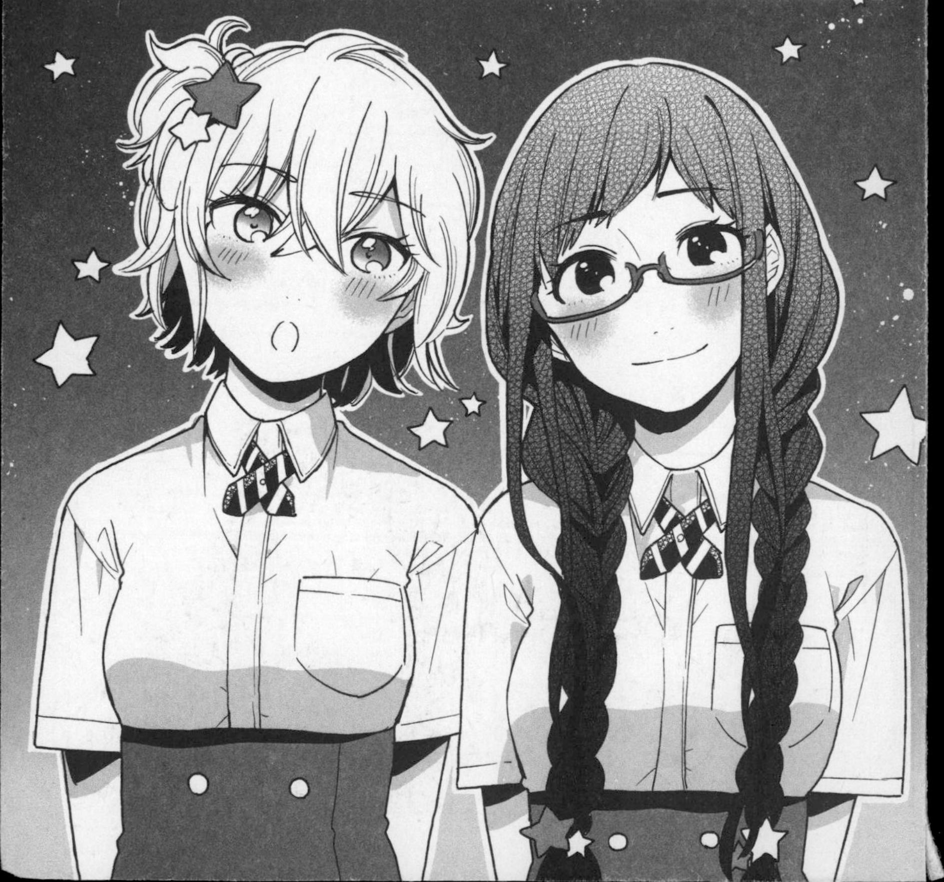

Kiss & White Lily for My...

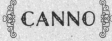
① CANNO

TRANSLATION: JOCELYNE ALLEN
LETTERING: ALEXIS ECKERMAN

ANOKO NI KISS TO SHIRAYURI WO Vol. 1
©CANNO 2014
First published in Japan in 2014 by KADOKAWA CORPORATION, Tokyo.
English translation rights arranged with KADOKAWA CORPORATION, Tokyo
through Tuttle-Mori Agency, Inc., Tokyo.

English translation © 2017 by Yen Press, LLC

Yen Press
1290 Avenue of the Americas
New York, NY 10104

Visit us at yenpress.com ⋅ twitter.com/yenpress
facebook.com/yenpress ⋅ yenpress.tumblr.com
instagram.com/yenpress

First Yen Press Edition: March 2017

Yen Press is an imprint of Yen Press, LLC.
The Yen Press name and logo are trademarks of Yen Press, LLC.
The publisher is not responsible for websites (or their content) that are not owned by the publisher.

Library of Congress Control Number: 2016958499

ISBNs: 978-0-316-55344-5 (paperback)
978-0-316-47040-7 (ebook)

10 9 8 7 6 5 4 3 2 1

BVG

Printed in the United States of America